John Douglas's love affair with Norway's Arctic Highway began as an undergraduate ambition to drive to the North Cape. This he achieved when the road was, for the most part, little more than a gravel track. He has since travelled in Arctic Scandinavia countless times, sometimes forsaking the road for canoe, RIB or light aircraft. He is the author of sixteen books including the definitive history of the route: *The Arctic Highway* (David & Charles).

Following a family tradition, he served as an officer in the British Army before embarking on a career in academia. Taking every opportunity to travel, he has travelled and photographed in over sixty countries in four continents. John is now a director of Geo Group & Associates, working mostly in Africa.

Norway's Arctic Highway – Mo i Rana to Kirkenes
First edition: October 2003

Publisher
Trailblazer Publications
The Old Manse, Tower Rd, Hindhead, Surrey, GU26 6SU, UK
Fax (+44) 01428-607571
Email: info@trailblazer-guides.com
www.trailblazer-guides.com

British Library Cataloguing in Publication Data
A catalogue record for this book is available from the British Library

ISBN 1-873756-73-9

Series editor: Patricia Major
Editor: Henry Stedman
Cartography: Nick Hill
Typesetting and layout: Henry Stedman
Index: Jane Thomàs

The illustrations on p10 and pp60-3 are reproduced from
Turi's Book of Lappland (Jonathan Cape, 1931)

Warning: motoring in extreme conditions can be dangerous
Please read the notes on when to go (p17).
Every effort has been made by the author and publisher to ensure that the information
contained herein is as accurate and up to date as possible. However, they are unable
to accept responsibility for any inconvenience, loss or injury sustained by anyone as a
result of the advice and information given in this guide.

Printed on chlorine-free paper by
D2Print (☎ +65-6295 5598), Singapore

NORWAY'S
ARCTIC
HIGHWAY

Mo i Rana to Kirkenes

JOHN DOUGLAS

TRAILBLAZER PUBLICATIONS

Acknowledgements

Over the years that I have travelled in northern Scandinavia and Finland I have received so much help and kindness that it is difficult to single out particular individuals or organizations. To the many Norwegians, Sami, Swedes and Finns who have willingly answered my questions, given me shelter or simply pointed me in the right direction, I express my gratitude.

Local tourist offices, hoteliers and flying clubs have generously assisted me. So, too, have the London embassies of Norway, Sweden and Finland and the national tourist boards.

Encouragement from the Army, from the Royal Geographical Society and from academic colleagues spurred me to make regular excursions across the North Sea.

My early research was greatly aided by the Norwegian Highway Authorities (Statens Vegvesen) at national and fylker level. They supplied my maps, let me see their plans for the future and expressed surprise and pleasure that a non-Norwegian should be interested in their road system. Information has come from many sources but any errors of fact or interpretation are mine.

Bryn Thomas has been an exceptionally patient and tolerant publisher and I thank him. I also acknowledge with gratitude the earlier encouragement to write this book that I received from Roger Lascelles.

Henry Stedman has been an eagle-eyed editor, tolerant of my careless errors, and Nick Hill has turned my rough maps into cartographic delights. Jane Thomas's index is the work of an expert. To all three goes a sincere thank you.

Three people deserve particular thanks. Ellen Anne Hatta, of Masi, herself a Sami, was my original guide and interpreter in Lapland. Amongst other things, she showed me just how tough are the Sami. It was she who introduced me to an area that has since become a second home. Ricky Wojciechowski was my field assistant during the early days of research. He drove me many thousands of miles up and down the Arctic Highway and its branches in the days when the roads were little more than tracks. Kelly White joined me as my research assistant in the field, experiencing the excitements, trials and tribulations of wild camping in the sub-Arctic. He then stayed to work with me on the final draft of this book, taking on the task of assembling the mass of data into a form that even I could understand.

To all three goes my deep gratitude, not only for their help but also for their friendship.

CONTENTS

Map Key

		$	Bank	✝	Church / Cathedral
⇧	Place to stay	☆	Police	◷	Bus Station
O	Place to eat	🏛	Museum	⛴	Ferry
⊠	Post Office	📖	Library	Λ	Campsite
⋰	Internet	ⓘ	Tourist Information	●	Other

INTRODUCTION

Norway's Arctic Highway is one of the world's great roads. For around 1500km it runs from Mo i Rana, just south of the Arctic Circle, north to Kirkenes on the Norwegian–Russian border. Seen simply in terms of latitude, the road gets to within nineteen and a half degrees of the North Pole; roughly as far north as central Greenland. Almost as remarkable, it reaches as far east as Istanbul.

The Highway is a relatively modern road; the product of an evolutionary process in the early days and then of a conscious aim to give Norway a coherent and unbroken land link through its most remote Arctic *fylker* (counties). Roads are dendritic, they have their branches, they grow and their shape changes and adapts to circumstances. In the case of the Highway, early development was characterized by the joining up of the links which were North Norway's historic local tracks. Nothing was to stand in the way. High plateaux and mountains were to be crossed; freezing and desolate tundra wastelands conquered.

Even when seemingly complete, the road had a further obstacle to clear. Norway's fractured west coast was seen to be the next challenge. When, just over sixty years ago, the Highway was deemed to have been completed there were still no less than ten sections where the link was not a road but a ferry. With the ingenuity and audacity which are the trademarks of Norway's road engineers, these were gradually reduced by bridging or tunnelling until today only one ferry remains in the Highway's path.

Judicious pruning, effected by straightening, widening, raising, re-routing and more tunnelling, has produced a road that, given the hostile environment, can be described as truly remarkable. And there's surely more to come. The Arctic Highway and its branches are still being developed. From the early, quite simple concept the Highway has taken root and refuses to stop its ambitious programmes of improvement.

When I first travelled the Highway just thirty-five years ago, the road for the greater part of its length was water-bound gravel and so narrow in parts that passing another vehicle could be difficult. Today the Highway is close to being an all-weather road suitable, at least in summer, for any roadworthy vehicle.

Is there still a challenge to drive the length of Norway's Arctic Highway and explore its branches? The answer has to be yes. This is, after all, a long road across one of Europe's most remote and least inhabited regions. It is even quite a challenge to reach its starting point, Mo i Rana. The surfaces, widths and configuration have improved but the natural hazards remain. The climate is unpredictable; mountains still have to be crossed. The old targets can still be set: to reach the top of Europe at North Cape, to make it to the border with Arctic Russia, to experience Lapland. And, of course, there is the stark beauty of the landscape. Arctic Norway must be one of the most beautiful places on the planet.

This book is written to guide you through this near-polar wonderland along a quite exceptional road. The first three parts deal with the practical matters of preparing for the journey and the logistics of getting to the Highway. A brief historical background to the Highway and its setting is also included. The main body of the book (Parts 4 to 9) describes the Highway from Mo i Rana to Kirkenes in six sections. It also includes descriptions of some of the Arctic Highway's more alluring branches which are easily accessible. It is unlikely that you will manage them all unless time is no constraint but, given their attractions, it is worth considering the merits of as many as can be fitted into your programme.

Although reference is made to conditions in winter, there is a general assumption that you will be travelling during the short summer period. After all, unless you live in a similar environment, driving the 1500km on snow and ice may well be a challenge too many. And why drive through such a beautiful land when it is dark for most of the day?

Norway is an expensive country by any measure but, like much of Scandinavia, there is a vast range of accommodation options including excellent self-catering cabins. Guideline prices are given but remember that prices change, usually upwards! Likewise, new options may become available and others may change character with new managements.

Part 2 contains a very brief note on the Sami but anyone interested in their background and culture will find that there is a wealth of literature to consult. A glossary of words and word endings is in the Appendix, p302. Most Scandinavian and Finnish place names are descriptive of their sites or locations and the glossary should help you interpret them.

No apology is made for the frequent references to the Arctic Highway's historical place in World War II. The German occupation of Norway is a largely forgotten chapter in an otherwise well-documented story. Not so to the North Norwegian; even by those who had no experience of the war, this period in their history is still vividly recalled from the accounts of those who lived through it. As time passes, it seems that consciousness of this horrific period grows rather than diminishes. New war museums open and new monuments are erected.

The Highway's place in the war is at once peculiarly poignant and ambivalent. It was the occupying power that carried out significant improvements to the road, but at a cost. The work was done by slave labour, largely Yugoslavs and Russians. Thousands paid the price of a better road with their lives. The people of Arctic Norway do not forget this. For them the Arctic Highway is the *Blodvei,* the Blood Road.

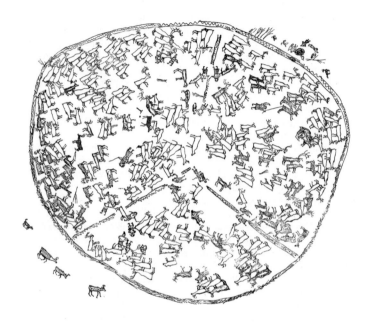

REINDEER STOCKADE IN AUTUMN

'In the autumn, when the reindeer are moving south, it is unavoidable that the herds get mixed. The various owners repair an old stockade, if it happens to lie in a convenient place, or build a new one, and into it they drive the mixed herd, and the 'separating' begins, so that each owner gets his own animals'. (From *Turi's Book of Lappland*, 1931)

This is one of numerous naïve illustrations that were made by Johan Turi to accompany his fascinating first-hand account of day to day Lapp (Sami) life. With the help of anthropologist Emilie Demant Hatt, the book was published in Norwegian in 1910 as *Muittalus Samid Birra* and later translated into English.

PART 1: PLANNING YOUR TRIP

Getting there

The Arctic Highway is accessible by road routes through southern Norway, Sweden or Finland. Despite the relatively long journeys involved, the standard of roads in all three countries is such that the average speeds which can be maintained enable you to reach either the northern or southern end of the Highway in a matter of just a few days (see Part 3, p65). But first, for non-Scandinavians, there is the matter of getting to one or other of these northern states.

It has now become possible effectively to ignore the seas, straits and channels separating Scandinavia from the UK and continental Europe. The Channel Tunnel and the new tunnel and bridge link across the Great Belt (Store Baelt/Storebelt) in Denmark have been complemented by the Öresund bridge from near Copenhagen to southern Sweden, just south of Malmö. The projected Fehmarn (Ferme) Belt Link between south-east Denmark and Germany will further ease the journey to the Scandinavian peninsula though this is unlikely to be built for at least a decade. Whether there will come a time when the sea ferries become redundant is another question. In the meantime it is a sea passage which figures in the itinerary of most UK travellers to Norway, Sweden or Finland.

The majority of those who travel the length of the Arctic Highway do so in their own vehicles or ones they have hired at home. Alternatives will be described and discussed but it is appropriate to deal first with approaches by vehicle ferry because this will be the choice of most drivers.

Anyone who is simply joining a party for the trip, or wishes to hire a vehicle, can opt to fly or use long-distance coach or rail and short ferry.

VEHICLE FERRIES TO SCANDINAVIA AND FINLAND

You are spoilt for choice. The Finns and Scandinavians are very used to ferry traffic and treat it with a familiarity reserved in most countries for the bus. The Baltic, the gulfs of Finland and Bothnia and the Skagerrak, have been crossed and re-crossed by traders and migrants for centuries. The average Norwegian is as much at home on a boat as on dry land. Today's trade and traffic may bear little resemblance to the days of the Hanseatic League but they are no less important.

The contact details of the principal ferries likely to be used by anyone making for the Arctic Highway are shown on p13.

All the ferries shown in the lists on p13 carry vehicles and provide a variety of accommodation. Some ships, notably those crossing from Stockholm to Turku, are like floating apartment blocks, able to carry 2000 passengers and 400 vehicles. The ships currently in use live up to their claims of luxury travel, at

PRINCIPAL FERRIES TO SCANDINAVIA & FINLAND			
From	**Route**	**Line**	**Approximate journey time**
Great Britain	Newcastle–Bergen (Norway) via Stavanger	Fjordline	24 hours
Great Britain	Newcastle–Gothenburg (Sweden)	DFDS	24 hours
Denmark	Frederikshavn–Larvik (Norway)	Colorline	6 hours
Germany	Rostock–Helsinki (Finland)	Silja Line	24 hours
Germany	Kiel–Oslo (Norway)	Color Line	20 hours
Sweden	Stockholm–Turku (Finland)	Silja Line	11 hours

least at the top end of the accommodation grading. The usual charging system which is employed consists of a basic fare with add-ons for the grade of accommodation booked. This varies from the simple airline-type seat to a suite of cabins. There is also a variety of discounts available on most lines for parties, students, seniors and infants, and for advanced return bookings. Vehicle charges depend on size of vehicle, especially height. Caravans and trailers attract higher fares but there are usually discounts for vehicles according to their passenger ratio. It is worthwhile looking carefully at what discounts are on offer.

Almost all the ferries run throughout the year but there is a reduction in frequency in winter. Fares, too, depend upon the time of year with, as a rule, three ferry seasons recognized. Peak times are normally from mid-June to mid-August. The intermediate or shoulder period is a month or two either side of the peak and low prices are charged during the rest of the year, the winter. Seasonal differentials are often quite substantial and it is wise to plan so that at least one journey is out of peak time. It is in the peak season that advanced booking becomes essential and it is not unknown for even these vast ships to be fully booked months ahead. It is certainly risky to turn up on the quayside for any of these ferries in the hope of finding an empty berth in early July.

The ships offer not only a variety of accommodation, but also a range of restaurants, cafeterias and entertainment. In almost every case the fare excludes meals which are purchased as and when taken on board. The à la carte restaurants could be considered expensive, especially if alcoholic drinks are purchased. The Norwegian cold table, however, is usually a visual and gastronomic delight. Breakfast is self-service even in the restaurants and can make a substantial and inexpensive meal. On-board entertainment, if any, is rarely as good as the brochures suggest and a pack of playing cards is useful on the longer journeys. The shops are worth walking round if only to reinforce the view that things are cheaper at home. The prices may attract the Scandinavians on board but will seem extortionate to almost everyone else. With Norway resisting membership of the EU, some of the ferries between EU countries call in at, for example, Kristiansand in Norway in order to legitimize the sale of duty-free goods. These are, of course, available on ferries going between EU countries and Norway. Even so, the prices always seem high, unless you live in

Norway. Any spare money you may have is more wisely spent on upgrading the cabin which at its best can be close to cruise-liner luxury.

In rough seas, the fact that meals are not included in the fare can seem a very real advantage. The North Sea can be very rough especially when winds are coming from the north over a long fetch. Even the Baltic can be choppy but for the most part these large ferries with their modern construction and stabilizers will not cause even the most sensitive of stomachs to complain. Some of the ships travelling from Bergen to Newcastle call in at Stavanger and up to that point are sailing in the protective shelter of off-shore islands. It may be advisable to wait until the ship sails out into the open North Sea before booking a table for dinner!

There is a general air of informality on board all the ferries and for most people it is clearly the start of their holiday. Public parts of the ship tend to be a little crowded during the day and, especially in the case of the North Sea crossings, the weather is usually such that only a few will be attracted to sit or stroll on the open decks.

Ships' officers and crew are helpful; once they even re-opened the vehicle-loading doors at Bergen when I arrived rather late for my ferry.

CONTACTS

Company	Address	Telephone/email/website
Color Line	PO Box 1422, Vika, N-0115, Oslo, Norway	+47 81 00 08 11 customerservice@colorline.com www.colorline.com
	Postfach 2646, 24025 Kiel, Germany	+49 (0)431-7300300
	Postboks 30, DK-9900, Frederikshavn, Denmark	+45 99 56 19 77
DFDS Seaways	Scandinavia House, Parkeston, Harwich, Essex, UK CO12 4QG	08705 333 000 (in UK) travel.sales@dfds.co.uk www.dfdsseaways.co.uk
	Utstikker 2, Vippetangen, Postboks 365, Sentrum, 0102 Oslo, Norway	+47 22 41 90 90 booking@dfdsseaways.no www.dfdsseaways.com
Fjordline	Royal Quays, North Shields, Tyne and Wear, UK NE22 6EG	+44 (0)191-296 1313 fjordline.uk@fjordline.com www.fjordline.co.uk
	Skoltegrunnskaien, PO Box 7250, N-5020 Bergen, Norway	+47 81 53 35 00 booking@fjordline.com www.fjordline.com
Silja Line	Mannerheimintie 2, PO Box 880, 00101 Helsinki, Finland	+358 (0)9-18041 www.silja.com
	Positionen 8, Hangovägen 29, S-11574 Stockholm, Sweden	+46 (0)8-222140
	Zeißstraße 4, D-23560 Lübeck, Germany	+49 (0)451-58990 info.germany@silja.com

CARGO SHIP

If the choice is a sea crossing from the UK but large passenger ferries don't seem attractive, then the alternative is to use a cargo ship. Perhaps the most enjoyable crossing I ever made was from Hull to Helsinki via the Kiel Canal and the Baltic Sea. With 'owner's cabin' accommodation and a maximum of just four passengers, nothing could have been more relaxing. We had our own steward, dined with the ship's officers, never seemed to stop eating and had the run of the ship.

This isn't going to be the quickest way to get to Scandinavia – we were delayed over 24 hours before we set sail – but it is a wonderful experience. Most of the vessels will be roll-on, roll-off (ROROs) so getting a vehicle on board is no problem and access to it may be possible throughout the voyage.

To ask about bookings, try the United Baltic Corporation in London (☎ 020 7265 0808). If you are making a return trip and already in Finland then try the Travel Center Helsinki Ltd in Helsinki (☎ 09-680901). Another company worth approaching is DFDS Tor Line (freight). They have cargo ships going into Gothenburg in Sweden and into Norwegian ports. They can be contacted and bookings made through DFDS (Seaways) whose contact details are on p13.

AIRLINE CONTACTS

Company	Location	Telephone	Website
BMI British Midland	UK	+44 0870 607 0555	www.flybmi.com
Braathens	Oslo	+47 67 59 70 00	www.braathens.no
	Bergen	+47 55 99 82 50	
	UK	+44 0870 607 27727	
	Sweden	+46 (0)40-6602900	
British Airways	UK	+44 0845 773 3377	www.britishairways.com
	Norway	+47 80 03 31 42	
	Sweden	+46 (0)563-541702	
	Finland	+358 (0)800-178378	
Coast Air AS	Norway	+47 52 84 85 00	www.coastair.no
Finnair	UK	+44 (0)20-7408 1222	www.finnair.com
	Finland	+358 (0)2-03140160	
KLM	UK	+44 0870 5074074	www.klm.com
	Netherlands	+31 (0)20-4747747	
Lufthansa	UK	+44 0845 7737747	www.lufthansa.com
	Germany	+49 0180-58384267	
Norwegian	Norway	+47 67 59 30 00	www.norwegian.no
SAS	UK	+ 44 0870 607 27727	www.sas.no
	Oslo	+47 64 81 60 50	
	Sweden	+ 46 (0) 770-727727	
	Finland	+358 (0)2-0386000	
Widerøe	Norway	+47 81 00 12 00	www.wideroe.no

For airport telephone numbers in North Norway see relevant location in Parts 4 to 9.

MAIN INTERNATIONAL AIRPORTS

Town	Airport	Location	Code
Oslo	Oslo International	47km north of central Oslo	OSL
Bergen	Flesland	19km south of central Bergen	BGO
Stavanger	Sola	14km south-west of central Stavanger	SVG
Stockholm	Arlanda	41km north of central Stockholm	ARN
Helsinki	Vantaa	21km north of central Helsinki	HEL

AIR ROUTES

If you decide to hire a vehicle in Scandinavia, then flying there is an option. The budget airlines have made this cost effective and the airfare should, in any case, be compared with the cost of the ferry price *plus* the cost of food and drink on board. As with other intra-European flights with no-frills airlines, it's useful to check the airports being used. Sometimes, when the journey between some outlying airport and the final city destination is calculated, it might well have been cheaper and less hassle to have used one of the mainstream airlines.

Norway is well served by the major airlines with most flights routed to Oslo's International Airport (code OSL). Other international flights touch down

USEFUL AIR SERVICES INTO SCANDINAVIA/FINLAND

From	To	Airline/s
Aberdeen	Stavanger	Braathens, Widerøe
Aberdeen	Haugesund	Coastair
Amsterdam	Oslo	SAS, KLM
Amsterdam	Bergen	KLM
Amsterdam	Stavanger	KLM
Birmingham	Stockholm	BA
Frankfurt	Oslo	SAS, Lufthansa
London Heathrow	Oslo	BA, BMI, SAS
London Stansted	Oslo	Norwegian
London Gatwick	Bergen	Braathens
London Heathrow	Stavanger	BMI, SAS
London Heathrow	Stockholm	BA, BMI, SAS, Finnair
London Heathrow	Helsinki	BA, Finnair
Manchester	Oslo	BA
Manchester	Stockholm	BA
Newcastle	Stavanger	Widerøe
New York	Oslo	SAS via Copenhagen or London
New York	Bergen	SAS via Copenhagen

at Stavanger (SVG) and at Bergen (BGO). If the approach to the Arctic Highway is to be via Sweden or Finland (see Part 3, p65), Stockholm and Helsinki are also on flight routes of a number of major world airlines.

National carriers provide the main services. Flights from UK regional airports to Scandinavia are possible with the airlines listed, but usually involve a change of aircraft at a hub such as Copenhagen. There are direct flights from London into some of Norway's regional airports, but others require a change. For up to the minute information, it will be best to consult the websites of the various carriers listed on p14. The current situation for direct, non-stop flights is given in the box on p15.

Domestic flights within Norway

If you intend to fly to one of the termini of the Arctic Highway before turning to road travel it will be least expensive to fly to Oslo, Bergen or Stavanger and then transfer to SAS domestic routes or those of Braathens or Widerøe, both part of SAS. A small company, Coast Air AS, also has a limited number of flights within Norway. Mo i Rana (lying at the southern end of the Highway) and Kirkenes (situated at the northern terminus) both have small airports with regular services. Between them, SAS, Braathens and Widerøe (all part of the SAS family) provide an impressive domestic network. Widerøe serves the short take-off and landing (STOL) airstrips, while SAS/Braathens link the larger airports. If you're flying into or out of North Norway, SAS/Braathens will get you to Oslo, and also to Bergen on some flights. Widerøe uses Trondheim as a hub and you must transfer there. The SAS/Braathens services in the table below are at least daily in and out of each of the airports shown with the exception of Lakselv (also, confusingly, called Nordkapp) which takes Sunday off.

Only those North Norway airports which are likely to be of interest to anyone using the Arctic Highway are shown in the table below.

DOMESTIC AIR SERVICES IN NORTH NORWAY

Airport	Airline	Telephone
Mo i Rana *	Widerøe	75 15 80 85
Bodø #	SAS, Braathens, Widerøe, Norwegian	75 54 28 33
Narvik *	Widerøe, Norwegian	76 92 22 00
Harstad-Narvik #	SAS, Braathens	76 98 10 00
Bardufoss *	SAS, Braathens	77 88 02 00
Tromsø #	SAS, Braathens, Widerøe, Norwegian	77 64 84 00
Sørkjosen *	Widerøe	77 77 16 60
Alta *	SAS, Braathens, Widerøe	78 48 25 00
Hammerfest #	Widerøe	78 41 25 82
Honningsvåg #	Widerøe	78 47 20 69
Lakselv *	SAS, Braathens, Norwegian	78 46 45 00
Vadsø #	Widerøe	78 95 22 88
Kirkenes *	SAS, Braathens, Widerøe	78 97 04 00

*=Airport on the Arctic Highway; #=Airport on one of the Highway's main branches

USING PUBLIC TRANSPORT: ROAD OR RAIL

European rail services and long-distance coaches are an inexpensive way to reach Norway if you are not taking your own vehicle. The final ferry crossing, from, say, Denmark will not add much to the cost. Once in Norway, you can reach the Highway by bus or rail (see Part 3, p111).

The great number of options, using bus or train, means that you are probably better off consulting a travel agent or the internet for the latest bargain prices.

When to go

The Arctic Highway is officially an all-weather road. The sections liable to closure in winter have been reduced in number and the length of any closure period is, today, very short. However, the entire Highway is not likely to be open every day of the year. The vulnerable sections remain the high plateaux, or *vidder*, including the Saltfjell (Nordland), the Kvænangsfjellet (Troms) and Sennalandet (Finnmark). Other sections may have to be closed for short periods in a severe winter and, of course, many of the Highway's branch roads will be impassable at times. Some of the approach roads to the Highway will also be subject to closure in winter. This is particularly the case with roads across the high plateaux of western Norway. To check on road closures there is an information line – Vegmeldingssentralen (☎ 22 65 40 40).

There's little doubt that a winter journey along the Highway will be an experience of a lifetime for most people. This is the Arctic at its harshest, yet it is a season which is the quintessence of all that is polar. The days are short and in midwinter almost non-existent. Midday is simply twilight and the land of the midnight sun is still half a year away. Few visitors, however, will choose to explore the Highway in winter. The locals keep their own journeys by road down to a necessary minimum and their winter driving skills are likely to be superior to those of the foreign traveller. Most of the Highway is kept almost clear of snow with the use of ploughs and powerful blowers. A thin cover of packed snow is left to protect the road and to give a better driving surface. Many sections of the north's roads are afforded some protection from drifting snow by high snow-fences placed back from the road, but the usual practice is to blow the snow into the bordering ditches. It is for this purpose that the Highway is often raised a few metres above its surroundings.

Driving in winter will take care and courage and, as has been said, the whole length of the Highway may not be open to traffic. The usual severe-weather precautions should be taken with regard to carrying some provisions and warm clothing, and it is advisable to include a shovel and sacks in case the vehicle should become stuck in snow or stranded on ice. Even better, sand ladders can replace sacks and are more reliable. It is only sensible to let someone at your destination know that you are travelling and to give an expected time of arrival.

MO I RANA

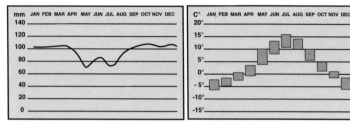

Average precipitation (mm)   **Average max/min temp (°C)**

Four-wheel drive is highly desirable for winter travel and chains or studs will be necessary. Some of the motoring associations will have chains for hire though they are not especially expensive to purchase. A very few hotels provide engine-heating points in their car-parks but, although quite common in Finland, this is not a regular feature of most Norwegian establishments. Diesel-powered engines may well cause problems because of the higher freezing point of the fuel. Daily journeys will need to be much shorter than in summer and accommodation should be booked in advance of each day's trip.

Unless you are used to similar conditions of snow and ice at home, a winter exploration of the Highway is not advisable and it certainly should not be undertaken by anyone who does not already know the route in the daylight of summer. (See also Convoy Driving, p27).

Spring travel has little to offer despite the cultural importance that season has in the north. Road surfaces are often at their worst as the effects of winter are revealed by the thaw. Days are longer but if spring is chosen then a late period of the season will be best, not least because this will be when the vegetation is recovering and often at its most attractive.

Autumn comes early and is the season when many of the more vegetated areas are at their most colourful as the greens turn to every shade of brown, red and gold. But it is also the period when quite severe frosts will be experienced. The *jernatter* (literally 'iron nights') may catch the unwary who have neglected anti-freeze in their car's cooling systems or some extra clothing.

It is arguable that there are only two seasons in the far north: winter and summer. The real summer is very short but a journey along the Highway is made particularly easy by the long hours of daylight. The north is the Land of the Midnight Sun. At least that is the theory but the chance of seeing the sun at midnight is dependent upon weather conditions and not just on latitude.

The best months to explore the Highway are June and September, bearing in mind what has been said about spring and autumn difficulties. In fact the road is most heavily used in the six weeks or so of July and early August. The omnipresent mosquito will be at its most bellicose at this time but the hotels will be offering accommodation at their lowest rates and campsites will be open.

KIRKENES

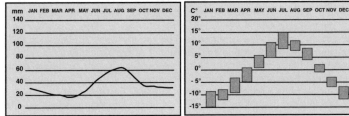

Average precipitation (mm)   **Average max/min temp (°C)**

There are some disadvantages in driving the Highway in late August and September. The further north you go, the shorter is the summer season. You can expect many camping sites, cabins and even some hotels to have shut down for winter by mid-August in the extreme north. Tourist information offices, as well as museums and other attractions, may also close from the latter half of August.

CLIMATE

North Norway has a climate which is unique. Nowhere else in the polar world has such relatively high winter temperatures. The temperature anomaly (the difference between the actual and the average for that latitude) is an exceptional plus 20C° in January. For example, while Narvik's lowest mean monthly temperature is just a few degrees below 0°C, comparable places in Canada's far north are experiencing -30°C. On a similar latitude, Verkhoyansk (Russian Federation) has temperatures below -13°C for no less than seven months in the year.

Away from the coast, the effects of the North Atlantic Drift diminished, temperatures in winter are noticeably lower. Hence, the Finnmark plateau has a more severe winter than most of the region through which the Highway passes. Karasjok, for example, has a mean minimum of -14.5°C but temperatures have been known to drop to a wickedly cold -50°C. Yet further north, Kirkenes, the Highway's northern terminus, has a mean temperature for the coldest month (February) as high as -10°C. The proximity of the sea makes all the difference.

As the winter turns into spring, temperatures rise only slowly. Much of the sun's radiant heat energy is lost in melting the snow or being reflected off the white surface. But as the days lengthen warmer temperatures return and by June almost everywhere along the Highway that is near the coast has means above 8°C. July is nearly always the warmest month with mean figures about 12°C. Some particularly favoured places are even warmer: Alta, for example, has a July mean of 13.6°C. Autumn, as the days shorten, can be cold. Tana Bru, in East Finnmark, has a mean of -5°C in November but Narvik, further south and more affected by the sea, does not have a daily mean below 0°C until mid-November.

Temperatures depend, as so often elsewhere, on the origin of the air-stream affecting the region. Certainly in summer it is very noticeable when the wind changes from north to east. The temperatures rise as one loses the cold air drawn off the Arctic Ocean. Windchill is important as far as perceived heat is concerned. Unfortunately, as wind speeds drop in summer mosquitoes become more active.

The long days (see box p20) make a considerable difference to average temperatures in summer. With the sun never or only briefly below the horizon, air temperatures show only a small diurnal range. For example, Tromsø has nearly 19 hours of daylight per day even in the first week of May. In these conditions, it can seem much warmer than the thermometer would have you believe. Of course, there are also days when the temperature can actually reach the mid-20s.

Precipitation figures in North Norway vary from the moderate (around 1000mm/40 inches) near the coast to the very low (300mm/12 inches) on the south-facing slopes of the Finnmark vidde. Even Alta, on the north-facing Finnmark coast, receives only 380mm/15 inches. It is along the more southerly

---

HOURS OF DAYLIGHT

To travel in northern Scandinavia and Finland is to journey in the Land of the Midnight Sun – or the midday darkness if you happen to go in winter. Put simply, if you go in summer, you'll probably never need to drive the Highway in the dark. If you go in winter, you'll have very few daylight hours and will not see very much. A winter journey may be a challenge and it will certainly let you experience the true Arctic but it isn't for those wanting to see something of the beauty of the north in easy driving conditions. Of course, you may be lucky enough to see the northern lights.

From the Arctic Highway's accepted starting point, Mo i Rana, you will effectively be in the Land of the Midnight Sun all the way to Kirkenes. Strictly, the phenomenon isn't experienced until you cross the Polar Circle but a few minutes of a degree of latitude aren't worth arguing about. In summer, the number of hours of daylight progressively increases as you go north and the same applies to hours of darkness in winter (see also p253). In practical terms, this means that travel and camping are especially easy when you have almost 24 hours without the need for artificial light. Until you've experienced these ultra-long days, it's difficult to appreciate what a boon they can be to the traveller. However, if you are sleeping in a tent and find that it's too bright to get to sleep, try using the shades that airlines provide for long-haul travellers on overnight flights. As a guide, the dates for the periods during which you can experience 24 hours of daylight (the midnight sun) and those for the polar night (24 hours of darkness) are shown below for some of the towns on the Arctic Highway or its branches.

Midnight sun	Location	Polar night
13 May–29 July	North Cape/Nordkapp	18 November–24 January
15 May–26 July	Hammerfest	20 November–22 January
16 May–27 July	Alta	24 November–18 January
20 May–22 July	Kåfjordbergan (Troms)	25 November–17 January
27 May–15 July	Narvik	4 December–8 January
4 June–8 July	Fauske	14 December–28 December

Note: the chances of observing the midnight sun are dependent upon weather conditions and may be no better than one day in five in any year.

sections of the Arctic Highway that precipitation is at its highest. Here the west-facing coast can receive the moist Atlantic air-streams any time in the year. Nordland and Troms are thus wetter than Finnmark. However, these *fylker* (counties) tend to be driest in spring and summer and wettest in autumn (eg Bodø: 50mm/2 inches in May, 130mm/5 inches in October). In Finnmark, totals are lower and the difference between the wettest and driest month is much less (eg Vardø has only half Bodø's annual total and the difference between the wettest and driest months is just 2.5mm). The heavy rainfalls associated with south-western Norway are not experienced in the north. Tromsø, for instance, receives just over half the total of Bergen: 990mm/39 inches against 1960mm/77 inches.

Some 40–50% of the precipitation will be as snow and, on high ground, light snowfalls may be encountered on a cold day even in midsummer. The low winter temperatures ensure that snow will lie for long periods of the year even at sea-level. In Troms and Finnmark snow will survive for more than half of the year but in Nordland the period is nearer to four or five months. Depths of lying snow vary but a metre of snow, excluding drifts, is not unknown in late winter.

The area through which the Highway runs is rather cloudy and base levels may be low enough to present a driving hazard over the vidder even in summer.

Like anywhere else where the climate is essentially maritime, there is a high degree of unpredictability about the weather. In some years the onset of winter will be delayed until late October; in others, the snow has arrived by September. Long periods of fine weather in summer are rare but not unknown. It is possible, with luck, to spend a month or so in North Norway without rain and with temperatures in the upper twenties most days. Yet in other years a glimpse of the sun will be a highlight of the tour. There is often a contrast, especially in summer, between the weather experienced in southern Scandinavia and that in the north. Driving up to the Polar Circle in unseasonably wet and cold conditions may well be a good omen for the journey along the Arctic Highway.

Driving the Highway

GENERAL

The improvements to the Highway (see p56) have produced a modern road which should not deter even anxious drivers. On the other hand, you should not expect to find anything even remotely resembling a motorway, autostrada, autobahn or equivalent. The only exceptions are stretches near to major towns in south and central Norway. Widths have been increased but there are still some stretches, especially in Finnmark and where the Highway runs along fjord edges, where the road is not wide enough for easy passing. In places the standard 6m may be reduced to 4.5m or less. Radii of curvature have also been increased but there will be blind corners – again chiefly when the road hugs the shore of a fjord. Gradients are moderate rather than severe but, if towing, the mountainous sections, eg north of Narvik and on the Kvænangsfjellet, may be troublesome.

❏ **CAR RENTAL** *(BILUTLEIE)*

Town	Company	Telephone
Mo i Rana	Avis	75 14 81 57
	Europcar	75 15 34 11
	Hertz	75 15 22 55
	Statoil	75 12 76 11
Kirkenes	Avis	78 97 37 06
	Bilrek AS	78 99 19 52
	Europcar	78 97 01 00
	Hertz	78 99 39 76
	Hesseng Auto Senter	78 99 80 21
	Kirkenes Motor AS	78 99 90 06
Oslo	Avis	23 23 92 00
	Budget	22 17 10 50
	Hertz	22 21 00 00
Bergen	Avis	55 32 01 30
	Budget	55 90 26 15
	Hertz	55 96 40 70
	Thrifty, Seim Bilutleie	55 90 22 50

One to avoid perhaps is a company I came across in Norway which traded under the name Rent A Wreck. Maybe they get the honesty prize!

Tarred road surfaces are usually good to very good but it must be remembered that the winter conditions and spring thaw can cause severe damage. Long sections may therefore be under repair or reconstruction during the summer – the only season when the work can be done. Coming across such sections, you should slow down to a crawl and not attempt to drive at speed across what may be simply a surface of high calibre rubble. Patience is never more of a virtue than when meeting a 2–3km stretch of road under repair.

On 16 June 1992, 25% of Norway's public roads changed their numbers. If using an old map printed before the changes, beware. Now all trunk roads (including the E6/Arctic Highway) are marked with white numbers on a green background.

The vehicle

An early decision will be whether to take your own vehicle or to hire. The days when four-wheel drive was necessary are past unless it is anticipated that off-road driving, for example for wild camping, is likely. The road surfaces and general conditions make almost any roadworthy vehicle adequate. Daily journeys may involve substantial distances so that a small, low-powered car which may become uncomfortable has little to recommend it beyond a favourable fuel-to-distance ratio. Travelling with a trailer or caravan was, in the past, considered unwise. It is still not common but if the towing vehicle is adequately powered there should be no problem on the Highway (see section on caravans, p29). One popular vehicle for the Highway is the camper or motorized caravan. While they may find little favour with tourist authorities, or even with other drivers, there is little doubt about their utility.

In summer, no special equipment is needed beyond that which you would be carrying for any long journey. However, because of the remoteness of the area and taking into account the relatively small size of its settlements, it's prudent to carry an appropriate selection of spares and to check that your tyres are in good order.

As already mentioned, special tyres with or without studs or snow chains will be needed in winter and may be required by law between 15 October and 15 May. Chains, because they are readily available and can be removed when there is no snow, may be the preferred option. Motoring organizations hire out chains but it may be cheaper to buy then re-sell after the trip. A UK source will be found on 🖳 www.carparts-direct.co.uk where the price should be below £60.

An international identity plate should be attached to the rear of the vehicle and a red hazard-warning triangle should be carried in case of a breakdown. Both are legal requirements. Some of the ferry companies will issue free deflector strips for the headlights of right-hand drive vehicles; otherwise, some sort of deflector should be fitted on arrival in Scandinavia. If you intend to drive only in daylight these deflectors are not strictly necessary.

There are strict rules forbidding the carriage of fuel in jerry cans on the North Sea ferries.

Car hire is an alternative to taking your own transport. There may be good reasons to hire from home but there are advantages in hiring in Norway, perhaps even at the start of the journey along the Highway. In this way time can be saved by using air travel and, in the event of breakdown, help should be at hand more quickly. The obvious arguments against hire are cost and unfamiliarity with the vehicle. Hire costs are comparatively high in Norway, some would say excessively so. As a guide, assume that the basic charge for the smallest car will be around NOK500 per day with perhaps 200km free of distance charges. There is a high tax on car rentals. It is also true that if a vehicle is hired in Norway, you will have to carry all you need for your journey in bags to the pick-up point rather than simply loading it into the boot or putting it on a roof-rack.

Most of the major international and European car-hire companies operate in Norway so bookings may be best done in your home country. Alternatively, if already in Norway, look for the word *bilutleie* in a telephone directory. Some of the smaller companies may well offer special, more favourable rates but it would be wise to take local advice. Norway has only a small population and there is not an abundance of vehicles for hire. Booking ahead is advisable especially in the high season. Some contacts in the towns most likely to be the point of hire are given on p22.

Rules, regulations and practicalities

The laws that are likely to affect the foreign driver are not restrictive or unusual but, it has to be said, they will be enforced rigorously. I recall a police official in Mo i Rana some years ago who, when asked what was his attitude to speeding, replied that he usually recommended a fine which would leave the driver with just enough money to leave the country.

❏ ROAD SIGNS

Sign	Meaning
Forbudt	Forbidden (eg *Parkering Forbudt* = No Parking; *Kjøring Forbudt* = No Entry; *All Stans Forbudt* = No Stopping; *Forbudt for syklende* = No cycling)
Redverk Mangler	No crash barrier. This generally indicates a temporary removal.
Kollektivfelt for buss og drosje	Stopping place for buses and taxis
Gatetun	Pedestrian space
Slutt	Finish (with a pictogram means the end of a restriction)
Kjør Sakte/Vegarbeidere	Roadworks.This may well be a section of road under construction for several kilome -tres. Look out for the students manning the walkie-talkies at the ends of the section.
Bomstasjon Toll plaza (also *Vegbom*)	Tollgate
Løs Grus	Loose chippings. Something of a misnomer, these may well turn out to be the size of small boulders.
Svake Kauter/Lose Vei Kauter	Soft edges. A frequent cause of accidents as a vehicle's nearside wheels collapse into the bordering ditch. Especially important to avoid in springtime if the surface is water-bound gravel.
Ferist	Cattle/reindeer grid. On minor roads and becoming increasingly common, these signs should be respected or your exhaust system may well part company with the vehicle.

● **Driving and alcohol** The simple rule is: if you are driving do not drink any alcohol before, during or even after the drive. Tests can be made up to 6 hours after an incident. The alcohol limit is just 0.5ml and the penalties are more severe than in most other countries. If you purchase a medicine in Norway which may affect your driving it will be marked with a red triangle.

● **Rule of the road** As with the rest of continental Europe, driving is to the right with overtaking on the left. Overtaking must not be across an unbroken central line; across a broken warning line it is to be carried out, if necessary, with extreme caution. Priority is given to vehicles approaching from the right but main roads have priority over minor roads.

● **Lights, belts and helmets** Norway has followed the long established Swedish rule requiring dipped headlights at all times. Flashing headlights as a warning or as an invitation to overtake should be avoided. Use of seatbelts is compulsory, including in the back seats of a car, if they are fitted. Crash hel-mets are required for drivers and passengers of motorcycles and mopeds.

A cautionary tale

Not so long ago my research assistant was driving me south along the E6 in our Land Rover. We were descending from the Polar Circle crossing of Saltfjellet on a road which was almost empty of traffic. We got no further than Krokstrand before we were stopped by the police and told that we had been recorded as travelling at 92km/h on a short, straight stretch of the Highway where the limit was the usual 80km/h. Therefore, there would be a fine to be paid on the spot, credit cards accepted. There was an alternative: five days' jail. My companion was somewhat relieved when I paid the fine: NOK800 for exceeding the limit by 12km/h (or less than 10mph). A few days later, I was caught: 61km/h in a 50km/h area: NOK1000 fine. In Norway, speed limits are intended to be observed.

● **Road signs** Most road signs conform to international standards but a few important signs may not carry a pictogram and these are given opposite. The placing of signs and their legibility are excellent.

● **Road numbers** Norway's main roads are classified as being in one of three categories: European routes, trunk routes or national roads. European routes (such as the Arctic Highway) carry the letter E before the number. The signs for E roads and trunk roads are green with white numerals. National roads are marked by black numerals on a white background. The Arctic Highway is the E6. Roads are very well signposted so you have to try quite hard to get lost.

Many of Norway's roads were re-numbered on 16 June 1992. Initially this caused confusion but only if you are using an old map will there be a problem now. However, some general road maps were re-printed after 1992 without the changes being made so check before you start out. Look at your map, check if the road entering Mo i Rana from Sweden is marked as the E79. If it is, throw the map away and buy one on which the road is properly designated as the E12.

To simplify matters, in this book all numbered roads are given their number preceded by the word 'Route' unless an 'E' road.

● **Speed limits** There is a confusing range of speed limits operating in Norway, from 90km/h down to 30km/h in 10km/h intervals. The highest speed allowed is restricted to motorway-standard roads and the 10km/h is an advisory speed on some sharp bends. There may be a temptation to put the foot down on the accelerator pedal when confronted by long-distance journeys and an almost traffic-free road. Don't. Even along the E6 Arctic Highway the speed limit is only 80km/h and in many places will be less. In built-up areas the limit is generally 50km/h. A built-up area may simply be a couple of farms 100m from the road, so beware. In 'residential' areas the limit drops to 30km/h. The speed limits are usually prominently displayed but may change suddenly and unexpectedly. In one or two places the Norwegians are adopting the sign, common in Finland and Sweden, of the silhouette of a town (building outlines and a church spire) to indicate a built-up area. The same sign with a red cancellation stripe indicates the exit from a town. Speed limits for caravans and trailers without brakes are a low 60km/h.

The sign *Automatisk Trafikkontrol* doesn't mean traffic signals. It indicates a speed camera which, unlike in the UK, is almost certain to be operating. There's not a lot of crime in Norway so there are plenty of police for traffic duty, operating even in the most remote areas.

● **Other rules** In towns, pedestrian have absolute right of way at marked crossings. Drivers observe this rule and driving along the Arctic Highway through a town like Narvik can mean you stop a dozen or so times. Watching Norwegian drivers, it sometimes seem that they stop in anticipation rather than waiting for a pedestrian to stand on the kerb.

There are frequent campaigns to cut the number of road accidents involving children. Motorists are warned in advance when a new school term is about to start. Norwegian children are no more or less cautious than other youngsters, but accidents to children are an especially sensitive issue in Norway.

There are lay-bys and picnic places on the borders of some roads, often well chosen beauty spots with good views. The best have tables, benches and a WC. It is important to note that it may be forbidden to use such lay-bys if it means crossing to the non-driving side of the road. As one goes further north, the frequency of stopping places diminishes markedly. In Finnmark there are very few.

On narrow sections of road there are very short sections of wider carriageway which might be mistaken for lay-bys. Marked with the letter 'M' (for *møteplass*), these are for passing only and stopping is forbidden.

● **Fuel and breakdowns** There is an adequate number of refuelling points along the Highway and its branches but some indication of their location will be given in Parts 4 to 9 where gaps between petrol stations are large. A fuel station can be assumed in the towns and larger villages.

There should be no need to carry spare fuel although a can for emergencies may be reassuring. (Remember, full fuel cans are not permitted on the North Sea ferries.) A sensible practice for most drivers is to refuel at the first opportunity when the tank is third to half full.

Only a few fuel stations are open for 24 hours and, on holidays and Sundays, may close by 18.00. What is more, they tend to make changes in opening times so that by the time you make the return journey some small but important alteration may have occurred. All the same, most will be open from at least 10.00 to 17.00, even in the most remote places.

Both leaded and lead-free (*blyfri*) petrol, as well as diesel, are available in North Norway. Petrol is usually available at 95 or 98 octane. Prices are some of the highest in Europe despite Norway's rich endowment in oil. There is a small differential in price in favour of lead-free but the low prices for diesel are long gone and the favourable differential is very small. Credit cards are usually welcome for payment; travellers' cheques *may* be accepted although ask first.

Breakdowns are a nuisance wherever they occur but the remoteness of North Norway presents additional problems. It is quite possible to find a point on a road where the distance to the nearest habitation, let alone garage, is 20km or much more. That's a long walk.

Another cautionary tale

I was camping along Route 95 when one evening, driving back to camp, we were stopped by a panic-stricken Italian who informed us that his four-wheel drive Mercedes was stuck in a bog on the top of a slope. The ground had looked safe enough and the party had assumed that a slope might well be drained. After reconnoitring a safe path towards their vehicle, I backed my Land Rover up the slope towards them but, despite every effort with a shovel and tow rope, we could move them only a few metres. Eventually we had to drive back to a telephone at Olderfjord, a round distance of 44km. Next morning a truck with a crane attached came out from Skaidi, 45km away, and dragged the Italians' Mercedes out of the bog. They had spent a very cold night regretting their lack of caution.

If a breakdown occurs, and the problem demands help, the best plan is to flag down a passing driver and either ask if he or she will summon assistance or beg a lift to the nearest telephone. Houses and other points where a telephone is available for public use may be indicated by road signs but these are few and far between so it is wiser to try to reach a village. To call up assistance it is best to enquire of a garage or look up the word *redningstjeneste* in a telephone directory. Even the smallest garage in North Norway will probably be able and willing to come to a driver's assistance but charges can be high. Because of the area's remoteness there is a general acceptance that everyone comes to the aid of another in need but, like anywhere else, it should not be taken for granted that the first vehicle to be waved down will actually stop.

The main motoring organization in Norway is the Norges Automobil-forbund (NAF, ☎ 22 34 16 00; 🖷 22 42 88 30) and, as a member of Alliance Internationale de Tourisme (AIT), it is affiliated to most national motoring organizations such as the AA and RAC in Great Britain and the AAA in the USA. Members of affiliated associations will be given help by the NAF, and I have personal experience of their efficiency and kindness.

● **Convoy driving** Winter driving may include travelling in a convoy behind a snowplough and there are a number of points to bear in mind if this should occur. You may be turned away if the number of vehicles is too great or if the snowplough driver (responsible for the convoy) deems your vehicle to be unfit for the trip – or even if the driver and passengers are inadequately clothed. Radiator grills should be covered and it is important to have a torch, tow rope and snow shovel on board. Once in the convoy, travel should be at a steady speed keeping sight of the vehicle in front and maintaining a warm air supply to the windscreen. Foglights, if fitted, should be switched on. It is forbidden to leave the convoy or to turn off and, if forced to stop, passengers and driver should not leave the vehicle.

● **Off-road driving** Even if not camping, there will be times when, either along the Arctic Highway or one of its branches, a driver will wish to pull off the road. Along the Highway this is becoming increasingly difficult as the road

❏ **DECANTING FACILITIES FOR MOBILE TOILETS**

Decanting facilities for mobile toilets on the Highway or its branches:

Facility	Telephone
Hauknes Kro & Bensin, Mo i Rana (5km south)	75 13 58 40
Sjøgata, Fauske Kommune, Fauske	75 60 06 00
Hunstad og Morkved Veisenter, AS Shell, Bodø	75 51 56 00
Hilling Shellservice Innhavet, Hamerøy	75 77 25 61
Statoil Norge Fagernes Autosenter AS, Narvik	76 94 71 80
Shell beisinstasjon, Setermoen	77 18 10 97
Gratangen Hotell, Gratangen	76 92 02 40
Sørstraumen Camping, Sørstraumen	77 76 99 10
Helligskogen Youth Hostel, Skibotn	77 74 54 60
Lyngenfjord Camping, Djupvik, Olderdalen	77 71 71 21
Alta Motor, Alta	78 44 40 50
Skaidicenteret, Skaidi	78 41 62 01
Shellstasjonen, Kautokeino	78 48 63 49
Shellstasjonen, Karasjok	78 46 60 03
NAF Nordkapp Camping, North Cape	78 47 33 77
Esso/Lakselv Auto, Lakselv	78 46 13 66
Shell Bensinstasjon, Kirkenes	78 99 33 10

is raised to prevent snow accumulations. On most of the minor roads this is not a problem. Even if driving a vehicle with four-wheel drive, the greatest caution should be exercised. Forest areas are usually safe but open ground, while appearing perfectly sound, may be little more than bog. It is foolish in the extreme to drive off the road without first inspecting the surface. Some areas are affected by sporadic permafrost and when the upper surface defreezes in summer the water is unable to drain downwards and the upper layers (the 'active zone') become waterlogged. If you wish to drive off the road the best plan is to make a careful inspection first by walking the path it is intended to follow. If there is any hint that the ground is unsound, do not attempt to drive on it. I always carry out this procedure using a pair of transceivers to communicate between the driver and the person inspecting the ground. If there is snow on the ground do not attempt to leave the road.

It's important to remember that the further north you travel the more fragile is the environment. It will take decades for the vegetation, and even the soil, to recover from being compacted or mangled by the wheels of a vehicle. This is especially the case where it is obvious that there is only the thinnest covering of lichens, mosses or grass. The rule must be to avoid driving over such surfaces even if they are solid enough to take the weight of the truck or car.

Off-road driving is best restricted to existing paths where it is clear that other vehicles have gone before. These include many of the old winter roads, often across the vidde, which may be marked by tall sticks or the slender trunks of stunted birch trees which have been cut for the purpose. One such route is described in Part 7 p230 as an alternative route between Alta and Kautokeino.

● **Caravans, campers and heavy vehicles** The E6 (Arctic Highway) from Mo i Rana to Kirkenes is deemed suitable for caravans and trailers for the whole of its length and only one or two of the major branch roads are classified as difficult. Some routes up to Mo may be best avoided by cars trailing caravans but alternatives will be described in the next part. A map showing routes to be avoided by caravans is available from the Norwegian Tourist Board.

The width limit for vehicles is 2.5m and if caravans or trailers are between 2.3m and 2.5m the towing vehicle must be at least as wide as the trailer. Caravan mirrors are compulsory but they must be removed when not towing. If your vehicle or trailer is greater than 2.5m wide you must seek permission from the **Directorate of Public Roads** (*Vegdirektoratet*): Statens Vegvesen, Norwegian Administration of Public Roads, Directorate of Public Roads, Box 8142, Dep N-0033, Oslo (☎ 22 07 35 00; 🖹 22 07 37 68; 🖴 frmapost@veg vesen.no). General information can be had on ☎ 22 65 40 40 but this is largely to detail winter road closures and getting anything other than recorded information in Norwegian may be difficult.

Contacting Statens Vegvesen can get you all sorts of information about road conditions and closures as well as a map showing permitted axle weights on roads. Alternatively contact a national office of the Norwegian Tourist Board (for addresses see p36). The only section of the Highway from Mo i Rana to Kirkenes where the permitted axle load is less than the national maximum (10,000kg) is across the Saltfjell north of Mo. During the spring thaw the limits may be reduced for short periods and many of the Highway's branches are unsuitable for heavy vehicles.

For those whose caravans or camper vans have built-in toilets, there are decanting facilities provided at a number of locations in northern Norway, almost all at petrol stations (*bensinstasjonen*, see p28).

● **Insurance, licences and documents** Third party insurance is compulsory. A full driving licence, valid for the vehicle being driven, issued by a national authority, must be carried by the driver. If the driving licence does not include a photograph, reference will be made to the passport which should, in any case, be carried at all times. Some evidence that the vehicle is owned by a member of the party or being legitimately driven (eg on hire) should be included in the documentation. For vehicles registered in the UK, the Vehicle Registration Document (Form V5), which is issued by the DVLA at Swansea, is the obvious choice if you own the vehicle. If not, carry the document plus a note from the registered keeper detailing all who are driving with permission. The police can be very finicky about minor details.

● **Animals** Even in the southern fylker it is quite possible that you will come across reindeer or elk on the road. While elk may be encountered singly, reindeer will usually be in small groups. If one reindeer crosses the road in front of you, you can be pretty certain others will follow. Both elk and reindeer are likely to dash out of roadside forests without warning. Caution signs are usually displayed by the roadside in southern parts of Norway but in the north, where the majority of reindeer are to be found, it's best to assume they might be anywhere. A fully grown reindeer may weigh 250kg; an elk much more. If you hit one it is not only the animal that will suffer. You should also report any fatal encounter, or instance when the animal is seriously injured, to the police.

Goats and cattle may also be found on some rural roads. Goats seem particularly fond of taking shelter in the entrances to road tunnels.

● **Tolls** The cost of new roads, tunnels and bridges is often partly offset by making a toll charge to users for some years after the construction is finished. The charges are modest but unavoidable. To discourage vehicles entering Oslo, Bergen and Trondheim, there are charges at some entry points. In the country there are still a number of private roads on which you'll find a toll being charged for the use of the road. Often there is no toll booth but payment is made by putting the charge into an honesty box and recording your registration number. These private roads are difficult and expensive to maintain and paying the fee is the least you can do to keep these tracks open. They often lead to some of the most interesting places in the area. If you see the sign '*Stopp, Bom*', don't be alarmed. *Bom* means barrier and you'll be approaching a tollgate.

It's important to have adequate small change ready at toll stations (and for ferries) or you'll incur the wrath of those behind you.

ACCOMMODATION

There is sufficient accommodation along the Arctic Highway to satisfy demand for most of the year but at peak season, late June to mid-August, it is wise to book ahead and in the low season the larger hotels may be fully booked for conferences. It has become quite fashionable in recent years for Norwegian and even international companies to hold conferences within the Polar Circle especially in towns served by airports. Paradoxically, the tourist peak season is the cheapest (look for *sommerpris* or *mini-pris*) and some hotels offer low weekend prices (*weekend tilbud*).

In Scandinavia it is difficult to classify the options in terms of price. Some would say that everywhere is 'expensive' and that none is 'budget'. The truth is that the standards are generally very high even for Europe and Norway is one of the most expensive places in which to travel. You cannot expect to find the US$2-a-night budget bed. It makes more sense to classify accommodation by reference to its type: campsite, hotel, guesthouse (called either *gjestehus* or *pensjonat*). Additionally, some private homes offer bed and breakfast (look for *overnatting* signs), and there is a good range of self-catering cabins (*hytter*) on the camping sites. Within these divisions there will be significant differences in price which largely reflect the quality and quantity of the facilities on offer as well as the location of the establishment. Thus, the large 300-room 'business' hotel in, say, Narvik, Tromsø or Bodø will be expensive but will usually have a range of eating places, and en-suite bedrooms with a television and so on. Almost all establishments will include breakfast in the price and you can assume the rooms are en suite unless otherwise stated.

In Parts 3 to 9, various options are described but it must be remembered that changes do occur quite quickly with, say, a change in management or owner-ship. Some of the smaller guesthouses may not be open at the time you pass by simply because the owner is away. As you travel further north the summer sea-son gets shorter and shorter. By late August some hotels and many guesthouses and camping sites will be closed until the following year.

Hotels and guesthouses

Prices are reasonable but rather on the high side of the European average. Almost all will include breakfast in the room price and rates are usually per room rather than per person so that a double room may be only a little more than the price of a single. Children will usually be accommodated at greatly reduced prices if sharing a room with adults. Combination (combie) rooms are common and provide an extra bed which converts into a settee in the daytime.

The larger hotel chains offer 'passes' or 'hotel cheques' which may be worth considering. These can be used only in the hotels of that group and at their best can be a real saving – often up to 50% on the usual rates. However, there are two points to note. Firstly, the number of hotels of any single group which makes these offers is small in North Norway. Secondly, it is essential to make it clear at the time of booking, or at least when signing the register, that you intend to use a pass or voucher. Some chains seem reluctant to acknowledge their own discount system. Because the 'hotel pass' systems vary from year to year it is best to make enquiries from the Norwegian Tourist Board's national office (see address section at the end of this part) when planning the trip.

If booking ahead, and this is wise, an international telephone call, a fax or an email is the simplest system and it is usually unnecessary to use an agent. Almost all hotels and even simple guesthouses will understand English and they will also confirm the booking in writing if asked to do so. If booking while in Norway a simple plan is to ask the reception at one hotel to telephone ahead to the next. They will usually do this free of charge. If you use local tourist offices, there may well be a small charge. Alternatively, there is a perfectly adequate public telephone system in Norway.

Accommodation standards in Scandinavia as a whole are high and North Norway is no exception. Most of the hotels are modern with en-suite facilities and small guesthouses will be clean and adequate. Throughout this book, you can assume that there are en-suite facilities unless stated otherwise.

It's worth noting that the exterior appearances of many of Norway's hotels are unflattering. They often manage to look bland at best and often drab. It's as well to go inside before you make a judgement.

Breakfast, not least because its cost is usually included in the room rate, is to be savoured. The average Norwegian breakfast is a major buffet meal. In the bigger hotels it is possible to eat enough to take you through to dinner in the evening!

The most expensive feature of hotels is the price charged for meals other than breakfast. A very ordinary evening meal may well be double the price of a more elaborate meal in a similar hotel in most of the rest of Europe. Alcohol prices, as is well known, border on the prohibitive. Entertainment, even in the largest hotels, is simple or non-existent. Occasionally there will be a 'group' playing in the restaurant. For reasons of cost these groups almost always seem to originate from Eastern Europe. Many hotels now feature a sauna and a very few have small heated indoor swimming pools.

Annual guides to hotels, motels and guesthouse accommodation are published and are available from the Norwegian Tourist Board. For reasons best known to the board they are usually not available until after Easter though the guides from the previous year will be quite adequate for most purposes.

Self-catering and camping

Undoubtedly, the least expensive way to travel the Highway is to use the cabins and campsites, or to wild camp (see p85), where self-catering is the rule. Most camping sites in North Norway are open only in the summer season and they will usually cater for those wishing to use cabins (*hytter*), to park a caravan or camper or to put up a tent. The cabins vary in size and quality and there is a somewhat unreliable star system for campsites. On some sites there may be a shop and, less often, a cafeteria.

A high standard of **hytter** can be expected anywhere in Scandinavia and they are ideal for families who want low-price accommodation and who are prepared to cook for themselves. The cabins accommodate between two and six persons and while bedding is not, as a rule, provided, almost everything else may be. This can include a well-equipped kitchen with sink and electric rings for cooking, bathroom with shower and WC, and a sitting area as well as bedrooms.

The spaces for **caravans** and **tents** are often rather poor quality although, on the better sites, caravans may be able to link up to the site's electricity supply. Tent spaces may be considered scruffy in comparison to those in more southerly countries because the climate does not favour the growth of a suitable grass cover. If travelling by caravan, you should note that most of the bigger sites have sewage disposal units. Additionally, there are decanting facilities as listed on p28.

Generally it is the cost of meals that you will find high. If self-catering, and space in the vehicle allows, it is wise to bring items of food that are cheaper at home. This includes tinned goods. Milk, bread, vegetables and fruit can be purchased locally. Many of the petrol/service stations have well-stocked shops.

Information about campsite locations and standards is available from the Norwegian Tourist Board or from the Norges Automobilforbund (see p27).

It is important to note that the electricity supply in Norway is AC at 220 Volts and the standard socket takes two round pins. Many campers experience difficulties in obtaining supplies of gas. For example, the standard cans of Camping Gaz International are not readily available. The best option is to make enquiries from suppliers in your home country and take sufficient stocks for the entire journey.

Rubbish!

Many years ago I used to bury all degradable rubbish when camping. On later visits I discovered that previous years' waste was as fresh as ever. I now bag all rubbish and put it in wayside bins or dispose of it in containers provided in the small towns. On one occasion, this system did not work quite as planned. Our rubbish bags were loosely tied to the back of the Land Rover for convenience while we camped. On an early morning departure, we forgot to put them in the vehicle with the inevitable result. Unknown to us the bags split open as we drove along leaving a trail of camping refuse in our wake! Stopping to pick up provisions later that morning, all that remained as evidence was a tiny fragment of plastic bag.

Wild camping

If wild camping is chosen, and there is a lot to be said for choosing your own site, there are remarkably few rules. Camping is permitted on any uncultivated land at least 150m away from any dwelling. Open fires are forbidden between mid-April and mid-September, and in a dry summer it is essential to be very careful, especially in forest areas. The water from most streams and rivers is quite safe to drink but any petrol station will gladly allow you to fill water containers. Camping in the wild is, perhaps, particularly appropriate to a journey along the Arctic Highway. There is an abundance of small streams, rivers and waterfalls and idyllic sites can be found off the Highway along some of the minor roads and tracks. Of course, the weather may not always be ideal for camping but on a fine day with only the sound of a bubbling stream and the thought that the nearest human being may be many miles away, it has a primitive attraction.

Thirty or forty years ago, when the Arctic Highway was little more than a gravel track, finding a place to camp just off the Highway was relatively easy. Today, it is much more likely that you'll need to make a detour along a minor road. As has been said, any farmed area should be avoided. It's important to recall that hay is a vital crop for the winter feed of stock. What may look like a rough grass field maybe someone's hay. If a farmed area cannot be avoided, you should seek the farmer's permission. It will probably be willingly given.

Ideal wild-camping sites are along rivers or by the side of lakes. The prospect of a swim is enticing but the water temperature is likely to be cold. However, in a country blessed with so many beautiful lakes, streams and waterfalls, the temptation may be irresistible. A further attraction, if wild camping, is the attitude to nude bathing which is not forbidden under Norwegian law, although one should, of course, avoid giving offence if others are around. There's something especially invigorating in taking a shower under a small waterfall.

The freedom to camp more or less where one likes places a special responsibility on the campers to leave the site as they found it. Rubbish degrades slowly in an Arctic climate.

MAPS

There is a very large range of maps available for the whole of Scandinavia and a rather smaller selection for the area traversed by the Arctic Highway. It might be best to select a fairly small-scale map for the journey up to the Highway and then have available more detailed sheets for North Norway.

A good general-purpose regional map is Michelin's *Scandinavia and Finland Map* at 1:1.5 million. For a simple, easy-to-read map for early planning there is Phillip's *Scandinavia Road Map*. Its weakness is the north for which a scale of 1:3.5 million has been chosen. The south is covered at an adequate 1:1 million and there are street maps of central Oslo, Stockholm and Helsinki.

If the approach is through Norway, then *Bilkart* (car map) *over Norge* at a scale of 1:1 million would be an inexpensive choice. This single sheet covering all of Norway is specifically intended for the motorist and is published by the Norwegian Tourist Board. Two features of this map are especially helpful: large-scale plans of the major towns, and distance charts. Because the map covers all Norway, it will put the Arctic Highway from Mo i Rana to Kirkenes into perspective but it is probably on too small a scale to be really useful when travelling the Highway itself.

For the Highway one of the best general maps is undoubtedly the Cappellen 1:400,000 (*Bil-og Turistkart*) series now published by Kümmerly and Frey. In the more recent editions sheets 4 and 5 will take in the whole length of the E6 from Mo i Rana to Kirkenes as well as covering the three northern fylker. In the older editions, which may still be available, the relevant sheets (sold as doubles) were 7/8 and 9/10. The particular merits of these Cappellen maps are their high cartographic standards, leading to exceptional clarity, their frequent revision and the fact that they are specifically aimed at the traveller. At 1:400,000, the scale allows most of the detail a driver will require and they are folded in a way as to make sequential use south to north (or north to south) particularly easy in a vehicle.

If more detailed maps are sought, then there is the official *Vegkart* (Road map), Norge series, at a scale of 1:250,000. This is published jointly by Statens Kartverk and Statens Vegvesen but it is quite expensive because no less than nine sheets (numbers 13–21) will be needed to cover the length of the Highway and its environs. It is a road map but there is a wealth of topographical information as well, although I have never found them very easy to use on the road because they are intended to be spread out flat rather than folded.

There is also a national 1:50,000 series but in an area as vast and uninhabited as North Norway, this scale would be of limited value to the traveller although it would prove helpful to anyone doing research in the region.

All the maps mentioned should be available in Norway or from any good cartographic retailer such as Edward Stanford in London (12–14 Long Acre, London, W2; ☎ 020 7836 1321).

A visit to the Map Room at the Royal Geographical Society (Kensington Gore) will give you a chance to consult detailed maps. The recently refurbished room is open to the public but check before visiting (☎ 020 7591 3050).

TIME ZONES AND TELEPHONES

Norway's time zone is GMT+1. However, because of its high latitude, North Norway stretches as far east as Cairo as the lines of longitude converge towards the poles. Strictly, therefore, East Finnmark should be GMT+2. For the purist, this will mean that the midnight sun will come early!

Sweden is in the same zone as Norway and Finland is GMT+2.

Norway's telephone system is efficient and, if there's habitation, there's probably a telephone. Telephone directories are regionally based with just two for the North of Norway: Nordland and a combined Troms, Finnmark and Svalbard directory. There are *Yellow Pages*, a commercial section and an alphabetical listing. A total of thirteen directories cover the whole country with Oslo being the only town to have its own edition. The directories list the numbers for the police (*politi*), the fire service (*brann*) and the emergency doctor service (*legevaktsentral*) in all the main centres of each region. In an emergency, the police can be called by dialling ☎ 112, with the fire service on ☎ 110 and the ambulance service on ☎ 113, from anywhere in Norway. Response times will be considerable in areas away from towns.

Check whether your mobile phone will operate in Scandinavia before you leave. Certainly it is helpful to have a mobile in the remote parts of the north. Finland is the home of the mobile phone and almost everyone has one.

For international calls into Norway, the country code is 47. Sweden's code is 46 and there are area codes. Finland's country code is 358 and, again, there are area codes. The country codes in Scandinavia and Finland have been omitted throughout the book, but area codes are shown for Sweden and Finland in Part 3. These area codes should be used when calling from one area to another. For international calls into Sweden and Finland, use the area code but omit the initial zero. Norway does not have area codes. To get an international connection when in Norway, Sweden or Finland the access code is 00.

LANGUAGE

Any English speaker will have little trouble communicating in Norway. It often seems as though English is the first language. Prior to World War II, German was the main foreign language taught in schools Now it is only the more elderly members of the population who don't have a remarkable fluency in English. Many Norwegians will start with an apology for their poor English and then proceed to show that they have a quite extraordinary command of the language. Some may have a slight American accent, depending on their teachers' educational background. If you travel through Norway you will find that it is quite easy to guess the meaning of many of the words on signs.

The same situation will be met in Sweden and the Norwegian and Swedish languages are very similar, so much so that they can generally understand each other except for the odd word or phrase.

In Finland there can be two problems. Firstly, the proportion of English speakers is somewhat less, at least on the level of general understanding.

Secondly, it is almost impossible for the native English speaker to guess at the meaning of words in Finnish. Pronunciation is easy: simply pronounce as you see the word written. But to understand is quite another matter. The Finnish language is one of the Finno-Ugrian group, as is the Sami language. It's sometimes said that only a Finn can understand Finnish and not even all Finns can! The reason is that Finland is strictly bilingual, Finnish and Swedish. Road names, for example in Helsinki, will often be in both languages. In fact, only some 5% or so speak Swedish and they live largely in the south and south-west.

❑ **NORWEGIAN NATIONAL TOURIST OFFICES**

For general information you can use the website: 🖥 www.visitnorway.com.

Country	Address	Telephone/email
Norway	Norges Turistråd, PO Boks 722 Sentrum, NO-0105, Oslo	+47 24 14 46 00 norway@ntr.no
United Kingdom	Norwegian Tourist Board, 5th floor, Charles House, 5 Lower Regent Street, London SW1Y 4LR	0906 302 2003 (Calls 50p per minute) greatbritain@ntr.no
USA/Canada	Norwegian Tourist Board, 655 Third Avenue, Suite 1810, New York 1, NY 10017	+1 212-885 9700 usa@ntr.no
Sweden	Norges Turistråd Sverige, PO Box 3363, SE-103 67 Stockholm	+46 (0)8-7918300 sweden@ntr.no
Finland	Norjan Matkailuneuvotso, PO Box 3363, SE-103 67 Stockholm	+46 (0)8-7918307 finland@ntr.no
Denmark	Norges Turistråd, Amaliegade 39, DK-1256 København K	+45 33 19 36 09 denmark@ntr.no
Germany/Austria /Switzerland	Norwegisches Fremdenverkehrsamt, Postfach 113317, D-20433 Hamburg, Germany	+49 (0)1 80 50 01 54 8 germany@ntr.no
Belgium/Nether -lands	Noors Verkeersbureau Benelux, Postbus 101, NL- 2460 AC Ter Aar, The Netherlands	+31 (0)900-8991170 norway@twi.nl
France	Office National du Tourisme de Norvège, BP 497, FR-75366 Paris Cedex 08	+33 (0)1-53 23 00 50 france@ntr.no
Italy	Ente Norvegese per il Turismo, Corso XXII Marzo, 4 I-20135 Milan	+39 (0)2-55193588 italy@ntr.no
Japan	Scandinavian Tourist Board Izumikan Gobancho 4F, 12-11 Gobancho, Chiyoda-ku, 102-0076, Tokyo	+81 (0)3-52121121 japan@ntr.no
Spain	Consejo de Turismo de Noruega, Real Embajada de Noruega, Paseo de la Castellana 31-9, E-28046 Madrid	+34 91-3197303 spain@ntr.no
Australia	Royal Norwegian Embassy, 17 Hunter St, Yarralumla, ACT 2600	+61 (0)2-6273 3444 emb.canberra@mfa.no

In reading this book you may well be puzzled by some of the spellings. The aim has been to spell place and feature names in the manner you are likely to find them on the ground, in street signs, local guidebooks and so on. Even so there may seem to be inconsistencies unless you remember that, in Norwegian, the definite article is given to a word by a suffix (-a, -en, or -et). Plural forms are generally given the suffix -er or -ene.

Hence *gate* = street but *gata* = the street. In some cases *gate/gata* is written *Gate/Gata* and may sometimes be merged with the street's name (eg *Storgata* = the High Street).

There are actually two forms of Norwegian still in use (especially in place names). These are *Bokmål* and *Nynorsk* and they often give a slightly different spelling to what is effectively the same word. For example, *sommer* (Bokmål) and *sommar* (Nynorsk) both mean summer. (Incidentally, the final -er is not the definite article here.) 'The summer' would be *sommeren*. When such words occur as part of place names (eg Sommerset/Sommarset) the local spelling has been used.

Because the stem of the words remain unchanged you shouldn't have any difficulty in understanding what is meant. When there might be a problem, the translation of the Norwegian word is given the first time it appears in the text.

There can be further confusion on the ground because the Sami and Finnish languages are also used, especially in Finnmark. But don't worry. Most of the people you'll meet speak excellent English!

GETTING ADVICE

This book is especially designed to guide the independent traveller who finds that much of the joy of travel comes from making plans. Anyone needing more advice can turn to a travel agent and there are a small number who specialize in Norway although few have detailed experience of the north.

The tourist board may be the first port of call when planning an Arctic Highway trip. There is an increasing number of national and regional tourist publications, most of them free, but do not expect the tourist board to make travel arrangements; that is not their function.

❏ REGIONAL TOURIST OFFICES FOR NORTH NORWAY

Organization	Address	Telephone/email/web
Nordland Reiseliv	PO Box 434, Storgarten 4A, N-8001 Bodø	75 54 52 00 nordland@nordlandreiseliv.no www.nordlandreiseliv.no
Destinasjon Tromsø	Postboks 311, N-9253 Tromsø	77 61 00 00 info@destinasjontromso.no www.destinasjontromso.no
Finnmark Tourist Board Ltd	Sorenskriverveien 13, N-9511 Alta	78 44 00 20 post@visitnorthcape.com www.visitnorthcape.com

❏ **LOCAL TOURIST OFFICES (TURISTINFORMASJON) ALONG THE HIGHWAY AND ITS BRANCHES**

Office	Telephone	Email
Alta*	78 45 77 77	
Ballangen	72 92 82 08	
Bardu	77 18 10 97	
Bardufoss/Målselv*	77 83 42 25	
Bodø*	75 52 60 00	
Fauske*	75 64 33 03	salten.reseliv@online.no
Hammerfest*	78 41 21 85	info@hammerfest-turist.no
Honningsvåg/Nordkapp*	78 47 25 99	info@northcape.no
Karasjok*	78 46 88 10	koas@koas.no
Kautokeino	78 45 65 00	
Kirkenes*	78 99 25 44	postmottak@sor-varanger.kommune.no
Kvænangsfjellet/Gildetun	77 76 99 58	
Lakselv	78 46 21 45	
Mo i Rana*	75 13 92 00	infomo@arctic-circle.no
Målselv/Bardufoss*	77 83 42 25	
Narvik*	76 94 33 09	post@narvikinfo.no
Nordkapp/Honningsvåg*	78 47 25 99	
Nordreisa/Storslett*	77 76 56 76	reiseliv@online.no
Olderdalen/Kåfjord	94 54 85 44	
Skaidi Info Senter A/S	78 41 62 80	
Skibotn	77 71 54 77	
Stabbursnes	78 46 47 65	stabburs@online.no
Storslett/Nordreisa	77 76 56 76	
Tana Bru	78 92 53 98	postmottak@tana.kommune.no
Tromsø Arrangement A/S*	77 61 00 00	info@destinasjontromso.no
Vadsø	78 95 44 90	museum@vadso.kommune.no
Vardø	78 98 84 04	contact@hexeria.no
Varangerbotn/Nessby*	78 95 99 20	info@varanger-samiske.museum.no

* Indicates offices currently staffed all year round

MONEY MATTERS

All prices in this book are in the currency of the country in which they apply.

Norway's currency is the *krone* (crown) divided into 100 øre. The shorthand for the Norwegian krone is NOK (sometimes Nkr) but within the country you'll see it as kr, followed by the number of crowns. Swedish currency is very similar, using the *krona* (crown) divided into 100 øre. SEK (sometimes Skr) is used internationally but simply kr within the country. Finland has embraced the Euro and this is shown internationally as EUR but within the country the symbol € is used. The shorthand NOK, SEK and € is used throughout this book.

In mid 2003 the exchange rates to the pound sterling (GBP) were such that, as a rough estimate, you could divide NOK by 11.5, SEK by 13 and € by 1.4 to find the cost in pounds. For the US dollar (US$) the comparative figures were 7 and 8 for the Norwegian and Swedish crown respectively. Of course these 'ready reckoner' figures are very approximate and become more and more misleading as sums increase. In any case, exchange-rate fluctuations may well render the figures obsolete.

Near the borders between Norway, Sweden and Finland, you may find shops willing to accept the currency of the neighbouring country but it is best to have made your own quick calculation regarding the rate of exchange before you make a transaction.

❑ **Exchange rates**
To get the latest rates visit www .xe.com/ucc. At the time of writing they were:

	NOK	SEK	Euro
NOK1	–	1.12	0.12
SEK1	0.89	–	0.11
€1	8.16	9.18	–
UK£1	11.62	13.07	1.42
US$1	7.21	8.10	0.88
Can$1	5.17	5.81	0.63
A$ 1	4.70	5.28	0.58
NZ$1	4.18	4.70	0.51

All three countries have generally adopted the use of international credit cards but don't expect them to be accepted by small traders, guesthouses and the like. The same applies to travellers' cheques.

Most banks have ATMs (cash points) where you can withdraw money direct from your account in your home country using a **debit card** with a Cirrus, Maestro or Eurocard symbol on it. Banks usually charge a small fee for this but their exchange rates are often the best available. It's also possible to use a **credit card** in these machines for a cash advance but you'll probably have to pay interest on this money so it's better to use a debit card.

PART 2: BACKGROUND
INFORMATION

The Arctic Circle lies at latitude 66.5° North, or approximately so, for it shifts very slightly from year to year. This circle round the North Pole encompasses most of Greenland (but not Iceland), the northern third of Alaska, the very north of Canada including the jumble of islands from Baffin Bay to the Beaufort Sea, and northern Siberia. In Europe, Sweden, Finland, Russia and Norway all have substantial areas inside the Circle.

Although all these lands are, in the strictest sense, Arctic, they vary enormously, from the uninhabited ice-cap of Greenland to the oil-rich regions of the Mackenzie and Prudhoe bays. Europe's Arctic is very special. It is unique among the polar lands.

Many roads now cross the Circle in Fennoscandia and in Russia, but only one can claim the title of Europe's Arctic Highway: the E6. This road, threading its way from Mo i Rana to Kirkenes through Norway's Arctic fylker (counties), is supreme. Over 1500km (900 miles) of road, getting to within twenty degrees of the pole itself and extending to an easterly point on almost the same longitude as Cairo – this is Europe's path to the Arctic: Norway's Arctic Highway.

Physical setting: geology and topography

What is so very special about the Norwegian Arctic, about the setting of the E6? Two features single it out, one climatic, the other topographic. Nowhere else in the world so far north enjoys such a relatively mild winter. The North Atlantic Drift, the tail end of the Gulf Stream, separates the cold waters of the Arctic Ocean from the warm waters of the eastern Atlantic. This warm current prevents the polar waters from mixing with those of the Atlantic and ensures that prevailing westerly winds draw warm air across Scandinavia and into north-east Russia. The seas and inlets remain ice-free throughout the year and nowhere do the winter temperatures fall to the levels achieved by the rest of the polar lands. Some of the climatic data has been given in Part 1.

The topographic singularity arises from the unrivalled fracturing of the coast and the recent modification of the land by the effects of the Pleistocene Ice Age. The area traversed by the E6 is in two distinct parts: the Baltic Shield and the Caledonian mountain system of the Scandinavian Highlands.

The Shield, which is the basis of south and east Finnmark and covers the northern stretch of the road, is an area of ancient rocks which have been eroded to produce a landscape like an upturned shield with its northern edge forming the coastal areas. Unlike the areas further south, the coast is broken, not by narrow and steep-sided fjords but by broader and less incised inlets. These are fjords but not the classic sort that you find illustrated in a school geography book.

The rest of North Norway consists of a range of mountains forming a backbone to the Scandinavian peninsula, the highest parts of which approximate to the Norwegian–Swedish border. These mountains present a steep face to the Norwegian Sea and are deeply dissected. As the name, Caledonian, suggests, this mountain range is part of the same system as that in Scotland. The trend lines (direction of the mountain ridges and valleys) is roughly north-east to south-west. This accounts for the alignment of many of the fjords.

Nordland and Troms are squeezed into a narrow coastal belt by the high ranges of these Scandinavian Uplands. When you drive through these counties you are never far from either the sea or the border with Sweden or Finland. Yet, the plateaux are often remote and the broadest, Saltfjellet, is further isolated by one of those relics of the Pleistocene Ice Age, the huge Svartisen ice-cap.

The northern areas of Finland and Scandinavia (Fennoscandia) formed the epicentre of the great ice masses which still covered much of northern Europe 10–12,000 years ago. Just as these regions were probably the first to be covered by ice, they were the last from which the ice retreated, just 8–10,000 years ago. The mark left by the ice on the landscape is everywhere evident and the land is still recovering from the weight of the ice. This can be seen in the emergence of parts of the coastal fringe; a process known as isostatic recovery.

During the Pleistocene geological epoch the old pre-glacial river-cut valleys were deepened and widened into classical glacial troughs with characteristic parabolic cross-sections. Near the coast they were drowned by the sea to form fjords; narrow and steep-sided in the west, but broader and with more gentle slopes in the north. Almost the whole area crossed by the E6 is blanketed by glacial drift: mixtures of sands, gravels and boulders deposited by the ice as it wasted away.

The geology of North Norway is interesting. The rocks include some of the oldest in the world, exposed by millions of years of erosion of the rocks which had been deposited on top. But there are also some of the youngest rocks, recent deposits from post-glacial times. This juxtaposition of the old and the new is especially well seen in the Lofoten Islands (just off the Highway) and in parts of the Baltic Shield in Finnmark.

The ancient rocks are igneous and metamorphic, while the younger include a variety of sedimentary deposits. Because the Highway runs though areas where the climate and steepness of slopes often leave little vegetation cover, the underlying rocks are exposed for all to see. One of the most fascinating stretches of road for geology buffs is the side trip up to the North Cape (see p243).

In summary, the Arctic Highway north of Mo i Rana crosses through three fylker: Nordland, Troms and, in the extreme north, Finnmark. The first two are narrow with nowhere far from the coast, and the mountains and sea come into conjunction. Finnmark, on the other hand, is broader and plateau-like. The plateau or *vidde* slopes southwards into Finland and the scenery, though less grand than in the southern two fylker, is more truly tundra.

❑ Glossary of geographical and geomorphological terms

ablation	Removal of surface snow or ice by any natural means (not simply by melting).
active zone	The relatively thin cover of soil or rock that overlays the permafrost. The active zone is likely to freeze in winter when it becomes 'inactive'.
bedding plane	The surface which separates one bed (layer) of a sedimentary rock from another.
bedload	Weathered and eroded rock and rock fragments carried along the bed of a river/stream.
calving	Process by which the front or snout of a glacier breaks off into the sea or a lake.
cirque	Rock basin in the side of a mountain which has been hollowed out by snow and ice. Often described as an armchair-shaped depression and may still contain ice long after the surrounding area is ice-free (hence: cirque glacier). Also called cwm (Wales), corrie (Scotland).
col	A pass or low-lying gap in a mountain ridge. In North Norway it is most likely the result of a break in the ridge caused by the passage of a glacier.
dead-ice	Stagnant ice mass.
diffluent glacier	Glacier leading away from a general ice mass.
dolomitic limestone	A limestone consisting largely of calcium carbonate and magnesium carbonate.
erratics	Rocks which have been transported from their place of origin by ice. Can include very substantial boulders.
esker	Narrow and winding ridge of sands and gravels produced by streams within an ice mass and deposited when the ice melts.
firn ice	Mass of granular snow that gradually transforms into true glacier (blue) ice. Sometimes known as 'last year's snow'.
glacier	A large body of ice on land which is moving down the slope under the forces of gravity and recrystallization of the ice.
hanging valley	A tributary valley which lies at a higher level than the main valley. The stream of the higher valley may join the lower by way of a waterfall.
ice caldera	Shallow, circular (say 4m diameter) depression in a snowfield.
isostasy	Strictly, the state of balance in the earth's crust. This is upset when large masses of ice accumulate on the land in an ice age. Initially sea level falls but this is followed by the land surface becoming depressed. When the ice melts, sea level rises but later, and slowly, the land surface rises now that the weight of ice has been removed. The rising of the land is called isostatic recovery. This results in wavecut platforms and other phenomena which are common in northern Scandinavia and Finland where the rates of recovery are some of the highest in the world.
knick-point	A break in the slope or profile of a river. May be characterized by a waterfall. In North Norway, these may be the result of a rel -ative fall in sea level as the land rises (see isostasy above) or glaciation (see hanging valley).

❑ **Glossary of geographical and geomorphological terms (continued)**

mica-schist	A metamorphic rock which includes the mineral mica. It splits into thin, almost wafer-like, layers.
moraine	Material carried along by a moving mass of ice such as a glacier. A terminal moraine is the deposit at the ice front or 'snout' of a glacier.
palsa	Mound of peaty soil containing ice lenses and an ice core.
peneplain	An area that has been eroded over a long period of time to form a near-plain with the occasional residual hill interrupting the general flatness.
periglacial	Strictly, near glacial. Areas which probably experience permafrost and have a number of characteristic features but are not permanently covered by ice or snow in all seasons.
permafrost	Permanently frozen ground. Permafrost areas usually have a relatively thin cover of soils and rock which defreezes seasonally. This is the active zone. Permafrost is quite common in the most northerly areas of Norway.
Pleistocene	Geological epoch in which the last ice ages occurred (the Quarternary ice ages). Probably lasted two million years.
re-entrant	A marked recess into any upland (or coastline)
rock bursting	When pressure is reduced on a rock surface, the rock expands causing surface layers to detach from the rock below. The rock is said to 'burst' and can happen naturally, as when surface ice melts, or can be the result of tunnelling.
syenite	A resistant rock similar to granite but without evident quartz.
talus	Loose, weathered rock
wavecut platform	Smooth, marine rock surface cut by waves. May be exposed above sea level if isostatic recovery has occurred (see isostasy).

Fauna and flora

FAUNA

Two mammals are especially associated with Arctic Norway; one very small, the other almost the largest to be found in this part of the world. The lemming is the former and the reindeer the latter.

Although well known, the **lemming**, a member of the *muridae* family, is not likely to be seen unless you happen to be in North Norway in one of those years that their population experiences explosive growth. The little rodent is generally rarely seen for it is nocturnal by habit, small in size and relatively uncommon. They grow to only about 10cm in length and are black and dirty-yellow in colour.

The years of rapid growth in numbers are associated with climatic conditions favourable to a matching growth in the lemmings' food supply. Then, as rapidly as this supply of food increases, so too does its consumption until the lemming finds that the food is in short supply once more. Now comes the reaction for which the lemming is most famous: its 'suicidal' marine excursions. There is, as so often, a certain element of truth in the stories of lemmings hurling themselves over cliffs and into the sea but the explanation is rather more mundane. Large numbers may well be found near the coast. Some of these may be forced over the edge in their frenetic search for food but the idea that there is some conscious decision made is more than a little fanciful. In fact, those that have a watery end are just unlucky. Some perish on the ice of glaciers such as Svartisen but most have a less dramatic end. However they die, the numbers of lemming rapid decrease and the quiet years return when there is food for all: a good example of the balance of nature and dynamic equilibrium.

If your visit to Arctic Norway coincides with that of the lemmings periodic explosive growth in numbers you may well see quite large numbers, especially in what passes for night in these regions. They can be a nuisance because they do not seem to be afraid of people and may run around your feet squeaking as they go in search of the diminishing food supply.

You'll certainly see **reindeer** (known as caribou in North America) as you travel the Arctic Highway and its branches. These relatively small deer are, almost exclusively, owned by the Sami (see p60) who herd them for their meat, antlers and skins. Although the animals are small their antlers are almost comically large. A fully grown male's antlers are magnificent, a sight to behold, and one wonders how the animal can support their weight.

Driving in the north of Norway in summer will give you the best sightings of quite large numbers of reindeer because this is the season that they will be nearest the coast. You may also see elk (moose in North America) but they will be more numerous on your journey towards Mo i Rana than when you're on the Highway. The coat of the deer will be dark in summer but close to all white in winter. Skins can be bought from the Sami, but beware: unless properly dressed you'll find you have just a bag of hair by the time you get home. Reindeer hair is hollow making it ideal for stuffing lifebelts but not necessarily for floor coverings. Reindeer skin is exceptionally warm to sleep on: campers please note.

Of the other mammals, one of the most endangered is the **brown bear**. If you want any sort of a chance to see one, the best bet is to take the side trip south from Kirkenes (see Part 9, p298). Also rapidly diminishing in numbers are **wolves**. Because they will attack reindeer and farm animals their protection is limited. **Red** and **Arctic foxes** may be seen and there are large numbers of small mammals such as **otters** and **hares**.

Birds and insects

The birds of Arctic Norway are notable for their variety and their uneven distribution. The super-abundance of sea food, along with the greater cover of coastal vegetation, gives rise to large numbers and greater varieties on the seaward margins of the area. Small **willow tits** to **golden eagles**, **oystercatchers** and **Arctic warblers**; birds of prey, town birds and sea birds – all have their homes in Arctic Norway. Thousands of **eider ducks**, single **sparrowhawks** and millions of **puffins** in a single colony; yet inland in the mountains of Troms and

Nordland or on the plateau of Finnmark a single bird may be a rare sight.

The **insect** world is rich. After your hundredth **mosquito** bite, you may well conclude that it's a little too rich. Much of the more tundra-like areas as well as the forests and boglands are ideal breeding grounds for a form of life that can easily withstand the long cold winters. Mosquitoes in the millions, as is common in all sub-polar regions, are a scourge to man and beast when the temperature and wind conditions encourage them to move freely and greedily. Fortunately they are non-malarial. Gadflies, ants, cockroaches and various beetles are among other insects which abound to delight the entomologists and plague the traveller.

Fish

Fish are indisputably the most important form of animal life in Arctic Norway – at least as far as the economy is concerned. The rivers and lakes provide some of the best salmon and trout fishing in the world while the sea fisheries are world famous and, more often than not, the *raison d'être* of much of the settlement.

The mixture of warm Atlantic and cold polar water is ideal and produces gigantic shoals of cod and herring as well as capelin, coalfish and haddock. Whales and seals can also be found, although in decreasing numbers.

It is seemingly quite rare to find a North Norwegian who doesn't fish, You will come across small cabins alongside the best rivers and frequently see cars parked for the day in remote areas as the owner trudges over the *fjell* (mountain, hill or plateau) to find his favourite fishing spot.

FLORA

In an area so scantily populated as North Norway, and with so little to attract the farmer or forester. the vegetation is largely natural. Regional variations occur with conifers in the southern fylker being replaced by birch in the north and altitude as well as latitude is a determining factor. All the same, the variety of vegetation is local rather than regional and the ever-changing microclimates produce a flora which is never wholly the same as you pass from one district to another.

Certain limiting factors are common: the very short but vigorous growing season, the general acidity of the soils, the waterlogged nature of the ground, the steep soil-free slopes and the wind-swept plateaux. Forests occur where shelter, latitude, altitude and soil depth permit. Nordland and Troms carry large stands of conifers, chiefly pine. This species extends only patchily into Finnmark where the world's most northerly pine forest is found bordering the Arctic Highway in Stabbursdalen (see p256), but in this fylke birch is predominant.

The topography of Nordland and Troms is such that commercial forestry is inhibited. The birch of the north has limited commercial value. Birch varies from scrub birch in the least favoured locations, through dwarf birch to taller trees in meadow woods. The cold and desiccating winds of the north greatly limit vertical growth and much of the birch you will see in Finnmark will scarcely reach the height of a man. Pine and birch are seen together in the south where transitional zones are found on the mountain sides. Other trees such as the alder and types of Arctic willow also occur but compete unfavourably with the dominant stands.

Peat bogs, with tufted sedge grass and delicate cotton-grass, give way to mosses and lichens where mountain vegetation borders the permanent snow line.

Much of Finnmark is true tundra and often waterlogged in summer or frozen in winter. Where it's better drained, heath plants prevail and edible berries are common. The delicious yellow/orange cloudberries (*moltebær*), sometimes known as Arctic strawberries, are much sought-after. In late August it is a common sight to see the local people tramping across country, armed with a plastic bucket, in search of berries.

Large areas, because of exposure, altitude or slope, are bare of vegetation and the country rock is open to rapid weathering.

The history of the Arctic Highway

Roads are like living organisms in a continuing state of evolution. It could be said that the Arctic Highway came into existence in the early 1940s when, for the first time, a journey by road was possible from south of the Arctic Circle to the north-easternmost extremity of Norway. Even then, it was necessary to take no less than ten ferry crossings to close the gaps left in the road by the fjords and inlets which rupture the coast. But, if the highway's birth was in the early 1940s, there had been a long period of gestation.

The E6 is essentially a joining together of innumerable old community (*kommune*) roads serving isolated settlements. For centuries, the north of Norway had no need for a trunk road. Its population lived in scattered villages and small towns most of which were either on the coast or a stone's throw from the sea. These littoral communities looked to the sea for their livelihood and its waters provided all they required for communication with their neighbours and the rest of the world. A tiny population, in a vast region in which land connection was inhibited by a difficult terrain, saw little point in engaging in a road-building programme which was as unnecessary as it was expensive. It must be recalled that, in stark contrast to today, Norway, even in the early part of the twentieth century, was, by European standards, poor. In North Norway the idea of regional land connections was not to be contemplated.

The Highway owes its existence to the foresight of a handful of local people, with the support of influential figures from the more prosperous and powerful south. From fragments of ancient paths the Highway has become one of the world's great roads with a history as fascinating as its setting.

There are four distinct periods in the historical development of what is today's European Route 6. First came the development of short sections of road serving local needs. The early 1930s saw the beginning of long linking sections to form a continuous highway. The next significant period is that of World War II when Norway was under German occupation. Finally came the slow and then spectacular developments which followed the war and which gave us the modern highway of today and which point the way to the future.

THE EARLY ROADS

The population density of North Norway today remains one of the lowest in the whole of Europe: less than half a million people occupying some 100,000 sq km (38,500 square miles). Living in a country where no less than two-thirds of the land lies above 300m (1000ft), and with one of the most indented coastlines in the world and over 50,000 off-shore islands, the population is squeezed into narrow patches of coastal lowlands or on to the islands. This pattern has always been so. Almost all the early villages in North Norway were on islands and nearly all had a maritime economy. This is especially so in Nordland and Troms but even in Finnmark four of the major settlements, Vadsø, Vardø, Hammerfest and Honningsvåg, all had island sites.

The need for roads was, in the past, limited to simple tracks within the villages and down to the quaysides. (Even today, some hotel descriptions include references to their distance from the harbour.) In the summer, the cart and horse made little demand on these pathways and, in winter, the sledge called for no more than nature eventually provided: a good cover of snow. Villagers were responsible for the maintenance of what few roads there were; maintenance being no more than the infilling of potholes and ditch clearing.

Most journeys were conducted by sea and, to a lesser extent, by river. This came naturally to a people who gained the greater part of their livelihood by fishing. Village to village communication was by boat and even the larger trading centres such as Alta and Tromsø attracted merchants and their customers not because they were a focus of land routes but because they offered good harbours. Despite the absence of roads, the settlements had excellent access to their neighbours which was at least the equal of that enjoyed by villages anywhere in Europe where land communication was the norm. Prior to the coming of the railway and the internal combustion engine, land movements were in any case slow and hazardous.

Even in the south of Norway, economic and physical conditions did not lend themselves to road building and the country entered the nineteenth century without even a rudimentary network of roads. It is true that there was legislation, some dating back to the twelfth century, dealing with the maintenance of what few trackways there were but new, continuous roads did not figure in any national plan. Bridges, very important in a land with a dense pattern of rivers and inlets, had, by law, to be maintained and ditches had to be cleared once a year. Trees had to be cut alongside the paths to permit the passage of a man riding with a spear lying across the pommel of his saddle! This was the level of development as Norway entered the 1800s.

In 1801, North Norway's population was served by nothing more than the most local of roads. Although the population was both scattered and small, even the large trading centres had no more than primitive tracks. Mo i Rana, with its neighbour Hemnes, was the home to rather more than 4500 as the nineteenth century opened and the more widely spread settlements of Alta district contained almost 2000 people, yet neither had anything more than rough paths between the houses. The only continuous trackways were the winter roads across the plateaux or mountains. In Finnmark, the vidde was crossed by a system of cairn-marked paths linking Kautokeino and Karasjok to each other and to the coast. Further south, similar trans-fjell snow roads brought people and trade across the Scandinavian Highlands and into Skibotn and Mo i Rana. But, of course, these winter roads could be used only when the snows came and sledges or skis could be employed. Winter, not summer, was the season for movement. When summer came and the snow melted, the sea and the rivers came into their own again and land communication virtually ceased.

This was the position at the start of the nineteenth century and little change occurred for another fifty years. Norway's 1851 Highways Act set up Highway Authorities which could rely, to some extent, on state funds to supplement locally raised revenue for road building and maintenance. But the effect of the Act was marginal. By the end of the century there were only some 9,600km of main road and 16,000km of minor roads. Given that the area of Norway is greater than that of the United Kingdom and Ireland combined, these figures hardly represent a network for the twentieth century. North Norway's share in these developments was pitifully small.

ONE HUNDRED YEARS AGO

By 1901, Finnmark, the most northerly of fylker through which the E6 was to run, had only 400m of road per square kilometre. The figure for Troms was little better at 2km but even in Nordland there was only 3.1km for every square kilometre. Not only were the densities low but the standard widths and surfaces of those roads that did exist make their claim to the status of road seem somewhat extravagant. They were still little more than cart tracks. There had been no officially designated main roads in the whole of Norway north of the circle before 1851. The few that did merit such a classification in Nordland at that date were all south of Mo i Rana and added up only to 240km. By 1915 the two most northerly fylker had a total just under 1200km of main road with all but 400km being in Troms. Very few of these roads were passable for traffic except in summer and some would be open for as little as four months a year.

Yet it was these roads or tracks which were to become sections of the E6. There is no record that anyone at the time foresaw this. The idea of a continuous route through Norway's Arctic fylker would, in 1915, have been seen as unnecessary and almost impossible. However, it is possible to identify these embryonic fragments of the E6, and the story of its building begins to unfold. Maps from the period 1910–15 reveal about a dozen sections of road already constructed which were later to be linked into the Arctic Highway. All of these served well-populated communities engaged in farming, fishing or trading. All were along the coastal edges of the region and none ventured far into the areas of upland or attempted to cross the interfluves separating the major fjords and river valleys. The fjells were still forbidden territory.

Today the road between Mo i Rana and its twin Mosjøen is quite heavily trafficked. In 1910 there was no road link. No road journey was possible to

Sandnessjøen from Mo and travel even to neighbouring Hemnesøya was by boat along the well-sheltered inner reaches of the Ranafjord. However, the north is the E6's destination and appropriately it is northwards from Mo i Rana that one has to look to find any extensive road construction. Over sixty kilometres of road had been built along the Rana valley to Krokstrand. The E6 follows almost the same route. Indeed it is largely built over exactly the same path as this early road. This is not surprising because the valley provides a naturally easy way into the interior of this part of Nordland.

This road had itself evolved from earlier inter-village paths and its construction reflected a generally prosperous economy. Farming on the river alluvial and glacial soils provided many with their livelihood and mining was also important. Along the valley of the Rana, in Dunderlandsdalen, sedimentary iron ores were extracted by the British-owned Dunderland Iron Ore Company. In order to export the ore a railway had been built to link the mines near Storforshei to the harbour at Mo. The roads followed the railway but on the other, western side of the valley.

The Krokstrand road was not difficult to construct. To the north-east of Mo two impressive gorges, the Rana and the Illhullet, limited the choice of route and one major river crossing had to be made just north of Mo at Reinforshei. It is here that the glacial outlet lake, Langvatnet, spills eastwards via the Langvassåga. Gradients, even in the gorges, were not excessive and many of the sections of road were built on near-flat river terraces cut in the glacial gravels.

Further river crossings, north of Reinforshei, had to be made but even these were easily effected by the building of stone arch bridges which were to survive for decades. Following the line of the Rana, as far as Storvollen, the road then swung south-eastwards towards Krokstrand. In so doing it followed one of the two major tributaries of the Rana, preferring the well-farmed lower valley and ignoring the mountain path links with Stormdalen and Tespdalen. By the time it reached Krokstrand, the road had risen to 330m.

The importance of this section of the E6-to-be cannot be underestimated. It gave Mo i Rana access to its natural hinterland and made the small town one of the most prosperous in all North Norway. Mo had been an important trading centre for a long time before the road was finally completed but its market and service functions had been limited by the absence of a land route to the north. Mo i Rana now entered the twentieth century equipped to grow in importance and influence. There is little doubt that other similarly placed settlements in the north were not blind to the developments made possible by new land routes. The road stopped at Krokstrand. There seemed to be no need or incentive to go further, to cross the Arctic Circle. To the north was the forbidding Saltfjell, a bleak, unwelcoming and uninhabited plateau which could be reached only by way of steep, broken slopes. Some winter snow roads and short tracks were all that one could find north of Krokstrand until one hit the northern side of the fjell.

North of the Polar Circle the region was dominated by the district of Saltdal. An 1852 English map of Scandinavia showed Salten in equal prominence with Bergen. It owes its fame largely to boat building though some of the sheltered valleys around Saltdalsfjorden have a long history of farming too.

The northern slopes of the Saltfjell are noticeably less steep than the southern flank. The watershed of the plateau is crossed at Stodi, two miles north of the Circle and from here the natural route down to Saltdal is via the Lonsdalen. This valley provides a winding natural path which falls some 200m in about 25km. Its steepness ruled out any early roads until it reached Hestbrinken. From here one road led east into Junkerdalen (the precursor of Route 77) while northwards, for fully fifty kilometres, a road ran through Saltdalen to the head of the fjord and the boat-building village of Rognan. It was this little road whose path became the E6. Again, the road had grown as village tracks became linked to give a continuous passage through the district.

Saltdalsfjorden prevented access by land to Fauske. The mountainous sides of the fjords drop almost vertically into the water. The only way to reach the northern side of the fjord was by boat and in this way Fauske or Finneid could be reached in half a day. Although the whole region around the fjord was settled centuries before the twentieth, there were few roads. Its prominence in boat building may have been the result of the lack of roads or was it the cause? The former explanation is the more likely because the width of the fjord and the absence of obvious national routes would, inevitably, have been deterrents to early roads.

Though it had no roads, Finneid did have a railway. It linked the port with the copper-mining village of Sulitjelma. It had originally been intended only for ore but the 0.75m gauge line was soon carrying passengers eager to exploit this new means of land travel. This railway was a replacement for a rough track originally built to carry the copper to the twin lakes of Øvrevatnet and Nedrevatnet. Boats then took the ore to Finneid for export. Once the railway was constructed in 1889, the road was allowed to decay and by 1910 had fallen into disuse.

Fauske, the neighbouring village to Finneid, had winter links with the north via the relatively low-lying Fauskeidet depression. These tracks linked the head of Sørfolda with the Saltdalsfjord and served the few farms and quarries which grew up there. Marble was quarried and, along with timber, could be carried down to the coast along these paths. Because the land rises to little more than 75m it was only marshes which inhibited road building and a number of roughly parallel paths crossed the lowland. One of these eventually became the E6.

Northwards from the Sørfolden inlet there were no roads for the next 200km. Few settlements existed here and those that did were exclusively concerned with fishing, necessarily on the coast, and relied on communications by sea. The coastline is especially deeply indented here and the mountains rise steeply from it. Few land routes offer themselves for road building and it is significant that this area had to await the end of the twentieth century and the development of modern building techniques for a truly integrated land route.

It is arguable that without the presence of Narvik, now the E6's largest town, no further continuous road would have been found before the Nordland–Troms border was reached. Even around Narvik the roads were of only local importance and, as yet, formed no part of any regional system.

Narvik relied on the Ofoten railway, completed in 1902. This brought

Swedish iron ore from across the border and it was the export of this iron that explains Narvik's growth from a clutch of farms to a population of over four and a half thousand in the succeeding twenty years. This explosive growth spread the settlement into communities between Rombaksfjord in the north to Grindjord in the south. Further settlement grew at the head of the Herjangsfjord. A road linked Grindjord to Ankenes and crossings of both Rombaksfjord and Grindjord were made by boat while a shore road ran around the east shore of

The Highway crosses the Beisfjord as it enters Narvik. A ferry crossed this stretch of water until after WW II.

Herjangsfjord to connect Bjerkvik with Rombaksfjord. North of Bjerkvik, just south of Ankenes, roads were conspicuously absent. Narvik was, in truth, a Swedish outpost. Deprived of land links with its Norwegian hinterland around Ofotfjord, Narvik lost its chance to become the natural regional capital of Nordland.

To the north of Bjerkvik, the high Gratangen ranges forbade a road in those early days. Beyond Gratangen the high Sølvfjell proved impassable but, more surprisingly, the more attractive Sangsdalen lacked a major road. Sangsdalen is separated from Bardudalen by an ill-drained depression and it is north of this that the 1910 picture changes significantly. The reason is not hard to find. Bardudalen and its tributary Målselv had been settled for well over one hundred years. The climate, despite the polar location, is conducive to farming, and quite extensive areas of lowland – the valley bottoms – not only foster cultivation and pastoral activities but also present land communications with few handicaps.

This was the most important farming community north of the Polar Circle and the relatively closely spaced villages were linked by roads along the valley courses. Often the broad valley carried more than one road. The easier tracks were close to the rivers but they were complemented by roads on higher ground which could be used during spring floods. Rivers were crossed by simple wooden bridges but at one point, Fredriksberg, a ferry was necessary to link roads on each side of the wide Målselv.

The E6 now uses precisely the same paths as some of these early roads, especially along the riverbanks. About 60km of the E6 follow the old road system. The particular importance of these early roads lies in the fact that it is here that the Arctic Highway forsakes the coast for one of its most important stretches.

Beyond Målselv in 1910 there was another break in the road north. A small lake-strewn plateau was the obstacle. Though its lowest point was only a little over 200m above sea-level, it was effective enough as a deterrent to road builders.

The next section of main road northwards started as a continuation of a forest path down Sagelvdalen and into Storsteinnes. From here another important

32km length of road linked Storsteinnes with Nordkjosbotn and on to Storfjord. As with all the roads in Bardudalen and along the Målselv, one of the incentives for local communication was a relatively well-farmed district along the shore of Balsfjorden but an even more influential factor was trade.

Storsteinnes had been a trading port from ancient times, ideally situated in a sheltered bay of the fjord but, more especially, the Lyngenfjord was important for trade over a much broader region. Moreover, there was a splendid natural pass between Nordkjosbotn at the head of Balsfjord and Storfjord on the Lyngenfjord. This low pass is cut by the Nordkjoselv in the west and by the Oterelv in the east. Rising to only some 100m at the watershed between these two rivers, it provides a natural route across the narrow-necked Balsfjordeidet. Mountains tower to over 1200m on either side of this beautiful pass and the ease with which the two fjords could be linked was an opportunity not to be ignored.

The Lyngenfjord at the beginning of the 20th century already had an unusually dense network of tracks, many of ancient origin. Paths led from the head of the fjord eastwards into what is now Swedish Lapland while trackways on the western side of the fjord followed each side of the Kjosen arm of the Ulsfjord and continued through the Breivikeidet pass and on to the mainland facing the important island-based settlement of Tromsø. Boats had to be used to cross the fjords and Tromsøysundet but this was common practice through all North Norway.

The Lyngenfjord had long been a centre for trade and cultural exchange between Norwegians, the Sami (Lapps) and the Kvaens (or Finns). In the ninth century a Norwegian outpost had been set up and by the Middle Ages trade was flourishing. Yet, despite all this activity and the already established tracks, the main road which was to be incorporated into the E6 stopped at Storfjord. The precipitous slopes of the mountains which enclose the Lyngenfjord to the east and, most especially, to the west saw to it that the boat should remain supreme and the only other road the fjord could boast was a short section from Årøybukt to Kvalvik, either side of Lyngseidet.

North of Lyngenfjorden: nothing, or almost nothing that in 1910 could claim to be the forerunner of the E6, the Arctic Highway. An exception was a short section of road linking the Tana and Varanger fjords. Here there had been settlement from ancient times and the Tana River valley was the natural route-way into interior Finnmark. Early tracks had developed along with reindeer migration routes and a continuous road had eventually been constructed to join the Tanafjord head with Karlebotn. Another branch led along the northern shore of Varangerfjorden through Vadsø, now moved from its original island site, and on to Norway's most easterly extremity, the mainland opposite Vardøya.

Such is the severity of the climate in east Finnmark that these roads were kept open only in summer when the ravages of the spring thaw had been made good. Elsewhere in the whole of this, the largest of the northern fylker, there were only four fragments of main road which were to become the E6. None was greater than 30km in length and all but one were focused on three important settlements: Alta, Lakselv and Kirkenes. The exception was an eight-kilometre section of highway across the narrow neck of the Økskfjordkollen in west Finnmark.

This little road used the low-lying Alteidelv valley and was constructed to join the trading port of Alteidet with its hinterland of Nordshov and Langfjordbotn.

Alta, as a single settlement, did not exist in 1910. Rather it was a collection of villages including Elvebakken and Bossekop and it was these that were linked by a road to Rafsbotn. Similarly, Lakselv was joined to Kvalvik by a track which scarcely merited the designation 'main road'.

In the east of Finnmark on the opposite, southern side of Varangerfjord to Vadsø and Vardø, Kirkenes was beginning to flourish as the outlet port for the rich iron ores of Sydvaranger. But its only road stretched just 6km westward from the village towards what, today, is the airport. Finnmark, deprived of any significant road building at the beginning of the century, continued to use its network of winter roads and reindeer paths. Yet Finnmark would eventually provide home for about 40% of the Arctic Highway's route.

So, a decade into the twentieth century and a continuous road through Norway's Arctic provinces was only a dream. Of the 1500km or so that were needed to provide such a highway, perhaps some 325km could be identified as potential links and no section was more than 65km long. As has been said, many of these links were little more than summer season tracks and the term main road had little real meaning. What is more, all these roads had been built along those parts of the route north which presented the least difficulties. No major fjell had been crossed or fjord bridged.

In the next twenty years lack of funds and economic incentives ensured that few changes took place. Two new sections of road were built around Porsangerfjorden and a five-kilometre road was constructed along Kåfjord. However, more important than these minor additions was the acceptance that the dream should become reality. By 1930 plans were being prepared to join the sections of already existing road and surveys had been completed. Furthermore, it had been accepted that the route would not be wholly coastal. The challenge of the mountains had to be met, the fjords must be crossed and there would be a continuous road through the Arctic fylker.

THE HIGHWAY COMPLETED

Work on the new stretches of road during the 1930s proceeded slowly. Even today, as in all polar climes, such construction activities have to be confined to the very short summer season. Money was short and it was quickly found that what had been set aside for new roads was often swallowed up in the cost of maintaining and repairing those already built.

Not surprisingly the lion's share of cash for roads went on the two southern fylker: Nordland and Troms. Finnmark was the poor relation but even here by the mid-1930s the only unplanned section was that between Karlebotn and Kirkenes. The route for the highway (by now classified as Route 50) was particularly difficult in this part of East Finnmark. The population densities were low and all the villages nestled in sheltered bays and fjord-heads unconcerned with a road which must largely cross the high ground some distance inland. Even Kirkenes had little use for a new road. It was adequately served by trans-fjord boats across the Varangerfjord to the well-settled northern shore and its iron ore continued to be shipped south by coastal carriers.

However, in southern Troms by 1935 much work had been completed and it was possible to travel by road from Grindjord (south of Narvik) all the way to Straumenfjord, well north of the Lyngenfjord. Of course, the major fjords required ferries but to a population so closely associated with the sea these were acceptable interruptions to an otherwise continuous road. Some of the earlier gaps were easily closed, as in the case of the link between Målselvdalen and the Balsfjord. The forest paths had simply been raised in status. Elsewhere problems were greater and called for ingenuity and high engineering skills. Such was the case with the crossing of the Gratangseidet mountains, across the Nordland-Troms divide. A steep and winding road carried the path of the highway up from Bjerkvik and northwards to link with the existing road in Bardudalen.

The five major high fjells – namely Saltfjellet, Sjettevassfjellet, Kvænangsfjellet, Sennalandet and Børselvfjellet – still blocked the path of the highway in the mid-1930s. Likewise, even such minor fjord crossings as that between Ankenes and Narvik were accepted as unbridgeable and ferries were employed. In fact no less than ten ferries were seen as unavoidable links if vehicle traffic between Mo i Rana and Kirkenes were to be possible.

Interestingly, in these early days, the actual ferry route was often being changed as new sections of the road came into use. An example was that across the Lyngenfjord where the first ferry link was between Årøybukt and Djupvik. As the new road south of Djupvik was completed, Normannvik became the eastern ferry point and later this was to be replaced by Olderdalen when it too found itself on the highway. At this stage the western ferry point was also changed and Lyngen took over from Årøybukt.

Lyngenfjorden illustrates another problem facing the road planners in the years before World War II. It might have been supposed that the highway should be built on the eastern side of the fjord. The presence of the trading post at Skibotn and a natural route from there into the Finnmark panhandle suggested this. But the mountains fringing the fjord between Skibotn and the Kåfjord arm of the Lyngenfjord were just too difficult to conquer and another forty years were to go by before the highway was to forsake the western shore of Lygenfjorden. Even this western road had its problems for there is almost no coastal strip and the eastern slopes of the Lyngen Alps are notorious for avalanches and rock falls.

The year 1937 was very special in the Arctic Highway's history for it saw the opening of the road across the Saltfjell and the crossing of the Polar Circle. King Haakon VII performed the opening ceremony of a road which at once symbolized the country's determination to carve a path through its Arctic fylker and, in reality, linked two of Nordland's most important towns, Mo i Rana and Bodø.

This trans-Circle route was to prove one of the most difficult segments to keep open during winter. Avoiding the higher parts of the fjell, the engineers had to choose between the two sides of dissecting valleys. Failing to heed the advice of Sami who seasonally grazed their reindeer there, they discovered too late that they had chosen that side of the valley most open to drifting snows. A quarter of a century later when the railway was built across the plateau the lesson had been learned and, ironically, cars began to be transported by rail between Mo and Bodø when the road was closed.

By the beginning of the next decade, as much of Europe became embroiled in war, almost all the major missing links had been constructed. The only breaks in continuous land communication, ferries excepted, were the uninhabited Lapland fjells of Sennalandet and Børselvfjellet in Finnmark and Mørsvik and Kråkmo in Nordland. Work had begun on these roads and was already completed along the difficult 110km stretch between Kirkenes and Karlebotn. Even the Kvænangsfjellet had been crossed by a road section forced to rise over 400m.

This was the Arctic Highway when, in the spring of 1940, the German Armies invaded and occupied the country for the next five years.

THE HIGHWAY IN WARTIME

From the very first days of World War II the Arctic Highway had a part to play. It gave the invaders access to Narvik, the primary cause of the invasion, and was later to figure prominently in the German strategy of exploiting their occupation by waging sea and air warfare from Norway's Arctic territories. The road became the lifeline of the occupying forces in the north.

The Germans' first task was to repair the bridges which the Allied forces had destroyed in their retreat following the abortive Narvik Campaign. The original bridges had largely been either masonry or steel girder constructions. Few of these fine bridges were replaced by replicas. Instead, wooden bridges using the original stone abutments were built. Most of these blown bridges were in the area between Mo i Rana and Fauske or around Narvik. As soon as this rebuilding had been effected, the German Army turned its attention to closing the few gaps that remained in the highway and to improving sections which suffered from long winter closure.

The perceived need to have an all-year supply line for their Arctic forces became a preoccupation of the Germans in Norway. From mid-summer 1941, when the final link was in place, up to the end of hostilities, when the Germans feared that a 'Second Front' would open in Norway, more and more effort was put into improvements with the aim of an all-weather road – an aim which was never achieved despite the high cost in human lives.

The labour force charged with maintaining and improving the road was not German, nor, in the main, was it Norwegian. Instead, thousands of Russian prisoners along with workers imported from central and southern Europe were to become the Highway's slave labour. As thousands perished from cold, malnutrition and arbitrary execution, the Arctic Highway became known as the 'Blood Road'. Evidence of this shameful episode in the Highway's history is still to be seen, ranging from simple monuments to extensive cemeteries. Many of them will be identified in Parts 4 to 9.

Despite the labour and the bloodshed, the road was never kept open along all its sections during winter. Only recently has the Highway come close to being an all-weather road for this was never the intention of the early planners.

However, some new sections of road were built during the war and none more important than that around the head of Saltdalsfjord. When completed the old ferry which had taken 20 minutes to cover the 5km gap in the road was no longer needed. Minor changes were made affecting other ferries. Bognes replaced Korsnes as the ferry point for Skarberget and another ferry, between Sørstraumen and Badderen, became defunct when new sections of road were built through Kvaenangsbotn.

As the war drew to an end the Highway played a different role. By the autumn of 1944, the German troops stationed in Finland were in full retreat. Their escape route took them through the Petsamo corridor and into East Finnmark. Here they were joined by the occupying German forces in a headlong dash to the relative safety of southern Norway. The line – and the means – of retreat was the Highway.

At first, in East Finnmark, the speed of retreat was such that little covering action could take place but soon a totally ruthless 'scorched earth and forced evacuation' policy was ordered by General Rendulic, the Germans' senior officer. All that could be destroyed – houses, churches, bridges – were burnt or blown up with high explosives. The people, or those who could not hide in the wastelands of the vidder, were required to move south.

As the German army fled it did as much as it could to destroy the highway it had been committed to improve. Not only was every single major bridge destroyed throughout Finnmark and North Troms but embankments were dynamited and barriers thrown across the roads for fear that the advancing Russians would catch them. Although the policy of retreat-and-destroy was effected to as far south as Lyngenfjord, the Russians did not follow. Instead they halted their advance at Seida in East Finnmark. By the spring of 1945 Norway was free from occupation and the work of rebuilding the Highway could start.

THE POST-WAR PERIOD

In the years immediately after World War II, work progressed slowly partly due to an unfavourable economic climate but also because the need for an upgraded highway was not self-evident. For the first ten years little was done except repair the damage caused in the retreat-and-destroy strategy of the German army. Cost, especially if measured per capita in the northern fylker, was the main limiting factor. In Finnmark alone, repair to buildings and roads was estimated to cost fifty million Norwegian kroner at 1945 prices, and this has to be seen in the context of a country struggling to rebuild its national economy.

Even by the mid-1960s the Highway, for much of its length, showed scarcely any real improvement and its standards resembled the pre-war road. Many of the major changes which have transformed the E6, as it became progressively from 1968, occurred in the 1970s and 1980s – and continue today. Transformation is not an exaggeration. Today's Highway would be unrecognizable by a traveller who remembered only the narrow, gravel rural road of the mid-1960s. The reasons for the changes lie in the opportunity afforded by the country's oil revenues and a growing awareness of the importance of North Norway in the West's defence strategy during the Cold War.

Norway's current expenditure on roads is massive by any standards. Per capita it is almost four times that of the United Kingdom. Although only 10% of the population lives in the North, the region receives about a quarter of the investment allocations. The problems associated with keeping the northern roads open in winter remain and solutions are costly. Until recently,

The Highway as it was in the 1960s. Summer grading work south of Skaidi.

some 40% of the maintenance budget went to winter maintenance whereas for the rest of the country the figure was less than 20%. Road-building projects, including new bridges and tunnels, become more and more ambitious but the aims and objectives have scarcely altered since the end of World War II.

On the Highway the three principal improvements have been in raising the road's general quality, in reducing reliance upon ferries and in keeping the road open for traffic throughout the year. To these may be added a fourth and most recent improvement: that of shortening and straightening the Highway's path, largely by tunnelling. The quality of the Highway has been improved, too, by programmes of widening, straightening, raising and resurfacing. The old bridges, often less than four metres in width, have been replaced and relocated. Difficult curves in the road, forced on it by its winding, fjord-edge paths, have been excised by blasting and re-alignment. Many sections susceptible to snow drifting have been raised to allow clearance into bordering ditches. Thirty to thirty-five years ago the most common surface of the Highway was water-based gravel. Such surfaces have been all but eliminated.

Many of the old sections of road, as well as abandoned bridges, can now be seen from the Highway. A few have been incorporated into today's road as lay-bys, but most are gradually being reclaimed by nature and will eventually be part of the lost history of the Highway. Former bridges are more likely survivors, their simple construction contrasting with their elegant replacements.

A few of the more important changes to the Highway are worth noting not simply because of their intrinsic interest but because they give today's traveller a retrospective view which puts the modern Highway into historical context. These are briefly described below, not in chronological order of construction, but geographically from south to north.

Leirfjorden originally demanded a significant detour for the Highway with a path leading around the 'wrong' western side of the Sørfoldafjord, of which Leirfjorden is a branch. An hour-long ferry journey from Røsvik to Bonnåsjøen was then necessary. In the 1960s a new section of Highway was built at a cost of nearly one and a half million kroner per kilometre, around the more rugged and precipitous eastern side of Sørfolda to Sommarset, with a shortened ferry passage up Leirfjorden, again to Bonnåsjøen. Thus, in 1987 a further section, again using tunnels, passed by Sommarset threading its way 29km round the head of Leirfjorden to Sildhopen where it rejoins the old route of the E6. With the road using no less than six major tunnels for one-third of its total journey, the 15-minute ferry has been made obsolete.

Almost 90km further north is the sole remaining ferry on the Arctic Highway's route north. This crossing of Tysfjord between Bognes and Skarberget will be eliminated only when the planned 700m-deep underwater tunnel is completed. But just 15km north of Skarberget, the Efjord was spanned by three bridges to make the 15-minute Saetran–Forsa ferry redundant.

In the early days Narvik was somewhat isolated. To the south of the town, two ferries, one across the Skjomenfjord and the other across Beisfjord, interrupted the Highway's path. The latter was superseded by a bridge at Akenes soon after World War II but it was not until the early 1970s that the short 10-minute Skjervik–Grindjord ferry fell to the building of an impressive 709m bridge some 35m above the inlet.

North of Narvik is the Rombaksfjord which proved to be more of a problem to the engineers than those to the south. Its very steep southern shore had forced the Highway to use a ferry between Vassvik and Øyjord. This ferry used to take 20–25 minutes to cross the deep waters of the fjord and a bridge at the same point was impossible. Instead a narrows in the fjord, Rombakstraumen, was selected for the largest suspension bridge in Norway. The magnificent bridge, fully 41m above sea-level, was constructed between 1961 and 1964. For a time a toll charge was made, but no longer.

Almost 200km to the north another, but more recent, re-routing has occurred. From the southern extremity of Lyngenfjord the Highway used to take a route which followed the western shore of this great fjord. A ferry crossing, first between Årøybukt and Nordmannvik, then between Lyngseidet and Olderdalen, gave the Highway access to the north. In the mid-70s an alternative route for the Highway was forged by extending an already existing east shore road into and around Kåfjord, an arm of Lyngenfjord. The merits of using this part of the Highway or taking the ferry, which continues to cross Lyngenfjorden, are discussed in Part 7.

The largest scale re-routing of the highway in modern times has been from Lakselv to the head of the great Varangerfjord in East Finnmark. For decades the route followed the eastern shore of Porsangerfjorden as far as Børselv and then turned eastward to the Tanafjord. This necessitated the crossing of two high plateaux, Børselvfjellet and Ifjordfjellet. These two high vidder, with highest points of 190m and 370m respectively, were a handicap in winter and closure was unavoidable. The gap in the old roads along the Tana River, notably that between Valjok and Levajok, had been closed in the 1970s. By the mid-1980s the whole route between Karasjok and Tana Bru had been sufficiently upgraded for the E6 to alter course from Lakselv, forsaking the high plateaux and adopting the Lakselv–Karasjok–Tana Bru road. As with the case of the new path round Lyngenfjord, the old path may well be preferred and this is discussed in Part 9.

These changes to the Arctic Highway have been paralleled, even exceeded, by work done over the last quarter of a century on the Highway's branches. Indeed, some roads have been built where there were none before. Two new roads in particular have been constructed to give access to Sweden. Both completed in the 1980s, these are relatively short but important roads.

Kirkenes, the northern terminus. Oslo is as far from Kirkenes as it is from Rome.

North of Narvik beyond the Rombaksfjord crossing, a road now links Norway with Sweden where previously there was only a railway. The distance is only 27km to the border by this road (E10) but the Swedish section (including a new road of some 132km) carries on as far as Kiruna. Further south the beautiful Junkerdalen is followed by Route 77. Again the major contributor was Sweden with a full 100km of road, while the Norwegian section is just 24km long.

Many branch roads have been improved. Among the beneficiaries of the millions of kroner that have been spent are the Highway's coastal rival, Route 17 (see Part 4), the Fauske–Bodø road (Route 80) and the important E69, with its submarine way to North Cape. Reference will be made to these changes, and to improvements to come, in Parts 4 to 9.

THE FUTURE

I have a recurrent nightmare that one day I shall arrive in southern Norway and find that the route to the North Cape is entirely through a tunnel. The climber's well-known rationale of his wish to scale a mountain 'because it's there' is matched by the apparent insatiable desire of every Norwegian road engineer to drill a hole through each and every hill, mountain and plateau encountered.

The early part of this century will undoubtedly see more and more holes. If the mountains become sufficiently perforated to allow the road system access to the otherwise inaccessible, then attention will surely turn to the construction of more undersea tunnels. All this tunnel building is something of a mixed blessing. It is true that journey times will be shorter and ferry delays will become part of history, but what can one see in a tunnel? One of the most beautiful countries in the world is in danger of losing its charm. Is the speed at which one can get from A to B the only consideration? The As and Bs of Norway, its villages and towns, have a limited attraction. What the traveller really wants to see is something of Norway's unrivalled wilderness, not a dimly lit view of its underlying geology. So make sure you travel the Arctic Highway now while it is still mostly above ground. By 2050 it may have become part of the world's largest underground transport network.

Many of the plans for changes to the Arctic Highway are still in an early stage of development, depending so often on financial constraints. The majority of those which will be referred to in subsequent parts (Parts 4 to 9) are likely to be built in the next half century, while others are less certain. The pace of change is rapid but the new projects and plans that will be described are those known at the time this book goes to press. Future editions will be updated as necessary.

The Sami

Much of the Arctic Highway and some of its approach roads (see Part 3) travel through Lapland and frequent reference has been made to the Sami. The name Sami has been used rather than Lapp, because it is preferred by the people themselves although, privately, few take much exception to being described as Lapps.

There is, of course, no national or ethnic territory which can properly be defined as Lapland although I am still occasionally asked if one needs a visa to visit the region. Rather, it is the area of northern Scandinavia, Finland and even Russia, which has traditionally been the homeland of the Sami.

The first recorded mention of the Sami was by Tacitus in AD98 when he referred to people he called the 'Fenni', a name which survived for at least 1000 years. The first use of Lapp or Lapland (also Lappland) seems to date from the thirteenth century. While Sami has overtaken Lapp as a name for the people, the area they inhabit is still generally called Lapland (occasionally, Samiland).

This isn't the place to give a complete picture of the history, culture and life of the Sami. There is a growing body of literature to which you can refer. It should be pointed out, however, that there has been a lot of nonsense written about these very interesting people. One very factual book which can be recommended is *The Sami People* (Sami Instituhtta/Davvi Girjiøs, 1990). A much older and quite fascinating book is *Turi's Book of Lappland* written in the period 1908–1910 but with an English translation published in 1931 by Jonathan Cape.

Travelling in northern Scandinavia you will probably gain a very superficial understanding of the Sami people and their way of life. It is even possible that you will return with a distorted picture.

The Arctic Highway and its branches have not been entirely good news for the Sami. In many ways the Sami have become at once victims and beneficiar-

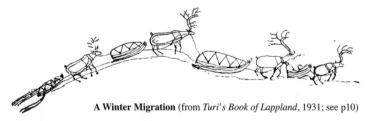

A Winter Migration (from *Turi's Book of Lappland*, 1931; see p10)

ies of the opening up of Lapland to outsiders. It is true that the small proportion who have remained reindeer herders find their sojourn in the summer pastures less lonely. It is undeniable that the influx of tourists each summer provides a market for reindeer skin, horns and all manner of supposedly Sami products. But the improved contact between the Sami and the outside world has done little for the preservation of their distinctive culture. Many years ago in *The Highway and the Lapps* I wrote:

> *How long will it be before the Lapp costume is abandoned, before reindeer herding ceases to involve transhumance, before the nomadic Lapp is finally and fully assimilated into the Norwegian population? Only time will tell. Isolation is the great safeguard of the traditional way of life and it is isolation that the Arctic Highway is committed to defeat.*

Time has told.

When I first travelled in Lapland thirty-five years ago, fulfilling an undergraduate ambition, the Sami costume was still to be seen as everyday dress. No longer. Highdays and holidays will see the colourful jackets, dresses and hats but it has become an increasingly rare sight except perhaps a bonnet worn by an elderly Sami shopper in the supermarket at Karasjok.

The Sami population today is unevenly distributed through the three Nordic countries and Russia. Exact numbers of those who would describe themselves as Sami are difficult to obtain but there are perhaps 30–40,000 in Norway, 17,000 in Sweden, 6000 in Finland and 2000 in northern Russia. Of these only about 10% in Norway, 15% in Sweden and 5% in Finland and Russia depend almost exclusively on reindeer herding. The great majority of these live in what can loosely be called Lapland (ie very roughly around or north of the Polar Circle). The largest concentration of Sami is in Finnmark and north Troms in Norway where there are over 30,000.

Specifically Sami settlements, of any size, are few with Kautokeino (see Part 7), Karasjok (see Part 8) and Enontekiö, across the border in Finland, being outstanding examples. Elsewhere, the Sami are almost fully integrated with the Scandinavian or Finnish populations and many have drifted into urban life, often in the south.

The reindeer herders, and it is this section of the Sami population which is closest to a traditional way of life, are transhumants rather than nomads. They follow their reindeer on their annual migrations to summer pastures but these are movements along traditional routes and between fixed points. There is no wandering. As a summer visitor to Lapland, travelling the Arctic Highway, you

see these summer pastures, often close to or straddling the roads. The deer's food is grasses, fungi and the foliage of trees on low ground near the coast. In winter they will be back on the high fjells, the vidder, where lichens and reindeer moss (also actually lichen) will be sought beneath the snow.

Herds vary in size and are often owned by Sami other than those who herd them. A herd of 300–500 is considered to be at the lowest subsistence level but some herds are as large as 1000 head or more. Most of the herders also mind deer of their sedentary neighbours. The summer huts that you see when driving the Arctic Highway and other roads are just that: summer huts. They will be occupied for about three months following the May migrations. They are the equivalent of the Norwegian *seter* (farmer's summer cottage). The few tents that will

In a Church Village

(from *Turi's Book of Lappland*, 1931; see p10 for more information about Johan Turi).

'Turi has drawn the Torne Lapps' yearly pilgrimage to the old church at Jukkäsjarvi; also called by the Lapps Susanna-church, after their custom of naming a church after the first person buried in the churchyard ... From all sides come the Lapps in their small boat-shaped sledges followed by their inseparable companions, the dogs. Several of the reindeer have their tongues hanging out as they always have when they have been running hard and are overstrained ... Between the steeple and the church itself Turi has drawn one of the fir trees which you find growing in that part. From the lowest bough of the tree hangs the figure of a man, and Turi explains that a man who had hanged himself in the forest was buried in the churchyard, and all by itself a fir tree grew out of his grave...a fir tree just like the one upon which he hanged himself. The figures without heads to the right of the church are ghosts wandering about in the churchyard' (From *Turi's Book of Lappland*, 1931, translated by ED Hatt and EG Nash).

be seen today are erected largely to attract tourists to buy skins and horn, although the tent is still used during the migration treks. Drive on the off-road route to Kautokeino or wild camp in this area (see Part 7) and you may well see tents awaiting the herders on their way back to the winter feeding grounds.

The Sami are a justly proud people who are increasingly jealous of their distinctiveness. There have been Sami parliaments in Norway from 1989 (Karasjok), and in Finland from 1975 (Enare). In Sweden there is a Sami Association (Umeå) and there has been a Nordic Sami Council, embracing all Sami peoples, since 1956.

In the autumn of 1989, the first Sami Parliament was opened by King Olav V of Norway. This was a logical step in the recognition of the Sami people and

their distinctive culture and origin. Dr Brian Sykes, a DNA expert, has written:

'Everywhere in Europe people have a bit of everything, even in the Scandinavian countries. The only group that doesn't seem to have any mixing is the Lapps in northern Norway and Finland.'

A variety of measures after World War II was enacted in law to give greater and greater status to the Sami, especially in matters of education and language. The Nordic Sami Conference and the Sami Council are cross-border bodies concerned with the interests of the Sami as a whole, irrespective of nationality.

The traditional Sami dress varies according to district but is always predominantly blue with red trimmings. There is also something of a 'national' difference. The blue of the Sami in Finland is usually a dark navy blue, that of those living in Norway a mid-blue and of those in Sweden a lighter blue. While the bonnet design of the women is generally a common pattern, the men's hats vary noticeably with each district. It is interesting to note that the 'traditional' dress is in fact quite modern and, most especially, the ribbon braiding is not strictly traditional at all.

The Sami are quite a shy people, the majority of whom tend to resent the attention they attract from the tourist. They do not welcome being the object of 'photo stops'. They take a long time to get to know and the tourist has only fleeting contact. The areas around their summer camps should be respected as should their herds of reindeer.

The deer are unpredictable creatures. One minute they will be feeding by the side of the road and in the next they take flight and become a danger to traffic and themselves. In summer they often use the roads to move from one feeding place to another, or even to sleep on. Whether encountered singly or in groups, as a driver you should slow to a crawl on approach and be prepared to stop suddenly. They should never be followed at speed even if they are in full flight in the road. The most dangerous situations occur when deer cross the roads. They are often hidden in the low birch forests when, without warning, they will run in front of a vehicle. Remember they are not large animals, that is why their enormous antlers are so remarkable.

Lapland without the Sami would be a nonsense. Travelling the Arctic Highway, you will have frequent reminders that its path is through the Sami homeland. Such easy access to Lapland is a privilege denied previous generations. Privileges are to be cherished and respected.

(Opposite): Sami boy in traditional dress with a gold and silver clasp.

PART 3: GETTING TO THE HIGHWAY

Part 1 described a number of different approach routes to Scandinavia. Various entry points were suggested and, in this part, the routes from them to Norway's Arctic Highway are discussed. In some cases, roads from different entry points will quickly join to give a common route to the Highway, but there remain significant differences between them. One of the first decisions you must make is that of a starting point for the Highway journey. The length of the Arctic Highway is over 1500km from Mo i Rana to Kirkenes. You may well prefer not to do some of the route in both directions. Each of the two termini, Mo i Rana in the south and Kirkenes in the north, is approachable by land, sea or air, so that a round trip can be made with no repeat journeys at all. The air option has already been described in Part 2 and the main land and sea options which will be described are shown below. Three of the routes are especially recommended (*).

The options

APPROACH ROUTES

I: Oslo to Mo i Rana by road (p66)
II: Larvik to Mo i Rana by road (p79)
III: Bergen to Mo i Rana by road (p79) *
IV: Bergen to Kirkenes by sea (p87) *
V: Stavanger to Mo i Rana by road (p89)
VI: Gothenburg to Mo i Rana (via Oslo) by road (p90)
VII: Gothenburg to Mo i Rana (via Stockholm) by road (p91)
VIII: Helsinki to Karasjok/Kirkenes by road (p97) *
IX: Turku to Karasjok/Kirkenes by road (p110)
X: Using public transport: rail or road (p111)   * = recommended route

It is not appropriate, nor does space permit, to describe each approach route in detail. However, the recommended routes (III, IV and VIII) have been chosen for their scenic interest rather than their shortness or convenience. We have not done justice to the larger towns, such as Oslo and Helsinki, in the very brief descriptions we have given them, and it's best to do a little research before you arrive and to head for the tourist office as soon as you get there.

(Opposite) Bridges span fjords and tunnels carve through mountains. **Top**: The 709m-Skjombrua at Grindjord (see p160). **Bottom**: Tunnel south of Narvik.

Accommodation options are described for the most likely stopping places along the routes but no attempt has been made to list every hotel, guesthouse or camping place. The same goes for places to eat. Suggested travel times will be dependent upon how much sightseeing you wish to do en route.

APPROACH ROUTE I: OSLO TO MO I RANA BY ROAD

A number of car ferries converge on Oslo (see Part 2) and you could make use of the opportunity to see Norway's capital with a stay of a couple of days before driving north. It is also possible to take a ferry into Gothenburg (Sweden) and then take the E6 to Oslo, a day's drive of some 315km (see Approach Route VII).

- **Route** Oslo–Otta–Trondheim–Mo i Rana: E6
- **Distance** 1035km
- **Summary** From Oslo you make for the famous Gudbrandsdalen before crossing the Dovrefjellet en route for Trondheim. From there, there are alternate valley and high fjell sections onwards to Mo i Rana.
- **Suggested travel time** Two to four days.
- **Road quality** Good to very good. The best stretches, on which speeds in excess of 80km/h will be allowed, are north of Oslo (approximately to Lillehammer) and immediately north and south of Trondheim. The rest of the road is variable but not difficult. Some relatively poor (narrow and winding) stretches will be encountered, especially north of Steinkjer. The steepest gradients will be found on the Dovrefjell (north and south of the plateau) and between Mosjøen and Mo i Rana (most especially south of Korgen).
- **Suggested stopping places** Oslo, Dombås, Trondheim and Steinkjer. This gives a long final leg but there are many camping and cabin sites along the route although their frequency decreases as you move north.

The route (south to north)

OSLO

Oslo is the capital and by far the largest settlement in area and population in Norway. It is built at the head of a broad fjord over 90km from the open sea. The Oslofjord is not like the ice-scoured inlets of the west coast of Norway but a broad, submerged and faulted valley.

For centuries it was overshadowed by Bergen but the city began to grow in importance in the mid-nineteenth century. When the railway system began to take shape, its links with the north, through the Gudbrandsdal, and also to the east and west, gave it the communications with its hinterland that were necessary if its superb harbour was to be exploited properly. A stay of two or three days will allow only a limited view of the city because of its dispersed form. However, the city centre, which still retains the grid pattern of streets which were laid out before the city was burnt down in 1624, contains a number of interesting features and other places well worth visiting, and all easily accessible in a morning or an afternoon.

Services

The most convenient **tourist office** (☎ 23 83 00 50) is near the harbour, close to the unmissable **Rådhus** (**town/city hall**) with its twin block-like towers. It's open until 19.00 in mid-summer. As well as a wealth of guides, information booklets and maps, the tourist office is also the place to get your 'Oslo Card' (NOK280 for two days) or 'Oslo Package' (from NOK395 per day). These tourist cards will save you a small fortune in parking fees, local travel and admission charges. They are also available from hotels, stations, post offices and most newspaper kiosks (*Narvasen*). The most convenient **post office** is on Karl Johans gate, the road leading to the Royal Palace, about halfway between the palace and the main **railway station**. The railway station is also the place to catch the city **buses**.

Around town

Oslo isn't a difficult town to drive around but parking is limited and very expensive (unless you've got your Oslo Card). Better to use the efficient bus service (free with the Oslo Card). There is much to see and it's probably best simply to walk in the central area with a map from the tourist office. Your walk could take in the **Royal Palace** (Stollet), the **town/city hall** (Rådhus), **Parliament** (Stortunget), **National Gallery**, the **Cathedral** (Domkirke) and some fine old buildings along and just off Karl Johans gate. There are also plenty of shopping opportunities. By the harbour is the fourteenth-century **Akershus Castle.**

A bit further afield but still within the town area there are places of interest such as the **Vigeland Park** (the famous erotic and primitive sculpture park) on the western side of Oslo. You could also visit: the **Kon-Tiki Museum**, dedicated to Thor Hyerdahl's exploits; the **Bislet Stadium**, scene of many records; **Holmen-kollen Tower**, which gives views of the city from 600m; and Oslo's oldest building, dating from 1080, **Gamle Aker Kirke** (church).

Accommodation

Two top-class hotels are the *Grand* (☎ 23 21 20 00; 🖾 23 21 21 00; 🖳 admin@grand.no), on Karl Johans gate and the *Bristol* (☎ 22 82 60 00; 🖾 22 82 60 01; 🖳 booking@bristol.no), on Kristian IV gate which runs parallel to Karl Johan's. Both have that old-world charm, beloved by some travellers, but with every modern amenity. Expect to pay around NOK1800 for a double though prices drop at weekends and in high summer.

If you really want luxury-plus there's the *Hotel Continental* (☎ 22 82 40 00; 🖾 22 42 96 89; 🖳 booking@hotel-continental.com), midway between the Royal Palace and the City Hall, on Stortingsgaten. It is a member of the Leading Hotels of the World, the only one in Norway, but remains family owned. A double room here will cost from NOK2400 to NOK2800 but you do get breakfast at no extra charge.

Mid-range hotels include the *Spectrum* (☎ 23 36 27 00; 🖾 23 36 27 50; 🖳 spectrum @os.telia.no), to the north-east of the centre on Brugata. It is one of the Tulip Inn Rainbow group so, if it's full, you could try their central reservations (☎ 23 08 02 00). In somewhat the same bracket is the *Travel Hotel* (a Rica property, ☎ 22 00 33 00; 🖾 63 92 67 00; 🖳 rica.travel.hotel.oslo@rica.no), on Arbeidergata, a turning off Karl Johan's gate. This is an especially good-value hotel with doubles around NOK600–800.

For bed and breakfast and small guesthouses, it's best to ask at the tourist office which will not only advise but also do bookings for you.

Of the half a dozen **youth hostels** (*vandrerhjem*) the all-round best is the *Haraldsheim* (☎ 22 22 29 65; 🖾 22 22 10 25; 🖳 post@haraldsheim.oslo.no). Although it is out of town at Sinsenkrysset, it is open all year and has nearly 300 beds. However it should be booked ahead in high summer. Doubles range from NOK350 to NOK460.

There are three camping places. The big *Bøgstad* site (☎ 22 51 08 00; 🖾 22 51 08 50), on the northern edge of Oslo, is open all year and has cabins at around NOK600 but its size is off-putting if you want a good night's sleep.

If you're driving in from Gothenburg, *Ekeberg Camping* (☎ 22 19 85 68; 🖾 22 67 04 36) is conveniently situated to the south-east of town between the E6 and the E18 but, like Bøgstad, it has all the disadvantages of being quite clearly an urban campsite. *Oslo Fjordcamping* (☎ 22 75 20 55; 🖾 22 75 20 56; 🖳 fjordcamping @online.no) is nearly 10km south of town on the fjord and has caravans rather than cabins to let at NOK400. It is probably the best choice.

Where to eat

You are spoilt for choice when eating out in Oslo but it all comes at a price: Oslo is one of the world's most expensive cities.

The *Theatre Café* in the Hotel Continental (see p67) is the smart place to eat. *Det Gamle Rådhus*, behind the Akershus Castle (see p67) is great for good Norwegian food, so too is *Kaffistova* on Rosenkrantz gate, just up from the Rica Travel Hotel (see p67). The cheapest places are the pizza bars, including *Peppe's*.

Round the town, it is possible to eat from Japanese, Chinese, French, Indian or Mexican menus.

For something inexpensive, there are plenty of takeaway cafés and, remarkably for Norway, vegetarians are well catered for: *Krishna's Cuisine* on Kirkeveien is a favourite with those shunning meat.

Perhaps the best plan of all is to wander the city-centre streets; you'll pass countless restaurants, cafés and bars and the choice is all yours.

Moving north

Leaving Oslo en route for Mo i Rana, any of the many roads leading to the east of the city can be used but it may be easiest to go direct to the E6. Leaving the town from a point outside City Hall, drive east to join the E18. Pass along Bispegata, taking care not to be diverted north on to Route 4. The E6 leaves the E18 at a point where the latter turns southwards. Once on the E6 you'll find signposting is excellent and route finding could not be more simple. There is no shortage of refuelling points or places to buy food or take meals.

The early part of the route, just north of Oslo, is not especially interesting but at least the road standard allows for relatively high speeds. Most of the route to **Lillehammer** (183km) is well settled and farmed with a number of large villages and small towns. The road now bypasses many of the smaller villages but access is not restricted. From this southern section of the road, the general prosperity of the region is evident with a mixture of farming, forestry and industry.

As the route approaches the southern tip of **Lake Mjøsa**, along the lake and into **Gudbrandsdalen**, so the area's attraction becomes clear. The lowlands at the southern end of Lake Mjøsa have one of the longest histories of settlement in the whole of Norway. Land was cleared for farming over one thousand years ago and there are twenty or so medieval parish churches in the region. The routes, either side of the lake, pass through further areas of prosperous agricultural land and north of the lake one enters the Gudbrandsdal, scene of many epic battles in the distant and more recent past.

Just 60km from Oslo is **Eidsvollverk** and, to the right of the road, **Eidsvoll Manor**. It was here that the country's constitution was proclaimed on 17 May 1814 – now National Day. Although it was to be another 90 years before Norway became fully independent, the house is one of Norway's most historic houses and beautifully preserved. If you can spare the time, it's well worth a visit.

The E6 bypasses Eidsvoll and, at **Minnesund** (71km), crosses the river Varma by a 600m bridge. It is this river which drains Norway's largest lake, Mjøsa. The lake, occupying a geological fault, has impressive dimensions: 100km long, 360 sq km in area and nearly 450m deep. It even has its equivalent of the Loch Ness monster. In recent years a different monster, pollution, has threatened the lake and, despite efforts to contain the problem, it remains an expensive business to effect a cure.

Mjøsa can be seen from the road to the left until just south of **Vikselv** (100km). For centuries the lake itself was the main artery for communications northwards. In summer there were boats but in winter the lake freezes over. Even today the lake can still be covered by ice in early May after a cold spring. It remains possible to take an old paddle steamer all the way to Lillehammer, from Eidsvoll (Route 81, to the right off the E6) but only for foot passengers. The lake is actually more direct than the road.

At Vikselv, to the left of the road, a choice of route can be made: the faster E6 or the more interesting Route 222 via Stange. Both will lead to the important town of Hamar. If using Route 222, another short detour is possible. At the village of **Stange**, turn left towards the lake and you can visit a thirteenth-century church as well as a row of preserved manor houses.

Hamar (122km) guards the approaches of the Gudbrandsdal, the valley which is followed northwards by the E6. The town shows its mixed fortunes over the centuries with modern buildings alongside ancient ruins. The old cathedral (the bishopric was founded by Nicolas Breakspear, the only Englishman ever to become pope) is part of an open-air museum. Another museum attracts railway buffs.

At Hamar, you have the choice of an alternative route to Trondheim, en route for Mo i Rana, if you use Route 3. This is just 33km shorter than the E6 and a fairly fast road. There are few steep gradients, the highest part of the road being only a fraction over 700m. Route 3 follows the broad and forested **Østerdalen**, running alongside the River Gläma until it strikes north-north-east after **Tynset** to make an easy plateau crossing. Most will agree that this is a route with far less on offer than the E6 but if you are towing a caravan or travelling in winter it may make for an easier trip. To take Route 3, you go through the centre of Hamar on the E6, turning right on to Route 25. This road links with Route 8 after about 15km and the road is now combined Routes 25/3. At **Elverum** (28km from Hamar), Route 3 leaves Route 25 before the bridge over the river on the outskirts of the town. Now Route 3 can be followed until it rejoins the E6 at **Ulsberg**.

If you stay with the E6, on leaving Hamar you'll find the road swings northwest round the Furnesfjord arm of Lake Mjøsa, bypasses the village of **Brumunddal** (135km) and strikes out to bridge the lake south of Moelv. A toll is currently charged for the crossing of the 1420m bridge which was opened in 1986; before that year the E6 kept to the eastern shore of the lake. After crossing the bridge, the E6 is joined by Route 4 which has reached here from Oslo on a journey 10km shorter than the E6.

The road continues, as the E6, along the western shore of Lake Mjøsa to **Vignes** (178km) where another bridge, replacing the more northerly 1930s' crossing, takes the road into **Lillehammer** (183km).

Lillehammer is still best known, outside Norway, as the home of the 1994 Winter Olympics but it was a health resort even before World War II and has been an important skiing centre for decades. It has managed to remain a typical Norwegian country town despite its involvement with tourism, though the imprint of the Winter Olympics is still clear. The quite extraordinary engineering triumphs include a massive underground stadium.

There is a **tourist office** on Elvegata, off the main road, Storgata (☎ 61 25 92 99; 📠 61 25 65 85; 🖥 info@lillehammerturist.no). It would be a shame to pass through the town without visiting the Sandvig collections at Maihaugen. Because the new bridge gives entry to the town at its northern extremity, to reach Maihaugen will entail turning back into the *sentrum* (centre) and taking Route 216 to this open-air museum, set on a hillside among trees and mountain streams. The museum is a collection of traditional and ancient Norwegian buildings: farms, a school-house, a twelfth-century stave church and well over a hundred other examples of domestic and vernacular architecture. All have been transported to the site, mostly from the Gudbrandsdal region, and lovingly reconstructed. This is a fascinating and absorbing collection.

As the E6 leaves Lillehammer there is, at first, little change in scenery. Although Lake Mjøsen is quickly left behind, the path continues through undulating countryside which is well farmed and forested. The road hugs Lågenelva for much of the way to Dombås and the river can be seen to the left of the road. Stretches with foaming rapids contrast with broader lake sections in the south. Much of the water comes from melting ice and snow off the Jotunheim mountains. Typically the meltwater is a beautiful milky blue-green.

The valley is the famous **Gudbrandsdal**, the historic route to the north and to Trondheim. Much of the valley wall is forested but farming is important on the glacial sediments which choke the valley floor. Only between Vinstra and Dombås does the valley narrow into what has all the feel of an important pass.

The road through Gudbrandsdalen passes through a number of small settlements, many of which have historical significance. At **Hindorp** (253km), there are said to be the remains of one Dale Gudbrand who gave his name to the valley. Dale was the heathen chief of the valley when, in about AD1200, the King-Saint Olav arrived to convert the people to Christianity. With the chief, he succeeded in his mission. Only 15km further north is **Vinstra** (268km). The road is now well and truly in Peer Gynt country. Indeed, in the village centre a minor toll road, the Setervei, leads off to the right to wind 2.5km up the hillside to Hågå, again to the right, the farm where Peder Olsen lived in the eighteenth century. Olsen was the model for Henrik Ibsen's Peer Gynt. If you can't afford a detour of 5km, take a look at the tourist office in Vinstra. It is a relocated cottage from Hågå.

Across the river bridge from Vinstra is Sødorp where the village's mid-eighteenth-century church was rebuilt in 1910. But it is the old churchyard where you'll find the Peer Gynt memorial. Also here is the grave of Captain Sinclair, the leader of a group of Scottish mercenaries who, en route for Sweden, were slaughtered in a famous battle with Norwegian farmers in 1612. The site of the battle was Kringen, nearly 30km further north.

North from Vinstra, the road continues alongside the river, sharing its route with the railway. After 5km it swings round a braided stretch of the Lågen to turn west and enter the village **Kvam** (278km). It was here that the British and Norwegian forces held back the German advance up Gudbrandsdalen in the spring of 1940. The graves of over fifty British soldiers who made the ultimate sacrifice are in the small cemetery by the village church. Examination of the gravestones in a number of villages in the valley will tell a similar story. The quiet and peaceful Gudbrandsdal is the resting place for many soldiers of British county regiments who found themselves in a less than peaceful Norway in World War II. The battles of the Gudbrandsdal and the action at Otta in late April 1940 are described in detail in *The Doomed Expedition* by Jack Adams (London, Leo Cooper, 1989), one of the best accounts of the Norwegian Campaign.

Continuing westward for about another eight kilometres, the road turns northward again just before **Sjoa** (287km) where the railway parts company with the E6 and chooses the right bank of the river. Just before entering the small town of **Otta** (298km), the road passes the memorial to the seventeenth-century battle of Kringen (295km) where Captain Sinclair's mercenary band met their deaths (see Vinstra, p70).

Otta is the first settlement on the road that merits the title town since leaving Lillehammer. Even so its population is only just over 2500. The town is spread across the confluence of two rivers for it is here that the River Otta joins the Lågen. The junction of two routes, the Gudbrandsdal and the Vågåmo route into the Jotunheim mountains, helps to explain Otta's importance. The town's other claim to fame is its slate quarries which lie up a steep winding route to the southwest, off Route 15. Slate from here has been used in buildings all over the world but most recently in the Olympic stadia in both Barcelona and Lillehammer.

The **tourist office** (☎ 61 23 66 50; 🖹 61 23 09 60; 🖳 post@visitrondane.com) is at the railway-cum-bus station.

The recommended route to Mo i Rana from Bergen (Approach Route III) and that from Stavanger (Approach Route V) join the E6 at Otta. See p87.

Leaving Otta, the road skirts the eastern side of marshland, the Selsmyr (now mostly drained) before entering the hamlet of **Nord Sel** (311km). In the graveyard of the tiny church is another reminder of Gudbrandsdalen's bloody past. In the shelter of the hedge and trees which border the little cemetery is a memorial to 25 of the British soldiers who gave their lives in the defence of Norway in 1940. It is here at Nord Sel that the minor road suggested as an alternative to Route 15, on the road from Bergen to Mo i Rana (Approach Route III), joins the E6. See p87.

From here the Gudbrandsdal is relatively narrow and the Lågen flows over rapids, the boulders of its bedload exposed when the river level drops. The valley sides are forested and, at **Rosten** (315km), there is a magnificent waterfall with a total drop of 115m. When you reach **Dovre** (330km) it is possible, without adding much to your distance or journey time, to leave the E6 and continue on to Dombås by one or two country roads which run parallel to the main highway but at a higher altitude. You can join the country roads, to the west of the E6, by turning left off the main highway about 1.5km after the village. However, the road on the eastern side of the valley is probably more attractive. This road, signposted to Tofte, leaves the E6 in the village. A kilometre or so north of **Tofte**, and to the right, is the King's Highway (Kongeveien) which leads up to the Dovrefjell mountains. This is not suitable for vehicles but can be walked. Today the car forsakes the King's Highway but it is said to be the oldest mountain pass in Norway. It strikes almost due north from Tofte, passing the peak of Hardbakken (1338m) on its western flank, and does not rejoin the modern fjell road until it reaches **Fokstua**. An even earlier track, now almost invisible, took a more southerly path on to the Dovrefjell via Foksa. These mountainous sections of the King's Highway are steeped in legend and are just a small part of what was the old route from Oslo to Trondheim (or Nidaros as it used to be called). Pilgrims and royalty used the route between Norway's two great cities.

DOMBÅS

Whatever route you chose, the E6 or its parallel country roads, the destination is **Dombås** (344km) – a tourist centre if ever there was one. It was already an important winter sports centre before World War II and today it is a bustling and lively stopping place for travellers on the E6 or Route 9 before they make an ascent on to the Dovrefjell. Cafés, gift shops and petrol stations seem to be forever busy during the day and tourism is clearly the village's raison d'être. The only quiet, unbusy spot is the village's delightful white timbered church to the western side of the E6 in the centre of the settlement. You can park here or in the big central car-park where you'll find the **tourist office** (☎ 61 24 14 44; 🖷 61 24 11 90; 🖳 touristoffice@dovrenett.no).

Dombås accommodation

If you decide to stop off at Dombås there's not a lot of choice but at least there is a range. The **Dombås Hotel** (☎ 61 24 10 01; 🖷 61 24 14 61; 🖳 dombas.hotel@ online.no) in the centre of the town. It is excellent but costs around NOK600 to NOK1000.

The youth hostel, **Trolltun** (☎ 61 24 09 60), is about 1500m off the E6, just out of town, and is not cheap. It is well appointed, with everything from dormitory accommodation to rooms of hotel standard. Prices are from NOK200 to NOK750. Seven kilometres south of the town is a camping site of superior quality: **Bjørkhol Camping** (☎ 61 24 13 31). The cabins are excellent and four can stay for around NOK500.

From Dombås the route changes, not only in direction but also in the character of the country it crosses. The road leaves the village by climbing the steep hill on its eastern side. It has begun its ascent to the top of Dovrefjellet and turned its back on the South.

The road is steep at first but gradually levels out towards **Fokstua** (354km). Now the E6 is in one of Norway's fifteen major national parks. In fact, this is the oldest, established in 1923. Its main attraction is the abundant birdlife. The blue throat, snipe, crane and the occasional red-necked phalarope can be seen, their nesting sites protected during the period from late April to early July. Short-eared owls swoop on lemmings and reindeer share their grazing land with elk. The birds are generally safe from the traffic hazards of the E6 but not so the reindeer and elk. You need to keep an eye out for both.

The Dovrefjell is a wild but not bleak mountain plateau of wonderful beauty as well as of interest for its fauna and flora. In bad weather it may look forbidding but when the sun shines you'll probably feel you should be walking and not driving across this unspoilt wilderness. The many marked paths leading away from the E6 may be too tempting to ignore.

Fokstua is where the old King's Highway joins the modern road and you can still see the old bridge which carried the former route. A little over ten kilometres further on is the Troll King's Hall (**Dovregubben's Hall**: 365km). The buildings here, to the left of the road, include a small museum, shop and café.

Route 29 joins the E6 at **Hjerkinn** (375km), just short of the E6's highest point on the Dovrefjell: 1026m. Hjerkinn is reputed to be Norway's driest point with only just over 215mm of rain a year. This may be difficult to believe. In the scores of times I have crossed the fjell, it has been raining more often than it has been dry but I have to admit it was usually little more than a drizzle.

Some 20km or so to the west you can see the two highest peaks of the region, Snøhetta and Svanåtind, both over 2200m. From here, the E6 soon begins its steady and winding descent from the plateau towards Oppdal. The railway has been a near companion of the E6 for much of the journey so far and it descends from the plateau to the left of the road. One of its most delightful stations can be seen from the road or reached by a minor track. This is **Drivastua** which, especially from the high viewpoint of the E6, looks exactly like a model railway station of an earlier era, its quaint turf roof and black timbers contrasting with its bright yellow paintwork.

Another short section of the King's Highway appears to the right of the E6 just 10km beyond **Kongsvold** (388km) where the old inn is now an environmental research centre. The King's Highway can be walked but not driven along. It is very narrow and has some vertigo-inducing drops at its edge.

Oppdal (423km) lies at the northern foot of Dovrefjellet and has many of the attributes of Dombås, to the south. Again, tourism is one of its major industries but it also acts as a service centre for the local communities and is an ideal place to refuel and restock before Trondheim. There are plenty of cafés and shops and, usually, adequate parking. Before leaving, have a look at the tree sculpture behind the newspaper shop to the left of the road. Close to the bus and railway stations is the **tourist office** (☎ 72 40 04 70; 🖻 72 40 04 80; 🖳 post@oppdal.com).

Route 70 joins the E6 at Oppdal and the latter continues northwards by crossing the low watershed between the Driva and the Byna. It follows the broad, tree-filled valley of the Byna then crosses the River Orkla by an impressive bridge and reaches **Ulsberg** (447km) where the E6 is joined by Route 3 (see p79). The scenery from here is outstanding with some excellent views and potential photo-stops. **Berkåk** (457km) is another small service village at the end of this section. The shopping area is a quiet backwater away from the E6 and to the left of the road.

Northwards the scenery is mixed but the winding descent to **Støren** (490km) through the Sokmedal valley is as good as any before Trondheim. Just after Støren the road passes through a narrow valley section infamous for its landslides which, in the past, have raised the level of the River Gaula and caused deaths by drowning among the local farming families.

As you approach Trondheim, the forests give way to farming and the influence of Norway's third city becomes more and more evident. Quite suddenly, the narrow highway becomes an urban freeway as you reach the new planned town of **Heimdal** (535km). The town is little more than an overspill suburb of Trondheim and will eventually house 50,000. Its shopping centre is called City Syd!

After crossing to the right bank of the Nidelv you are presented with a choice. Leading off to the right is a branch of the E6 which bypasses central Trondheim and its traffic but prevents you from seeing one of the most interesting cities in northern Europe. To go into the town, continue on the left-hand branch of the E6. Trondheim was the first town in Norway to introduce a toll for entry into the city centre, but this shouldn't put you off.

TRONDHEIM

Trondheim (542km) is cosmopolitan like no other Scandinavian city, not even Stockholm. If it were transplanted into, say, northern France or the Low Countries it would, you feel, be quite at home. Perhaps it is the mediaeval cathedral or the large population of students from the university and technical college. Perhaps it is the colourful open market in the central square (Torvet). Whatever it is, Trondheim has an unrivalled charm and attraction. It is a very European town.

There is so much to see in Trondheim that it makes an ideal stopping place en route for Mo i Rana. There are plenty of hotels but on a short stay parking can be difficult and the town's road system takes some getting used to. If staying in a hotel, abandon the car and walk or use public transport. It's quite a large town with a population around 140,000. If you plan to stay at Steinkjer, your next leg is going to be a drive of just over 100km only so you can afford to linger in Trondheim.

The jewel in Trondheim's crown is the **Nidaros Cathedral** where fine views of the town can be had from the tower. Despite periodic fires over the ages, parts of the building date from the twelfth century and its weathered green roof and spire can be seen for miles around. The cathedral is the traditional and constitutional place for the coronation ceremony of the Norwegian royal house. Although a service of consecration has replaced a formal crowning since the 1950s it is none the less an important occasion on the accession of a new monarch. The most recent consecration was of King Harald V and Queen Sonja on 23 June 1991. The crown jewels have been on display in the cathedral since 1988.

Other attractions offered by the town, apart from its many fine buildings, are a number of museums and an attractive river frontage where the city section of the E6 crosses the Nidelva. Tall warehouses, some preserved from the 18th century, flank the river and, when reflected in the calm waters of the river, are a photographer's delight.

Views of the town when the cathedral tower is closed are best had from the rotating restaurant (Egon Tårnrestauranten) set at 80m above the ground in the Tyholt Tower. The shopper is well catered for and the pewter- and silverware is as good here as in any town in Scandinavia. No need is forgotten: there is even a *kondomeri*.

The **tourist office** (☎ 73 80 76 60; 🖹 73 80 76 70; 🖳 touristinfo@taas.no) is on the southern side of the main square (Torvet) where Kongensgt meets Munkegata.

Accommodation

As befits a town of this size and importance there's a good choice of accommodation of which the following are examples.

The best hotel is the **Radisson SAS Royal Garden** (☎ 73 80 30 00; 🖹 73 80 30 50; 🖳 trondheim@radissonsas.com) which overlooks the river. Here the prices hover around NOK1000 and at weekends the hotel has the annoying tendency of shutting down some of its facilities. The **Britannia** (☎ 73 80 08 00; 🖹 73 80 30 50; 🖳 brittania @britannia.no) on Dronningens gate is good value at NOK800. It is a favourite with British visitors who seem to like the fact that it's over 100 years old!

For the great range of small hotels and bed and breakfast accommodation, it's best to go to the tourist office who will advise.

To the east of the town is the *Vandrerhjem* (Youth Hostel, ☎ 73 87 44 50). It is open all year except around Christmas and New Year and offers a great range of accommodation, some of which is hotel quality. For camping and cabins, again excellent quality, there is *Sandmoen Camping* (☎ 72 88 61 35; 🖪 72 59 61 51; 🖳 tras@online.no). The site is by the E6 as you come into Trondheim, 10km out of town.

The E6 leaves the city by way of a very good urban highway, which seems to improve year by year, and descends into **Hell** (566km). Besides being the obvious place to stop and send a postcard of the 'wish you were here' variety, there is now a very modern shopping centre and hotel at this amusingly if ill-named little settlement. To be assured of getting a Hell postmark it is best to drive off the highway to the railway station which was Hell's original claim to importance. The post box there should ensure the desired franking.

Passing the Hell Hamburger Bar, on the left, the highway slips under a bridge which carries the main runway of Trondheim's airport. For the next 100km there is little of riveting interest along the route. This is a region of rich farming land which stretches eastward through a break in the highlands and into the lake area of Jämtland in Sweden. It was Bronze Age man, living by the lakes, who first ventured into the Trondheim region, Trøndelag, and settled along the deeply indented coastline. The area is now one of the most populous in central Norway. The E6 is often crowded with traffic on the section between Trondheim and Steinkjer and the road is in urgent need of widening and general upgrading. It is not that the road is poor. Quite simply it is inadequate and to travel many kilometres behind a farm tractor with no possibility of passing because of heavy oncoming traffic is one of the most frustrating experiences on the E6.

Soon after Hell a major route from Sweden, the E14, joins the E6 at **Stjørdal** (577km) which then runs along the relatively minor fjord Fætten where the German battleship *Tirpitz* was unsuccessfully attacked by mini-submarines of the British Royal Navy in 1942. At **Åsen** (600km) a minor road leads left off the E6 towards Frosta. If you make this detour to this historically interesting village it entails a round trip of 45km but you would be rewarded by a visit to Frostating. This is the site of Trøndelag's first parliament (or *ting*) which exercised authority from AD940 to the seventeenth century. There are other historic sites here and an open-air museum.

Back on the E6, the importance of forestry as well as farming is evident at **Skogan** (615km) which lives and breathes wood products, and is especially important for newsprint. The road bypasses the next major village, Levanger, and moves on to **Verdalsøra** (636km). As the E6 enters the village, Route 72 branches off to the right to cross the Swedish border 50km away. In the village a minor road leads left to Skiklestad (4km from the junction with E6). It was here that King-Saint Olav was killed in a battle on 30 July AD1030. It is a sacred place in Norwegian nationalism. The E6 route northwards now leaves the coast and runs behind a peninsula (Inderøy) only to find itself back with the sea as it turns into **Steinkjer** (664km) along the southern shore of the sheltered Beitstadfjord. Even Steinkjer's loyal citizens would not claim that it is an attractive town. More than three-quarters of the town was destroyed in World War II and rapidly rebuilt. Its modern industrial plants do little to enhance its appearance. As the E6 enters the town, a large barracks is passed to the right of the road. Many a Norwegian conscript has memories of the town as a none-too-popular posting. The E6 runs through the centre of the town and, apart from an attractive modern church (to the right of the highway) with a tall detached belltower, there is little reason to stop unless you are seeking accommodation here.

That said, there's not much choice if you want a hotel: there's really only the **Tingvold Park** (☎ 74 16 11 00; 🖹 74 16 11 17; 🖳 guldsho@online.no). Prices are around NOK800 for a double. For camping and cabins there's **Guldbergaunet Sommerhotel og Camping** (☎ 74 16 20 45; 🖳 guldsho@online.no).

You leave Steinkjer by climbing the hill that marks the town's northern boundary. At the top of the hill, however, as the road swings to the right, a small road leads off the E6 from where panoramic views of the town can be had. Leaving Steinkjer behind, the E6 is now very evidently in different country.

The road descends gently through a forested valley to **Asp** (671km). From Asp there is an alternative to the E6 – Route 17. This route, which in pre-war times was the better road and held the title 'Northern Trunk Road', is the more interesting and leads through the mountains to the coast near Namsos. At various points along the route the E6 can be rejoined. If you ignore the E6 and take Route 17 to Mo i Rana, it will involve an extra 100km and four ferries. The ferry journeys alone take nearly two hours, excluding waiting time. If there is plenty of time to spare, choose Route 17; if not, the E6 still has much to offer.

Along the E6, the scenery at first is largely forest with small farms occupying clearings. Near **Føling** (676km) the road levels out through what was marshy country, passing Lake Lømsen on the left to reach the south-western extremity of Lake Snåsa near **Sem** (677km). Snåsavatnet, fully 36km long and Norway's sixth largest lake, is set in near perfect alignment with the Caledonian (NE–SW) geological grain of the country. Unfortunately, views of the lake from the car are few and far between for the road follows an undulating course behind woodlands and is often forced away from the lake's shore by its many indentations.

You can get a view at **Kvam** (687km) but the road climbs away from the lake through a col and once again only tantalizing glimpses of the vast stretch of water are to be seen until you reach **Holmen** (712km). From this point, to the right of the road in a well designed lay-by, you can view the lake in all its magnificence. It is at its best when placid and mirror-like. When wind conditions exploit its great NE–SW fetch, substantial waves disturb the surface.

The road descends from Holmen to the northern end of the lake and then turns up the valley of Bruvollelva, one of the feeder streams. Rising steeply at first, the E6 runs through countryside which is a mixture of forest and bog. Reaching a height of 246m it descends again via the Sanddøla valley to Formofoss (738km). You might consider a stop here worthwhile to see the famous waterfall. A path leads to the falls away from the road.

Nine kilometres further on the road passes through **Grong** (747km), a quite important railway centre for the timber industry and a junction between the northern line and the route to Namsos.

Shortly after Grong and the junction with Route 760 (to Namsos), the E6 strikes north-westward along Namdalen. The scenery along this part of the route is undistinguished, mostly forest, marsh and lake, but some of the small villages bordering the road are of interest. At **Gartland** (753km) the old church (parts dating from the late seventeenth century) has Sami (Lapp) connections and the interior has a relic of an old stave church in the form of a column in front of the choir.

At **Lassemoen** (782km), Route 764 leads off to the east and towards Skorovatn where copper and zinc were once mined. The overhead cable which carried the ores to the coast passes over the E6 a little beyond the junction. With mining diminishing in importance in this area, forestry is dominant and **Namsskogen** (820km) is a regional centre for the industry. Beyond **Mellingsmoen** (838km), the E6 leaves Namdalen over a low col and joins the valley of the River Mellings in the fylker of Nordland. The next section of the road threads through forested and marshy valleys alongside a string of lakes, the largest of which is Store Majavatnet.

In the village of **Majavatn** (850km) is a monument (to the right of the road) to 24 members of the Norwegian Resistance who were executed here in World War II. Also in the village are preserved buildings of the old Sami market which used to be held here.

Just six kilometres further on, near Sefivatn, a path leads off the E6 to the right and down to an impressive canyon. It is something of a scramble to reach the edge of the great gorge but it is a spectacular sight.

Northwards the road enters Svenningdal, a fairly narrow, forested and marshy valley. To the left of the road high mountains, retaining their snow-caps in summer, rise to over 1200m.

The valley begins to open out to allow more farming but the road keeps close to the river. This is fortunate because one of the great waterfalls of Nordland is only a stone's throw from the highway at **Laksfors/Laksfoss** (910km). A minor road leads off the E6 to the left and down to the falls, a distance of about 200m. Although not especially high, the falls' attractions are the enormous volume of water they spill and the possible sighting of salmon leaping at their foot. (*Laks* is Norwegian for salmon.) What was a very natural beauty spot has now been spoilt by the erection of a café, but the falls are still worth a visit.

Beyond Laksfoss the E6 climbs away from the river before rejoining it along low terraces to enter the industrial town of **Mosjøen** (937km). The town is at the head of Vefsnfjord around the Skjeven River. It has a forbidding air about it and I have always found it especially unattractive. Across the narrow fjord, black mountains rise to well over 800m, presenting a sheer wall to the west. Behind the town, to the east, the land rises almost as steeply to over 300m. Mosjøen's setting is this steep-walled corridor. It is not the place for the claustrophobic.

Mosjøen was little more than a hamlet at the start of the nineteenth century. A population of just sixty-three was recorded in 1801. It now houses some 10,000 thanks largely to the implantation of an aluminium refinery in 1940, based on cheap hydro-electricity. Three industries dominate – and that is an appropriate word – the town: aluminium, saw mills and textiles. The E6, following improvements in recent years, passes easily through the town and if you wish to make use of its shops and banks (note there is no petrol station) you must turn left off the E6 shortly after reaching the town (look for the hospital/*sykehus* on the right) and make for the sentrum. There are ample services in town, including one of the very few state alcohol shops (Vinmonopolutsalg) in North Norway. Apart from the services and an interesting collection of 19th-century domestic and commercial buildings around Sjøgaten, there is little reason to leave the E6 as it runs across sand and gravel flats to the east of the town centre.

The road leaves the town after passing the giant aluminium works (left) just beyond the main timber quays and then pulls away from the fjord and turns to the north-west across a low but boggy depression before descending into the Fusta valley. Narrow and forested at first, the valley widens towards Fustvatnet and Mjåvatnet, two lakes to the east of the road, and on to Lake Ømmer. The scenery is quite pretty along this stretch in summer when the calm waters of the lakes reflect their forested borders.

Leaving the lakes behind, the E6 starts to ascend as the valley again narrows and the road runs along the western shore of yet another lake, Luktvatnet, and into **Osen** (973km). This little settlement has a story to tell because it was here that the German occupying forces in World War II built a camp for Yugoslav prisoners who were shipped to Norway to work on the road through to Korgen. Many failed to survive.

Shortly after Osen you begin a steep climb up to Vesterfjellet and Korgfjellet where the road reaches 550m. The views along this stretch are spectacular in fine weather. To the east is Okstind with ice and snow peaks of over 1900m, visible as the summit of the road is attained.

At the top of the fjell (to the right of the road) is a modern hotel and restaurant (985km). As the road winds its way down a very steep incline you can see the shimmering white surface of the distant Svartisen ice-cap to the north. On the right of the road is a simple memorial to the Yugoslav prisoners who died as their forced labour built the road.

The road now follows the Røssågo valley to one of the inner arms of the Ranafjord, Sørfjord. Just after **Bjerka** (1002km) there are good views to the west into the fjord. Through the village of **Finneidfjord** (1009km) the E6's path is now the shore of the main fjord which it shares with the railway. In 1997 the E6 was slightly re-routed between Bjerka and north of Finneid. It runs on a straightened path from Bjerka to Bredvika and includes a new bridge. Via two tunnels and a new road section, the village of Finneid is bypassed.

Crossing the bridge over the Dalselv brings yet another reminder of the battles of 1940. The Scots Guards were involved here (see *One Boy's War* by John Douglas) but it is peaceful now and it is the views across the fjord and towards the Svartisen ice-cap that catch the attention. A memorial to those guardsmen who lost their lives in the battle was unveiled on Norwegian National Day in 1993. To see it, go right off the road by the bridge.

By now the road is running into what are the outskirts of **Mo i Rana** (1035km) and the E6 is about to become the Arctic Highway.

APPROACH ROUTE II: LARVIK TO MO I RANA BY ROAD

This route adds a further 130km to the Oslo–Mo i Rana journey but the Frederikshavn–Larvik ferry crossing (see p12) is one of the shortest from continental Europe to Norway and one of the cheapest.

● **Route** Larvik–Oslo: Route 40–E18; for Oslo to Mo i Rana see Approach Route I.
● **Distance (Larvik–Oslo)** 130km
● **Total Distance (Larvik–Mo i Rana)** 1165km
● **Summary** Near coast route along Skagerak and Oslofjord, then as Approach Route I.
● **Suggested travel time** 2 hours from Larvik to Oslo. For Oslo to Mo i Rana see Approach Route I.
● **Road quality** Good to very good. Much of the E18 is classified as motorway.
● **Suggested stopping places** See Approach Route I.

The route (south to north)
Larvik is the centre of an industrial and commercial area near the mouth of Oslofjord. From the town centre, follow Route 40 to join the main road (turn right) to Oslo, the E18. The E18, although often described as a coastal road, for the most part runs well away from the sea over undulating but attractive country. All the major coastal towns and villages are bypassed and the road is relatively fast.

A substantial new section of road is being built which will take the E18 to the east of its present route. When completed, the E18 will swing east just south of **Holmestrand**, avoiding the built-up areas by the fjord before it re-joins the current route as it goes into Drammen. At **Drammen** (90km), one of the arms of the Oslofjord is crossed by Norway's largest single-span bridge (toll payable). The road remains of a specially high standard and the congestion of central Drammen is avoided by the E18. Drammen is a major industrial centre and port, its growth coinciding with the general industrialization of the Oslofjord area.

At **Fossekollen** (98km) the E18 passes through a 550m tunnel and, 10km further on, the road heads into the south-western suburbs of Oslo as it sweeps through **Asker** (110km) and **Sandvika** (117km) and into central **Oslo**. (There is a toll charged on entry to Oslo.) From here you can follow the Oslo–Mo i Rana route (see Approach Route I).

APPROACH ROUTE III: BERGEN TO MO I RANA BY ROAD. A RECOMMENDED ROUTE

This is a popular route to the north because of the importance of Bergen as the terminus of North Sea ferries and because the journey provides some outstanding and varied scenery. It is arguably the most interesting of all the road-approach routes.

● **Route** Bergen–Voss–Vik–Sogndal–Lom–Otta: E16–Route 13–Route 55–Route 15; for Otta to Mo i Rana see Approach Route I.
● **Distance (Bergen–Otta)** 417km (or 432km using mountain alternative – p82).
● **Total distance (Bergen–Mo i Rana)** 1214km plus 15-minute ferry (or 1229km plus 15-minute ferry using the mountain road alternative).

● **Summary of the route** Bergen to Voss: heavily tunnelled route along E16 (or mountain road alternative for part of the way). From Voss, valley and mountain route across Fossfjellet. Sognefjord crossed and followed east on northern side. Route leads over Jotunheim mountains and into Ottadalen from Lom to Otta. Joins E6 at Otta (see Approach Route I above).

● **Suggested travel time** 1 or 2 days up to the junction with E6 (Otta). Then two days on E6 from Otta to Mo i Rana.

● **Road quality** Very good along E16 to Voss but the mountain alternative is winding, narrow and with steep gradients. Steep gradients over Fossfjellet and over Jotunheim mountains (road may be closed at times in winter). Narrow on north side of Sognefjord. Good road from Lom to Otta.

● **Suggested stopping places** Bergen, Voss, the Jotunheim (also see Approach Route I). There are plenty of camping sites along the route, including mountain wild camping in the Jotunheim.

The route (south to north)

BERGEN

Bergen is Norway's second largest town with nearly a quarter of a million inhabitants. The settlement is spread widely and untidily across seven hills and along the fjords which fracture the coast. Central Bergen, however, is compact and lies largely around and behind Vågen, one of the two main harbours, with the industrial district around Puddefjorden. All in all, the town has a spectacular setting, especially when viewed from the sea.

The North Sea ferries dock on the northern side of the entrance to Vågen. The central area of the town is very picturesque and full of bustle. It is well worth spending at least a day in the city before you move north. Its historic links with the Hanseatic League and, more recently, Edvard Grieg are well known but there's a lot more of interest.

Services

The town's **tourist office** (☎ 55 32 14 80; 🖹 55 32 14 64; 🖳 info@bergen-travel.com) is in Vågsallmenning, a small square behind the fish market. Simply go down the harbour road (Bryggen) away from the ferry terminal and you reach the end of the harbour. Turn right and you're in the Torget Fish Market. The information office building is the imposing **Fresco Hall**. In high summer

(June–August), the office is open from 08.30 to 10.00. In the rest of the year it opens at 09.00, closing at 20.00 in May and September and at 16.00 in winter. It carries information brochures not only for Bergen but also for most of western Norway. You can get a Bergen Card here which will give you substantial discounts on many attractions, free parking and a host of other privileges. At NOK150 for one day (NOK230 for two days) it is well worth the investment. Tours of the town also start from the information office. The staff are helpful if you need accommodation advice.

For internet access, try the **library** on Strømgaten, near the railway station. The main **post office** is on Småstandgaten, the first turning left as you come out of the fish market away from the information office. The **bus station** is close to the library.

Around town

Getting round the town, it is probably best to walk or use public transport. The town has a good road system but it is confusing if it's your first visit. There are good bus services but many of the attractions can be reached on foot from a base in central Bergen.

The **fish and flower market** (see above) is a must and best seen early in the

---

(Opposite): Snow can affect approach routes even in summer.

day. To get a bird's-eye view of the town, take the **funicular railway** to the top of Fløyfjellet (320m). The station is off to the left at the end of **Bryggen**, the road into town from the ferry terminal. The Bryggen is Hanseatic Bergen, the old wharf buildings now a mix of smart shops and craft workshops. To get to Edvard Grieg's house, **Troldhaugen**, take a bus from the bus station (see above) and there's a 20-minute walk after that. The main shopping centre is in the pedestrianized square, **Torgelmenningen**, up the rising road beyond the fish market, away from the harbour.

At the ferry terminal end of Bryggen are a 12th-century **church** (St Mary's/*Marikirken*) in Dreggen, and the **Bergenhus Fortress**, which includes the 13th-century **King Haakon's Hall** or *Håkanshallen*, and the 16th-century **Rosenkrantz Tower**.

Listed in the town guide (available from the information office) are more museums than a short visit here will allow time to visit. Just one word of caution if planning to walk round the town: the annual rainfall is nearly 2000mm or 77 inches. Pray for a sunny day but take a suitable rain jacket.

Accommodation

There are some 25–30 hotels to choose from with the majority near the city centre. Even so booking ahead is even more important than in Oslo. The tourist information office has details of scores of bed and breakfast or guesthouse options. If you fly in to Bergen airport, there's the *Quality Hotel Edvard Grieg* at Sandsli, only 5 minutes from the airport (☎ 55 98 00 00; ▤ 55 22 01 50; ▣ booking@edvard grieg no). This is an all-suite hotel where a double with breakfast will be about NOK1000. Accommodation in Bergen is quite expensive even by Norwegian standards.

Occupying the more expensive end of the market are two Radisson SAS hotels: the *Norge* (☎ 55 57 30 00; ▤ 55 57 30 01; ▣ info.bergen@radissonsas.com), in the middle of town, and the *Royal* (☎ and ▤ as Norge; ▤ 55 32 48 08), very close to the

ferry terminal. The former is thought of as Bergen's best but the Royal has a good carpark and its position is ideal if you're coming in by North Sea ferry. The Royal's only drawback is the rather small size of the rooms. Prices for both will just break NOK1000 for a double with breakfast.

A more modest price for a double, around NOK650, can be found at the *Bergen Gjesthus* (☎ 55 31 96 66; ▤ 55 23 31 46) on Vestre Torggate but they only have 46 rooms, so book ahead.

Campsites and caravan parks are plentiful with the majority to the south or east of the city. Two large sites that are open all year are *Lone Camping* (☎ 55 24 08 20) and *Midttun Camping* (☎ 55 10 39 00). Both are situated on Route 580 between Nesstun and Indre Arna, and both have cabins.

Where to eat

There's no shortage of restaurants, cafés and bars in Bergen. There's even a 'Scottish Pub', on Valkendorfsgata.

For a real treat of Norwegian seafood in a wonderfully restored, 300-year-old building on the quayside, Bryggen, go to *Enhjørningen*. It's not cheap but the food and the ambience are priceless. It's probably best to book (☎ 55 32 79 19).

In the big shopping centre, *Galleriet*, in the pedestrianized Torgalmenningen, there's a range of eating places including Chinese. Galleriet stays open until 20.00 except Saturdays when it shuts at 18.00. It's closed on Sundays. Around the town there are four of the ubiquitous *Peppe's Pizza* bars and two *Burger Kings*. Even if you only walk along Bryggen, go though the fish market area and up into Torgalmenningen, you'll have an extraordinary choice of menus and bars.

For the vegetarian, *Den Gode Klode* is a little away from the centre up by the Museum of Natural History on Fosswinckels gate. At the other end of the taste spectrum, there's an *Angus Steakhouse* on Valkendorfsgata, three streets back from the other side of the harbour to Bryggen.

(Opposite) Farming and fishing characterize the northern economy. **Top:** Badderen (p209). **Bottom:** The tiny fishing village of Seljenes, south of Repvåg on Porsangerfjord (p245).

Moving north

If you've come into Bergen by North Sea ferry, the route to take out of town couldn't be easier. Simply turn left from the terminal, away from Bryggen (which leads down into Bergen along the harbour side). You are now on the Route 585/E39 and you will find that you are driving through tunnels more often, or so it seems, than on open road.

Route 564 leads off to the left and you swing right past the Åsane Senter. Then the E39 goes off left as you join the E16 to go past **Ytre Arna** (22km). More tunnels, and you quickly reach a major junction, **Indre Arna**. This is where Route 580 (see Approach Route VI, p90) joins the E16. In fact, if you go straight on here you'll be returning to Bergen. Instead, follow the E16 by turning left.

Almost immediately there is a series of tunnels taking the E16 to **Trengereid** (31km). From Trengereid the road goes through more tunnels and you will see only glimpses of the fjord, Veafjorden. It is the fjord shore that the road follows as far as **Stranghelle** before turning north-west to **Dale** (57km). Between Trengereid and Dale there are seven long tunnels and numerous short sections where the road burrows into the steep rock-face of the fjord's edge. The

---

The alternative mountain route

The main reason for choosing this route will probably be to see some of the wild country of the Bergsdalen plateau. However, the route adds a further 15km to the journey and it includes a very narrow and steep section east of Dale. It's not the route to take if you've a trailer or you're in a hurry.

If you decide that scenery is more important than speed, follow the E16 as far as Dale (see above) but turn off, right, through the village. You are now beginning the mountain route. Leaving Dale, and after a short tunnel, the road climbs up through Bergsdalen. It is this next section which is unsuitable for caravans and large camper vehicles. Not only is there a steep gradient but the road winds through hairpins and is exceptionally narrow in places. With luck, and if the traffic is light, it may be possible to make the ascent without reversing but, in order to allow passing, backing the vehicle may well be necessary. Having once had to drive this route, downhill, in a rainstorm with a broken and opaque windshield, I know how difficult it can be!

Passing a hydro-electric power reservoir on the right of the road at **Hamlagrøosen** signals that the most difficult section of the road is over but the whole of this route, almost into Voss, is narrow and driving should be done with special care. Much of the journey from Hamlagrøosen is across a high mountain plateau with an untidy scattering of small settlements and the weekend cabins of Bergen's residents. Most of these cabins have been built to provide a base for sports-fishing and at weekends the road can be quite crowded. Forests, lakes, rivers and bogland make up the rather bleak scenery and farmland is rare. At Lake Svarta the road reaches an altitude of 625m but the scenery is unaltered.

The descent down into the Voss valley begins soon after Svartvatnet and, although it is not quite as steep as the ascent from Dale, it is narrow and winding. If you're driving, you'll be concentrating on the road, but your passengers will get some splendid views into the valley to the left of the road. At the foot of the mountains, the road bridges the river and turns sharply to the right as it joins the E16 (see above).

longest tunnels are Stavenes (2750m) and Dalevågen (1380m). This road did not exist except as a plan before World War II. After the war the tunnels were cut but the original plan to take the road beyond Dale along the same path as the railway had to wait until the 1990s. Dale has a quite extraordinary setting, jammed into the narrow valley bottom at a river confluence. To appreciate its site it is really necessary to fly over the village. Industry is here, mostly textiles, because of the abundance of hydro-electric power. From Dale a minor road branches off through the village giving you an alternative and mountainous route to Voss (see p82). Meanwhile the E16 continues northwards.

The E16, as far as Voss, is now either a completely new road or an improved and widened surface. This section of the route is quite exceptionally good and fast. Just a few years ago there was no road east from **Dalseid**. Now with the aid of tunnels the E16 follows a path along Bolstadfjorden towards **Evanger** (78km). The road passes through the largely forested and steep-sided valley passing few farms and fewer villages. From Evanger there are more signs of agriculture but the valley remains narrow and somewhat awesome. At **Bulken** (90km) the E16 is joined by the alternative mountain route. Now the road runs along the very beautiful north shore of Vangsvatnet to reach **Voss** (99km). Parts of this final section of the road into Voss are still being widened. You come into Voss (99km) from the west on the E16 and pass by Fleischer's Hotel (to the left) and Appartments (to the right).

VOSS

If you've come into Bergen on the North Sea ferry but don't want to stop there, Voss is the obvious alternative place to stay as you make your way north. On the other hand, if you've been staying in Bergen, you can afford to leave late knowing that you can overnight in Voss. The little town is unashamedly catering for tourists. Its streets are lined with shops selling carved and moulded trolls of incredible ugliness and attraction. Pewter and silverware are as important as postcards and guide maps. As you enter the town from the west, an attractive church dominates the view and splits the road into two. Voss is a good place to check your needs for the drive ahead. It will be a long journey before you come to another place with as good a range of stores.

All the same the town is small enough to drive through with ease and the E16 is well signposted.

Accommodation

Fleischer's Hotel has to be the place to stay if you can afford it. The building dates from 1889 and has the appearance of a middle-European mansion. The Fleischer family still own and run the hotel. The public rooms are quite splendid and the bedrooms are large and well-furnished. A swimming pool is on the lower ground floor. Prices are around NOK600–800.

If the hotel is too expensive, an alternative is to use the *Fleischer Appartments* on the opposite side of the road. The well appointed cabins used to be described as a motel and they are excellent when you're driving because you can draw your vehicle right up to the front door. If not self-catering, you can use the hotel's excellent restaurant. If you use the apartments, try to get a cabin which overlooks the lake (☎ 56 52 05 00; 🖷 56 52 05 01; 🖳 hotel@fleischers.no).

For camping, there's a site, *Voss Camping*, at the end of the lake (☎ 56 51 15 97; 🖷 56 51 66 75). However, there's a wonderful camping place just 10km further on: *Tvinde Camping* (see p84, ☎ 56 51 69 19; 🖷 56 51 30 15; 🖳 tvinde@tvinde.no). Although it can become a little crowded in mid-summer, the site is stunning. Cabins come out at NOK300–400.

As you leave Voss, Route 13 joins the E16 on the edge of town to become a single road for the next 20km. The road standard is good as it runs above Lønavatnet to **Tvinne** (109km) where, on the left of the road, by the cabin and camping site, there is an impressive and much-photographed waterfall. From here the farms are left behind and the steep-sided valley narrows. The road climbs alongside the River Stronda which tumbles over small falls and rushes over rapids. At **Vinje** (120km) the E16 turns east to Gudvagen and you take the Route 13 branch as it continues on its own towards the north and the Sognefjord. This next stretch of Route 13 is past a long lake, Myrkdal, and then into the broad Myrkdalen. This valley is a typical glaciated U-shaped trough with a near-flat floor and towering walls. At the head of the valley the climb to the Fossfjellet mountains begins.

To reach the top of the fjell involves a climb of about 500m with the steepest section coming first. From Hola, the road has four main hairpin bends with excellent views of a really impressive waterfall to the left. There are conveniently situated viewpoints, in lay-bys along the road, which is just as well because you need to drive this section of Route 13 with care.

This part of the road was built in the mid-1950s and, with altitudes well over 1000m on either side, it often retains snow patches close to the road even in summer. Much work has been done to improve this section of Route 13 but its modernization has not detracted from the beauty of the very wild landscape through which it runs. The road reaches an altitude of 986m just after the fylke boundary is crossed and Route 13 enters Sogn og Fordane.

The descent from the mountains used to be difficult, even dangerous, but the road has been widened and the crash barriers strengthened. There are spectacular views across the village of Vik (Viksøyri) into Sognefjorden and to the Jostefonn ice-cap. This is a detached glacier from the giant Jostedal ice mass. There are viewing places, well constructed to give space to park a car off the road. The best occurs about halfway down the mountain slope as the road turns sharply left at ninety degrees. The village of **Vik** (167km) lies in a sheltered inlet off the main Sognefjord – it is actually a partially drowned hanging valley. It is a useful place to restock and refuel before you continue along the edge of the main fjord to **Vagsnes** (178km). This edge-of-fjord road is rather narrow and in the rush to the ferry it can be frustrating. You'll find that passing is almost impossible for much of its length.

The ferry point at Vagsnes lies at the end of the road. The service is frequent and, if you miss the ship, you'll soon see another crossing the fjord to take its place. The journey time is about 15 minutes to Hella. You need to take care not to catch the wrong ferry because other routes go to Dragsvik and to Balestrand.

The crossing allows you to see something of the magnificence of the Northern Hemisphere's largest fjord. The statistics are impressive: Sognefjorden stretches 300km inland, is flanked by mountains rising to well over 1200m, and has a depth of nearly 1000m. Unfortunately, a dog-leg bend in the fjord at this point obscures the view westward and the full length of the Sognefjord has to be imagined rather than seen.

Camping in comfort
For many years I used to wild camp everywhere I went in Arctic Norway – it was much easier than today – and my Land Rover would be loaded with boxes of food carefully arranged in meal packs. These would supply all my needs other than a relatively meagre ration of fresh food to be bought as I travelled. I could make my boxed food last for six weeks or more. I even used to carry boxes of wine (alcohol is prohibitively priced) stored under the false floor I had built in the vehicle to provide an emergency sleeping area on the occasions the weather ruled out pitching our tent. Whether the wine really travelled well hardly mattered. A glass of wine with dinner is a wonderful prelude to a night in a tent under Arctic skies.

On arrival at Hella there is only one way to go. Route 55, the road to Sogndal, is narrow and winding along the shore of Sognefjorden and into its tributary branch, Sogndalsfjord. This road is undulating as it passes through some very beautiful countryside and the views to the fjord are excellent. Small villages line the route and orchards overlooking the road make it possible to pick fruit from a car's open window – possible, but not encouraged! **Leikanger** (191km), with an interesting church sitting above the road, and **Hermansverk** (194km), are two of the larger villages before the road turns up the narrow Sogndalsfjord and crosses the river to **Sogndal** (216km).

Sogndal is a sizeable town with all services and, if you've not refuelled in Vik, this is the most convenient place to do so before Lom, which is almost 140km away. From here you continue on Route 55, one of the most impressive sections of road in all Norway. You can think of this part of the journey as being in two sections: the first is an easy route along the picturesque inner-arms of the Sognefjord while the second is the crossing of the Jotunheim mountains. The latter is Norway's highest mountain crossing by a major route.

As far as **Gaupne** (246km), Route 55 winds through undulating countryside where farming and forestry compete. From Gaupne there is a toll road to Nigardsbreen, a diffluent glacier of the Jostedalsbreen. If you make this excursion, be warned that although the glacier can be seen from the end of the road, you'll need half a day to reach the ice

After swinging round the head of the little Gaupnefjord, the road joins Lustrafjorden where fruit farming is again important despite the relatively narrow strip of lowland allowed by the high-rising and forested mountain slopes. You pass through a pretty village, **Luster** (262km), with a restored church (Dale Church), to the left of the road, before the sides of the fjord become even steeper and more rugged.

At the head of the fjord is **Skjolden** (272km), a village which marks the beginning of the mountain section of Route 55, starting with a relatively gentle climb to **Fortun** (278km). Now, for the next 11km, 10 hairpin bends, with a maximum gradient of 1:9, ease the road up to the Jotunheim (literally Home of the Giants) mountains and to the Jotunheim National Park. The road is one of the most famous in Norway and was opened just before World War II. There are breathtaking views to be had back into the valley of Fortunsdal but you should stop only where lay-bys widen the road.

Near the top is the **Turtagrø** mountaineering centre (289km). To the southeast is Norway's third highest peak, Skagastøl, which rises to 2405m. It was first climbed by an Englishman, William Cecil Slingsby, who is revered as the father of Norwegian mountaineering (see also p201). Four kilometres further on is a commemorative stone marking the 1860 ride across the mountains of Sognefjell by Crown Prince Oscar who was later to become king of both Norway and Sweden. This is a great place to stop for even more splendid views.

Route 55 next crosses the dam of the Hervass Reservoir (295km) before climbing to its highest point, 1400m, near the fylke boundary. This part of the route is a glaciologist's delight: cirque glaciers, snowfields, periglacial landscapes, even ice calderas. The road is open from June to October only and in some years, even in midsummer, high snow walls may line the road, and lakes may remain partly frozen throughout the year. Peaks and valleys break the skyline and this must be one of the most beautiful and inspiring of Norway's many outstanding scenic offerings. The road skirts round the Finnårken ice mass and drops down to **Krossbru** (309km) where there is a small mountain hotel much in favour with mountain walkers and climbers. Now the road falls again, more steeply, along the barren Bøverdal (also known as Breiseterdalen) before passing over a col and into Leirdal.

If you're not in too much of a hurry, you can make an interesting short excursion by turning right off Route 55 down a small toll road (clearly marked) which follows the Leirva River to Leirvassbu. To go to the end of this road would involve a round trip of 35km but there is a mountain hotel at the end and even this short drive into the Leirva valley will give a flavour of this very impressive mountain country. The owners of the Leirvassbu Mountain Hotel are also the proprietors of a hotel at **Elveseter** (332km). A stop here is a 'must', even if only for coffee. Better still, stay the night.

Elveseter accommodation

Elveseter Hotel (☎ 61 21 20 00; 🖷 61 21 21 01; 🖳 elveset@online.no) is to the left of the road and consists of a group of old farm buildings which have been transported here from the Otterdalen district and sympathetically restored. The interiors are wonderful if you don't mind feeling you're in a museum. The hotel has rooms in the main buildings and also in self-catering apartments up the hill to the left. There is even a small swimming pool in one of the old farm buildings. Don't miss (you can't miss) the great column, *Sagasøyla,* 33m of carved syenite telling the history of Norway from AD872. The hotel and the erection of the column here were the work of Jessie and Åmund Elvæseter and the family still runs the hotel. Rates are around NOK750 for a double but note that the season is from 1 June to late September only.

From Elveseter the road runs through the village of **Galdesand** (336km) in the shadow of Norway's highest peak, Goldhøpiggen (2469m). A minor toll road leads off to the right to climb up towards the Juvbre glacier. This is one of the most extraordinary roads in western Norway. A steep zig-zag path carries you up to over 1800m in a distance of 15km. You need to drive this road with care; coming down will test your braking system. There is skiing throughout the year from a centre built at the end of the road.

Continuing along Route 55 you come to **Røisheim** (340km) where there is another hotel, similar to Elveseter but not really in the same league. Fifteen kilometres and a fairly rapid descent gets you to the village of **Lom** (355km). Lom is most famous for its mediaeval stave church (turn left on to Route 15, cross the bridge and the church is on the right). It is also a good service centre with a tourist office in the shopping complex. Despite its capitulation to tourism, this is an interesting village and a useful stop. There's accommodation in the village but nothing to match Elveseter.

From Lom join Route 15, a major road; this is the link with the E6 at Otta. Leaving Lom, you start the journey to Otta by turning right on to Route 15 which runs along Ottadalen. The River Otta flows through a long lake, Vågåvatn, at this point although farmland separates the road from the lake for the most part. Indeed, at **Graffer** (362km) it runs briefly behind a ridge and you lose sight of the lake. As it returns to the lakeside at **Garmo** (369km) it passes by the cottage birthplace of the famous Norwegian writer Knut Hamsun. All along this part of Route 55 there are some well-preserved old farm buildings, many still in use.

Just before **Vågåmo** (388km), a bridge carries the road to the northern side of the valley where it makes a sharp turn to the right after passing an old church (to the right of the road) which was rebuilt in 1625 from its original stave form.

After five kilometres, and just before Route 15 turns through a right-hand bend, a steep road leads off to the left up the side of the valley. This is **Vågårusti**, a short cut to Nord-Sel (see Approach Route I, p66). If you use this minor road you save 26km but the initial slope is steep and it's a winding climb. The road is very narrow and, if you're pulling a trailer, stay with Route 15. If you do take this route you will find it leads through forest and past isolated farmsteads. It has just a little magic of its own.

Most traffic stays loyal to Route 15 and continues along the farmed valley to **Otta** (417km) where it joins the E6 for the rest of its journey to **Mo i Rana** (1151km). For a continuation of this route, see Approach Route I, p66.

APPROACH ROUTE IV: BERGEN TO KIRKENES OR KIRKENES TO BERGEN, BY SEA – A RECOMMENDED ROUTE

To combine a sea journey with a drive along the length of the Arctic Highway may be the ultimate experience of Norway north of the Polar Circle. The sea trip is by the Coastal Express Steamers, Hurtigruten, and is an all-year-round service. It is often described as 'the local boat' and the service pre-dates the completion of the Arctic Highway. In fact the centenary of the service occurred on 2 July 1993 and, appropriately, a new ship to join the fleet that year was named after the founder, Richard With. The first service was between Trondheim and Hammerfest but was extended north and south to give today's Bergen–Kirkenes route. The service is subsidized, partly because of the competition offered by the Highway. The daily service takes seven days northward and six travelling south, with around 30 ports of call. In fact, the best plan is to drive north and sail south. This is for two good reasons: firstly, the ships don't call in at Mo i Rana so it's impossible to join the Arctic Highway at its southern limit; and, secondly, the fares are less on the voyage south.

Currently, there are twelve ships involved in the service. All can carry vehicles but the number of car spaces varies from 4 to 55. The *MS Lofoten* is the last remaining traditional ship and the smallest at 2,600 tonnes. But if you favour small and traditional over large and modern, book early because the *Lofoten* is the ship with only 4 spaces for cars. All the other ships have at least 40 spaces. Even so, book well ahead of your planned trip because the largest and most modern ships can take a maximum of 50 cars despite their 15,000 tonnes and 1000-passenger capacity. The most recent addition to the fleet is the *MS Midnatsol* whose maiden voyage was in 2003. It might seem surprising that these new generation ships are so large. The reason will be evident as soon as you arrive at the dockside. The majority of the passengers are using the service as a holiday cruise. The days when Hurtigruten was simply a local service and most passengers were making short journeys from port to port are gone. The improved road system, including the Arctic Highway, has transformed communications in the north and radically reduced the need to travel by sea.

If you decide to use the Hurtigrute, you could join at Bergen, sail to Kirkenes and then travel south on the Arctic Highway. But, as explained, it may be better to drive to Kirkenes and then sail south. This has the added attraction of providing you with a relaxing week after the stresses and strains of the drive north. Whichever direction you use the ship, it will be a fascinating journey and complement the drive with a coastal perspective of the north.

The cost of such a journey by sea depends upon the time of year and the quality of the onboard accommodation you choose. The fare rates are so varied that it is best to contact the company running the service close to the time you book. Also, ask what concessions are available. If you travel in the high season (June to mid-August) expect to pay perhaps 175% of the fare in the winter. Likewise the cheapest cabins are only half the cost of the dearest. Of course, fares must be set against the cost of fuel plus accommodation which would have to be paid on the equivalent road journey.

Vehicle costs remain the same through the year: NOK2050 for a car carried all the way from Bergen to Kirkenes, and the same for a southward voyage.

The ships can be joined at any of the intermediate ports so there is a high level of flexibility. For example, you could use Trondheim as the embarkation/disembarkation point even if you entered Norway through Oslo.

The quality of accommodation and food aboard is good to very good.

This is certainly an alternative to driving all the way north and south that is worth considering. It will not be cheaper if you propose to camp or use cabins when driving, but is less tiring, takes less time and a quite different experience.

For booking or other enquiries in the UK: ☎ 020 8846 2666; 🖷 020 8846 2678; 🖳 sales@norwegian-coastal.com. In Norway the contact is: ☎ 81 03 00 00; 🖳 info@hurtigruten.com.

APPROACH ROUTE V: STAVANGER TO MO I RANA BY ROAD

Stavanger is an international airport as well as a ferry port for the UK–Norway crossings. There is little point in starting a road journey to the Arctic Highway from Stavanger if the North Sea crossing has been used because the ferries also call at Bergen, but if you're flying into Norway with the intention of hiring a car, then Stavanger may be an option.

● **Route** Stavanger–Bergen: E39; for Bergen to Mo i Rana see Route III above.
● **Distance (Stavanger–Bergen)** 172km plus 3 ferries (total 1hr 45min for ferries).
● **Total Distance (Stavanger–Mo i Rana)** 1386km plus 4 ferries (total 2 hours).
● **Summary** The whole route to Bergen is coastal or near so; this is its charm and attraction. If you want an appreciation of Norway's fractured west coast, this is it.
● **Suggested travel time** Best part of one day from Stavanger to Bergen. For Bergen to Mo i Rana see Approach Route III, above.
● **Road quality** Very good with only occasional narrow sections. Much of the first part of this route has been constructed only in the last few years.
● **Suggested stopping places** See Approach Route III.

The route (south to north)

The E39 leads north out of **Stavanger**, past some large oil industry stores, to slip down into a tunnel (8km) under Byfjorden. From here, the road leapfrogs a series of islands by bridge and tunnel to reach the ferry point of **Mortavika** (31km). This is a busy but frequent ferry crossing which gets you on to your next island, Vestre Bokn, in under thirty minutes. Now the E39 is running almost due north, away from the coast but still with innumerable inlets and islands in view.

The Oslo–Haugesund road (E134) leads off to the left at **Aksdal** (62km) and for the next five kilometres the E134 and E39 become one before the E134 continues its journey eastward (right) to Oslo. The next section of the road continues to be dominated by water and only one sizeable village is on the route, **Førde** (87km). At 102km there is a ferry crossing between **Valevåg** and **Skjærsholmane**, the ferry point for **Leirvik**. A new under-sea tunnel is being constructed to take the E39 just west of the ferry crossing. The new road will take a slightly longer route than the boat but there'll be a saving on the 20 minutes the ferry normally takes – not to mention the waiting time.

Now on Stord Island the E39 avoids much of the large village of Leirvik by skirting round it to the west. Your route then follows close to the island's shore until it reaches **Sandvikvåg** (136km). The third and last ferry on this route leaves from here for **Halhjem**, a journey of about one hour.

By now the E39 is practically in suburban Bergen but you've still another 26km to cover before **Nesttun** (162km) and the junction with Route 580. Central Bergen is a further 10km. (There is a toll charged on entry to Bergen.)

You can stay on the E39 through Bergen and you'll be able to continue your journey out of the town on the same road (see Approach Route III above). Alternatively, if you want to avoid central Bergen and continue north without staying in the city, turn on to Route 580 at Nesttun and join the E16 at Indre Arna (see Approach Route III above).

APPROACH ROUTE VI: GOTHENBURG TO MO I RANA (VIA OSLO) BY ROAD

Gothenburg is a major ferry port for entry into Scandinavia (see Part 1) and you can take a variety of routes to the Arctic Highway from this major Swedish city. The chief attraction is that Swedish roads provide easy driving. The scenery is less of an incentive. The road is the E6 which becomes the Arctic Highway from Mo i Rana. In addition to this route, via Oslo, an alternative, via Stockholm, is described as Approach Route VII.

● **Route** Gothenburg–Oslo: E6; for Oslo to Mo i Rana see Approach Route I above

● **Distance (Gothenburg–Oslo)** 316km

● **Total Distance (Gothenburg–Mo i Rana)** 1351km

Summary Whole route runs behind the coast but little is seen of the sea.

● **Suggested travel time** Best part of one day from Gothenburg to Oslo. For Oslo to Mo i Rana see Approach Route I above

● **Road quality** Very good, with sections of dual carriageway and motorway for much of the journey.

● **A note on driving in Sweden** As in Norway, except near the large towns, the volume of traffic is small. Driving standards are high and generally courteous. Headlight and seatbelt rules are as in Norway. Drink-driving is considered a major offence. The limit is 0.02%, even lower than Norway.

Speed limits are generally higher than in Norway with substantial sections of the excellent roads up to 110km per hour. The limits are enforced. On many of the major roads you'll come across what appear to be hard shoulders marked by a broken line. You should pull over on to these paths if another driver clearly wants to overtake and then resume the main carriageway.

The route (south to north)

Most of this route lies away from the coast which you can reach only by taking side trips down minor roads. Leaving Gothenburg, the E6 follows the same line as the Göta River (Göta älv) until it bridges the Nordre River and bypasses **Kungälv** (17km). The road is classed as motorway as far as the bypass of Uddevalla and is good for the rest of the journey to the Norwegian border, just south of Halden.

The Norwegian section of the E6, all the way to Oslo, is again motorway. Because it bypasses or skirts the edges of such towns as **Fredrikstad** (226km) and **Moss** (260km) there are few impediments to legal fast travel except the volume of traffic which can be relatively heavy. On the other hand, the unvarying scenery of farmland and forest does little to capture your imagination or catch the eye.

The E6 enters Oslo (316km) through its south-eastern suburbs and you have to make a decision as to whether to go into the centre of the city or to continue north-eastward, on the E6, to the Gudbrandsdal route to Mo i Rana. (See Approach Route I.) There is a toll charged on entry to Oslo.

APPROACH ROUTE VII: GOTHENBURG TO MO I RANA (VIA STOCKHOLM) BY ROAD

This route makes sense if you've come into Scandinavia at Gothenburg and would like to see more of Sweden. It certainly isn't for those who are anxious to get to Norway's Arctic Highway by a direct route.

● **Route** Gothenburg–Stockholm–Gävle–Umeå–Mo i Rana: E20–E4–E12
● **Distance** 1552km
● **Summary** The first part of the route crosses west to east through Lakeland Sweden. From Stockholm the road runs behind the coast of the Gulf of Bothnia. The final stretch turns inland, north-west, to Mo i Rana, rising eventually to 650m after crossing the mountains separating Sweden from Norway.
● **Suggested travel time** 5 days (6 days would give you time to see something of Stockholm).
● **Road quality** Good to very good throughout. Hardly any gradients until the last tenth of journey.
● **Suggested stopping places** Stockholm–Sundsvall–Umeå–Storuman

The route (west to east to north)

The route suggested is not the shortest but it is the easiest to navigate and drive, and gives the opportunity to see Stockholm. It also incorporates part of another suggested route to the Arctic Highway (see Approach Route IX: Turku to Karasjok/Kirkenes).

This route might mislead and disappoint you because it crosses the Swedish Lakes Region with scarcely a glimpse of the lakes and follows the Gulf of Bothnia without giving you a good view of the sea. Most of the Lake Region route avoids towns and villages of any size but services (fuel and food) are readily available without the need to take a detour from the E20.

There is plenty of accommodation and camping along or just off this route in addition to those suggested. The exception is the section from Umeå to Mo. On the other hand, this is the only section along which you will find wild camping relatively easy.

Leaving Gothenburg The exit from Gothenburg is of motorway standard but beware: if you go into the centre of the city it is easy to get lost. It will be a long drive if you want to reach Stockholm in the same day.

The E20 runs between two of the largest lakes (Vänern to the north-west and Vättern to the south-east), threading its way around some of the 8000 smaller lakes littering the landscape. There is some variation in the scenery as low plateaux and characteristic flat-topped hills rise above the plains. The first town is **Skara** (126km), an interesting, attractive place to visit if you are going to break your journey to Stockholm. It boasts Sweden's oldest cathedral, parts dating from the 11th century, as well as some interesting domestic architecture.

At **Mariestad** (172km) the E20 gets to within a stone's throw of the great Lake Vänern but again skirts around the main built-up area which separates it from the lake shore. Eighty-five kilometres further on, past yet more farms and forests, and the E20 becomes a motorway again as it runs through the north-western suburbs of the important industrial town of **Örebro** (284km). Örebro was very much a railway town and today retains that link in its engineering industry. It is also a centre for shoe manufacture.

From here on Stockholm begins to exercise an overwhelming influence. The E18 joins the E20 as far as **Gravudden** (317km). Then there is a choice between these two roads. The E20 takes the more southerly route into Stockholm running past the industrial and engineering town of **Eskilstruna** (345km) and, on a motorway section, into Sweden's capital via **Södertälje** (421km). Central **Stockholm** (456km) is well signposted but is broadly spread across the archipelago and can be a confusing city in which to drive.

The alternative, E18, takes the traveller around the north of Lake Mälaren and into Stockholm from the north-west. If time is short and Stockholm is not on your itinerary, it is best to turn left (north) off the E18 just 7km after leaving the bypass around **Enköping** and make direct for Uppsala. This is Route 55 and, at Uppsala (see p93), you can join the E4. If you use this short cut, there is a saving of 95km compared with the route through Stockholm.

STOCKHOLM

Stockholm is Sweden's capital and largest city with a population of about a quarter of a million. Unless you're in a hurry, stop for a least one night so that you can have a day's sightseeing. Stockholm has been dubbed the Venice of the North because of its archipelago site. The old town is especially attractive and is the place to make for.

Services

As befits a capital city, there's everything you might want. The best plan will be to abandon the vehicle and take to the underground railway (*tunnelbana*) using a **Stockholm Card**. Make straight for the main **tourist office** (Stockholm Information Service, ☎ 08-7892490; 🕮 08-789 2491; 🖳 info@stoinfo.se) on Hamngaten. Take the underground to Kungsträdgården station and turn up Kungsstrsädgårdengaten. Turn left into Hamngaten and the information office is at the first left turning. There can't be a more comprehensive information office anywhere. From getting your Stockholm Card (about SEK200 per day) to booking your accommodation and changing money, it's all here. The card will not only get you round the town but also into most museums and some other attractions.

There are **post offices** at the Central station and just north of this point on Drottinggaten. **Banks** abound and there's a good choice in the central area and the historic old town.

Around town

If you're in Stockholm for a day only, the best plan may be to get a street plan from the information office and take a walk round the old town on Stadsholmen, the *City Island*, on which the mediaeval town was built. If travelling by the metro, get off at Gamla Stan station. If you walk from the tourist office, you can also take in the **Opera House**, **Sophia Albertina Palace** and the **parliament** building (Riks-daghuset).

Having crossed one of the bridges to Stadsholmen, you can view the **Royal Palace** (the world's largest still in occupation), watch the changing of the guard, visit the **cathedral**, wander through narrow streets and take in countless **museums**. It's all very tourist friendly with lots of places to eat and some internet cafés.

If you decide to spend two days or more in the city then a trip around the water-ways in a boat is many people's choice.

Accommodation

The best that can be said about accommodation prices is that they are a little lower than Oslo (and London). However, there's an enormous variety from which to choose.

If you want to pamper yourself, try the **Grand Hotel Stockholm** (☎ 08-6793500; ▤ 08-6118686; ▱ reserv@grandhotel.se), one of the Leading Hotels of the World group. This is a hotel which lives up to its 'Grand' title with the charm and service of an earlier era. However, you'll pay from SEK1400 for a double on a summer weekend to a bankrupting SEK24,000 for a suite. It is located in the old part of the town and has parking.

Right in the centre of Stockholm, near the Central station, is the **Kom Hotel** (☎ 08-4122300; ▤ 08-4122310; ▱ bokningen@komhotel.se). It's as well to book ahead here because it's popular with businessmen. Check, too, that you can get a parking place in the garage. The breakfasts are very generous and at SEK950 for a double at the summer weekend price, it's good value. During the week the price goes up some 50%.

Central and inexpensive is the evocatively named **Hotell Tre Små Rum** (☎ 08-6412371; ▤ 08-6428808; ▱ info@tresmarum.se). It is on the big island just south of the old town in the Södermalm district. The price here for a double is only SEK600 but there are no meals served except breakfast.

A useful service is provided by BBA (Bed and Breakfast Agency, ☎ 08-6438028; ▤ 08-6438078; ▱ www.bba.nu). They have a large number of private rooms on their lists, both in the suburbs and (slightly more expensive) the city centre. The only snag is that stays have to be a minimum of two nights but there are some real bargains to be had.

There are five STF/HI hostels around Stockholm. Prices for dormitory accommodation will be around SEK165 per person with breakfast. The best plan is to book ahead especially if you are going to arrive late in the day. To see what's available, try the website ▱ www.stfturist.se or telephone ☎ 08-4632270. Standards are good to satisfactory.

The easiest campsite to find is **Bredäng Camping** (☎ 08-977071; ▤ 08-70 72 62; ▱ bredangcamping@Swipnet.se). If you've come towards Stockholm, as described above, on the E20, turn off (right) on to the E4 at Södertälje and the site is just 10km south of Stockholm. It's doubly convenient because it is the E4 you need to take going to the north for the rest of your journey. To get into Stockholm city, there's just an eighteen-minute ride on the underground railway from Bredäng station, five minutes' walk from the camp. It's a nice site with excellent fully fitted cabins/cottages at between SEK620 and SEK820. There's a licensed restaurant and the main site is open from April to October inclusive. Rooms (without facilities) come at SEK450 and the site has a youth hostel (SEK125 for a bed). Booking ahead is a wise move.

Where to eat

As with accommodation, the choice is almost overwhelming. There are lots of fast-food outlets like **McDonald's** and **Burger King**, simple cafés and plenty of fine dining. The top hotels also boast some of the best restaurants and the Opera House's **Operakällaren** is hard to beat. For mid-priced meals it's really best to select from what you see on, say, a walk round the old town. If you are looking for a vegetarian menu go to **Hermans Hermitage**.

The town's not short of bars. There is an increasing number which resemble the British pub. Typically Scandinavian, it may be as well to leave before closing time when things can become a trifle rowdy. If you intend driving the next day, remember the drink-drive rules.

Moving north

Moving on from Stockholm towards the goal of the Arctic Highway, the next road to be taken is the E4 north out of the city. This will be signposted 'Uppsala' or to the city's airport, 'Arlanda' (also 'Älingshundra'). The road is excellent and of motorway standard all the way to **Uppsala** (428km), Sweden's fourth largest city and most important university town. Traffic may be heavy up to the turning (right) for the airport, 41km out of Stockholm. The area is rich in history and, just north of Uppsala – itself thirteenth century in origin and a former capital – is Gamla (Old) Uppsala, a religious centre from AD500. Uppsala is often compared with Trondheim in Norway: an embodiment of the national spirit. It is at Uppsala that Route 55 (see p92, alternative route) joins the E4.

The E4 north of Uppsala is less heavily used but also not as wide or as fast as it continues to **Gävle** (535km), a regional centre with an ancient core (Gamla Gefle). The countryside is one of small farms and scattered villages as the urban influence of Stockholm diminishes.

From Gävle, the E4 route gets close to being a coastal one without ever quite achieving it. This is now the shoreline of the Gulf of Bothnia, minutely fractured and with an untidy scattering of tiny islands. You won't see much of the waters of the gulf unless you make a short detour down one of the many small side roads (to the right) that lead off the E4.

The climate here is mild enough to give prominence to farming over forestry. The frost-free season leaves enough time for cereals to ripen and cattle to be grazed out of doors for a good part of the year. Gradually, however, the ubiquitous conifer forest takes over, farmland becomes more patchy and the higher ground to the west (left) of the road is blanketed with spruce and pine.

By the time you reach **Sundsvall** (735km), timber is king and the town's forestry industry is evident in the harbour area. There's an **information office** in the centre of town (Torget, ☎ 060-671800). Sundsvall is a suggested stopping place on this route.

Sundsvall accommodation

The top hotel is probably the *Hotell Baltic* (☎ 060-155935; ▤ 060-124560; ▱ info.baltic@swedenhotels.se), close to the E4. Look for the harbour and railway and you'll find Sjögaten; the hotel is 50m on the left of this road. Comfortable and convenient, the summer prices are very reasonable at SEK500.

If you're camping, stop around 4km short of Sunsvall (731km). *Fläsians Camping* (☎/▤ 060-554475) is here and there are cabins as well as tent places and rooms. The cabins vary in quality and facilities; the best cost SEK120. The site is open from mid-May to the end of August.

Northwards, after a short motorway section, the E4 is forced along a curving path, slipping uneasily around the broken coast and pushed back from the sea in order to cross the many rivers running off the highlands and into the gulf. It avoids Kramfors, a mid-nineteenth-century timber town, to press on to **Örnsköldsvik** (827km). This is a pleasant little place and one of the few towns, anywhere, in which I have been told by a traffic warden that visitors are welcome and parking fees are waived! Sports facilities are immediately evident with a large hall and a ski jump which seems to threaten to project its users into the centre of the town. The E4 runs tangent to the shopping area and continues north past some high-rise apartment blocks towards Umeå.

Umeå (939 km) – the Town of the Silver Birches – is entered by another short motorway section of the E4. The town marks the beginning of the 'true' north: Norrland. It was founded in 1622 as a regional centre and port. Today it is a thriving, though small, university and industrial town, as well as retaining its market function. It is a good place to stop for refuelling and for buying provisions. Turn off into the city centre as signposted, before you reach the junction with the E12. For the **information office** (☎ 090-161616), turn right off the E4 into Skolgaten. The office is about 150m down this road on the right. There's a very pleasant shopping precinct providing a range of shops and services and with an interesting civic building, the **Town Hall** (1892). A good place for you to take a lunchtime picnic is the park with a lake and fountain nearby.

Umeå can also be considered for an overnight stop.

Umeå accommodation

A hotel with a good summer discount is the **Quality Royal** (☎ 090-100730; 🖹 090-100 739; 🖳 royalhotel@telia.com); easy to find if you've been to the information office. It is further down Skolgaten and also on the right. A double room here may come in at SEK600 which is good for what you get.

Parallel to Skolgaten but two streets further north is Norrlandsgaten and the **Comfort Hotel Dragonen** (☎ 090-125800; 🖹 090-141075). You should be able to get

a room here for around SEK500 or less in summer. You need to go a further 5km beyond Umeå, passing the junction with the E12, if you're looking for a cabin or camping. Off the E4 to the right is **Umeå Swecamping** (☎ 090-702600; 🖹 090-702610). The site is open all year but with full service only in mid-summer. There are excellent cabins with all facilities at SEK500 to SEK725. There are also rooms, with shared facilities, and tent places.

From Umeå the route to the Arctic Highway changes. Not only do you leave the E4 to take to the E12, but you turn through ninety degrees from north-east to north-west. To reach the E12, simply continue to the junction in Umeä and turn left. This is the Blue Road (*Blå Vägen*), so-called because of its companion lakes and rivers throughout its course.

The E12 links the Gulf of Bothnia with the Norwegian Sea. It cuts across three main geographic regions: the coastal plain; a plateau of ancient rocks and the *fjäll* (Swedish for fjell). The slopes of the fjäll rise high to the Swedish–Norwegian border only to drop again to the Norwegian coast and Mo i Rana. This is an area of great forests. Regiments of pine and spruce in lines of martial straightness stretch back from the road seemingly to infinity. As the coastal plain is left behind, farms become increasingly rare but rivers and lakes provide a source of hydro-electric power to satisfy the needs of the coastal towns and their timber industries.

The E12 is just one of a number of roads which run at right angles to the coast back into the interior of Norrland and Lapland. Each follows the line of a major valley and each is remarkably straight. The E12 runs parallel to the Umeå River, remaining faithful to it and its lakes all the way to the border. There are not a lot of petrol station on this section so don't let the tank run too low.

At **Norrfoss** (954km) a turning to the left is a minor road to Sörfoss and one of the largest hydro-electric stations in northern Sweden: Stormorrfoss. Opened in 1959, this power station utilizes a natural head of 75m.

The first small town you'll reach is **Lycksele** (1071km) over 130km out of Umeå. This little regional centre owes its importance to the junction of the E12 and Route 90. The latter runs parallel to the coast but on the edge of the plateau. Here the E12 leaves the left bank of the Umeälv and bridges the river to its right bank. From Lycksele the route is especially scenic for the next 30km or so, with good views to the right and left across the valley.

When you reach **Hedvik** (1107km) you are at the beginning of the lakes section of the route. From here on, long ribbon lakes join the Umeälv or actually replace it.

From the village of **Storuman** (1179km) the road runs along the largest of these lakes, Lake Storuman. Not by any means the largest of all lakes in northern Sweden, it is none the less 30km long and, when there's a wind blowing the full length of the lake, it develops frighteningly large waves.

Storuman is worth considering for an overnight stop.

Storuman accommodation

There is limited accommodation but the *Hotel Luspen* (☎ 0951-33380; 🖹 0951-10800) near the station is comfortable enough. The price is a very modest SEK300. The **tourist information office** (☎ 0951-33370) is in the hotel. There is camping near the lake: *Storumans Bad och Camping* (☎ 0951-10696; 🖹 0950-8095). The site is just 200m north of the town centre and has cabins, with or without full facilities, for self-catering. Prices are from SEK250 to SEK550.

From **Strömsund** (1210km), at the north-west end of the lake, the road runs a little away from the river and lake and the forests begin to thin as the fjäll is approached. Soon bog and more scattered trees replace the thick stands of trees and, by the time you get to **Tärnaby** (1431km), you are well into the mountain section of the route. In the distance are the high peaks of the Scandinavia Uplands appearing a shadowy blue in the haze. Could this be another reason for the route's nickname of the Blue Road?

Tärnaby is actually the joint Swedish–Norwegian customs post although it is still some 80km from the border. For the average traveller, there are no customs formalities. This area provides excellent skiing and there is a very 'touristy' feel about the place. Small hotels abound.

The international boundary is crossed just before reaching **Umbukta** (1514km) after the E12 has made some steep climbs along a lake-strewn mountain path. Road-signs will alert you to the fact that you're close to the border where Norwegian driving regulations will apply.

A further 35km or so and you arrive at the road into **Mo i Rana** and Norway's Arctic Highway. For a description of this short section, see the side trip from Mo i Rana to the Swedish border, Part 4, p119.

APPROACH ROUTE VIII: HELSINKI TO KARASJOK BY ROAD – A RECOMMENDED ROUTE

This route, travelling from the UK or continental Europe, involves a vehicle ferry from Rostock in north Germany or a direct service from the UK by one of the cargo shipping companies which link the UK with Finland (see Part 1, p11). Alternatively you may have travelled by ferry from Sweden or arrived by air intending to hire a vehicle. Although these approaches may seem to be taking you out of your way en route to Norway's Arctic Highway, this overland route by road through Finland allows for very easy driving and actually saves time on some of the alternatives. However, you should note that this suggested route to the Arctic Highway does not bring you directly to either of the Highway's termini, but close to Karasjok, a Sami village on the Highway (see Part 8). The reason that this route is recommended is because it allows you to see a comprehensive cross-section of Finland before the wonderfully contrasting scenery of Norway's Arctic Highway.

● **Route** Helsinki–Jyväskylä–Kuopio–Kemijärvi–Ivalo–Karasjok: E75–E63–Route 81–Route 945–E63–E75–Route 92
● **Distance** 1432km
● **Summary** This route starts in the capital and runs through the heart of the Lake Region. It takes an easterly course beyond the lakes before striking north through Finnish Lapland and across the border to Norway. Much of the journey north is on roads which did not exist until after World War II. This isn't a journey for anyone who doesn't like driving through forests! If you like wild camping alongside a lake, however, it's for you.
● **Suggested travel time** 3 to 4 days (4 to 5 if you include one day in Helsinki).
● **Road quality** Good throughout. The roads narrow and are increasingly lower in quality as you get further north but traffic diminishes in the same direction. No major gradient whatsoever. This is a good caravan or camper route.
● **Suggested stopping places** Helsinki, Javäskylä, Kajaani/Kuusamo, Ivalo or Inari
● **A note on driving in Finland** Rules and regulations are much the same as in Norway (see Part 1, p23) and Sweden (see p90). Finnish roads outside the main towns carry less traffic than do those of their Scandinavian neighbours but the quality of roads is not quite as good. This is especially so in the north and many minor roads are gravel. Relatively narrow roads can seem a problem when you come across an enormous timber-carrying truck; simply let them have priority, they'll take it anyway. At junctions, it is usually best to give priority to vehicles on your right and not to bother about who is on the minor road. Alcohol limits are strictly enforced and are the same as in Norway (see Part 1, p24). Speed limits rise to 120km/h on motorways in summer, but are the standard 50km/h in built-up areas. Where there are no speed signs in open country, assume an 80km/h restriction. Finland uses the town pictogram at the beginning of the town limit and the same sign with a red cancellation stripe as you leave.

If you have a breakdown, getting help may be more of a problem in Finland than in Sweden or Norway because you may experience language problems. (See also Part 1, p35.) All petrol sales are unleaded.

The route (south to north)

HELSINKI

Helsinki is Finland's beautiful capital with a population of rather more than half a million. However you arrive in the city it would be a lost opportunity not to spend at least a day here – preferably two – before driving north. The most thrilling way to see the city for the first time is to approach by ferry and dock in Eteläsatama (Söra Hamnen), the main ferry harbour. Right in front of you, across the **Norra Esplanaden**, are the **State House** and the **President's Palace**. Behind is the towering **Tuomiokirkko**, the Lutheran Cathedral, with its splendid duck-egg blue dome.

On a short visit you should probably go straight to the **tourist information office** (☎ 09-1693757; 🖳 tourist.info@hel.fi). The office is just off the Norra Esplanaden on Pohjoisesplanadi. The office, open on weekdays until 19.00 in summer (15.00 at weekends), will provide city maps and other information about Helsinki. You can also get a **Helsinki Card** which gives you free bus travel and entry to some 50 museums. It costs around EUR25 for a day but proportionately less for additional days. If you cross over to the southern esplanade, directly opposite the information office, you'll come to the offices of the **national tourist board** (☎ 09-41769300; 🖳 mek.espa@ mek.fi). It could be helpful to call in here if you need maps of, or information about, the rest of your journey north. The main **post office** is near the **railway station**, on Postikatu which lies off the city's main highway, Mannerheimintie.

Armed with a map there's plenty to see within walking distance. Places and features not to miss include the **Senate Square** or **Senaatinori** (Senatsторget); the **Uspenskin** Orthodox Cathedral just to the east of the ferry harbour; the remarkable **Temppeliaukio Church** carved out of a rock outcrop; and the **Kiasima Museum**, lying near the post office and housing the city's contemporary art collection. If you want to travel further, use your pass to travel on route T3 of the tram system. You can hop on and off, see the **Sibelius Monument** and **Finlandia Concert Hall** and much of the splendid architecture dating from 1808, the great fire, and the Russian connection from 1809. There is an interesting mix of classical and modern styles and monuments galore around the town. Helsinki is always lively in summer, from the harbour market to the al-fresco eating on the esplanade.

If you've more than one day in Helsinki, take a **boat trip** round the archipelago which is the city's site or perhaps go out to **Tapiola** to see a suburb as all suburbs should be. The Finns are famous for their design and architecture as well as for their rally drivers and athletes.

Accommodation

Accommodation in Helsinki varies from the luxurious to the very ordinary. Remember, there's an enormous choice, except for camping, and, of course, there'll be a sauna everywhere you stay. There is a **Hotel Booking Centre** (☎ 09-22881400; 🖹 09-22881499; 🖳 www.helsinkiexpert.fi) at the railway station. The top end of the range includes the centrally located *Radisson SAS Royal* (☎ 09-69580; 🖹 09-69587100; 🖳 helsinki@radissonsas.com), a favourite of mine because it has a sauna suite – ideal for a sauna party. This luxury has to be paid for. Room prices are around €225 (all are doubles) but there are summer discounts up to 50%. Free parking is available.

More modest prices can be had at the privately owned *Hotel Authur* (☎ 09-173441; 🖹 09-626880; 🖳 sales.department @hotelauthur.fi) on Vuorikatu, just north of the railway station. It has a large number of single rooms at €85 and doubles come at only €15 more. Most rooms have showers rather than baths. As usual there should be some weekend and summer rates at a discount. Even cheaper, but still quite central, is *Finnapartments Hotel Finno* (☎ 09-774980; 🖃 09-7016889). It's on the northern side of city centre, close to the main fire station and the high-towered Kallio Church. Prices here are about €60 for a double and non-en-suite singles start at just €30. There's only a cafeteria but there is parking.

There's a good range of youth hostel accommodation augmented by student hostels in summer. Nicely central, but on Katajanokka (Skatudden) island on the east side of the ferry harbour, is *Eurohostel* (☎ 09-6220470; 🖃 09-655044; 🖳 eurohostet@eurohostel.fi). The prices here start at €25 but there's no en suite and parking could be a problem. However, there is a café.

If you're self-catering the best place for cabins and campers is some 10km east of the city at *Rastila Camping* (☎ 09-316551; 🖃 09-3441578). It is open from mid-May to mid-September, has limited cabin accommodation but ample space for caravans. Rastila is reached by leaving the ferry harbour area and driving north and east along the main coast road. This leads, by turning right, on to Route 170 and out across an island, towards Herttoniemi. Branching right towards Puotila, a turning right leads to Rastila after bridging an inlet. The campsite is to the left of the road after crossing a bridge. Cabin prices will be up to €100, depending on facilities and size of cabin. It's important to book ahead in the summer.

Where to eat

As with accommodation, there's a wealth of choice when it comes to restaurants, cafés and bars. Generally speaking prices are less than in Sweden or Norway. Perhaps that's another reason to choose this Approach Route. Bars stay open until the early hours of the morning. Finns are serious drinkers.

For a gourmet meal, try the *Amadeus*, on Sofiankatu, a street leading from Senate Square to the ferry harbour. Game is the speciality here.

For excellent seafood there's *Havis Amanda*, on Uninoninkatu. This street is south from the information office, past the delightful statue after which the restaurant is named. Throw some money in the fountain pool which surrounds the maiden and go on to your meal.

Helsinki has a broad range of restaurants serving a variety of national dishes. In addition to the expected Chinese and Thai, there is Californian, Austrian and Japanese. For authentic Sami food there's *Lappi*. It is two blocks up Kalevankatu from the main thoroughfare, Mannerheimintie, on Annankatu.

The best Russian restaurant is probably *Saslik*, but it's pricey. The restaurant is on Neitsytpolku which you'll find by going down the western ferry harbour road and turning up Fabriksgaten.

There are at least four **vegetarian** restaurants. Choose *Kasvisravintola* (just north of Saslik – see above) for dinner and *Tempura* (off the Esplanade Park) for lunch.

There are lots of fast-food outlets and cafés often with tables on the pavement in summer. There's a concentration of small eating places near the ferry harbour market and a choice of cafés in the big Forum shopping centre off Mannerheimintie.

Moving north

To begin the journey north, drive out of the city along routes signposted for the E75 or Lentaasema airport, but watch out for the turning at Vallila where the airport road turns off to the left. (Note: this is not the international airport of Vantaa.)

Accommodation on the journey north should not be difficult but you should really try to book ahead. Campsites often have a limited season (early June to mid-August) and wild camping is difficult south of Jyväskylä. You should have few problems with refuelling or other services but note that their frequency is much reduced north of Käjaani and, more especially, beyond Ivalo.

The E75 out of the city is an excellent, motorway-standard road and in no time suburban Helsinki is replaced by some of the best agricultural land in Finland. These post-glacial clay plains slope gently upwards towards the Salpausselka. This double-ridged terminal moraine marks the separation of the coastal plain from the Lakes Region. From **Mäntsälä** (58km) the E75 is not classified as a motorway but is still of a high standard as it crosses the first of the Salpausselka ridges and runs into **Lahti** (104km). With a population of nearly 100,000 this is Finland's seventh city. The country's main railway to St Petersburg in Russia travels east from Lahti and the town is also an important road junction. Lahti sits at the southern end of Lake Vesijärvi; the Lakes Region has been reached.

Saunas

The Finnish sauna is often misunderstood and its importance in Finnish culture underestimated. It is a Finnish institution. Any self-respecting Finn will take a sauna bath at least once a week. The sauna has been credited with winning wars and Olympic gold medals.

Wherever you go in Finland, and also in northern Norway and Sweden, you'll find a sauna; in hotels, alongside lake cottages, at every farmhouse and in a good number of private homes. In central Finland there is a sauna for every four inhabitants. In hotels, you will come across electrically heated saunas; in the countryside they will be heated by log fires, sometimes with a chimney to let out the smoke, though occasionally there's no chimney. The smoke saunas are not to everyone's taste and are relatively rare but they have their supporters.

Some of the mechanics, rituals and practices of the sauna are often misunderstood. In the first place, saunas are not Turkish baths; they are not steam baths. The heat is dry – that is the essence of the sauna. Yes, water is sprinkled on the heated stones but this is only to raise the temperature as heat is given off when the steam evaporates. The human body is able to withstand temperatures close to 100°C simply because the air is dry, allowing sufficient cooling through perspiration.

Except within the family or with very close friends, mixed-sex saunas are not the practice. Men and women use different cabins or bathe at different times and always completely naked. It is expected that you will take in a small towel, not to wrap round you but to sit or lie on and, being Finland, you may take in your mobile phone! In public saunas most people take a shower before entering the cabin. In hotels you can shower after or during a session but in the countryside you'll be expected to leap into a lake (or roll in the snow in winter) after a sauna. Your body will have retained sufficient warmth easily to withstand a drop in temperature of perhaps 130C°.

The sauna is a wonderful antidote to the rigours of wild camping. After a couple of weeks of living close to nature, call in at a farm and ask if you may use their sauna. Invariably the answer will be yes, although a small gift or payment is usually made to compensate for the work needed to get the fire prepared. Now all the grime of camping will vanish, laundry can be done and beards shaved off without the need of a lather. Finish with a leap into a lake and you will never feel more refreshed.

Forget the sleazy image of 'saunas' outside Finland and Scandinavia; go for the real thing and you'll want to build your own cabin when you get home.

Finally, it's worth pointing out that the first syllable of sauna should be pronounced 'sow' – as in female swine – not 'saw'. But even the Finns have almost capitulated to the non-Finnish pronunciation.

Finland claims to have 187,888 lakes but quite who counted them is less clear! Fortunately, no one has counted the trees! For the next 500km the scenery is dominated by lakes large and small, and, increasingly, by forest. If the sublimity of such landscape is not appreciated, this route is not for you. Maybe you will never want to see another conifer again. But this is Finland! The tranquillity is undeniable and for many it has a captivating beauty.

Driving north of Lahti, still on the E75, the lake is some distance to the west of the road and it is not until you reach **Vääksy** (127km) that you can appreciate the magnificence of the lakes. At this point the E75 bridges a narrow gap through which the waters of the lakes Vesijärvi and Päijänne are linked. The latter lake extends northwards across a full degree of latitude and is over 1000 sq km in area.

Although your route follows the west shore of the lake, you'll see little of its waters behind the trees. Only at **Kuhmoinen** (179km), just south of **Jämsä** (220km) and as you approach Jyväskylä can you see something of this extraordinary lake system. The whole of the Lakes Region is actually a low plateau on which rest the lakes, themselves split by shallow moraine and esker ridges. The latter are the sand and gravel deposits of glacial streams. It is not far from the truth to say that the whole plateau would be covered with water were it not for these deposits. Some of the eskers are so narrow that they provide little more than a causeway for the roads.

Some 12km before arrival in Jyväskylä, the village of **Muurame** (266km) is a place of pilgrimage for sauna lovers. In the village (to the right of the E75) is a collection of some two dozen old saunas dating largely from the 18th and 19th centuries. Some are still in working order; the collection is open only in summer. The Approach Route to Karasjok/Kirkenes from Turku (Approach Route IX, see p110) joins the E75 just south of Jyväskylä (278km).

JYVÄSKYLÄ

The university town of Jyväskylä is sandwiched between three lakes. To the south-east (right of the E75) is Jyväsjärvi. To the north-west are Tuomiojärvi and Palokkajärvi, divided by an esker along which the E75 travels north towards Oulu. Jyväskylä is a cultural centre and there are a number of museums. The population is a touch over 75,000. Before leaving the town you can get a good view from the park on the Harju Ridge behind the town centre and to the left of the E75 route. The **tourist office** (☎ 014 -624903/4; 🖹 014-214393; 🖳 markailu@ jkl.fi) is on Asemakatu, near the railway station. The **post office** is on Vapaudenkatu which is the E75 as it goes through town.

Jyväskylä accommodation

There are a dozen hotels to choose from. The **Sokos Hotel Alexandra** (☎ 014-651 211

🖹 014- 651200; 🖳 sales@jyvaskyla.sok.fi), although not a large hotel, is conveniently located near the centre on Hannikaisenkatu, by the railway station. There is a small restaurant and limited car-parking in a secure place behind the hotel. Prices are around €140 for a double but ask for discounts in summer. A cheaper alternative is the **Hotel Milton** (☎ 014-3377900; 🖹 014 -631927; 🖳 hotel.milton@kolumbus.fi) on the same street. Here you'll pay about half the price of the Sokos but there are only 33 rooms so book ahead. There's no restaurant.

An excellent campsite, named after the lake on which it is situated, **Tuomiojärvi** (☎ 014-624895/6), is easily reached by continuing on the E75 north of the town. There are cabins as well as spaces for tents and caravans. The 4-bed cabins cost around €50 with facilities.

On leaving Jyväskylä you leave the E75 and follow the E63 eastward through the suburbs of Vaanjakoski. By taking this path it is possible to keep well within the beautiful Lakes Region. The E63, as it is today, is a much improved road. Since I first travelled here, the road through to Kuopio has been upgraded and re-routed. The old winding path around hundreds of lakes has been replaced by a much shorter and direct road of high standard.

Because the road is relatively new it is almost totally free of villages or even farms. It crosses some lakes by causeways and runs tangent to others. This section of the route north offers you especially fine opportunities for wild camping although it is not always easy to find a path off the road. Forests thick and thin line most of the route and glacial erratic boulders litter the ground between the trees. The area is particularly attractive for the semi-wilderness it offers but, like much of Finland's open countryside, it is inhabited by mosquitoes. You'll probably find it necessary to take some protective measures. You won't get malaria from these mosquitoes but some people find them an almost unbearable nuisance.

Just short of **Suonenjoki** (374km), the E63 is joined by Route 69, its former path. Suonenjoki is a pleasing little town with a vast market square, recently repaired. It is probably an easier place to stop for services than its larger neighbour, Kuopio. The E63 runs round the town to join Route 5 (402km) before approaching and swinging round to the northern perimeter of **Kuopio** (434km) on a stretch of motorway. If you do stop here, you'll find the town to be a busy regional centre with a near-insular location. If you've time, visit the **Puijo Tower**. To reach the tower, continue along the E63 round the outskirts of the town until you get to the Puijontie turning, signposted to the left. The tower is at the end of this road. From one of the tower's two observation decks (75m) there are splendid views of the endless lakes and forests. There is also a revolving restaurant in the tower in which you might sample *kalakukko*, a fish and pork pie for which the town is famous. On the other hand . . .

North of Kuopio, the E63 crosses a causeway to reach dry land and then proceeds on a fairly straight course to Iisalmi. The railway is the road's companion to the right as far as **Siilinjärvi** (448km) and then to the left until almost at Iisalmi. The first part of this stretch is very pretty with a mix of forest, farm and lake. The forests tend to dominate the further north one goes but innumerable small lakes and watercourses are never far from the road's edge. Just before Lapinlahti, you can see the largest lake, Onkïvesi, to the left. **Lapinlahti** (484km) is a reminder of the Sami presence in the area; the name means Lapp Bay.

Just as you reach Iisalmi the road and railway interweave several times over level-crossings. **Iisalmi** (509km) is a small market town almost completely surrounded by water and was a centre for lake traffic. The E63 runs through the middle of the town and, further north, parts company with the railway to follow a lonely path towards Kajaani. There are lakes and rivers here but the lakes are small and the rivers are hidden by the omnipresent forest. The stands of trees along this part of the route form an almost unbroken wall either side of the road.

There are few farms and fewer villages. The only settlement of any size is **Sukeva** (550km), a village with a **café**. If your fuel is running low, this is a place to fill the tank because north of the village is even more devoid of services than the area to the south. You meet the railway again in the village, crossing over it in the northern outskirts before losing sight of it again as it makes its own, more direct journey north. At **Mainua** (580km) the E63 is joined by Route 85 and as a combined road of good quality they make the journey north-eastwards into **Kajaani** (598km).

KAJAANI

Kajaani is an attractive and well served town on the Kajaaninjoki, a river which links two lakes: the immense Oulujärvi, to the west of the town, and the smaller Nuasjärvi, to the east.

Its main claim to fame must be as the birthplace of Elias Lönnrot who gave Finland its greatest literature in the *Kalevala*. This epic collects together Finnish traditional folk poems and was the foundation of the revival of Finnish culture in the mid-nineteenth century.

Today, the small town is a market and tourist centre making full use of its watery setting. The market runs down to the river and along the waterside, in summer, women come to wash the rugs which are so characteristic of Finnish homes.

To the right of the main road through the town you'll find the **tourist information office** (☎ 08-6155555; 🖷 08-6155664; 🖂 kajaani.info@kajaani.fi) on Pohjolankatu. The **post office** is on the next, parallel, street away from the high road.

The town can be used for an overnight stop if you don't want to press on to Kuusamo.

Kajaani accommodation

The *Scandic Hotel Kajanus* (☎ 08-61641; 🖷 08-6164505; 🖂 kajanus@scandic-hotels.com) is good value. You can reach it by coming off the E63 in the town and taking the westerly bridge over the river. You'll see the hotel immediately to the right after crossing the river. A double in summer will be around €75; parking is easy and, if you're there in winter, there are no less than 100 power points for car heaters.

A less expensive alternative is the *Hotel Välskäri* (☎ 08-6150200; 🖷 08-629005) on Kauppakatu which is three streets back from the river on the left of the main road. Prices are about half those at the Kajanus and there's no difference in price between doubles and singles. It's a fairly simple hotel but there's a full restaurant and parking facilities.

There is a large campsite to the east of the town, *Onnela* (☎ 08-622703), with log cabins and caravan spaces. It is on the south bank of the river and can be reached by taking the last turning right off Route 5 before it bridges the Kajaaninjoki and keeping to the road nearest to the riverbank. Cabins range from €25 to €50.

The E63 leads out of Kajaani across the river and heads north-east. Just before reaching **Kontiomäki** (619km) you come to the junction with Route 22. Up to this village the area has been well settled with farms but from now on there are fewer houses and the opportunities for wild camping increase. In fact, from here all the way to the Finnish–Norwegian border you'll find wild camping, away from organized sites, is a very attractive proposition.

Along this route to the Arctic Highway the road is now adequate but there are some narrow stretches. Only nearer the more important settlements does it widen into a carriageway where passing is easy. With fewer villages and towns it becomes more important for the rest of this route to check fuel tanks and not to assume that there will be a filling station around the next corner.

As far as **Hyrynsalmi** (647km) the northern railway again follows much the same route as the road but from this village it branches off to the west to its terminus at Täivalkoski while the road swings eastward to **Ämmänsaari** (704km). This is a major tourist area with the accent firmly on outdoor pursuits. There is a well-equipped leisure centre-cum-spa in the village and small boats line the lake's edge.

The E63 bypasses the more important twin village of Suomussalmi but you could go north through the village using Route 915 and rejoin the E63 a few kilometres north at Veikkola. This is an especially pretty area with the usual jigsaw of lakes, islands and tree clad promontories. In tragic contrast it was in these parts that in the Winter War of 1939–40 about 15,000 Russian troops froze to death at their posts in the forest.

From Ämmänsaari to Kuusamo (843km), the E63 runs almost parallel to the Russian border which lies some 30–40km to the east. It is possible to reach close to the border down a number of roads eastward but you are not permitted to cross into Russia. The roads on the Russian side of the border are unkempt. For some 130km the E63 passes through no settlement which can claim even village status. The path is slightly undulating but never hilly.

KUUSAMO

Kuusamo is a prosperous, modern little town which the road does its best to ignore. The town's buildings are almost all post-World War II, because the Germans torched the old town in 1994 as they retreated from the Russian army. To reach the town centre, turn off the E63 to the right at the signposted junction. The large, impressive **tourist information office** (☎ 08-8502910; 🖷 08-8502901; 🖳 info@kuusamo.fi) is on the right just after this junction.

Despite its small size (population just 11,500) Kuusamo has seven hotels and a camping site so it is good for a stopover before the next 400-plus kilometres to Ivalo.

Kuusamo accommodation

The hotels are mostly either side of the E63 about 5--6 kilometres north of the town centre. The *Holiday Club Kuusamon Tropiikki* (☎ 08-85960; 🖷 08-6521909; 🖳 myyntipal velu.tropiikki@holidayclub.fi) describes itself as 'A four-star paradise spa'. Perhaps no further description is necessary. In fact it is a hotel with a large pool (almost as big as its email address) complete with a long water slide. There are also 17 cabins on the adjoining **campsite** (☎ 08-8596404). Prices are quite high with hotel doubles charged at around €115 but all the facilities of the so-called spa come free. The cabins are around €50 but you pay to use the spa. To find the hotel and camp, travel north on the E63 for about 5km and look for the signs to the right.

Despite its rather strange appearance, the *Sokos Hotel* (☎ 08-85920; 🖷 08-8521263; 🖳 sokoshotel.kuusamo@sok.fi) is very comfortable and situated within the town. To find it, look for the street Kirkkotie (left) as you enter the town from the south. The hotel is about 300m up this road and on the left. It's quite large, with nearly 180 rooms of which just eight are singles. It has a number of attractive facilities including a swimming pool. The restaurant is good.

Beyond Kuusamo, the E63 can be used for the journey to Kemijärvi but an arguably more scenic path is along Route 81 and the minor Route 945; this is the one which is described on p105.

However, a short distance up the E63 is a large **national park**, Oulanka, and the holiday village of **Juuma**. If you've got the time to visit Juuma, continue on the E63 past Ruka, a skiing resort, and take the next right turn beyond the junction with Route 8694. Juuma is 6km up this road, clearly marked to the right. There are camping sites, a lakeside sauna and the opportunity for white-water rafting. If you decide to stay overnight, *Oulanka Camping* (☎ 08-863429) is about half a kilometre inside the park where cabins cost €35. There's a **café** and the inevitable sauna so, even if you are not self-catering, a stop here is practical. A drawback is that the camp shuts towards the end of August before the park is at its autumnal best.

The real attractions of the national park are its peaty boglands and forests (uncut since World War I) through which there are marked walking trails. Within the forests are two important rivers, Aventojoki and Oulankajoki, which flow eastward through Russia to the White Sea. Their courses are over rapids and small falls and through canyons. To add to all the natural sights, I once met a rather large Finnish lady on one of the trails, wearing hiking boots, a too-small bikini and carrying an umbrella! For information about the park you can contact the visitor centre on ☎ 016-839651.

Returning to the recommended route, ten kilometres north of Kuusamo turn left off the E63 on to Route 81. For the next 66km this road travels westward through pretty wooded lakeland scenery. At **Mourusalmi** (891km) you can get particularly good views of two lake complexes. There are some wonderful picnic spots on this part of the route. Route 81 continues through **Ahola** (902km) but at **Perä-Posio** (919km) you should join Route 945 (turning to the right). This minor, very rural road is of adequate standard but narrow in parts. Again, the path is attractively lined by lake and forest, the road often crossing lakes and river courses by narrow strips of sand and gravel eskers. After 32km, the road makes a sharp turn to the left (at the junction with Route 9451) and heads for the **Polar Circle**.

A moment's loss of attention and it is possible to cross the Circle and not know that you have done so. It cuts across the road at the hamlet of **Lehtula** (981km) and is marked by a simple sign, in Finnish, Swedish and English, at the side of the road. Nothing else. What a contrast this is to the new Polar Circle Centre which you will see on Norway's Arctic Highway (see Part 4, p131).

Less than 20km further on, the road runs along Lake Kemijärvi and meets the E63. Take the turning to the left on to that road. Almost immediately, you pass through **Isokylä** (1003km) and then cross a perfectly straight causeway with the distant steeple of Kemijärvi church acting like a marker.

Kemijärvi (1007km) claims to be Finland's most northerly town. Like many Finnish towns, its importance was derived from its function as a lake and river port. With the lake, whose name it shares, and the Kemijoki River, it links this interior part of Finnish Lapland to the port of Kemi at the head of the Gulf of Bothnia. The E63 out of Kemijärvi turns north and follows the lake complex and Kemijoki, never far from its right bank. The valley is well farmed and has been noted for its grain cultivation although now it is dairy farming which dominates. You'll see some old farm buildings among the post-war constructions. The largest village is **Pelkosenniemi** (1059km) but just after the junction with Route 965 (1064km), the E63 runs through **Kairala** (1071km) an interesting 17th-century village. It was a Lapland centre for barley up to World War II.

Although the route through northern Finland is one of generally increasing elevation, the gradients are gentle and any rise scarcely perceptible. On the other hand the evidence of a colder climate and severe conditions is clear in thinning forest and a greater proportion of wilderness and bogland. Pine and birch become the dominant species rather than spruce and, not surprisingly, forestry is more of a state enterprise than in the south.

Sodankylä (1116km) is a village with Sami connections. It makes a worthwhile short stop if only to see one of Finland's oldest wooden churches, dating from 1689. (The log fence round the church, despite its old style, is modern.) The district around Sodankylä was home to Olaus Sirma who passed on much of the information and poetry that appeared in Johannes Scheffer's book *Lapponia* which was published in 1673.

At Sodankylä the E75 joins the E63 and it is the E75 that you follow due north out of the village. After some 35km the modern road bypasses the village of Petkula (to the right, signposted) where there is an impressive 1900m-long dam which holds back the waters of the Kitisenjoki to provide hydro-electric power. If you want to see the dam, it is a simple excursion because the Petkula village road rejoins the E75 north of the village.

Much of the road's margins, often behind thin stands of pine, is peat: soggy, boggy and with a monotony relieved only by cotton grass. These peatlands constitute 40% of the northern provinces of Finland. Near **Peurasuvanto** (1170km) is an important floatway station where logs begin their journey to coastal sawmills. The use of floatways has declined in recent decades, most timber being transported by road. Here, however, on the Kitinen River, the logs are floated to the main artery, Kemijoki, in stages, avoiding the power stations along the route.

Continuing northwards, the road runs near-tangent to the Porttiphata Reservoir (to the left of the road), bridging an arm of it at Lohijoki. At **Vuotso** (1205km), the E75 crosses a canal. The Vuotso Canal links Porttiphata with another reservoir, Lokka, to the east. Both reservoirs feed the northern hydroelectric system. At **Tankavarra** (1216km) is the visitors' centre for the **Urho Kekkonen National Park**, named after the long-serving Finnish President (1956–81). A **Gold Museum** (Kultamuseo) is also here and you can try your hand at gold panning for just €4.

From here you can see the high fjells, stretching to the Russian border and rising to over 700m, to the right of the road. It is this high ground that comprises most of the park. The region is steeped in Sami history. Two to three kilometres after the National Park Centre, a minor road leads left off the E75 to the most southerly of the truly Sami villages in Finland, **Purnumukka**. The village was deliberately avoided by the E75 but its population has none the less diminished as reindeer herding has declined. The village lies some two kilometres up the minor road. Don't miss the chance to see a genuine Finnish Sami settlement.

Another very short excursion that you can take off the E75 is from **Saariselkä** village (1247km). A short minor road immediately after the village on the right of the E75 curves clockwise to bring you to the top of Kaunispää. This hill is a modest 438m but it provides very good views over the surrounding country.

Before reaching Ivalo, the E75 passes the small village of **Palkisoja** (1257km). This area has been reforested since a disastrous fire in the summer of 1960 in which 260 hectares of trees were destroyed. Locally the village is known as Palkisojapalo (*palo* = fire).

Shortly after Palkisoja, there is a small lake close to the road (left) and then you are in the scattered outskirts of Ivalo. The road is now alongside the Ivalojoki (left) which follows a convoluted course of intricate meanderings towards the great Inari Lake.

Ivalo (1276km) is the largest 'village' in Finnish Lapland. It is now the centre of a tourist industry which includes Inari, Lake Inari and the skiing regions of Saariselka, as well as the Kekkonen National Park. Before World War II Ivalo was the gateway to the Finnish Arctic coast through the Petsamo corridor along what was Finland's Arctic Highway (see p271). When that territory was annexed by the USSR at the end of the war, Ivalo reorientated not only its hinterland but also its economy.

The Sami call Ivalo *Avvil*, and there is a small Sami museum and an Orthodox church (post-war) in the village. Although Ivalo is often seen as the centre of the region, you may think it's better to go on to Inari for an overnight stop. However, for camping, the place to go is 2km north of Ivalo: the Ukonjävi Camp (see p108).

Ivalo accommodation

Within Ivalo an attractive place to overnight is the *Hotelli Ivalo* (☎ 016-688111; ▤ 016-661905; ▣ hotivalo@netti.fi). Operated by the Finnish Travel Association, it is situated to the left of the E75 near the entrance to the village and is recognizable by its umbrella-like roofs over the reception building. Rooms are small but with all facilities and there are two restaurants and three saunas. It is not a large hotel, just 94 rooms, so book ahead. Like many hotels in northern Finland and Scandinavia which cater for visitors on tour, it fills up rapidly from mid-afternoon. A telephone call to a hotel in the morning preceding an overnight stay is often all the notice you need give.

The E75 from Ivalo to Inari runs parallel to the shore of Lake Inari but you will see little of the lake until you get to **Inari** village (1315km). This previously insignificant little village is now full of life and bustle thanks to tourism. A **tourist information office** is run by Northern Lapland Tourism (☎ 016-668402, ▤ 016 668403; ▣ northern-lapland.tourism@co.inet.fi). It is excellent for maps and guides for all northern Finland.

Inari is not an especially attractive village but the white wooden church, with a separate belltower, is interesting. It is a Sami church with a particularly attractive painting showing a Sami family with Christ. The little war cemetery is, as is common with Finnish churches, immaculate. Along with the usual range of services in the village are shops selling snow scooters. Another visit worth making is to the **Sami Museum** (Saamelaismuseo). The open-air section has been open since 1962 but the main building dates from only 1992.

The main attraction at Inari is, of course, the great lake, third in size of the Finnish lakes at 1386 sq km. It is 80km long, half that width, and fully 95m deep – a natural down-warped basin in the Baltic Shield peneplain. Inari will be the best point on the route to see something of the lake. You can make short float-plane trips from the village as well as longer boat trips. You can take a boat out to an island on which there is an ancient **Lapp shrine** (Ukonkivi).

Before tackling the last leg of the journey to Norway's Arctic Highway, Inari makes an attractive place to stop, not least because there is a selection of accommodation. There are over a dozen hotels from which to choose.

Inari accommodation

A pleasant little hotel (just 12 rooms) is *Lapinleuku Wilderness Hotel* (☎ 016-666208; 🖷 016-666214). Despite its size and price, rooms are en suite with showers. Prices start at €60 for a double. Much larger and with far more add-on facilities is *Hotel Riekonlinna* (☎ 016-6794455; 🖷 016-6794456; 🖃 riekkohotels@riekkoparvi.fi). Doubles here cost €125.

There are a number of campsites but one of the better equipped (including cabins) is *Ukonjärvi Camping* (☎ 016-667501; 🖺 016-667516), referred to above. To reach the site, drive through Ivalo village and continue on the E75. After about 2km the road passes under a power line which will now be to the left of the road. The turning for the campsite is the next right exit from the E75. The camp itself is on an arm of Lake Inari a further 2km up this minor road. This camp stays open from May until late September – a long season in these parts. The big cabins come in at about €120 with the small ones at only €50.

Inari marks a very special point in this whole route from Helsinki to Karasjok. Even the relatively sparsely inhabited route that the E75 has followed so far is nothing compared with the real wilderness to come.

The E75 rises away from the village and runs at first across gravel ridges which thread through Lake Vuådasjärvi. The forest is already beginning to thin away from the sheltered basin of Lake Inari. At **Mukkaniemi** (1341km) a minor road (971) leads off the E75 to the right. This is one of the alternatives to this recommended approach route to the Arctic Highway (see Options box opposite).

From the junction with Route 971, the E75 continues a further six kilometres to **Aitajärvi** (1347km). Two kilometres along this stretch is the tiny village of **Kaamanen** (1343km). This is an important centre for the Skolt Sami living in the district. Some are descendants of Sami who left Russia on the setting up of the Soviet Union. There is a Sami school in this village.

At Aitajärvi what was Route 970 is now the continuation the E75 – another alternative to this Approach Route (see the Options box opposite).

If you decide to stay with this recommended Approach Route, from Aitajärvi you are on Route 92. This road branches north-westward as it leaves the E75. From here there is virtually no settlement to speak of for the next 70km. The road rises and falls over undulating countryside. Although the road has been widened and improved in recent years, some surfaces are still gravel and, on a dry summer's day, vehicles send up clouds of dust and windscreen-shattering stones. However, the road is remarkably straight for significantly long sections and, with little traffic, driving is easy. Some of the improved stretches are exceptionally wide. (Some of the roads in northern Finland have been constructed to be wide and straight enough to act as emergency runways for aircraft.)

> **Options**
>
> There are several choices facing you both as you enter Norway and as you approach the Arctic Highway. The recommended route for this Approach Route leads to Karasjok, on the Arctic Highway. The other options also get you to the Highway but aren't perhaps so good. If you take the path to Neiden, for example, the road is not especially attractive, while if you decide to continue on the E75, you'll enter Norway with no prospect of a choice of accommodation for some distance from the border.
>
> All the same, the choice is yours and a brief description of the options is given here.
>
> To get to Neiden: Turn on to Route 971 at **Mukkaniemi** (see p108) as it strikes north-eastward towards a link with Norway's Arctic Highway at **Neiden** (see Part 9, p292). This 134km journey is not an easy one. The road is rather a poor one, especially beyond Väylä and is often badly affected by the spring thaw. There is no accommodation or easy camping near the frontier on the Finnish side, and unless you arrive at the frontier post, **Näätämö**, between 07.00 and 22.00, the hours when the frontier is open, there will be a long wait in your vehicle.
>
> To get to Utsjoki: The route is the continuation of the E75 which takes you to the crossing of the Tana River at the **Utsjoki/Ailigas** Norwegian–Finnish border. The road was upgraded before the bridge over the river was completed (see Part 9, p270). This 100km stretch is quite fast but of no intrinsic interest. The disadvantage of using this road is that you are a long way from a choice of accommodation after you arrive on Norwegian soil.

As might be expected, in an area where winter temperatures regularly drop well below -20°C, when the thaw comes the dirt roads can be badly affected.

At the roadside, spruce is absent from the forest cover. Birch, including dwarf birch, and pine forest grow in the more sheltered parts but much of the surface seen on either side of the road is bog, low shrubs and bushes and bare rock. In one or two places, especially on the left of the road after Kabmasmohkki, and it may be possible to see defoliated stunted birch. These trees were attacked by caterpillars of the epiritta moth in the mid-1960s and have never recovered.

Other interesting features on this part of Route 92 are to the right of the road just beyond **Kielajoki** (1371km). These are fossil dunes. Appearing as undulating ground with an amplitude of 7 to 8m, these dunes, now vegetated, were formed from sands laid down in a post-glacial lake. In the dry climatic period which followed, the glacial winds blew the sands into dune forms.

At **Muotkan Ruoktu** (1375km) to the left of Route 82 there is a **café**.

Although this remote part of Finnish Lapland has proved uninviting to human habitation, some areas, where reindeer moss carpets the birch forest floor, have become feeding grounds for the Sami's reindeer. Close to the Norwegian border you can see a few corrals and slaughterhouses set away from the road but along driveable tracks.

The Finnish–Norwegian border is reached at **Karigasniemi** (1413km). Vehicles may be stopped at the customs post (to the left of the road) or waved on, though it is sensible to get some sign from the border police before driving over. Compared with Norwegian–Swedish border posts, the Finns tend to take the crossing more seriously. I once saw a German car being systematically dismantled by three border guards at this post.

There is a petrol station at the border, on the Norwegian side, but little else. Route 92 continues into Norway and covers the next 19km to Karasjok. The road is a good though winding road from which there are excellent views of the Karasjoki River with its complex of meanders and point bars. In summer the water will be low but in springtime its extensive width just accommodates the flood waters of the snow-melt. Farms, mostly owned by Sami, increase as you reach **Karasjok** (1432km). You've finally met with Norway's Arctic Highway (see Part 9, p262). You can now continue eastward towards Kirkenes, one of the Highway's termini.

APPROACH ROUTE IX: TURKU TO KARASJOK BY ROAD

You can use this route if you've come into Scandinavia via Gothenburg (see Approach Route VII, p91) and Stockholm or direct by Turku. There are frequent and convenient ferries from Stockholm to Turku (see Part 1). A night crossing from Stockholm saves time but deprives you of good views of the Åland Islands, an archipelago which almost links Finland and Sweden. There are over 6500 islands of various sizes, mostly small and uninhabited.

The route briefly described below is from Turku to Jyväskylä. From there you can use Approach Route VIII, p97.

● **Route** Turku–Tampere–Jyväskylä: E63; for Jyväskylä to Kirkenes see Approach Route VIII above.
● **Distance (Turku–Jväskylä)** 307km
● **Total distance (Turku–Karasjok/Kirkenes)** 1461km
Summary Route to Jväskylä is almost due north-east and avoids central Tampere.
● **Suggested travel time** One day from Turku to Jyväskylä. For Jyväskylä to Karasjok/Kirkenes see Approach Route VIII on p97.
● **Road quality** Good to very good. Fast sections in environs of Turku, Tampere and Jyväskylä.
● **Suggested stopping places** Jyväskylä, then as for Approach Route VIII (for details see Route VIII)

The route (south to north)
Turku was Finland's capital until early in the nineteenth century and it's the country's oldest town. If you can spare the time, it would be rewarding to have a look at some of the sights. There's a **castle**, a **Lutheran cathedral** and an **Orthodox church** as well as a clutch of **museums**. The ferry docks at the mouth of the River Aura and there is a **tourist information office** (☎ 02-2627444; 🖷 02-2336488; 🖳 tourist.info@turku.fi) at the harbour (on Aurakatu) which will provide you with a street map and information on opening times.

Leaving Turku, you should use Aninkaistenkatu which leads north over the main river from the centre of the town and bears right after bridging the railway. The E63 is well signposted from here. The road runs through alternating farmland and forest. Over the years the road has been reconstructed to avoid settlements. There is an important junction near **Humppila** (85km) where Route 2 crosses over the top of the E63.

Beyond **Urjala** (104km) the road runs through particularly well-farmed country before it begins to get entangled with a scattering of small lakes and watercourses which signal the start of Finland's **Lake Region**.

At **Kulju** (142km) the E12 joins the E63 and, as an urban motorway, they enter **Tampere** via a complex system of over- and underpasses. The second largest city in Finland, **Tampere** (157km) has spread east and west from its original site along the Tammerkoski rapids. The E63 turns right rather than entering the town centre and slips away through the suburbs to find its way along the edge of a lake, Näsijärvi. You'll get only an occasional glimpse of the lake (to the left).

The road from Tampere runs through country noticeably less well farmed and much of its journey is through forest unrelieved by settlements. Some 40km north of Tampere the road cuts by an underpass through **Orivesi** (119km), a busy place, half town, half village. The road on from here becomes much more rural in character and some pretty forested terrain leads to **Jämsä** (249km). Here the E63 meets the E75 (junction from the right) and the combined roads lead to **Jyväskylä** (307km). From Jyväskylä the route to the Arctic Highway is the same as Approach Route VIII on p97.

APPROACH ROUTE X: USING PUBLIC TRANSPORT (RAIL OR ROAD)

To experience the Arctic Highway and all it has to offer you really have to drive it. However, it is possible to reach the Highway by train and bus, and even to travel the length of the road by public bus. Anyone who is hiring a vehicle, or is not the main driver, may prefer to wait until Mo i Rana is reached before turning to their own transport.

Norway's main **railway** network stops at Bodø. There's nothing further north but the line into Narvik from Sweden and the mineral line at Kirkenes. So Mo is almost at the limit of the network as well as being the starting point for an Arctic Highway drive. In fact there are two rail routes: Oslo–Dombås–Trondheim–Mo, and Oslo–Røros–Trondheim–Mo. The fares are identical and the journey times similar but the former route, via Dombås, following much the same path as the E6, is the more interesting. There are daily services taking about 14 hours and you can travel overnight using a sleeping car.

The advantages of rail are speed and lessened fatigue. On the other hand it is expensive as railway fares go in Europe. First class is about 150% of standard class. For up-to-the-minute schedules, fares and reservations log on to 🖳 www. nsb.no. If you are already in Norway when you want to book, call ☎ 81 50 08 88 and dial 4 for an English speaking operator. Of course, you can call by telephone from outside Norway (the country code is 47) but that can be expensive unless you have already got the basic information from the website.

There are very comprehensive public **bus** services in Norway which include long-distance coaches. No single company takes in the whole of Norway but the individual companies work well together to produce a pretty seamless system.

With a little advanced planning, it's not difficult to go by bus all the way from Oslo to Kirkenes. Of course, you are something of a prisoner once you're on a particular leg of the journey and you have none of the flexibility or independence of vehicle travel. All the same, if well planned, you can make good use of the stops. It is difficult to compare bus travel with car when it comes to costs. Using a bus will mean fares are proportionate to the number of passengers in the party. By car the costs can be shared.

If you do decide to travel the length of the Highway by bus, the most convenient starting point is Fauske, picking up the long-distance bus coming from Bodø. Fauske to Narvik takes about six hours, Narvik to Alta is a twelve-hour run and it's another eleven hours on to Kirkenes. You can also use a bus for some of the Highway's branches. For example, the journey to Tromsø from Nordkjosbotn is around 45 minutes. On these buses you can break your journey at intermediate locations.

Keen cyclists might like to note that buses will usually accept bikes, carried on the front of the bus. I've seen cyclists on the Highway but I'm not sure if anyone has ever done the whole of the road on a bike. There would inevitably be quite a lot of walking and pushing involved!

For information on bus services the company to contact is Nor-Way (☎ 82 02 13 00 or 81 54 44 44 for international bookings – the domestic information service costs a punitive NOK10 per minute; 🖹 23 00 24 49; 🖳 ruteinformasjon @nor-way.no).

PART 4: MO I RANA TO FAUSKE

Route guide introduction

In the following six parts, the Arctic Highway (the E6) will be described from south to north (Mo i Rana to Kirkenes) in roughly equidistant parts.

DISTANCES

Distances given in the text along the Highway are given as **from the start of each part**. Because the Highway is frequently being upgraded, often by minor re-routings and straightening, all distances should be taken as approximate. However, as explained in Part 1, roads in Norway, even minor ones, are usually well signposted and there is little likelihood of an observant driver losing his way.

The more interesting minor roads, offering possible **side trips**, are described with distances given from the junction with the Arctic Highway. Again, quoted distances should be treated as approximate for the reason given above. To avoid confusion in the text between these side trips and the descriptions of the Arctic Highway, shaded bars run down the edge of the page next to the side trip.

JOURNEY TIME

The question most often asked, for obvious reasons, is 'How long will the journey take?' The standard of the road is such that it could be done in three days but this would give you no opportunity to appreciate properly the Highway as one of the world's most fascinating roads and would certainly rule out the exploration of the alluring side routes. Six days might be sufficient to see much of what is along the Highway itself; ten would allow you some time in the more interesting small towns and larger villages; and two weeks should be sufficient for you to sample a range of side trips. Recalling the vast area through which the Highway passes, it is not surprising that many travellers return time and time again.

ACCOMMODATION

As in Part 3, reference is made to accommodation options. The choices are described at the end of each section of the Highway and in the order they will be reached if travelling from south to north. In the case of the towns, the accommodation is described towards the end of that town's account. In the accommodation sections which follow, where a price is indicated it should be taken only as a rough guide. Prices alter with season, with availability and, most especially, over time. On the maps the following symbols are used: **hotel or guesthouse** ⇧ and for a **campsite** (usually with cabins as well as caravan or tent spaces): △ .

The guide

MO I RANA

It is from Mo i Rana that the European Route 6 can properly be called The Arctic Highway. Mo is at the geographical centre of Norway and the last town on the journey north before the Polar Circle is crossed. It deserves to be better known than it is, not simply because of its size but because it is becoming a very attractive settlement in its own right as well as a good base for touring.

Its relative anonymity may have something to do with its isolation at the head of the Nord-Rana arm of the deeply penetrating Rana fjord and the fact that it is off the track of the Coastal Express (the Hurtigrute). Mo is some 100km from the open sea but only 30km (40km by road – see side trip on p119) from the Swedish border. The town has spread around the fjord-head and, to some extent, along the Highway to Selfors and astride the E12 in the direction of Gruben. The greater part of the town lies south of the Rana River and its heart remains close to Moholmen, the original trading point and *raison d'être* for Mo's modern growth.

Because the town has such a wealth of interesting features, and because you are about to embark on the drive up 1500km of Arctic Highway, you might consider stopping for at least two or three days in Mo.

History

Mo is not an old town although there is evidence of some Viking settlement along the Ranafjord and a Sami market was established in 1730. In the eighteenth century the majority of the people still lived at Ytteen, now a north-west 'suburb' of Mo. Here were the boathouses of the local valley farmers. Hemnes at this time was the prime settlement of Ranafjord, essentially a fishing community and, typically, built on an island. The farmers of Dunderlandsdalen were few in number even in the early 1700s.

Three events stand out in Mo's history: the founding of a church, the establishment of the town as a trading centre and the building of a giant steelworks after World War II.

Thomas von Westen, the Lapps' Apostle, was responsible for the church. He first came to Mo in October 1716 on one of his missionary journeys north. A mission school had already been opened for local Sami children at Moholmen (near to the centre of the modern town). By 1722, and after two other visits, Westen had persuaded the local community of farmers to contribute enough money to construct a church on the rising ground to the east of the present Arctic Highway. Today's church (see p116) is on the same site.

Although now with its own church (independent of the Hemnes church since the mid-eighteenth century), the settlement grew only slowly. By the beginning of the nineteenth century, the combined population of the Hemnes and Mo parishes, a quite vast area, was only 4561 persons and Hemnes was still the larger of the two. Sixty years later saw the beginnings of growth with the arrival of one Lars Aagaard Meyer.

Lars was in his twenties, a son of the renowned trading family, when he moved to Mo from Vikholmen in 1860. The Meyers had traded in the region for decades, mostly at Nesna at the mouth of the Ranafjord. He obtained a trading licence on 21 May 1860 and in a short time had purchased almost the whole of the present town area which, at the time, consisted of just a few houses. From then on the town proceeded to grow.

As well as founding a boat- and coffin-building industry, Meyer was a skilful and successful merchant. Acting as a middleman he found markets for the produce of Mo's hinterland and stored in his warehouses the goods needed by the local community. This hinterland included bordering areas of Sweden and a road was built across the frontier (now, with some re-routing, the E12). It became known as the 'Butter Road' as Swedish dairy produce was brought into the town. When Lars' son, Hans, took over the business in 1902, Mo was already known as Meyer's Town and the family has continued to exercise an influence over the town to the present day.

In 1923, with a population of 1457, the town separated from the Nord-Rana Kommune with plans for growth to a target figure of 5000. However, the depression of the early 1930s and the declining output of iron ore from Dunderlandsdalen held back development.

By 1935 the population had reached only the 1500 mark and there it stayed until after World War II despite the coming of the Nordland Railway and the construction of the Arctic Highway across the Polar Circle on Saltfjellet.

The North Norway Railway, which crosses the Arctic Circle and terminates at Bodø, was the brainchild of Ole Tobias Olsen who is commemorated in a number of ways in the town. An interesting character – parish priest, teacher and visionary – he saw his scheme for this railway approved by the Storting (Parliament) but died before it was built.

The most significant date in Mo i Rana's post-war development was 10 July 1946 when the Storting unanimously passed a bill to set up a national ironworks (A/S Norsk Jernverk) in the town. This act foreshadowed the 1952 North Norway Economic Development Plan which addressed the problem of developing the seriously under-populated and vulnerable northern fylker (counties).

A new hydro-electric power station, a coking plant for coal from Spitsbergen and iron from Kirkenes (and, later, from Dunderland) combined to create the largest steel plant in Norway. The massive works occupied about 40% of the town's area to the east of the town and in the 1970s more than half the working population were employed in steel. Meyer's Town became Steel Town and, ominously as it turned out, people spoke of Mo as Norway's Sheffield.

The industry brought prosperity at first. The dominating rolling mills, the largest covered building in Norway, and huge chimneys were tolerated as necessary nuisances. Even the pollution, which coated streets, gardens and lamp-posts with a grey-pink dust, was accepted. Sales of steel from Mo went round the world from China to the USA. Output doubled in the ten years from the mid-1950s to the mid-1960s, but ten years later, just as the atmospheric pollution was beginning to be conquered, Mo's products no longer found easy markets.

The industry went into decline and diversification was the order of the day. A ferro-silicon works was established and there were feasibility studies for the setting up of an aluminium works to take up the surplus hydro-electric power. However, the threat of massive unemployment spurred the state into relocating a number of civil service departments to the town and the construction of a vast industrial park, largely on the land where the steelworks had once flourished. Once again Mo showed itself equal to the task when disaster loomed.

Despite the setbacks to Mo's most important industry in the late 1980s and early 1990s, the town shows no scars. The population in the town proper exceeds 10,000 and there are over 25,000 in the municipality. Every year seems to see the construction of at least one new prominent building and the town is the most attractive of all those along the Arctic Highway.

Services

Entering Mo i Rana from the south along the E6 the centre is reached after passing under a railway bridge and crossing directly over the first of three roundabouts. At the second roundabout the re-routed E6 bears off to the right but, to go into the town, take the second exit to the last of the roundabouts where the route is the third exit. This is Ole Tobias Olsensgate.

For anyone who knows the E6 route from earlier days, it may come as a surprise to find that it is re-routed to the east of the town. It now loops in an arc past the new industrial area before it rejoins its old path by the junction with the E12.

If coming into Mo from Sweden on the E12 (Approach Route VII) it is best to turn left on to the E6 and then follow the signs south until reaching the second roundabout referred to above. To continue south is to leave by the third exit but to go into Mo take the second exit and continue as though coming from the south, as above.

The very helpful **tourist office** (☎ 75 13 92 00; ✉ infomo@arctic-circle. no) is just to the left on entering Olsensgt. The office is open from 09.00 to 20.00 (to 21.00 in July) Monday to Friday in summer (mid-June to mid-September) and from 09.00 to 16.00 for the rest of the year. It closes at weekends in the winter but in summer opens on Saturdays from 09.00 to 16.00 and on Sundays from 13.00 to 19.00. It's worth calling in if only to collect a parking permit, free visitors during the summer.

Continuing down Olsensgate leads directly past the modern **railway station** (☎ 75 15 01 77) with a striking hexagonal main building (left). The somewhat rundown **bus station** (☎ 75 12 87 00) is just beyond the railway station with, appropriately, a bust of Ole Tobias Olsen gazing at the railway between the two stations. The town's **taxi** (*drosjer*) rank (☎ 75 15 23 33) is by the railway station. To the east of the road is a small square with a garden (Railway Station Square). This is the heart of the town. On one side of the square is the railway and, opposite, the **Meyer Store** with more shops on the third side. At the more open end of the square are the Rana Museum, alongside a garden, and the Meyergården Hotel (see p118).

Almost everything one might need from stores to services is within a pedestrianized block east of the square, behind the Meyer store. The store is on the site of the original Meyer family shop but, massively enlarged, it is now the **Meyersenteret**. There is a **library** on Torrgata (☎ 75 14 61 00) which has internet facilities which can be used for emails. Close by is the **police** (*politi*) **station** (☎ 75 15 08 22), a modern **post office** (☎ 75 12 95 00) and a **medical centre** (☎ 75 15 17 00). There are several **banks** in the centre. The town hall (**Rådhus**) is also here. A two-screen **cinema**

with a **theatre** (☎ 75 14 60 50) is on Jernbanegata. Most days in summer there's a variety of market stalls in the pedestrian area selling all manner of goods from strawberries to audio tapes. If the prices are not a deterrent, then alcoholic drinks (wines and spirits) can be purchased at the very modern (1999) **Mo Center** down by the tourist information office. The **telephone office** (*Televerket*) is at the point where the pedestrianized Jernbanegata meets Sørlandsveien.

Around town

As stated, there is so much to see and do in Mo i Rana that it would be a pity to drive straight through without stopping. It is a place to gather your strength before setting out on the journey to the north along Norway's Arctic Highway.

The town church is partly hidden by some unattractive apartment blocks. It stands to the east of the Arctic Highway and can be approached from the square by continuing along the pedestrianized Jernbanegt to its upper end, where it meets Sørlandsveien. The road to the church is on the opposite side of Sørlandsveien. **Mo Kirke** is on the site of the original 1722 church. The first building, despite its drab tarred exterior, was easily visible from the fjord. Today's church, although a more imposing structure, is dwarfed by the modern buildings which surround it. It dates from 1801, when the old church was pulled down, but alterations were made in 1832 and again in 1860. It is simple in design, with a high gabled roof and an onion-spired low tower. Originally it was red (painted with a local dye), but in 1908 it surrendered to the fashion that the House of God should be white.

Inside there are some interesting relics dating from the first church. These include a pauper's purse and a poor box. There is a fine painted altar-piece in the main body of the church and an even more fascinating simple carved altar-piece in the chapel behind the choir. The latter dates from 1768.

Outside, the churchyard is well kept and on the far side are the simple graves of British soldiers killed in the Battle of the Dals Valley in 1941 (see p78). There is also a Russian war memorial.

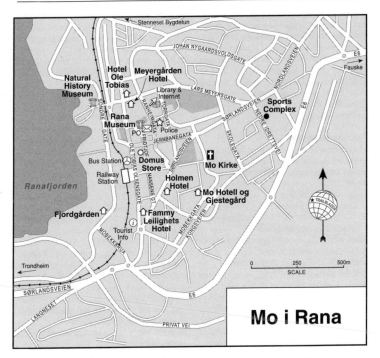

Mo i Rana

There is a really magnificent new **sports complex** (☎ 75 14 60 68), including a heated swimming pool, a little further north than the church. It is easiest to find by continuing up Sørlandsveien from the turning to the church. After 200–300 metres is a right turn, Nedre Idrettsvei. The sports complex is on the right. A **ten-pin bowling alley** is situated between the Abelone and Elvinds restaurants (see p118).

For the hardy, shunning the comfort of a heated pool, there are beaches from which swimming in the fjord is possible. **Hauknes Bathing Park** is in a suburb of Mo off the Arctic Highway 5km south of the town centre. More attractive, to the west of the town along Route 12 is **Altern Beach**, larger and with more facilities. It is popular on hot days in summer.

There are three museums in or near Mo i Rana. The **Cultural Museum** (☎ 75 14 61 70) is by the post office in the town centre (Museumveien). Exhibits trace the history of the town and Sami culture and there is the Lars Meyer collection. Crossing the railway, from the roundabout towards the northern end of OT Olsengt, leads to the small **Moholmen** peninsula where there is an interesting **Natural History Museum** (☎ 75 14 61 80). Moholmen was the original trading post of Mo i Rana. Some of the old buildings still remain. Out of town is **Stenneset Bygdetun** (☎ 75 14 61 70), an open-air museum of 22 relocated but authentic domestic buildings which chart the variety of vernacular architecture in the Rana area. The museum is clustered around a restored parsonage and is certainly worth the 8km journey by Route 12 along the fjord to Båsmoen. For the opening times of all the museums it is best to ask at the tourist office.

'Street sculpture' is a feature of Norway and there's an interesting example in the town market square: a prancing horse facing the fjord. Even more impressive and best seen from Moholmen is **Havmannen** (The Sea Man). This is one of those like-it-or-loathe-it works of art, a giant stylized stone figure of a man standing out in the fjord. It is the work of the English artist Anthony Gormley.

Accommodation

Mo is a busy commercial centre so there are times when, unless pre-booked, accommodation may be limited. However, there is a wider range of hotels, guesthouses and camps than might be expected in a town of this size. *Meyergården Hotel* (☎ 75 13 40 00; 🖹 75 13 40 01; 🖃 meyergarden@meyergarden.no) is probably the 'top' hotel in town. It was the former home of the Meyer family and is set in a small garden at the north side of Railway Station Square. The original section of the hotel, including the dining-room, is very attractive but the modern extensions are nothing very special, with some of the bedrooms small and the décor institutional. Rates will be of the order of NOK500-plus with breakfast but in summer the lowest rate may drop to a more reasonable NOK400.

The *Fjordgården* (☎ 75 15 28 00; 🖹 75 15 43 70; 🖃 jjacobsen@meyergarden.no) is a modern hotel built in 1994 and formerly known as the Rica. It is on the fjord side of the railway off Søndregt almost opposite the tourist office. This is a well-designed and attractive hotel with 160 rooms, six of which are singles. There is an unusual galleried lounge. Next door is a sports hall and the hotel will organize access for guests. Currently the hotel is open only between May and late August or early September. Arrangements can be made for guests to use the Meyergården as an alternative. The rates of these two hotels are the same.

On the old E6 road, Sørlandsveien, to the east of the town centre, there's the *Holmen Hotel* (☎ 75 14 14 44; 🖹 75 15 18 70; 🖃 holmenho@online.no). It is on the corner with T V Westensgt. There are just 44 rooms of good mid-market standard, all en

suite but most with showers and not baths. The restaurant is noted for its buffet lunches and there is a pub attached to the hotel. The hotel is open all year except Christmas and is a member of the Rainbow Group. Prices are from NOK500 per person with breakfast.

Mo Hotell og Gjestegård (☎ 75 15 22 11; 🖹 75 15 23 38) was the Rana Gestervi and is just behind the Holmen Hotel on Hans Wølnesgt. It is mid-market, charging NOK500 per double room. Rooms are a bit small but it's clean, comfortable and showers are en suite.

Without a restaurant and somewhat overpriced is the *Hotel Ole Tobias* (☎ 75 15 77 77) just behind the Meyergården but facing on to OT Olsengt. There is a buffet breakfast but for an evening meal it is necessary to eat out. The rooms, particularly on the top floor are small. The hotel is a member of the Choice Group.

An interesting option is *Fammy Leilighets Hotel* (☎ 75 15 19 99) almost opposite the tourist office. One shouldn't be put off by the rather drab exterior. Inside is bright, cheerful and spotlessly clean. Much use is made of wood in the beautifully furnished interior. In fact, Fammy isn't really a hotel but a self-catering establishment which serves breakfast. The rooms are well equipped for self-catering and the best look out to the fjord. If eating out at the Abelone restaurant next door there's a 15% discount. A double room will be about NOK800 and a triple can cost NOK1000: not cheap but very friendly.

On the road into Sweden north-east of the town there is *Bech's Hotel* (☎ 75 13 02 11; 🖹 75 13 15 77). Modestly priced and long established, its only disadvantage is its location away from the centre of town.

Where to eat

Most of the hotels (see above) will serve meals to non-residents but are less helpful if you just want a snack. Buffet meals in hotels are often quite good value although à la carte may seem expensive.

There is a quite large number of cafés, restaurants and 'pubs' in Mo i Rana. The *Abelone Restaurant* (☎ 75 15 38 88) is conveniently situated near to the Fammy

Hotel (see above) and has the **Punktum Pub** above. Meals are à la carte (plenty of meat dishes) and cost around NOK175. It is open from 14.00 to 23.00 (to midnight on Friday and Saturday). It is neat, clean and the décor is slightly Germanic.

Close to the Meyergården Hotel is **Dolly Dimple's** (☎ 75 13 93 00), one of a chain, which is locally popular for its pizzas. **Karen's Babettes Bar** (☎ 75 15 16 08), in an unmistakable orange and brown building by the police station, is one of the more popular bars, very like a modern English pub. For fast food, there is **Elvinds** (☎ 75 15 04 33). Essentially a takeaway, there are a few tables too. A plate of chips costs NOK20. It is on the corner of Heltzens gt (off OT Olsensgt) and Fridtjof Nansens gt.

With something of a nautical theme is **Fembøringen** (☎ 75 15 09 77). It is on the first floor above a shop and below a night-club bar, very centrally located on Jernbanegata. As the name suggests, this road is up from the railway station in the pedestrianized area. As well as full meals, this café serves pizzas, salads and sandwiches.

There are lots of cafés providing light meals and snacks. In shopping hours, the **Domus Store's** café is where everyone in town gathers for their morning coffee and gossip. It's good value – probably the gossip is too! Between the railway and bus stations the younger generation prefers **Mix Scene I** opposite Domus on the north-east corner of Fridtjof Nansensgt and Kirkgata. It's more of a shop than a café but there are a few stools and it does serve snacks and drinks. It's open until 23.00 every night including Sundays.

At the bus station is the **Caroline Café** with plenty of the cream cakes favoured by Norwegians. It's clean, bright and reasonably priced. Another quite smart-looking café is the **Conditoriet** opposite the Fembøringen (see above). You can sit outside, weather permitting, and it's a favourite of the locals for their morning coffee. A coffee and a Danish pastry will cost NOK20.

SIDE TRIPS FROM MO I RANA

There are a number of side trips that can be made from Mo before setting out on the long journey north. It's unlikely that there'll be time for all those described below. It is largely a matter of taste. However, if time is short, forego those direct from Mo i Rana and at least take the Svartisen and caves visit, described from Røssvoll (see p124).

1 – Side trip to the Swedish Border
Map 1a

To reach the Swedish border is only a half-day trip with a distance of only 86km there and back. It is a trip of modest interest but there are good views in fine weather. The road is part of one of the routes suggested as an approach to the Arctic Highway. (See Approach Route VII, p91). Many years ago this was known as the Butter Road. Butter was bought in from Sweden for trading in Mo i Rana. As late as the 1960s it was still a very difficult path, narrow and with many very sharp hairpin bends. I was once told of an English motorist who actually abandoned his car and walked into Mo, so scared was he of negotiating the bends with precipitous drops to one side or the other. Today's road is a transformation on a new, slightly more

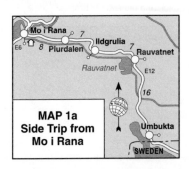

MAP 1a
Side Trip from
Mo i Rana

northerly path. It is still fairly steep in places but the notorious bends have gone.

The route out of Mo is the E12 which joins the E6, Arctic Highway, near the northern exit from the centre of town. The road goes eastwards as it passes through straggling suburbs, with a number of side roads. After 5km, a road leads off to the right into the high Mofjellet which rises to almost 750m. At **Plurdalen** (8km) is a road (Route 352) to the left which might be explored as an alternative to the E12. On the 352, after 34km, you arrive at Kaldvatnet, a very large lake, after passing a waterfall, Sprutfossen. The last stretch to the lake is on a minor road. You can also use Route 352 to reach the caves mentioned later (see p125).

Staying with the E12, the route climbs up into the mountains, swings briefly right (south) and reaches **Ildgrulia** (15km) before turning left again. Here there are good views to the west. The Ranafjord and the Svartisen glaciers can be seen. This could be a point to turn back if your time is limited.

The rest of the journey is across the plateau past innumerable fish-laden lakes and streams. The countryside is wild and rather bleak. You need the sun if you're to see it at its most attractive. The next section of road runs eastward towards **Rauvatnet** (also Raudvatnet, 22km). The hills to the left of the road contain iron and the weathered pyrites provided the ochre used in paint for the houses of Mo i Rana. The distinctive colour is still visible on a few of the older buildings although there are hints of a revival of the custom.

On reaching Rauvatnet, the road turns south towards the border. To the south-west are the Okstind mountains containing a large ice-cap. The immediate landscape remains one of scattered lakes, bogland and trees seeking shelter. At **Umbukta** (38km) there is a *fjellstue* (mountain hostel) and three kilometres further on, the E12 becomes a Swedish road as the border is crossed. Remarkably, the customs post is still some 80km away at Tärnaby.

2 – Side trip to Nesna   Map 1b

This is a half-day journey to the coast. The round trip is 132km.

The attraction of the trip is the view it gives you of the Helgeland Archipelago. Route 12 is the route. It is the natural extension of the E12 (see above) but to reach the road take the Arctic Highway (E6) north out of Mo and join Route 12 by continuing straight on at the Selfors bridge instead of branching right for the Highway.

Route 12 is known as the Blue Road. It is relatively modern, passing through scattered settlements and alongside farms. There is only one steep gradient and the latter half of the journey is on a well-surfaced road.

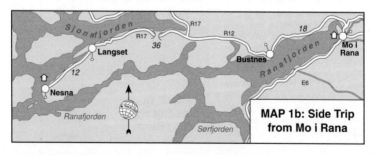

MAP 1b: Side Trip from Mo i Rana

After running through the suburb of Yetteren on the northern outskirts of Mo, the road follows the edge of the Ranafjord towards the open sea. Although rarely far from the fjord, your view is often obstructed by trees and only occasionally is it easy to see the full length of Ranafjorden. You'll probably get the best view at **Bustnes** (18km), but even here you need to leave the main road. From this point, Route 12 pulls back from the fjord and access is by minor roads to the left.

After crossing the Sjoneidet isthmus, Route 12 joins the relatively modern (late 1980s) Route 17. This is part of an alternative to the recommended Approach Route I (see p66). The path is the southern edge of Sjonafjord but, as with the Ranafjord, it is not always possible to see the fjord itself. However, the road rises steeply on to the Sjonfjellet and at a height of 356m there is a good viewpoint from which you can see across Sjonafjorden. To the north-west you can see Høgtuvbreen, a glacier standing at over 1200m above sea-level. To the west are the Helgeland Islands.

The destination is **Nesna** (66km) at the very end of the peninsula which separates the Rana and Sjona fjords. Today it is a fishing village of about 1000 people but there has been some sort of settlement here since Viking times. Evidence of even earlier inhabitants lies in the caves on some of the off-shore islands where traces of Stone Age man date back 5000 years. The islands are quite large near the mainland but diminish seawards to a myriad of tiny rock platforms just keeping their heads above water. The islands form the Helgeland Archipelago, a sort of miniature Lofoten but very beautiful even when viewed from the Nesna shore.

The larger islands are the homes of fishing communities but there are also several bird colonies including the rare puffin. Daily boat trips are possible to the islands. Route 17 continues south by way of a ferry (25 minutes) to Levang (also Låvong). This ferry has been in operation only for the last forty years and has dramatically reduced Nesna's traditional isolation.

Nesna has a small **museum** (at the junior school) and there is an old parsonage which dates from the time Petter Dass was a curate at the village. Dass, a celebrated poet and writer of the seventeenth century was actually the son of a Scot but the family name of Dundas was changed to the Norwegian Dass. Much loved and respected, when he died in 1707 it is said that Norwegian ships carried a black patch on their sails for the next 100 years. His writings provide a graphic account of the daily perils encountered by the fishermen on this part of Nordland's coast.

The village's other claim to fame is the production of *nesnalodder*, a sort of warm oversock.

There are services in the village for fuel and refreshment. For a longer stay, there are camping, cabins and rooms at *Nesna Feriesenter and Motel* (☎ 75 05 65 40; 🖷 75 05 66 97; 🖳 nesnafer@online.no).

3   Side trip to Stokkvågen and the Helgeland Islands   Map 1c
You'll need time to spare for this trip as it will take anything from the better part of a full day to two days. Just going to Stokkvågen is a round trip of 148km.

If you do have the time, then this is an especially interesting alternative to the Nesna side trip described above. The first part of the journey, as far as Sjoneidet, is on Route 12 as for Side trip 2. At Sjoneidet, take the right turn on to Route 17 instead of continuing westward on the road of the same number.

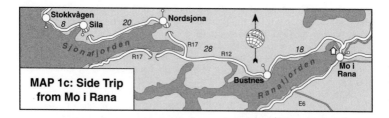

MAP 1c: Side Trip from Mo i Rana

From now on the road runs close to the Sjonafjord and there are wonderful views of the fjord and across to the Helgeland Islands. It is a good road, much of it dating from 1990, with a few short tunnels. **Stokkvågen** (74km) is a small ferry point with few services and infrequent ferries to the islands. On a short visit, your best plan may be to take a round trip on the ferry (a couple of hours or so) to one of the nearer islands such as Onøya. To reach Lovund, the puffin island, requires more time, not least because the ferry schedules mean an overnight stay is unavoidable.

Whether taking a ferry voyage or not, it is well worth continuing a couple of kilometres on Route 17 beyond Stokkvågen to the top of the promontory. Here you'll get quite spectacular views of the off-shore islands.

The Highway: Mo i Rana to Røssvoll
MAP 1

The journey north along the Arctic Highway/E6 leads through Mo i Rana town. From the centre of town, you can join the Highway by going to the roundabout at the southern end of Ole Tobias Olsensgt (near the tourist information office) and following the signs to the next roundabout where the E6/north is the third exit. This is now the new bypass route which skirts Mo's impressive industrial estate and passes the junction with the road to Sweden (E12 on the right). At the **Selfors bridge** it sweeps right leaving behind Route 12, the road to Nesna, described above. The bridge takes the Highway over the Rana River and it was at this junction where, in the past, small boys would stop foreign cars to ask for autographs and coins. Today they have other things to do or perhaps there are just too many cars.

Selfors is little more than a factory estate, home to a number of small industries and to the town's small hospital (to the left). Once clear of Selfors the scattered outskirts of Mo are left behind and the Highway follows the course of the Ranelv. With the road on its right bank and the railway on its left, the river runs through a magnificent gorge. The Highway is high above the turbulent and turquoise river which can rise suddenly after heavy rain, and campers using paths to get down to the water's edge are warned of the danger should this happen. Depending on the light, the Ranelv can seem menacing as the low sun reflects off the blue-black faces of the gorge and its glacial meltwater.

Paths for the Highway and its companion railway on the other side of the river have been engineered out of the sides of the gorge. The railway makes use of some short tunnels to reduce its gradient but the Highway clings close to the canyon's walls. The railway is of special interest, being part of one of only a handful of passenger lines which cross the Polar Circle anywhere in the world. It will never be far from the Arctic Highway for the next 200km.

Beyond the gorge the railway stays close to the river but the Highway strikes a route which is directly northward through a landscape of rocky outcrops and glacial deposits. Here and there are signs of realignment as narrow tracks lead off the Highway to the left only to rejoin it some 500m or so further on. You may find it hard to believe that these tracks were the early Arctic Highway.

Passing small farms and patches of mixed conifers and birch, the Highway turns sharply right to cross a narrow bridge. This is the crossing of the Langvassåga, a river whose lactescent waters are witness to their source: the meltwaters of the ice-cap Svartisen.

It is worth stopping near the bridge for there are beautiful views eastwards across the Rana valley towards the Kjerringfjellet peaks rising to over 1200m. A few hundred metres further on, a scattering of buildings including a petrol station signals your arrival at the small village of **Røssvoll** (12km).

At Røssvoll a small white octagonal church stands to the left of the Highway near the junction with a minor unnumbered road (see side

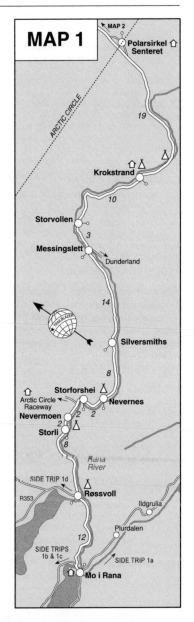

The old railway
The stretch of railway track running through the gorge was originally simply a mineral line carrying iron ore from Dunderlandsdalen into Mo. In the 1870s Ole Tobias Olsen (see p129) and Consul Nils Persson, alerted by Swedish geological surveys to the existence of iron, competed for the rights to mine. Persson won the battle and persuaded a British company to set up the British Dunderland Iron Ore Company. One of their first tasks was to build a standard-gauge railway to take the ore to Mo from the mines at Storforshei. Although mining was not entirely successful – the ore is phosphoric and difficult to gain – the mines remained in operation until World War II. By that time plans were already afoot to incorporate the 30km length of track into the national system.

After the war, work on the railway went ahead and by 1962 the line (Nordland Railway, part of Norwegian State Railways) had crossed the Polar Circle and reached Bodø. Today the railway is much more important for freight than for passengers and some of the stations built on the section between Mo i Rana and Bodø have never opened.

trips below). The attractive little wooden building was erected in 1953 on a concrete base. The interior is painted in typical light pastel shades and the whole church is floodlit in winter.

Accommodation: Mo i Rana to Røssvoll
Opposite the petrol station at Røssvoll is a camping site with a few cabins. This is *Anna's Camping* (☎ 75 14 80 74). The *Røssvoll Senter* (☎ 75 14 81 57; ▤ 75 14 83 90; ▣ jostrand@monet.no) is just down the road with fourteen, four-bed, comfortable cabins. These two sites make Røssvoll an excellent alternative to Mo as a place to stay at the start of a journey north on the Arctic Highway. Prices at both sites are attractive but vary according to the quality of the cabins.

SIDE TRIPS FROM RØSSVOLL

You can take the trips described below using either Mo i Rana or Røssvoll as your base. If you are going to the caves only, a half day might suffice, but to get to see Svartisen glacier you'll need a whole day even though the driving distance is a modest 40km round trip from Røssvoll. The trip out to Melfjordbotn (round trip distance: 84km) might be done in half a day.

1   Side trip to Limestone caves and Svartisen   Map 1d
On the side trip to the limestone caves and the glacier you'll be using minor roads, narrow and winding, and you will need to drive with special care. They are not really suitable for caravans or trailers. In parts there are sections of water-bound gravel surfaces. While at times it will be almost traffic-free, it is possible to encounter a sudden surge of cars and even a small bus when visitors to the glacier have disembarked from the ferry (see p126). The roads also run past small farms where children play on the road and cattle roam.

Route 353 is a left turn off the Arctic Highway at Røssvoll and will be clearly marked for Svartisen and the airport. The road leads past **Mo's airport** (1.5km; ☎ 75 15 80 85) to the left. This little aerodrome (*Lufthavn*) has daily services linking with international flights. In the mid-1960s when I first flew over Svartisen, there was only a landing strip cut out of the forest by local amateur pilots. The runway at that time was a dirt surface. Near the airport entrance it is possible to park a camper/caravan overnight. Just beyond the airport at a sharp bend is a large and unsightly municipal rubbish dump, now a seagulls' restaurant.

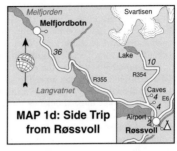

MAP 1d: Side Trip from Røssvoll

The early part of the journey is past one or two isolated houses and farms. At about 6km there is a junction with Route 355 at a bridge across the Røvass, a river carrying meltwater away from the glacier. (For this route see Side trip 2 p127.) The road to Svartisen goes straight ahead but is now in a narrowing valley, almost a gorge, with especially steep forested slopes to the right. This is Røvassdalen. A signpost (10km) pointing right indicates arrival at the limestone caves, *grotter*. Park here and it's is just a short walk to the caves.

These cave systems in the limestone were discovered in 1750, and have been open to the public since the early 1900s. It must be said that they aren't particularly spectacular and the dripstone formations could be described as ordinary. **Grønligrotta** (☎ 75 13 25 86) is suitable for a quick visit by anyone who can tackle a slightly difficult walk and some scrambling. These caves are lit (the only caves in Scandinavia with electric lighting) and a guided tour takes only 20–30 minutes. There is a tour starting on the hour from 10.00 to 19.00. As well as the usual dripstone formations, this set of caves contains a really extraordinary feature. This is a large granitic, glacial-erratic boulder. Just how it got lodged in the caves is something of a mystery because it is larger than the entrance to the passage it occupies. For these caves you need stout footwear and, be warned, it isn't easy-going in one or two places.

Setergrotta (☎ 75 13 92 00) is for the more adventurous. The trip takes about two hours and full equipment and clothing is provided. The features of these unlit caves are on an altogether grander scale, but be prepared for more scrambling and a tougher trip. There are guided tours twice a day.

Both these cave systems are open from mid-June to the end of August. There's a café and very limited, simple accommodation at the caves.

(Budding or practising speleologists might also like to visit a further set of caves near the Swedish border. These will be found at the end of a minor road leading to the right from the Highway just before Røssvoll. After a rough journey of some 25km you'll reach **Krystallgrotten** and **Jordlaugrotten**. If you intend making a visit, check with Mo i Rana tourist office before making the journey. Note: the road is private from Jordbru.)

From the caves you now take Route 354 but don't expect any signposts. It continues along the right bank of the river to pass through more open but very wild country – Svartisdalen – with many a twist and turn on a gradually deteriorating path. After a further 10km (20km from Røssvoll), **Lake Svartis** is reached. There is a small café and sundry other wooden buildings together with parking spaces. To reach the glacier you have to take a small (and usually crowded) motorboat, *Svartis III*. This runs from late June to late August between 10.00 and 16.00 hours only. There is usually one boat each hour in each direction but check with Mo i Rana's tourist office for exact times because they vary. There's a kiosk and a small camping place at the jetty.

It is possible to walk all the way and avoid the boat but the path round the lake is difficult and 2–3km long. The journey by boat takes about 20 minutes. On arrival on the far side of the lake, the really hard work begins because there is a walk of some three kilometres to reach the ice.

It is advisable to be well prepared for the walk. There is no shelter whatsoever if the weather should be unkind. Much of the walk is uphill over ice-smoothed rocks which can prove a problem, especially if wet. I have seen elderly visitors turn back when less than half-way to the ice but children seem to enjoy the challenge. The ice is in retreat so hurry, the walk will only get longer in the years to come.

The glacier itself justifies the effort expended. What you are seeing is just one of 60 or more outlet glaciers, **Østerdalsisen**, which lead off Norway's second largest ice mass, **Svartisen** (Black Ice). Østerdalsisen calves into a lake.

On the ground, you see only the snout of Østerdalsisen but this will not be a disappointment. The surface of the ice may be dirty from the wind-blown

---

Svartisen

The whole of the ice-cap of Svartisen covers an area of well over 500 sq km but it is divided into two almost equal parts by a deep valley, Glomdalen. To the west is Vestisen or Engabreen but it is the eastern half, Østisen, from which this diffluent glacier spills. Each of the large ice masses is like an upturned shield occupying a vast plateau. Although they are classified as dead-ice, the caps have a well documented recent history of change.

The present size of Svartisen is approximately what it was in the late seventeenth century, but shortly afterwards accumulation exceeded ablation and the mass began to grow. The most northerly tongue, Engabreen, pushed its snout towards the coast in Holandsfjorden, overwhelming two farms in its way. Another major growth was the valley glacier, Østerdalsisen, which is the objective of this side trip. It moved south towards the lake, Svartisvatn.

This was the situation up to the beginning of the twentieth century but there has since been a fairly rapid retreat of the outlet glaciers at a rate of some 800m in the last 25 years or so. Every time I visit Svartisen it seems to have shrunk and the approach walk gets longer – or is it that I am getting older?

Soon after the start of World War II a dangerous situation developed when, for a reason not fully understood, Østerdalsisen's summer meltwater failed to discharge westward and Lake Østerdalsvatn grew. Eventually the lake itself discharged eastwards, under the glacier and Røsvassdalen flooded. A 2000m tunnel had to be built to relieve the pressure and make safe the valley floor.

The immense size of Svartisen can only be properly appreciated from the air. Flying a light aircraft over the ice-cap for the first time is an experience I shall never forget. There is an annual precipitation of up to 15m depth of lying snow and only the highest peaks, *nunatakker* (Inuit: lonely peaks) penetrate this blanket rising to over 1500m.

'rock flour', but at the edge of the ice the high-density glacier ice can be seen in ice-blue caves. Glaciers are, of course, moving masses of ice and it is dangerous – and wet – to enter the caves. Ice movement is sudden, especially in summer. You should not attempt to climb on the surface of the glacier without a guide and proper equipment. Even with an ice-axe, as I have discovered, the weak firn ice quickly breaks up under stress.

The glacier calves into the lake to give small icebergs. A calving cannot be guaranteed on a single visit but it is worth listening for the creaking, rumbling sound which heralds a massive block of ice parting company with the ice-front and plunging into the water. If you hear the sound, get the camera ready.

A visit to Svartisen, even if only for an hour or so, could be a highlight of the Arctic Highway.

2   To Melfjordbotn   Map 1d

This trip is rarely taken by tourists, but it has a lot to offer. It has only been possible since the early 1980s when the road was completed. You'll find the older parts of the road are poor in sections but the new, latter stretch is beautifully engineered.

To reach Melfjordbotn you take the same minor road off the Arctic Highway as for Svartisen (see above) but after 6km turn left on to Route 355 over a long bridge. Much of the first part of the journey is along the northern shore of Langvatnet, a lake which is fed by ice and whose waters flow into Ranaelva near the Highway, south of Røssvoll.

The lake is not continuously visible from the road but there are some small farms as well as very attractive and partly forested wilderness. Something of the isolation of the families living here can be appreciated, even in summer. The road should be driven with care, not least because the lack of traffic (you can drive the whole 40km in mid-summer and see no other vehicle) may lead to over-confidence.

After about 30km the new section of road is reached as it begins to climb up on to Melfjellet. Now the scenery is quite unusually spectacular. What you are seeing is an extensive mountain plateau at only the early stages of recovery from its complete cover by ice. This is really wild country, totally untouched and unspoilt by man. Ice-scoured and scarred rock surfaces, pools and small lakes, waterfalls and magnificent peaks – in any weather this is a thrilling place to be. To the right you can glimpse the large western ice mass of Svartisen.

Suddenly, before a steeply descending path off the plateau, the Melfjord can be seen hundreds of metres below. **Melfjordbotn** is the little village at the bottom of the slope and at the head of the fjord.

Until 1982, when this road was completed, its only link with any other community was by water. It keeps the sea connection with regular ferry services but the fishermen and their families who live here know that, in summer, they can drive to Mo i Rana if they miss the ferry. Not so in the depth of winter: the road capitulates to nature.

You can make the trip to Melfjordbotn and a visit to the limestone caves, described above, in a single day but this would be to ignore the main attraction, Svartisen.

The Highway: Røssvoll to the Polar Circle
MAPS 1–2

The E6 continues north from Røssvoll along the Rana valley with the railway for company on the other side of the river. **Storli** lies 8km along the road, where there is a **campsite** to the right of the road.

Two kilometres further on is a cluster of houses, **Nevermoen**, and in another two kilometres, to the left, is one of those surprises that enriches the experience of driving the Arctic Highway. A road off to the left leads to the spanking new **Arctic Circle Raceway**! This is a 3750m race-track which is said to meet the standards of Formula One racing. The whole concept is quite extraordinary when you remember that this is only a snowball's throw from the Polar Circle. In winter, racing is with snow scooters. In summer, everything is catered for from formula racing to saloon cars to go-karts. There's a 60-bed **motel**, conference facilities and **restaurants** (☎ 75 13 45 00). It has to be seen to be believed.

Back with reality on the E6, the Highway swings almost south as it passes through the village of **Storforshei** (24km). This is a small mining community which has grown since the working of new iron-ore deposits from 1964. The opencast quarries provided ore for Mo's steelworks but it has suffered from the demise of the industry, described earlier. It is a fairly typical mining village of undistinguished buildings and a certain untidiness. However, it is well served by shops, a **post office**, petrol station and a school.

Beyond Storforshei the Highway enters Dunderlandsdalen on its way to the Polar Circle. Although called the Dunderlandsdal this is still the valley of the Rana. The valley is generally broad with high mountains lying back from the river, road and railway. The river has cut deep terraces in the glacial deposits and it is these flats which, along with the road, have attracted small farms.

Just out of Storforshei is **Nevernes** with a church to the right of the road. A kilometre further on is **Skogly Camping**. Some ten kilometres from Storforshei is a small but interesting silversmith's workshop (to the right of the road). Silver was first mined in this area in the early seventeenth century. There is a small exhibition at the workshop and you can purchase some quite beautiful pieces of silver at very reasonable prices. It is perhaps worth noting that silversmiths often sell goods at below shop prices and, in particular, will often make a reduction if a number of pieces are bought.

As the Highway pushes on through Dunderlandsdalen you'll see the high mountains of Ørtfjellet (to the left) and Jarfjellet (to the right), rising to over 1400m and 1100m respectively. Ørtfjellet is permanently capped by ice. Although the valley is generally broad, there are narrow sections, such as at the Illhullet gorge, where road and railway come together and farming is impossible. The railway uses tunnels through the most difficult parts although the old rail line can still be detected as a ledge carrying telegraph poles.

An ambitious railway plan

In 1862, after a visit to the London Exhibition, Olsen (see p124) conceived the idea of a great international railway through northern Europe. Seeing fish arrive in London by rail from Scotland, he foresaw a time when Norway could likewise export fish to Russia. Ten years later, when he became involved in the mining of Dunderland iron ore, he wrote enthusiastically of a railway linking northern Norway with St Petersburg through Happaranda at the head of the Gulf of Bothnia. The idea, far from being ridiculed, was met with support. The London *Times* had even more visionary ideas: a continuation of the route to St Petersburg through to Peking and with a branch to India. By 1874, Olsen had produced a blueprint for his scheme. Sadly it took the Norwegian parliament another fifty years to approve a North Norway Railway. This was 1924 and two years later the 94-year-old Olsen died, some twenty years before the railway was to pass through Storvollen.

The story of the Northern Railway had a further extraordinary twist during the German occupation of Norway in World War II (see p150).

There are very few settlements that can be called villages; most of the small farms are quite isolated. The Highway rises and falls as it crosses hummocky moraine and, where the valley widens, both sides of the river are farmed with small bridges providing the necessary links. Almost all of the farming is for dairy produce. The cattle roam the roadsides and patchwork forest in summer and the land is cropped for hay to provide winter feed. There is little commercial forestry on anything but the smallest scale. There is plenty of tree cover but the land is too steep to be economically exploited. In fact about 120 hectares of trees are actually protected. This is Norway's second most northerly spruce forest. Only in Pasvik (see p299) is there a more Arctic stand of spruce.

At **Messingslett** (48km) the Highway bridges the River Rana. Before World War II there was an attractive stone-arched bridge but this was blown up during the German drive northwards towards Narvik. During the war it was replaced by a simple wooden structure; the modern bridge is post-war.

Now the Highway is on the Rana's left bank and a minor road leads away from the E6 towards the rather sad little railway village of Dunderland. Rotary blowers which are harnessed to the railway engines in winter in order to keep the line free of snow are stored here. The Highway and the railway run for a while some 60m above the river but then descend to the village of **Storvollen** (51km).

Storvollen (also Storvoll) is at the confluence of two glacial valleys, Dunderlandsdalen and Tespdalen, a meeting point characterized by terraces of glacial debris and well farmed. In the village is a monument with a bust of Ole Tobias Olsen. Olsen has been described as the father of Nordland. He was a parish priest and teacher with a passionate interest in the development of North Norway.

The first crossing of the Polar Circle

When the Highway was first built across the Saltfjell in the late 1930s it followed a path which avoided the lowest ground because of the way in which it acted as a snow trap. Instead the engineers chose the western slopes only to find them the most affected by snow throughout the winter. Had they heeded the advice of the Swedish Sami family, Blind, who regularly used the vidde to graze their reindeer, they would have selected the eastern slopes and the snow problem which caused the Highway to be closed for long periods each winter would have been greatly reduced. It was as late as 1968–9 before the road was first kept open throughout the winter months.

As soon as the Arctic Highway was opened to traffic across the Polar Circle, its tourist potential was appreciated by the local people. As early as 1937, souvenir sellers sat out in the open during the daylight hours of the tourist season. In 1956 a café-hut was erected and staffed from the nearby Høyfjellshotell. This could still be seen high above the present tourist centre on the old road until it was demolished in 1992. This simple café served the needs of travellers through the next two decades with parking on the road outside. With an increase in the number of tourists, a car-park was then built and later an untidy collection of seasonal Sami stalls were set up selling a variety of genuine and factory-made Lappish souvenirs. Perhaps this was the beginning of the end for the old café.

Just outside Storvollen the railway passes over the Highway and both begin a gentle climb through the wooded Randalselv valley. The valley sides are steep and gullied. To the left of the Highway is Ranfjellet and to the right Kjerringfjellet. Both exceed 1100m and, especially during spring, produce melt-water streams which cascade down scores of waterfalls.

Gradually the farms become less frequent and smaller. Altitude and isolation are taking their toll. In winter the small communities may still be cut off for short periods by heavy snow.

The Highway crosses the Randalselv above the Silfoss waterfall. **Krokstrand** (61km) is the last settlement before the Arctic Circle and the crossing of Saltfjell. The village is set in a clearing in the forest. Despite its pleasant setting, the village always seems a little untidy and unsure of itself. It is as though it were uncertain of its future and no one is confident enough to smarten up the village. On my last visit I could find nowhere to get fuel. There is accommodation in a motel attached to the **Krokstrand Kafe**, to the right of the Highway, with the alternatives of **Krokstrand Camping** or **Elvemøthei** 3km further up the valley.

Some 15km north of Krokstrand is a road-closure barrier. In times of severe winter weather, the Highway may be temporarily closed to traffic for almost 20km, up to the northern side of the Saltfjell.

At 600m the trees have been left behind, the road is now up on the *vidde* (plateau) and the landscape has taken on a strange lunar quality. There is a sense of exposure and nakedness: little soil and only a partial cover of peat. What little vegetation there is finds a home on the blanket of peat bog and returns to life when the snow recedes in late spring. The Saltfjell is uninhabited – there is even a restriction on the building of summer cabins – and no branch roads to tempt the driver away from the Highway.

In the 1980s a decision was taken to re-route the Highway across the Arctic Circle and the new road was completed in the early 1990s. It has transformed the important Circle crossing. Today the Highway is as broad and modern here as any section along the whole of its length. Its path is on lower ground and to the east of the old road. You can see the old Highway to the left. At the crossing of the Circle a new tourist centre has been built with a massive car-park and shrubs have been planted in soil brought from afar to landscape the surroundings. It is the new **Polarsirkel Senteret** that has caused the greatest controversy. The road is undoubtedly an improvement. It is broader, better engineered, less liable to closure and clearly meets the needs of an increasing traffic flow across the vidde, but the centre is not to everyone's taste.

The **Arctic Circle** (80km) is marked by a line of cairns and the Centre, only too clearly seen from the road, straddles this significant line of latitude of 66° 33' North. The altitude has reached almost 610m.

The controversy which surrounds the building of the Centre has little to do with its design which most would agree is pleasing enough. It is the dominance of the building and its car-parks which attracts the greatest criticism. The surrounding landscape is unspoilt, raw nature. The Centre, it has to be said, is intrusive. It is a piece of structural graffito. Something of the magic of the Polar Circle crossing and even of Saltfjellet has been lost.

In the car-park are **memorials** to Yugoslav and Russian prisoners who died working on the Arctic Highway crossing of the Saltfjell during World War II (see p55). The Yugoslav memorial is to the south of the car-park, the Russian is to the north near the entrance to the centre. Up a slope to the east of the centre is the interesting kommune monument with the local *kommune* (district) shields surrounding it.

The centre, a dome-shaped building of some individual merit, was opened in 1990. It is deceptively large inside, accommodating a **café**, shop, **museum** and a small cinema in which a regular wrap-round screen presentation of film and stills of North Norway is shown. There is a small charge to enter the building but the parking is free. You'll probably find that a stay of perhaps 30 minutes to an hour is adequate depending on the timing of the cinema show.

The new section of the Arctic Highway continues north from the Centre until the old road is re-joined close to **Stødi** (85km). This marks the watershed between north- and south-flowing streams and it is also the highest point the Highway reaches on the vidde, at just over 692m.

Now you begin a long descent through Lonsdalen. There are some splendid rapids and small falls to the right and, mirroring the situation on the southern side of the vidde, trees return to the landscape as the altitude falls. At about 600m the northern winter-closure barrier is reached (97km). An area to the east of the road has been declared a nature reserve (**Semska-Stødi Nature Reserve**). To the west of the road are marked walking trails. There are some fairly steep

road gradients but nothing to worry you, even with a caravan or trailer.

Less than 5km further, and to the right of the road, is a small **café** perched on a ledge. It is a pleasant and quieter alternative to the Polar Circle Centre. Unfortunately it doesn't seem to have very regular opening hours.

A kilometre further along a tree-lined road, a turning to the left (103km) leads up a steep path to a small railway station and the **Polarsirkelen Høyfjellshotell**. This hotel lies some 400m from the Highway and is well signposted. It would make a very good choice for a short stay if you want to explore the area of Saltfjellet. There are beautiful views of the surrounding peaks, especially eastwards towards Sweden, from close to the hotel.

Beyond the hotel turning the Arctic Highway continues its descent on an undulating course. The tree cover is thick and obscures the view of all but the highest peaks. You can see something of the bleak exposed face of Solvagtind to the north of Junkerdalen but as the valley narrows and conifers replace birch, there is little distraction from the road itself.

As Lønsdalen becomes Saltdalen there's a petrol station; a turning to the right of the Highway (112km) leads east towards Sweden. This is Route 77 (see side trip p134).

Less than a kilometre north from the junction with Route 77 is a road-condition sign which informs drivers of the state of the highway across the Saltfjell in winter. Almost immediately after the sign, on the right, is the **Saltdal Turistsenter** and nearby is **Polar Camping**. Even if you are not using these accommodation options, it is worth calling into the centre because it gives access to **Junkersdalsura** (*ur* = scree). There's a large car-park and on its eastern side is a marked path leading to the screes and to the **Junkersdal Canyon**. A quite short walk down this path is a fascinating excursion. There's a suspension bridge over the Junkerdalelv and the screes are home to rare plants, including orchids. The canyon is spectacular and it's amazing to recall that this footpath, less than 2m wide, was once the only road into the valley. This 1871 'road' is now, of course, replaced by the modern Route 77.

On the other side of the Highway to the Turistsenter is a path leading to **Kjemåfossen**, a waterfall which carries the outflow of streams draining off the Saltfjell. A further place of interest is the **Storjord Arboretum**, also to the west of the Highway here. All the trees are clearly identified.

The number of walks which can be done from the Turistsenter make it an attractive place to stay for at least one night.

Accommodation: Røssvoll to Saltdalen

The only place to stay near the Arctic Circle is the Polarsirkelen Høyfjellshotell but there are camping sites and cabins on the way up to the Saltfjell and more sophisticated accommodation on the north side of the plateau at Saltdalen.

Storli Camping (☎ 75 16 00 65) off the Highway 8km north of Røssvoll, has a beautiful setting alongside a crystal-clear river. There are cabins as well as the campsite but Storli is open only for three months, June–August.

Skogly Camping/Overnatting (☎/🖹 75 16 01 57) is some 2km north of Storforshei. Here there are twelve cabins, some of which are adapted for wheelchair users. There are electric sockets for caravans and camper vans. Skogly is open from mid-may to mid-September.

Krokstrand Kafe (☎/🖹 75 16 60 02) is in the middle of the village and has a variety of accommodation on offer, from nine double rooms and four self-catering motel rooms. It is open all year and there is a caravan parking place. It all seems a little untidy and Krokstrand Camping may be a better bet.

Krokstrand Camping (☎ 75 16 60 74), open all year, is an attractive site with 15 well equipped cabins in the shelter of trees with space for tents and camper vans. There are electric sockets for caravans.

Elvemøthi Fjellgåard (☎ 75 16 60 25) is a small camping place with five cabins, three kilometres north of Krokstrand along the river. Again, this is a none-too-tidy site. It claims to be open all year but you shouldn't bank on this.

Polarsirkelen Høyfjellshotell (☎ 75 69 41 22; 🖹 75 69 41 27) is a turning off the Highway E6 on its path down the northern side of the Saltfjell. This is the nearest you can get to staying at the Arctic Circle. The hotel is up a 400m gravel road to the left of the Highway; the turn into the car-park is to the left of this minor road. The railway station is further along the same road. Polarsirkelen is essentially a winter-sports hotel from mid-December to mid-February but the standard of accommodation and its facilities make it an attractive proposition in all seasons. All 50 rooms (six singles) have showers and prices are reasonable at NOK490 for a single including breakfast; rates are reduced when the hotel isn't busy. The hotel's a member of the Global Hotels group.

Unmissable is the ***Saltdal Turistsenter*** (☎ 75 69 41 00; 🖷 75 69 41 18). It is to the right of the Highway just after the junction with Route 77. It is remarkably large with a big shop selling provisions for anyone on a self-catering trip. There is also a **café** seating 180! Built in 1990, the centre is smart but only just escapes the description 'brash' because its accommodation is fairly discreetly hidden by trees. There are 12 cabins, each sleeping up to five people at about NOK650 per night per cabin. Each cabin is en suite, very well equipped and even has telephone and television. They are excellent. A giant camping area lies to the right of the entrance to the car-park. It consists of 120 individual plots for tents or caravans/camper vans. There is open space for children to play and a mini-golf course. The centre closes only for Christmas.

A less expensive option at Saltdalen is ***Polar Camping*** where there is camping space, caravans and cabins. It is a neat and tidy site.

SIDE TRIP FROM SALTDALEN TO SWEDEN Map 2a

Route 77 leads off the Arctic Highway at Saltdalen to travel through Junkerdalen towards Sweden. It is a short distance to the frontier and, time allowing, makes an interesting break from the Highway. The distance is 24km, or 48km for the round trip. You should allow one to one and a half hours.

This is a relatively new road. Until the mid-1970s there was no cross-border road. The Norwegian section went only 12km through the valley to Gamfossbru with a rough track extension to the Graddisfjellstue (a mountain hotel). In Sweden there was no road beyond Merkenes, some 20km or so from the border. Sweden built 100km of new road as its contribution to the project and Norway expanded and partly re-routed its existing 12km, adding a further 12km to make the link with Sweden.

The first stretch of Route 77 from the Arctic Highway is a steep and winding climb with some splendid views, first to the west and then to the east. There is an adequate number of widened sections of the road to allow for stops and enjoyment of scenery. The valley of Junkerdalen is unique in the flora it supports. A combination of mica-based soil and shelter gives a mixture of Arctic and lowland plants. This unusual combination has been protected by law since 1928. The botanic reserve has an area of over 400 sq km. There is also an interesting juxtaposition of wilderness and prosperous farming. It is a pretty and quiet valley, off the beaten track. Short of the border are

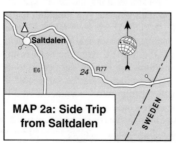

MAP 2a: Side Trip from Saltdalen

a camping site with cabins and a motel. The customs post is on the opposite side of the road. It is worth going a few kilometres beyond this point for the view, the road running through an impressive gorge.

Crossing the **border** (24km), the road becomes the Swedish Route 95. A further 365km away is Skellefteå on the Gulf of Bothnia coast.

The Highway: Saltdalen to Fauske
MAPS 2–3

From its junction with Route 77, the Arctic Highway continues on its largely tree-lined path with only the occasional clearing for forestry or farming. Much of this part of the Highway was greatly improved in the 1990s. Another of the memorials commemorating Soviet prisoners who died in forced labour on the road stands by the side of the Highway (116km). Three kilometres further on (118km) is a different memorial, this time to a certain Nieuweejaar who was an early proponent of reforestation. The valley is narrow as far as **Bleiknesmo** (125km) but, as it begins to widen, the forest has been cleared and farms stand on dry patches of terrace above the boggy river bottom. The river, Saltdalselva, is noted for its salmon and there are some pretty stretches to the left of the Highway. In the summer, the heavy bedload, brought down from the Saltfjell when spring-melt occurs, is exposed and the river is braided. The farms are isolated; there are no villages here.

At 130km is **Nordnes Camp** which is the last accommodation along the E6 before Fauske.

The first village of any note is **ov-Saltdal/Storalmenningen** (133km) where there is a small church, and about 1500m further is the beginning of an entirely new section of the Arctic Highway, known locally as Ny E6 i Saltdal (the New E6 in Saltdal). There is fuel to the left of the road here.

This new E6 section of the Highway in Saltdal is nothing if not majestic in concept. The old road served a string of ancient villages in the valley. That remains its attraction, but for the engineer the challenge of improvement could not be ignored. Hemmed in by farms and other buildings the old road defied straightening and widening so, at a cost of NOK340 million, this new section bypasses all the villages by taking the near-direct line of the Saltelv, keeping as close to the river as possible and crossing it no less than four times.

The new road departs company from the old by a 160m bridge (Almenningen Bru) taking it to the west bank of Saltelva. From here it runs tangent to the village of Røkland (see p136) before recrossing the river at Kvæle Bru. A brief stay on the east bank brings it to the next bridge (Nes Bru). Bypassing the little village of Nes, and having crossed back to the west bank, there it remains for the next nine or ten kilometres before it swings round to the right and makes its last crossing of the river by the Kvalnes bridge, fully 140m in length. Two new access roads link the new Highway with the old. The first, to the left, carries you into Medby (see p136) while the second, to the left just before Kvalnes Bru, carries you on to the old Highway just south of Rognan (see p136).

From Kvalnes Bru the new road runs along the east bank of the river before running through two short tunnels: Saltnes (465m) and then Dalmavikhaelsen

(145m). Now the old and the new Highways have merged round the innermost bay at the head of the Saltdalsfjorden towards Botn.

Although this new section of the Highway gives very good views of the river it lacks the charm of the old road. Undoubtedly the new route is the quicker alternative and an excellent example of Norwegian road building in the 1990s, but for interest the old Arctic Highway route has the edge.

The old and new Arctic Highways join at **Botn** (155km) is reached. The railway rises a few metres above the road and to its right. A signpost indicates a nearby **cemetery**; this is no ordinary graveyard and a visit involves only a kilometre detour. Turning off the Highway to the right and crossing the railway a minor road runs up a steep slope to the last resting place of over 4000 bodies,

THE OLD ROUTE

To take the old route, instead of turning left to cross the river by the Almenningen bridge (see above), stay on the east bank of the river and follow the signs to Potthus and Røkland.

At **Potthus** (also Pothus, 136km) the road bridges Saltdalselva and the railway too is crossed to bring both to the right of the road. Potthus was the scene of fierce fighting in May 1940 when the Irish Guards attempted to delay the advance of the German army en route for Narvik. (For a graphic account, see *The Doomed Expedition*, J Adams, Leo Cooper Ltd.) Today it marks the beginning of a stretch of the old Highway which is more like a country road in rural Sussex as it threads its way through a clutch of small villages: **Røkland**, **Venesmoen** and **Kvæle**. Farms and other houses stand close to the road and with a combination of farm vehicles, children and other pedestrians using it, you should exercise care in driving this section. A minor road leads off to the east at Potthus and continues a short distance, through the Flågan ravine, before reaching the very beautiful Evensdal valley. If using this road, take the right fork after about 2500m. This road stops short of the mountains after some 12km but there are marked mountain paths beyond.

Today, this part of Saltdalen has a general air of prosperity. In its long history – the area has been well settled for centuries – it has had changing fortunes. In the past, its claim to fame and fortune was its boat building but this industry declined in the early years of this century leading to a fall in population through emigration. The construction of boats continues here but no longer dominates. Other forest products such as fibreboard have grown in importance as have service industries.

At **Medby** a new and improved road, Route 812, leads off to the left of the Highway and provides an alternative path to Bodø. Although the distance to Bodø, 100km, is almost the same as that described on p142 using the Arctic Highway and Route 80, the 812 is slower because of its more mountainous, winding route. All the same it is a picturesque road with added attractions such as the Graddstraumen maelstrom (a rival to Saltstraumen, see p142) at Skjerstad and a magnificent bridge crossing the Saltfjord as the road links with Route 17 on its final kilometres into Bodø.

The old Arctic Highway continues beyond the junction with Route 812 into **Rognan**, a substantial village at the head of Saltdalsfjorden, the most easterly arm of Skjerstadfjord. In 1940 Rognan was already a regional centre; for the Highway, it was also an important ferry point. Construction of the road northwards had been inhibited by the almost sheer mountain walls which plunge into the Saltdalsfjord north and east of Rognan. This was a difficult engineering problem and the ferry none Norwegian. There are two cemeteries side by side. Buried here are 1657 Yugoslavs and 2732 Germans, all victims, in contrasting circumstances, of World War II. The chapel was closed the last time I visited but the story behind these burials is worth contemplating.

Below the hill and the cemetery, the Arctic Highway continues northwards along the edge of the fjord on a path blasted out of the cliff face. This is still part of the new, improved road although it remains on the same route as the old Highway. Having circled round the bay, and reaching **Saksenvik**, the new route again leaves the old to enter a tunnel just 1148m in length quickly followed by another short tunnel, the 183m **Setsåshøgda**. The old ferry point of Langset is bypassed but there are good views to Rognan which you can see against a

---

❏ **THE OLD ROUTE (continued)**

between Rognan and Langset bridged the gap in the Highway. Work on the Arctic Highway to eliminate this twenty-minute ferry had begun before the war but the German occupying army, using forced labour, made its completion a priority and within twelve months the ferry was no longer needed.

Rognan is a good service village for travellers on the old Highway but is otherwise undistinguished apart from an interesting church, built in 1862. However, not to be missed is the **Blood Road Museum** (see p139). The road runs straight and quietly through the village on an easterly path before it turns northwards along the steep fjord edge. The railway keeps it company but is forced to tunnel through the more difficult promontories. The Highway has been re-constructed along the edge of Saltdalsfjorden and this is where the old and new (see above) highways merge. Travellers coming from the north can choose between the old and new routes here.

Just before the junction on the edge of Rognan is a very interesting collection of reconstructed old houses, barns and a schoolhouse. The oldest is from 1680 but most are nineteenth century. This is the **Saltdal Historical Museum** (☎ 75 69 06 60) on the site of an eighteenth-century farm, Skippergården. The old schoolhouse (from 1899) has original desks and teaching materials. Local children are brought here to experience something of life over two hundred years ago. In one of the old buildings is a café with lace cloths on the tables. A British connection is seen in the cabin taken from the *Quest,* the vessel which carried Sir Ernest Shackleton to the Antarctic. When the ship was rebuilt in Rognan in the 1920s, Shackleton's cabin was replaced but the original preserved in the museum.

Also here is a monument to a prominent politician, Erling Engon (1910–1982).

Accommodation on the old Highway

If taking the old Highway's route there are accommodation options which will be missed on the new route.

Nordlandia Hotel (☎ 7569 00 11; 🖻 75 69 13 72; 🖳 rognan@norlandia.no) is in the middle of Rognan. This is the expensive option with singles at NOK995 and doubles at NOK1195, though it's cheaper at weekends (about NOK300 less). This is a smart place to stay. The rooms are well appointed and there is a sauna, solarium, a cafeteria and a restaurant that stays open until 02.00. On the downside, there is no adequate parking. Very much cheaper are the cabins and camping facilities at *Medby Camping* (☎ 75 69 03 15) in the village of the same name. Run by Inge Jansen, this camp, away from the Highway, makes a good retreat.

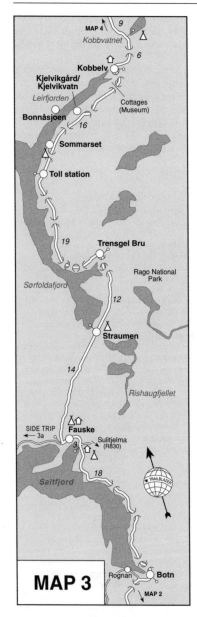

mountain backdrop. Two kilometres further is yet another tunnel, the 1747m Kvængflåg.

The exit from the tunnel marks the end of the Saltdal Highway improvement. Signposted to the left is Leviset, home of what is believed to be a four-hundred-year-old **Sami ritual site**. Two stone slabs stand inside a circular mound.

As the Highway turns around a small bay, Fauskevika, there is **Fauske Camping** (171km). Two kilometres further is an important junction with Route 830 (173km) at the small port of **Finneid**. The 830 leads off to the right of the Highway and eastwards to **Sulitjelma** (36km from the junction with a quarter of the distance in three long and one short tunnels). The path of the road follows the railway line which pre-dates the road and leads to the former copper mines of Sulitjelma, an unlovely little settlement whose future is now in question.

It is from the Arctic Highway's junction with Route 830 that a new bypass is proposed to carry the E6 around the north-eastern outskirts of Fauske. This new section, planned but lacking funding, would be some 3km in length; 2.4km will be through a single tunnel. When opened this will save time rather than distance. After rejoining the present Highway just north of the town the bypass will continue westward to link up with Route 80 just to the west of Fauske. This will enable traffic to use the Highway and Route 80 for journeys to Bodø (see p142) without passing through Fauske. All this is pretty unlikely in the next decade. The present path of the Highway remains

The Blood Road

In June 1942 three German troop-ships set out from Stettin on the southern Baltic coast with 8000 Yugoslav prisoners. These were industrial prisoners who had been rounded-up without warning and with no knowledge that their destination was to be the Arctic. Wearing their best clothes and carrying what few possessions they had been allowed to keep, they embarked for northern Norway. They arrived in summer when conditions were bearable and large numbers were brought to this district of Saltden to improve the Arctic Highway by completing the Rognan to Langset section (see p137) and by keeping the trans-Circle route open throughout the winter. The first of these tasks they accomplished. The second proved impossible. The prisoners were housed in crowded camps often without food and with totally inadequate clothing for the long Arctic winter. Disease, especially TB, claimed hundreds of lives; others died of malnutrition, were summarily executed or died from constant beatings. The people of Saltden who are old enough to remember still have horrifying stories to tell, none more poignant than that of the young Yugoslav who mistook the time of day and opened the door of his prison hut before the appointed hour. He was shot dead.

The local Norwegian population, especially the women, did what they could by taking food to the prisoners but were powerless to prevent this local holocaust in which less than 1000 of the 8000 prisoners survived.

Here in the cemetery at Botn, the Yugoslavian section is now neatly kept by those who remember. The German area is altogether more grand. There is a small chapel of remembrance with a visitors' book. The German graves are individually numbered and a clear record has been kept. The Yugoslavs were buried in a mass grave, no names, not even a number. Theirs is the dignity of the unknown.

In 1995 the Arctic Highway was officially recognized as the Blodvei (Blood Road) and a museum was opened in Rognan (see p136). Part of the museum is in an old German army camp. Called **Blodveimuseet**, the museum contains artefacts, photographs and reconstructions from those terrible times. This shameful period of the Arctic Highway's development is vividly portrayed here. It was not only Yugoslavs who were involved in the slave labour; Russian and Polish prisoners were also forced to work on the Highway. A total of 18 prison camps were in Saltdal alone. Despite the enormous loss of life, there were no less than 34,000 prisoners who survived to see peace come to Norway and the Highway. The museum is only open between mid-June and mid-August and only in the afternoons at weekends. I believe these rather limited visiting schedules are being reconsidered. There is a NOK 20 admission charge.

through **Fauske** (176km) reached by swinging around the bay. From the middle of the town, it then branches northward on the next leg, to Narvik.

Accommodation: Saltdalen to Fauske

Before reaching Fauske, there is just one campsite on the new Highway and there are further options along the road to Bodø (see side trip, p142).

Nordnes Camp (☎ 75 69 38 55; 🖹 75 69 39 60; 🖳 post@nordnescamp.no) is reached just before the new section of the Highway where it bypasses Rognan. A small but well equipped group of cabins, permanent caravans and tent sites, it has the convenience of a shop and café.

On the southern edge of Fauske just 3km before the town centre is *Fauske Camping and Motell* (☎ 75 64 84 01; ▤ 745 64 84 13; ▤ fausm@online.no). The motel has just six double self-catering rooms at NOK550 per room. There are 44 cabins for which the charge is NOK200 for doubles and NOK900 for large 8-person cabins. The 19 larger cabins are en suite. There is plenty of space for caravans and camper vans. This is a well managed camp nicely set among birch trees.

FAUSKE

Fauske is an important route centre: the junction of routes E6 and R80, and the junction of the old mineral railway line from Sulitjelma and the main line to Bodø.

It is also the town from which you can access a bus service which offers you the opportunity to travel the rest of the Highway, to Kirkenes, in three easy stages (see p111). You'll find the **bus station** (☎ 75 64 30 11) is by the T-junction where the Highway turns north and the E80 leads off to Bodø.

History

The town was almost totally destroyed in a bombing raid in May 1940 but has been completely rebuilt and continues to expand. As well as being an important municipal and educational centre there are a number of industries. One of the better known, internationally, is the preparation of marble which is quarried locally. Some of Fauske's marble graces the United Nations building in New York. The **Rådhus** (town hall), which is to the north of the Highway in the centre of Fauske, has examples of pink marble. A variety of marble products is available for sale at **Ankerske Naturstein** (☎ 75 60 01 50) to the left of the Highway as you enter the town.

Services

Fauske may be a good place to take a break from driving the Highway, especially if the journey from Mo i Rana has been completed in one go. Most of the services are along the Highway and its continuation, Route 80, here called Storgata (High Street) or on its parallel street, Sjøgata, which runs along the fjord's edge. There is a helpful **tourist office** (☎ 75 64 33 03; ▤ 75 64 32 38; ▤ salten.reiseliv@online.no) to the right of the Highway as you enter the town (almost opposite the Fauske Hotel). From

mid-June to late September it opens from 08.30 until 19.30 but closes at 16.00 during the rest of the year. I was able to pick up and send emails here but I'm not sure if this service is always available! The **library** certainly does have free internet access.

The **post office** (☎ 75 64 38 55) is on the left of the R80 (Storgt) as it goes towards Bodø. There are shops of every kind and a number of vehicle service stations. In common with most modern Norwegian towns, Fauske has an excellent sports centre, **Fauske Fritidssenter** (☎ 75 64 45 00). It is to the west of the town off Route 80 on the left by the fjord edge. There's an impressive range of facilities from billiards to international-standard indoor tennis courts. It is open from 11.00 to 23.00.

Around town

For something of intellectual interest, there is the **Fauske Museum**, situated at the western end of Sjøgata in a park alongside the fjord. There is a marble and aluminium sculpture of a boathouse by Per Barclay (1995) but the main museum has some 3000 exhibits. The rather eclectic collection includes wartime artefacts, textiles (said to be the best in Nordland), telecom equipment and farm implements. It's open all year. The opening hours are longer in summer than winter when it is closed at the weekend. Admission is NOK15 (☎ 75 64 46 98).

If staying in the town for any length of time, it is possible to drive 36km up Route 830 to **Sulitjelma**. This is an interesting old copper-mining town. The whole place has become something of a museum since the mining stopped in 1991. The surrounding area is wonderfully wild. Accommodation is possible at the *Sulitjelma Hotel* (☎ 75 64 04 01) or at *Sulitjelma Camping and Fritidssenter* (☎ 75 64 04 33).

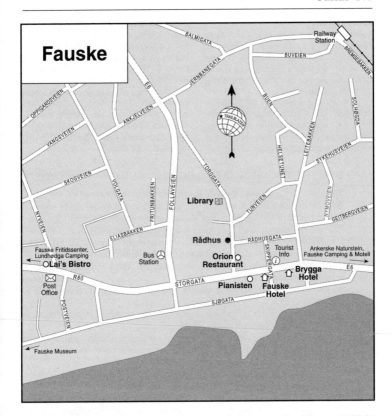

Accommodation

There is less choice than one might expect in Fauske and there's a real temptation to go on to Bodø especially if you want to use a hotel. *Fauske Hotel* (☎ 75 64 38 33; 🖷 75 64 57 37; 🖳 firmapost@fauskehotell.no) is the top accommodation in town. It has a central position on the Highway almost opposite the tourist office. There are 92 rooms including 12 singles; all are en suite. Most simply have showers but a few also have baths. The best rooms overlook the fjord. The hotel's open all year and although without any special merit it is comfortable enough. Prices are about NOK800 for doubles and NOK675 for singles. Close to the Fauske Hotel and under the same management is the summer hotel *Brygga* (☎ 75 64 63 45; fax and email same as Fauske Hotel). This is a cheaper option but it's more of a popular pub than a hotel and is open only from June to mid-August.

Off the road to Bodø (R80) and only just over 2km from the town centre is *Lundhøgda Camping* (☎ 75 64 39 66; 🖷 75 64 92 49; 🖳 lundhogda@c2i.net). The site lies to the left of the R80, going west, and some way from it by the fjord's edge. The very pleasant camp has 36 cabins, a store and a café. Some of the cabins are en suite and all are well equipped but bedclothes are not provided. There's ample room for tents and caravans. Payment can be by credit card. The camp is closed October–March.

Where to eat
There is a large restaurant in the *Fauske Hotel* with an à la carte menu. There's usually a band, except on Sunday, or you can go to the basement nightclub. The restaurant in the *Brygga Hotel* is comparatively downmarket but cheaper.

The *Pianisten* (☎ 75 64 36 21) is further west down Storgt from the Fauske Hotel but on the same side of the road. As the name suggests, it's a piano bar, but has a restaurant too. It may seem a little dark

inside and rather scruffy outside, but it does have Elvis impersonators as a consolation.

On Torggata, to the north of Storgt, the Highway, is the *Orion Pizzarestaurant* (☎ 75 64 66 60), opposite the Kino (cinema). This is more of a pub-cum-café than a restaurant but it's popular with Fauske's younger set. The café serves pasta and snacks as well as pizza. Almost opposite the post office on the R80 towards Bodø is *Lai's Bistro and Restaurant* (☎ 75 64 70 44) which specializes in oriental dishes.

SIDE TRIP FROM FAUSKE TO BODØ   Map 3a

The journey from Fauske to **Bodø** is 63km (126km for the round trip). It might be a day's outing from Fauske, or you can make use of Bodø's wide range of accommodation for a night's stay. Whatever you decide, it's worth the effort because the journey itself is of interest as is the destination.

The road is Route 80. This is a fjord route along the inner Skjerstadfjord and outer Saltfjorden. Its main attractions are the Saltstraumen and the town of Bodø. Although the road keeps fairly close to the fjord's coastline and thus is winding, it was greatly improved in the 1980s and is now a good quality route almost without gradient. There may be quite heavy traffic at certain times in the day.

The railway, here on its final stretch, follows an almost identical route to the road except between Røsvik and Straumsnes.

You'll have good views to the south of the high mountains which include Børvasstinden (1176m), and some views to the north of Kistrandfjellet only slightly lower and still over 1000m.

The road initially follows closely the edge of Klungsetvika and the Skjerstadfjord. This is quite a difficult path and only a narrow ledge is available above the steep shore. Turning north on Route 80 leads across the neck of the boggy Alvnes promontory before passing through **Valnesfjord** (18km). Side roads to the right take you round an attractive lake, Valnesvatnet.

From Valnesfjord, the road passes through more open country and farmland as far as Mjønes when, again, it has to rely upon a narrow fjord-side ledge for its path. After **Vågen** (36km) the road moves away from the coast and cuts across the partly drained marshland of Tverlandet peninsula. At **Løding** (44km) there is the junction with the important Route 17. A short detour down this road is well worthwhile.

Just 13km down Route 17 is the **Saltstraumen Eddy**, one of the world's strongest maelstroms. Four times a day, 80,000 million gallons of water foam and swirl through a strait only 150m wide and 45m deep. The strait links the open Saltfjord with the inner Skjerstadfjord. The tourist offices in Fauske or Bodø will provide timings of this phenomenon but it is seen at its best on the incoming current of a spring tide. Ships have been known to be smashed to pieces on the rocks when caught in the whirlpools and gulls circle overhead ready to dive on the thousands of fish which follow the bait-fish sucked into the sound.

Cones (red balls by day and lights by night) are hoisted on each side of the strait when the current is too strong for cargo ships. Passenger ferries used to have to wait for the calmer waters which follow the maelstrom but modern roads and bridges have made these boats obsolete.

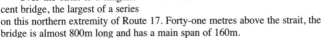

MAP 3a: Side Trip from Fauske

Over the strait is a magnificent bridge, the largest of a series on this northern extremity of Route 17. Forty-one metres above the strait, the bridge is almost 800m long and has a main span of 160m.

Returning to Route 80, en route for Bodø, the road continues north out of Løding before turning west along a narrow ledge backed by steep hills. For its final stretch it uses a broader coastal terrace where farms and forest compete as far as Bodø. Just ten kilometres before the town, at **Bertnes** (53km), a small road leads down to the fjord and a burial mound dating from the Iron Age. Early settlers in North Norway, having moved up the coast from the south, are known to have made their home here as long ago as AD200.

BODØ

Bodø is a town that increases in importance as the years go by. Its modern growth dates from after World War II; its earlier history was one of mixed fortunes.

History

In 1803 a group of merchants from Trondheim set up a trading post on the peninsula thrusting westward into the open sea. The site was well chosen with protection given by two rugged off-shore islands, Store and Lille Hjartøy.

By 1816 the settlement housed a hundred or so souls and was granted the status of a town with an administrative role over the Bodøgård estate. The aim was to make Bodø a major fish-exporting centre for the fylke of Nordland. This proved wildly over-optimistic. However, by chance, from 1864 to the late 1890s there was an unaccountable increase in the herring population of the local waters. The town grew ten-fold in this period to a substantial 3000 but fell again when, equally unaccountably, the herring decided to move south.

To compensate for the lack of herring, the export of Sulitjelma's copper ores (see p50) helped to sustain the town's economy

in the first half of the twentieth century but it was necessary to exploit its administrative and commercial importance in order to prevent a decline in population.

Comparable with Bodø's misfortune in losing its herring shoals was its almost total destruction in World War II. The scene of a major withdrawal of Allied forces, in the early evening of 27 May 1940 Bodø was almost completely destroyed in a rain of German incendiary bombs. The wooden buildings burnt furiously, fanned by a strong on-shore wind. Even the hospital, on high ground and clearly marked with red crosses, was reduced to ashes.

The post-war reconstruction saw concrete replace wood for most of the larger buildings. New buildings still seem to sprout in Bodø like flowers in spring. One of the recent improvements has been in the harbour area where an attractive marina has been built. The air of prosperity in the town is almost tangible. It has made very good use of the benefits of its position as the major town of Nordland, its service industries, its importance to NATO and its role as a leading academic town. Bodø is, of course, also a communications hub.

Services

Route 80 runs through 10km of built-up area as it makes towards the sentrum via Sjøgata. The town's **tourist office** is alongside the Diplomat Hotel on the east side of the road on Sjøgata and there are parking spaces signposted nearby. The office is open all year (☎ 75 52 60 00).

As befits a town of Bodø's importance, there's a wealth of shops and cafés.

Around town

Off Sjøgata, beyond the tourist office is Torvgate which leads to the imposing Town Hall (**Rådhuset**). Turning right after passing the building will take one to the **Domkirke** (cathedral). This basilica was built after the wartime destruction of the town and completed in 1956. It is an impressive building, not least for its pillar-less nave and beautiful rose window. Behind the altar is a stained-glass picture of the Ascension of Christ. It is a full twelve metres high. A separate tower stands alongside the cathedral's main building.

The other noteworthy church in Bodø is in the district of **Bodin** to the south-east of the centre. Part of this church dates from the thirteenth century and survived the bombing. The carvings are exquisite and it is worth the short journey from the town centre; check opening hours with the tourist office. The cathedral closes at 15.00. (When in Scandinavia, you soon learn that closing time for many buildings is as early as three or four o'clock in the afternoon.)

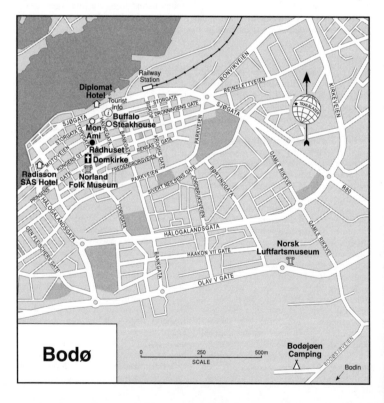

Across the road from the cathedral is the **Nordland Folk Museum** in Prinsens gate. This is one of Bodø's oldest buildings and houses some interesting exhibits which show something of the life and times of old Bodø, especially as a fishing settlement. There is also an exhibition of Sami culture. The museum has an open-air section alongside the Bodøjøen camping site (see below).

Very different is the modern and fascinating **Norsk Luftfartsmuseum**. Take a left turn off the R80 as you come into central Bodø on to Olav V gate; the museum is about 500m on the right. Built on the site of the WWII German airfield, the museum seems to have everything one can think of to do with aviation. There are aircraft from the past and the present and even a flight simulator that can be tried out. It isn't a place just for aviation buffs – only those with no imagination should stay away! There's a **café** and shop as part of the museum.

On the northern side of the town (take the road signposted Route 834) about 3km from the centre is Rønvikfjellet, a hill some 150m above sea-level with a **restaurant** at the top. It is an ideal point to view the distant south-east extremities of the Lofoten Islands, the nearby Landegode Islands and, at the right time of year and in good weather, the midnight sun. The full disc of the sun is visible from 3 June to 8 July but only when cloud permits.

Accommodation

There is a greater variety and number of hotels here than in any other town on or near the Arctic Highway, except Tromsø. In addition to eight hotels there are a number of small guesthouses and two campsites. Only the three largest hotels are described. It is especially important to book ahead because Bodø is a major business centre.

Top of the range is the *Diplomat Hotel* (☎ 75 54 70 00; 🖹 75 54 70 55; 🖃 hotel@ diplomat-hotel.no) where prices will be over NOK1000 but you can be assured of luxury. It is on Sjøgt near the fjord and by the tourist office.

A less expensive alternative, on Storgt, is the *Radisson SAS Hotel* (☎ 75 52 41 00; 🖹 75 52 74 93; 🖃 sales@radissonsas.com) with nearly 200 rooms. Rooms, except on the executive floor (Royal Club) are not especially large but it is otherwise a very comfortable place to stay, with lots of facilities.

A cheap self-catering option is *Bodøjøen Camping* (☎ 75 56 36 80; 🖹 75 56 46 89) which is open all year. The camp has 45 cabins. It is near the Bodin Church so not far from the centre of town, and payment can be made by credit card. Also close by is an open-air museum.

Contact details of other options are:
Best Western Hotel (☎ 75 75 54 53 00; 🖹 75 52 42 66; 🖃 central.hotel@nl.telia.no)
Bodø Hotel (☎ 75 54 77 00; 🖹 75 52 57 78; 🖃 booking@bodohotell.no)
Comfort Home Hotel Grand (☎ 75 54 61 00; 🖹 75 54 61 50; 🖃 unni.olsen@comfort.choicehotels.no)
Norrøna Hotel (☎ 75 52 55 50; 🖹 75 52 33 88; 🖃 elsa.karlsen@radissonsas.com)
Bodø Gjestegård (☎ 75 52 04 02; 🖹 75 52 04 02; 🖃 johnst@online.no)
Midnattsol Gjestegård (☎ 75 50 49 00)

Where to eat

There are over fifty restaurants and cafés – excluding those in the hotels! The range is impressive, from the *Buffalo Steakhouse* (☎ 75 52 15 40), on Havnegt to *Mon Ami* (☎ 75 52 24 80), on Glasshuset where – no surprise – the menu features French dishes. There are plenty of pizza restaurants but a better bet is to try the superb fresh-fish dishes which are available at most of the better establishments.

PART 5: FAUSKE TO NARVIK

The Highway: Fauske to Ulsvåg
MAPS 3–4

The Arctic Highway strikes north-east out of Fauske on its long journey to Nordland's second city, Narvik. This is an interesting section of the Highway's path with some excellent scenery. It is also the first of the three legs of the **express bus service** which links Fauske (and Bodø) with Kirkenes. The bus leaves Fauske from the terminal in Follaveien. This is part of the Highway as it turns north in central Fauske. The bus station is to the left immediately after the T-junction linking the E6 to Route 80. The bus arrives in Narvik less than six hours after leaving Fauske.

Once through the industrial suburbs, whether travelling by bus or car, the journey along the Highway from Fauske carries you across the Fauskeidet (*eid* = isthmus). Perhaps the least interesting stretch of the Highway to Narvik, this flat neck of land links the Saltfjord to the Sørfoldafjord. Its flatness leaves it ill-drained and even marshy but land improvement has enabled a number of farms to line the road and forestry is also practised. Fauskeidet is wide enough to carry other roads parallel to the Arctic Highway and numerous linking minor roads lead off the Highway to the left and right. You can see some quarries, chiefly marble, to the left of the road while to the east rises Rishaugfjellet, a somewhat strange-looking conical mountain whose steep bare sides are often free of snow even in midwinter. In summer, however, its summit, at almost 850m, is cold enough to develop a banner cloud on its lee side giving it the appearance of a smoking volcano.

At **Vargåsen** (8km), the Arctic Highway swings towards the east at its junction with Route 826. This road was the original path of the Highway making towards Røsvik where, until the early 1960s, if you were travelling north you had to cross the Sørfoldafjord by ferry to Bonnåsjøen. About a kilometre north of Vargåsen, a road leads off to the right to Grønnås and the Highway makes a gentle ascent above the valley floor as the river broadens before it flows into Sørfolda.

There is industry here. With an impertinent incongruity, factory chimneys break the horizon at the fjord and belch white smoke into the otherwise pure Arctic air. These are part of the Valljord ferro-silicate works, Elken Salten Verk. In simple economic terms, this is a perfect site for such a plant. The raw materials can be shipped in along the fjord and six kilometres away to the east is a large hydro-electric power station, at Siso, to supply the energy needs. Taking a more aesthetic view, the factory is something of an eyesore even though it is dwarfed by the scale of the landscape in which it is set.

On the Highway, you cross the outlet from a substantial lake, Straumvatnet, as it runs into the Sørfoldafjord. The village here, **Straumen** (14km), lies to the right of the Highway, the turning just before the bridge. It is a pretty little village with a cluster of shops and services. There is also accommodation at **Strømhaug Camping**.

From Straumen, the Highway's relatively modern path begins a section characterized by some finely engineered tunnels and bridges. For the next 40km or so the Highway carefully negotiates its way around the fjord Sørfolda. It reaches the fjord first by way of a rising, curving path before falling towards the sea. The road was literally blown out of the rock face which forms the fjord's edge.

All of the tunnels reach or exceed the standard four metres height and most are well lit. However, you should take care using all tunnels in Norway. The tunnels on the E6 are hewn out of the rock leaving bare, unlined sides and roofs. Only where the phenomenon known as rock bursting is likely or where there is the possibility of excessive water seepage is there any lining. Stopping is, of course, prohibited and you are expected to dip headlamps for oncoming traffic. The very occasional cyclist can easily be lost in the general gloom but, in these cave-like tunnels, it is trolls that you'll expect to see hiding in the rocky crevices.

Surrounding this tunnel section of the Highway are some prominent high fjells. To the east the land rises to over 1000m but you can see little from the road. The peaks to the west, only just below the 1000m mark, are more visible when the road leaves the tunnels and there are views across the fjord. The peaks are cloaked in a snowy blanket by early winter but in summer the snow is gone and the mountain-sides are streaked with silvery waterfalls.

The 1960s' series of bridges and tunnels, costing, at 1960s' prices, NOK58 million, starts with the Torfjorden bridge. As the Highway skirts round the eastern edge of Sørfolda, climbs a ridge and then drops down it arrives at the bridge which spans the fjord-head. You travel along the water's edge before the Highway next runs through a relatively short (386m) and absolutely straight tunnel, the Megården. On emerging, the Highway skirts round a narrow branch of the Torfjord, Nordfjorden, and then into Tennflåget tunnel (800m). At the northern exit, after a short road section, the road crosses the longest (approximately 180m) of the many bridges in this section, Trensgel Bru (*bru* = bridge, 26km).

There is a minor road to the right at the bridge. It leads, partly by a tunnel, to Lakshola some 6km away and from here there is access to the **Rago National Park**. This is contiguous with two Swedish national parks across the border: Sarek and Stora Sjøfallet. These parks are good examples of Scandinavian wilderness at its most attractive.

After the Trensgel Bru, the Highway rises to 75m before entering two more tunnels, Daumannvik (822m long) and Løkthaugen (725m). Now the Highway is crossing a spur between Torfjorden and the Aspfjord. Here, after a short tunnel, at **Gyltvik** (34km), there is a shop but the old fuel station is closed. To the side of the Highway the hummocky glacial headland is farmed around **Kvarv** while, to the right of the road, mountain lakes rest like jewels enclosed by tree-covered slopes.

North of Gyltvik you go through the short 40m Eva tunnel before entering the Aspfjorden tunnel, the second longest of the series and one with a steady gradient. This tunnel, running for 1496m, winds down to sea-level. The Highway leaves it to cross a small bridge before quickly returning to the longest of all the section's tunnels, the Kalvik (2700m). This tunnel has been cut through the headland to the Leirfjord arm of Sørfolda. It is straight and level and, because of its length, has five lay-bys in case of breakdowns. When the Highway breaks out of the tunnel you are alongside the fjord shore.

Now there are another seven tunnels along the following section of the Highway and these are preceded by a **toll station** (45km). New roads in Norway, especially those involving expensive tunnels and bridges, are often partly financed through toll charges for some years after their construction. The charges here are: motorcycle, NOK29; car, NOK40; car plus trailer, NOK55; car plus caravan, NOK90.

This comparatively new section of the Highway, which includes some tunnelling originally intended for a railway (see p150), is explained by the previous path of the road. Until 1986–7, the Highway slipped down to the fjord shore at **Sommarset**, almost half-way along Leirfjorden. From here a ferry sailed down and across the fjord to Bonnåsjøen. This 15-minute ferry journey had succeeded the longer Røsvik-Bonnåsjøen route just twenty years earlier and it had long been the plan to replace the ferry entirely by a bridge or a road. There might be some regrets about the passing of this short water section on the Highway's route north. Only from the ferry could you appreciate the magnificence of the fjord's setting. To the north-west rise Rismålsfjellet and Grønfjellet matched to the south-east by Sommarsettinden. These mountains, often clothed in snow and shrouded by cloud, so dominate the deep waters of the fjord that to cross it is like sailing on the waters of a deep well.

The case for a replacement for the ferry lay largely in the difficult path for the Highway beyond Bonnåsjøen. In fact, from across the water at Sommarset it seems as though there is no way through the mountain wall on the northern shore. The old road had to climb steeply away from the water's edge and up through the narrow and winding Bonnelv valley. This was a difficult stretch for the Arctic Highway, especially in winter. The altitude, combined with the narrowness of the valley, made it a snow trap and winter closures were common.

As elsewhere along the Arctic Highway, the re-routed road actually adds to the distance travelled. From Bonnåsjøen to Sildhopen is 18km but the new road is 11km longer. This extra distance, costing NOK1,000,000 per kilometre, is justified by the easy driving and all-weather route it offers. It is a triumph of engineering. In fact a third of the journey to Sildhopen is out of sight through these finely cut rocky burrows.

The first tunnel you meet is Berrflåget (1400m). The little village of Sommarset is now bypassed but as you leave the tunnel there is another of the many war memorials that are found along the Highway's length. To the left of the road is a plaque commemorating eleven Russian prisoners of war who were shot here by the occupying German army during World War II. The simplicity of the memorial adds to its poignancy. The plaque was placed by the prisoners' comrades.

Just before this point is a turning (left) down to the old Sommarset ferry point. There is a **campsite** in the village.

The next tunnel, Kannflåget, is reached over a slight rise followed by a fall in the road through a broad valley with a lake to the right of the road. Although rather less than 800m long, the tunnel has quite a steep ascent.

As the road leaves the tunnel it continues through a narrow defile and climbs steeply in a landscape of rocks and scattered trees. The next tunnel, Gleflåget, is the shortest of the seven, only a little more than 500m. Again the tunnel is cut to facilitate the climb upwards and, shortly after the road breaks out into the open again, it reaches its highest point near **Kjelvikgård** (55km). The lake here, Kjelvikvatn, is peculiarly placid in its rocky setting.

About 2km after leaving the Gleflåget tunnel to the left of the road is **Husmannsplasen** or the cotters' homestead. This little open-air museum consists of peasant cottages with turf roofs (see below). There are guided tours in summer costing NOK30 for adults with children charged half price. It is open from late June to late August. The sour-cream waffles and coffee available here make a stop even more attractive.

Continuing along the Highway, there is a descent towards the next tunnel, Rauhammaren. There are views across Leirfjord, to the left, and when the sun

---

Kjelvik's cottages

For a wonderful insight into a way of life now gone, stop for a while at Husmannsplasen (Kjelvik's cottages). What is more remarkable is that, belying appearances, you are looking back not centuries but less than forty years. The tenancy finally fell vacant only in 1967 on the death of the last farmer to work the land near here. The site had been occupied for 220 years.

In 1967, there was no Arctic Highway here (the E6 was re-routed to its present path only in 1986) and the tenants of Kjelvik saw the boat and the fjord as their sole means of communication. Everything they needed had to be carried up from the fjord a distance of almost two kilometres and a climb of 300m. The only alternative was a trek over the hills to Sommarset or to Sørfjord at the head of the fjord. For these even longer journeys a horse was often used. The isolation of the cottages is difficult to imagine in modern Norway but was the way of life here until the late 1960s.

The exhibits are simply the everyday furnishings, the goods and chattels of the cottages, just as they were. Particularly interesting are old farm implements, some over 200 years old. It is possible to examine everything in the buildings without constraint.

The old paths used by the cotters have been cleared to allow you to experience even more of the surroundings. On the last Saturday that the 'museum' is open (the third or fourth Saturday in August) it becomes a working farm for the day. The mill is put to use, butter is churned, the kitchen produces griddle cakes and the blacksmith is at work in the smithy. This is the day to be at the Cotters' homestead and to enjoy a bowl of sour-cream porridge.

shines, you can see a string of houses on the other side of the fjord reflected in its deep, dark waters. The road, remaining high above the water, slips into the tunnel and the view is lost. For the next 1250m or so, you see nothing but bare rock, dimly lit in the shadowy confines of the tunnel. After leaving the tunnel, the Highway continues its descent to the head of Leirfjord.

In just 200m the Arctic Highway (61km) reaches **Kobbelv** where there is fuel, a shop and, to the left, a modern restaurant and accommodation at the **Kobbelv Verthus**, which overlooks the Sørfjord head of the Leirfjorden. By the side of the hotel is an exhibition on the theme of the **Northern Wartime Railway**. Close by is one of the old railway tunnels. Across the fjord the old ferry point at Bonnåsjøen can be seen.

Beyond Kobbelv is an 830m tunnel, Kobbhammaren. This takes the Highway under the headland which separates Sorfjord from the arm of Leirfjord at Elvkroken.

The Northern Wartime Railway

The story of the **Northern Wartime Railway** is one of quite extraordinary audacity bordering on fanaticism. It is told in the Kobbelv Verthus exhibition of photographs covering the time of the German occupation of Norway to the present day.

In World War II, the Germans were anxious to extend the railway beyond the Mosjøen–Mo i Rana section which had virtually been completed before they invaded Norway. The Dunderland line could be linked but the ambition of the occupying force was to take the railway to Fauske and then onwards to Narvik. From there it could be linked to the Swedish iron-ore fields which were feeding the German war machine (see p163). An even more incredible aim was to continue the railway beyond Narvik to Kirkenes. This would have been a railway to rival today's Arctic Highway.

The scheme was overseen by Fritz Todt, who had masterminded the pre-war autobahn network in Germany as well as the construction of the Siegfried Line.

The railway never did get built beyond Fauske. The task was enormously over-ambitious even allowing for the fact that thousands of prisoners of war were used as slave labour and further hundreds of Norwegian forced-labour prisoners were drafted in from as far away as Oslo. The conditions these workers endured have already been touched on in connection with the building of the Highway (p139). Here, 1,200 died out of a labour force of 11,000. The brutality was reminiscent of that experienced by prisoners of the Japanese working on the Burma Railway, yet the Norwegian story is hardly known.

Albert Speer took over the project when Todt died in 1942 but the railway line was defeated by the twin forces of nature and the Allied armies.

The whole concept was probably doomed to fail in any event. Despite meticulous planning and the construction of railway stations, power plants and fjord-side quays, this is not railway country. Today, it seems quite extraordinary that in the middle of a war the Germans embarked on such a scheme and pursued it so ruthlessly.

Not all the work has gone to waste. Some of the tunnels and associated land-fills are incorporated into the Highway's tunnels between Fauske and Kobbelv.

This narrow stretch of water is rapidly silting and as the Highway runs east away from the fjord it enters a narrow, tree-filled valley with the pine trees cleared in patches to allow for the building of a farm. A gentle climb up the valley takes the Highway into its second longest tunnel of this stretch, the Middagsfjell, which is over 2km long.

The road rises at first in the tunnel then flattens before coming out to views of a large lake, Kobbvatnet, on the right. This is, perhaps, scenically the most attractive part of the Highway's journey on this modern section. The setting is mountainous to the west and to the east and, shortly after leaving the tunnel, at Kobbvangrenda, a turn to the right leads down a gravel track to some small farms and the possibility of **accommodation**. Two kilometres further on is a **café** and kiosk with great views across Kobbvatnet. A steady climb along the longest of the non-tunnel stretches of this part of the Highway, about 5km, takes the road to Kobbskardet tunnel. This is over 4km long and slopes downwards to the north permitting the Highway to reach sea-level near the tunnel exit at Sildhopen (76km). Leaving the tunnel there is a **campsite** to the right of the Highway.

From here the road returns to its former path with the old Highway from Bonnåsjøen joining it on the left. You now skirt the head of Mørsvikfjorden though the dog-leg shape of the fjord obscures your view to the open sea. At **Mørsvikbotn** (78km) there is a service station and shop. There are a significant number of settlements around the head of the fjord. Much of the building is on delta flats and terraces but none of the settlements is really large enough to be called a village, simply a handful of little houses, brightly painted yet somehow part of the natural scene.

Overshadowing the inlet are massive rock faces, some with screes which spill off Sildhopfjellet to the south-east; and beyond, into the fjord, the unsettled mountainsides are streaked with impressive waterfalls.

Leaving Mørsvikfjord behind, you ascend the deep and narrow valley of the same name and continue on to Mørsvikvatnet. To the right of the road (83km), almost hidden in the trees, a small rough road leads round to a clutch of farms which nestle in the shelter of the steep mountains by the side of the lake. This little road is worth following for a short detour. After rather less than a kilometre, the road – little more than a track – reaches an open lake terrace, cleared of trees. About 50m further on there are notices pointing to a simple monument erected in the woods by local people. Following the line of the notice into the trees for about 50m, a search reveals a small pyramid of concrete which holds a pole topped by the Red Star. On the concrete is a simply carved plaque with an inscription in Norwegian: 'Here lie Russian Prisoners of War who fell by the bloody hand of Fascism'. It is a touching and solemn lesson in history.

Returning to the main road, the Highway continues to climb to its highest point (86km from Fauske) on this stretch, 390m, above another large lake, Tennvatnet, to the right of its path. To the west and to the east, the mountains rise to over 1000m but, closer to the Highway, water dominates the scene. Inky blue lakes fill every hollow and lie at every altitude. Some are fringed by narrow beaches of white quartz sand. Waterfalls are everywhere. Some crash over

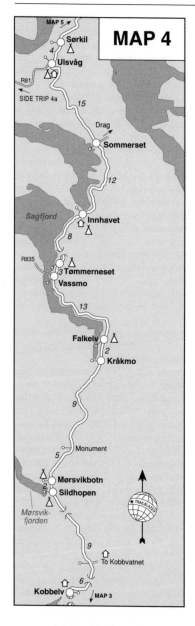

precipitous slopes while others spill gently over huge slabs of black rock racing over the bedding planes and falling over the edges. This is wild untamed country but, where shelter is available, short birch trees have colonized the slopes. Where the ground is flat, the moist, peaty forest floor is covered by a thick fern carpet in summer.

As the Highway descends from its high point there are good views of the lakes and especially the seven lakes of Sagvassdal, each linked to the next like pearls on a string. The Highway picks its way carefully over shallow cols and through knife-cut valleys down to **Kråkmoen** (92km).

Dominating the scene here, but best viewed from the Highway north of **Kråkmo**, is Kråkmotind. The suffix *tind* means mountain peak but this is no ordinary peak. The top of Kråkmotind appears to have been sliced off giving it a peculiarly truncated, sugar-loaf appearance. Its sides are so steep that the scree it produces can only find a resting place at its base. Only its exfoliated surface prevents it from being totally smooth. Like most of the summits here, it rises just to or above the permanent snow-line. Most of the mountain peaks wear their snow caps at a jaunty angle with the snow-line noticeably lower on the north-facing side. At a lower level, scree girdles encircle the mountains and below them is thin forest.

The streams and lakes around Kråkmo are noted for their red char and brown trout. Through the crystal-clear waters of the streams, quartz veins in the beds glitter as they catch the light of the sun. The abundance of water has not been ignored and you'll see a hydro-electric station just north of the village, its huge pipe stretching upwards and out of sight over the shoulder of the mountain.

Kråkmo is proud of its connection with the novelist Knut Hamsun (1859–1952). His Nobel Prize winning work *Markensgrøde* (*Growth of the Soil*) was partly written in the village and the area provided inspiration and settings for some of his other works.

From here onwards the Highway runs along the side of the seven lakes you saw on the descent. The short streams linking the lakes run over low glacial moraines which are sometimes steep enough to give rise to rapids. The lakes lie to the left of the road and, for some reason I have never discovered, only three are named and the other four are known by numbers. There is not much room for the Highway and its path is often little more than a ledge above the lakes. There is even less room for settlement, and farms are rare.

About two kilometres north of Krakmo you come to a lakeside **camping site** at Falkelv and the Highway then skirts Sandnes. Thirteen kilometres further and the open Sagfjord is reached – or, rather, its southernmost arm. The hamlet here is **Vassmo** (107km). To the left, a side road leads off to the Steigen peninsula. This is Route 835, a new road completed only in 1990 and noteworthy for its tunnel section just west of Vassmo. The tunnel is over 8km long and is currently the longest in North Norway.

The shelter of the fjord arm has long been an attraction to settlement as witnessed by ancient rock carvings.

Three kilometres further north the Highway passes Tømmerneset. To the right of the Highway is a graveyard and, nearby, a monument. To reach the monument you need to turn on to what was the old Highway which runs parallel to the new to the right. It is then 150m up the road and to the left. The monument is inscribed: '*To the memory of the Soviet soldiers who gave their lives in Norway 1941–5 and who are buried here.*' These were prisoners of war brought here from the Russian campaign and employed to maintain the old Arctic Highway. Yet again one is reminded of the Highway's other name: The Blood Road.

Back on today's Highway and a further 500m north are some 8000-year-old rock carvings of two reindeer. The site is Helleristringer. There is a small carpark on the left of the road. Another 500m or so and on the other side of the Highway is **Tømmerneset Camping**.

Shortly after the campsite, the Highway passes through the 700m Tømmerneset tunnel and generally keeps close to the shore of the head of Sagfjord until it reaches **Innhavet** (118km) where it turns inland. Innhavet is a small village with a supermarket, fuel and the **Hamarøy Hotel**. The hotel has a café open to non-residents and there's a campsite, **Notvann Camping**, on the edge of the village. There is an important local fish-farming industry here.

Across the Sagfjord to the west you have views of the islands and skerries which fringe the coast. At sunset or in the low winter sun the islands have a special beauty. The inlet is, however, too deeply indented to allow a sight of the

Lofotens. To the east are some massive *roches moutonnées*, ice-scarred hump-backed rock outcrops. A reminder, if one were needed, that the landscape bears all the marks of recent glaciation.

The coast is intricately fractured north of Innhavet and as the Highway runs towards Sommerset you can see something of the twisting inlets, to the left. The immediate surroundings of the road are characterized by bare rock surfaces. Where soils have not been stripped away, trees and bog occupy the lower ground. **Sommerset** (130km) is a village at the neck of a peninsula with Drag just 4km across the narrow strip of land to the east. The importance of the short road link (Route 827) is likely to increase with the completion of new road-works on the eastern side of Tysfjorden.

Drag is linked by a ferry across the fjord to the village of Tysfjord/Kjøpsvik. A new road with seven tunnels has been built to **Sætran** (see p158). This may be considered to be an alternative to the Arctic Highway and, although the ferry journey is longer than the Bognes to Skarberget crossing, it is possible that this may eventually be designated as the E6 and the Arctic Highway will again have shifted its path.

If this were to come about the plans to realign the Highway north of Sommerset will surely be scrapped. The plans, which have been on the drawing board for years, include two new tunnels (the 147m Tjukkskjømning and the 321m Middagsfjellet) as well as a by-pass around Ulsvåg.

As it is, the Highway presently winds its way north from Sommerset along the edge of a large lake, Skillvatnet, and then though some very attractive country with excellent views as it slips down to the open sea facing the Lofoten Islands. The village here is **Ulsvåg** (145km). There is a **guesthouse** and a **campsite** to the left of the Highway.

Just before entering the village centre you pass the turning (left) on to Route 81 which gives an opportunity for a side trip. There is a fuel station at this turn.

Accommodation: Fauske to Ulsvåg

Only 14km out of Fauske is *Strømhaug Camping* (☎ 75 69 71 06; 🖹 75 69 76 06; 🖳 stromhaug@pluscamp.no) in the village of Straumen. Open all year, this is one of the Plus Camp group and is very popular, especially with anglers. There are 22 well-equipped cabins, 4 rooms and space for camping. It is a pretty enough site but anyone looking for isolation will be disappointed: it's impossible not to notice that you are in a village. Prices range from NOK250 to NOK800 depending on the size of the cabin and its equipment.

There is a small but beautifully located group of cabins at **Sommarset**, 47km north of Fauske and just off the Highway. The cabins are simple but, strung along the fjord, have splendid views.

Kobbelv Verthus (☎ 75 69 58 01; 🖹 75 69 57 07; 🖳 vert.as@online.no) occupies one of the most attractive settings of any along the Highway. It overlooks the Leirfjord, 61km north of Fauske. Alongside, to the south of the hotel, just 20m away, a waterfall, Baggfossen, thunders fjordwards. Below the hotel there is a delightful sandy beach. There are 26 en-suite rooms of good standard, costing around NOK750, and a licensed restaurant. It's important to book ahead because the hotel is a favourite with groups. The café-restaurant serves meals and snacks throughout the day and there's a shop here. Apart from the state of the public toilets, this is a good place to stop off for a break.

An inland beach camp is available at **Kobbvaten Camping**, about 6km north of Kobbelv and down a track to the right of the Highway. The beach is that of a large lake of the same name where there are cabins and spaces for tents and caravans. The communal ablutions and kitchens are adequate and, although simple, the site is cheap (under NOK500 for a cabin) and in a most attractive setting. It's ideal for children. The site is open from mid-May to the end of September.

Nyheim Camping is at Sildhopen. It is a simple site of cabins with camping available and it has some superb mountain scenery to look out on. However, the quality of the cabins and the management of the site may mean that it's worthwhile going on a further two of three kilometres to the camp at Mørsvikbotn.

Mørsvikbotn Camping (☎/🖹 75 69 51 18), run by the Jensen family, is to the left of the Highway just beyond the shop and fuel station. It is nicely laid out with about a dozen cabins and plenty of space for tents or caravans. The cabins are simple but there's a decent kitchen and ablution block. It is possible to use a washing machine and spin dryer. Prices for the cabins are under NOK500. The site is open through June to mid-September.

Falkelv Camping is an inexpensive campsite just north of Kråkmoen. The largest of six cabins sleeps eight, has cooking facilities and is a bargain at NOK400. The other cabins each sleep three and cost just NOK250 but are only primitively equipped. On the edge of a lake, Falkelv's site is its strong point.

Just south of Innhavet and 110km out of Fauske is *Tømmerneset Camping* (☎ 75 77 29 55; 🖹 75 77 29 65). Here, to the right of the Highway, is a well-kept site with a mountain backdrop. There are 16 cabins and room for tents. Prices range from under NOK500 to NOK750. It is near enough to the Bognes–Skarberget ferry to make it a convenient overnight stop.

In Innhavet village, 118km from Fauske, is the small and inexpensive **Hamarøy Hotel** (☎ 75 77 25 60; 🖹 75 77 26 22; 🖳 hamaroy.hotell@narviknett. no). There are 29 double rooms, 5 single and three family-sized. All are en suite and with TV, but, although nicely furnished, they are rather small. It has an indoor swimming pool (closed in summer – use the fjord!), a sauna, a café and a restaurant. A bar and dancing are further attractions. The hotel stands to the left of the Highway and has two strange-looking wooden figures outside.

Also in Innhavet is *Notvann Camping* (☎ 75 77 25 36). As well as places to pitch a tent or park a caravan, there are four big cabins and a number of very small ones. The site is alongside a small lake. Although it proclaims to be open June–August, the last time I passed it in mid-August it was closed down.

There's a choice in Ulsvåg (145km from Fauske) between a guesthouse and a campsite.*Ulsvåg Gjestgiveri and Camping* is to the left of the Highway in the village. The guesthouse has 9 rooms, 6 double, a single and a triple. The rooms are quite simple but that's reflected in the modest prices. Doubles are NOK350 and the single is NOK250. However, breakfast is an extra NOK45. The café serves all meals. Outside there are 17 cabins and all have refrigerators and cooking facilities. Those with toilets and showers cost between NOK450 and NOK475. The rest cost NOK225. The guesthouse is open all year but the campsite is closed October–May unless there's a whale-watching party in residence.

SIDE TRIP FROM ULSVÅG TO NORDNESET PENINSULA   Map 4a

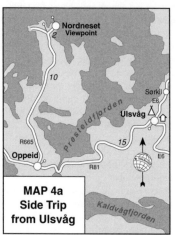

MAP 4a
Side Trip
from Ulsvåg

Good weather is needed for you to appreciate properly the scenery and make this trip worthwhile. A drive on Route 81 leads to the **Nordneset Peninsula** at Tranøy and some splendid views. The round trip is 58km. Although this journey takes you away from the Highway for two or more hours, the views it affords across Vestfjord and to the Lofoten Islands justify the additional time. To follow this route, drive along Route 81 as far as Oppeid. The road keeps fairly close to the shore of Presteidfjorden and the scenery, with fjord to the right and mountains to the left, is impressive.

At Oppeid (15km), you turn right on to a minor road (Route 665). This leads to the end of the peninsula. There is a Y-junction at 27km and, for the best views, it is the left-hand branch which you should take. When the road runs out, there is a viewpoint to some truly beautiful scenery to the west and to the north (29km).

The Highway: Ulsvåg to Narvik
MAPS 5–6

Moving north from Ulsvåg, the Highway is more or less direct to Bognes: first along the coast, with the Stordjupet inlet to the left of the road, and in just under 4km, through the little settlement of **Sørkil** where there is a **campsite**. Sørkil was formerly a trading post. Looking north from the hamlet, you can see the impressive peak of Tilthornet (850m). In another kilometre, the Highway begins its crossing of yet another peninsula neck; up through a narrow forested depression which rises to 150m before its descent to Bognes.

Ten kilometres after Sørkil, to the right of the Highway, is the **Tysfjord Turistsenter** at Storjord. It comes as quite a surprise to come across such a large complex of buildings in an otherwise totally natural environment. However, this is an exceptionally comfortable establishment offering a variety of accommodation and activities including whale watching. There is a growing settlement at Storjord with a useful store.

Driving north from the Turist-senter it is easy to miss a very good viewpoint on this stretch of road. Some 12km beyond Ulsvåg, the Highway sweeps round a rising curve to the right where there is a picnic place to the right of the road. From this point there are fantastic views westward. This has to be a compulsory stop even if it means missing the ferry. Once again it is the Lofoten Islands that can be seen but, for me, they never fail to impress no matter how many times or from where I see them.

As the Highway descends to Bognes it skirts a little inlet, Bessfjorden, on the right of the road. This is a popular place for summer cottages, some quite grand and others tiny. As **Bognes** (164km) is entered, the mountains on the northern side of Tysfjord come into view.

Bognes is a ferry point. There is a ferry to the Lofotens, to the village of Lødingen and to the E10 (via Route 85), the Lofoten Islands' main highway. There is also a shorter ferry connection to Skarberget. It is the latter that remains the Arctic Highway's only ferry section. Fifty years ago ten ferries were necessary to close the gaps in the Highway. Just how long this ferry will remain is uncertain. There have long been plans to provide an alternative route with an undersea tunnel but the Tysfjord may be deeper than the State's resources. One day, for sure, the Highway will be an all-road route and the new road between the village of Tysfjord and the Highway at Sætran is the precursor of a 700m-deep tunnel.

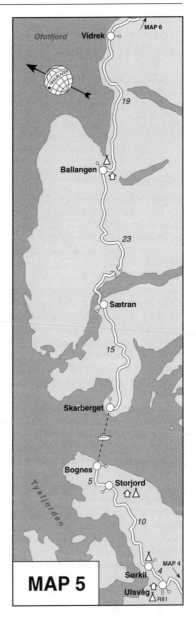

> ### The Skarberget–Bognes Ferry
> The **Skarberget–Bognes Ferry** uses two large ferry ships, the *Hamarøy* and the *Honningsvåg*, with a smaller ship, the *Røsund*, on standby. The ferry frequency is about fifteen each day in each direction (rising to 21 between early June and late August) between 01.00 and 23.35 (from Skarberget), and 00.15 and 22.45 (from Bognes). The service is very restricted at Christmas and the New Year. The frequency is highest during the day, fewer at night.
>   The 25-minute sailing time goes only too quickly. The ships are well appointed with lifts, a café, a large lounge deck and toilets. Subsidized, the costs are modest. For example, a car plus driver and two passengers is only just over NOK100.
>   It should be possible to get schedules from any local tourist information office or nearby hotel. Alternatively, telephone ☎ 76 96 76 00.

In fact the ferry makes a welcome break from driving and, in summer, two ships ply the route so that waiting times are not too lengthy. There is also a **café**. It takes about 25 minutes to make the crossing to Skarberget and the views from the ship make a visit to the deck compulsory in any weather.

After crossing the narrows of Tysfjorden, the ferry enters the Skrovkjosen inlet. On all sides the mountains rise vertically out of the sea. The great peaks of Tepkiltinden and Breiskartinden dominate the north shore. To the west of Skarberget, great clefts in the mountain face leave you with the impression that some giant has been at work with an axe. To the south-east is Stetind. At almost 1400m it is claimed to be the world's finest natural obelisk.

Skarberget has a **café** but no settlement and the Highway climbs away from the pier into the mountains. The next 15km take the Highway through some of the best scenery on the whole of the journey from Fauske to Narvik. Running across a mountain pass the road passes towering mountains denuded by ice, their flanks now peeling as the rock surfaces exfoliates in what is known as rock bursting. This is wild country with no settlement or significant economic use. Again, there are constant reminders of the work and power of ice. The Highway rises to 255m before it is able to take a winding path down to Efjord.

As the fjord comes into view so too does the conical Eidetind to the west and the smooth slopes of Huglhornet to the east. There is little vegetation save the occasional stunted pine sheltering behind the loose rocks which litter the surface. Across the fjord the mountains rise to over 600m.

The Highway descends to **Sætran** (179km – NB distances exclude the ferry crossing) and the junction with the new road, Route 827, which links it to Tysfjord village (see p154). Sætran was formerly a ferry point for the crossing of Efjord. The ferries ran down the length of the fjord to Forså in the late 1960s. Today, three bridges span the fjord using islands as stepping stones. The longest of the bridges is over half a kilometre in length and crosses the Kjerringstraumen, a significant maelstrom when the tidal waters stream through the narrows.

Having crossed the fjord, the Highway turns right to run down the fjord's length before turning into the Forså tunnel (685m). From there it turns away

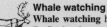

Whale watching

Whale watching has become increasingly popular in recent years in Tysfjord and east of the Lofotens. The season is determined by the vast numbers of herring that move into the area in the autumn. The whales are killer whales and the best time to see them is between mid-October and mid-December.

Killer whales are members of the dolphin family and their numbers worldwide exceed those of any other whale species. They are impressively large with a length of up to eight metres and a weight of around four tonnes. Their diet is not restricted to the herring and to make up the 100kg or so of food they need daily they will eat other fish, birds and even seals.

Killer whales live in family groups called pods but they find their mates in other schools. Undisturbed, they have a life expectancy of over 75 years in the case of females and some 15 or 20 years less for males.

The whales have their own special calls with each pod having its own 'dialect'. In Tysfjord, watching is from boats which track the whales just as they are tracking the herring. The most exciting experience is to use large, rigid inflatable boats but other, larger craft are also employed. In addition to seeing whales, there's a good chance of sighting one or more of the 250 white-tailed eagles which are native to these shores.

from the fjord towards Ballangen. Now there is increasing settlement and farming returns to the roadside. At first, thin forest vies with farming and the farmhouses are widely spaced. But, as you approach Ballangen, the scene changes and the wild country is left behind until after Narvik.

Ballangen (202km) is on an inlet of the same name which itself is an arm of the great Ofotfjord. It started life as a port exporting the products of the Bjørkåsen pyrite mines to the south. The mines have long since closed. It has a largely industrial population of rather more than 1500. I once described it as having a shabby appearance, much to the annoyance of its inhabitants. It is pleasing to say it has smartened itself up and it is a good place to take refreshment and refuel, especially if a stop in the town of Narvik is not intended. In fact this is the last opportunity to do so before Narvik, over 40km away.

Most of the useful shops and stores, as well as the café, are to the left of the Highway as it enters Ballangen. The **post office** and **information office** (☎ 76 92 82 08) are also here as is a **guesthouse**. There's a large fuel station on the corner (right) as the Highway turns north out of the town and it is here (left) that you find **Ballangen Camping**.

As the Highway swings right and then left through the little town it passes along the southern shore of the Ballangen inlet. From here the influence of Narvik is obvious. The area is generally well settled and there is no longer any real sense of isolation. The road is quite heavily used but it is well engineered and adequate for the volume of traffic it has to carry.

Much of the route is along the fjord shelf as it follows the shoreline of Ofotfjord. This is a broad, open fjord unlike those of western Norway but very similar to those that you will see in the north in Finnmark. If the shelf narrows the line of farms which border the Highway is broken and the road is left to its solitary self. The area around **Vidrek** (221km) is well farmed but, as the Highway temporarily turns south along the narrow Skjomen arm of the fjord, farms are absent, squeezed out by the steep mountains which form the coast. These mountains are high enough to be topped by snow even in high summer.

Where Skjomen narrows, at Grindjord (227km), a bridge spans the milky meltwaters of the fjord. The bridge was not built until the early 1970s. Before this, a five- to ten-minute ferry linked the two parts of the Arctic Highway. Looking at the bridge today it seems very strange that such an important stretch of the Highway relied on a ferry for so long.

The site for the bridge was well chosen for it is here that two small promontories face each other across the water. Skjombrua is 709m in length with a main span of 525m. It rises a full 35m above the rather forbidding-looking waters. Having made the crossing, the Highway is again on a narrow shelf by the fjord's edge. Turning right here, instead of staying with the Highway, would take you south-east along Skjomenfjord to the world's most northerly 18-hole golf course.

As the Highway gets ever closer to Narvik, farms begin to be replaced by the houses of Narvik's workforce and, later, greenhouses, evidence of the town's market influence.

What might be described as outer Narvik is reached at **Ankenesstrand/Håkvik** (233km), a settlement which is strung out around a headland leading into another fjord arm: Beisfjord. There are many stories from World War II associated with Beisfjord and Ankenesstrand. This was the scene of fierce fighting during the Narvik Campaign but the local people remember it most for a prisoner-of-war camp housing Yugoslavs who were used as slave labour. It was here that, on the pretext of preventing the spread of typhus, over 300 prisoners were machine-gunned to death by their German guards in a single night.

A ferry crossed the Beisfjord until after World War II when a bridge was built. Engineering work here, including tunnelling, is in progress.

As you enter **Narvik** (244km) you'll be left in no doubt that this is the most important town on the whole length of the Arctic Highway between Mo i Rana and Kirkenes.

Accommodation: Ulsvåg to Narvik

Sørkil Fjordcamping (☎/▤ 75 77 16 60) is just 3–4km out of Ulsvåg. Thirteen simple cabins line the fjord beach with a café on site. Tents and caravans have their place and prices, for cabins, range from NOK500 to NOK750 depending on their size. Some sleep up to five. There are glorious views of the Lofoten Islands and the site is well kept. Sørkil is open from June to the end of August.

The very substantial *Tysfjord Turist-senter* (☎ 75 77 53 70; ▤ 75 77 53 75; ▣ post@tysfjord-turistsenter.no) is about 14km north of Ulsvåg and to the right

---

(**Opposite**) **Top:** Narvik (see p162), the largest town on the Highway. **Bottom:** Østisen spills off the Svartisen icecap (see p126).

of the Highway. It offers a great range of accommodation from hotel to motel, cabins to camping places. There's a sauna and solarium, a piano bar in summer and a band in winter! The café is open 24 hours a day in summer and until the last ferry passengers have been catered for in winter.

The tourist centre organizes a comprehensive variety of activities: whale watching, walking on marked trails, birdwatching, fishing and hunting. Because it houses whale-watching groups, it remains open all year.

The hotel has 23 double rooms including 5 suites at NOK700. There are 18 rooms in the motel, each with four beds (two in a gallery). The seven cabins are quite small but each has a refrigerator and cooking facilities. Showers and toilets are in the hotel.

Prices rise in winter during the whale-watching season (late October –mid-December) but for NOK1000 the whale safari is included. I have yet to come across a better range of facilities and activities in any other place along the Highway. It's also spotlessly clean and well managed.

Ballangen may be too close to Narvik to be attractive when one considers the choice the Highway's largest town has to offer. In the centre of Ballangen is *Solheim Gjestgiveri* (☎ 76 92 81 06; 🖹 76 92 81 16), a small guesthouse with a bar and café. Its position rather detracts from any charm it might have had but its claim to *rimelige priser* (reasonable prices) is accurate.

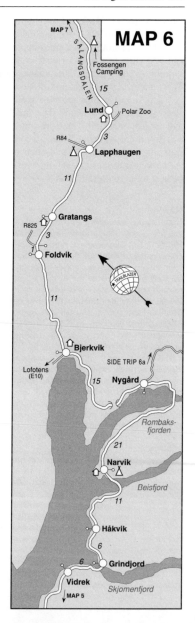

(Opposite) Top: Peaks and sandy shores near Ulsvåg (see p154). **Bottom:** Skarberget: only one ferry now breaks the Highway's path (see p158).

Out of Ballangen, bordering the Highway (left), is ***Ballangen Camping*** (☎ 76 92 76 90; 🖹 76 92 76 92). I'm afraid this isn't for anyone seeking a peaceful wilderness. The one word which sums up the site is 'brash'. The camp has 50 cabins and 120 caravan places, as well as a rather crowded tent area. There is a big swimming pool, tennis courts, sauna, solarium, trampolines… the list is endless. There are even pet rabbits. In fact it has a 1950s or 60s holiday-camp air about it.

The largest cabins are very well equipped with toilet and shower. They sleep six and cost NOK650. The smallest sleep four but have no water supply and are just NOK250. There are communal wash places and washing machines and dryers are available. There's a café and a restaurant. Remarkably, Ballangen Camping is open all year and often very full in summer. However, unless you are very gregarious or travelling with children who need to let off steam, it may be best to drive on to Narvik.

NARVIK

Narvik is the best known and the largest of the few towns that actually straddle the Highway. Not surprisingly, it is also a modern creation. Nearly all the older settlements of any consequence in North Norway lie well to the west of the Highway, out towards the open sea, even on islands; such are the sites of the great Arctic towns of Tromsø, Hammerfest, Harstad and Bodø. The maritime economy of North Norway demanded easy access to the fishing grounds of the Norwegian Sea.

Narvik's site is distinctly cramped. Backed by high mountains, there's little room to expand beyond the tip of the peninsula on which the modern town is built. The Arctic Highway is the town's high street, Kongensgate. It rises and falls over the spur that forms the headland.

History

Just over a hundred years ago there was not even a village where today there is a town approaching 20,000 inhabitants. Just a couple of farms stood at the head of the Rombaks inlet. Narvik's history as well as its future are inescapably bound to Swedish iron ore. The Swedish border lies just a few kilometres to the east and beyond the border, in the Swedish province of Norrland, are some of the richest sources of iron in the whole of Europe. These are the great iron hills of Gallivarra and Kirunavarra.

For a long time the ores, known to have an iron content of 60–70%, remained untouched because of their phosphorus content. Then in 1878–9 a certain Sydney Gilchrist Thomas, an English scientist, discovered a process to remove the phosphorous impurities. The scene changed. Now came the difficulty of exporting the ores. To the east was Luleå on the Swedish coast of the Gulf of Bothnia – but the Gulf freezes over in winter. Just across the border to the west, however, was the ice-free Norwegian coast. Here at Rombaksbotn was a suitable inlet and site for a harbour. The new town was conceived but the birth was to prove more difficult.

The harbour was originally named Victoriahavn after a visit in 1887 of the Crown Princess Victoria but the locals still called it Narvik after the farmland on which it was built. By the time it was officially given the status of town, on 29 May 1901, Narvik was the accepted name.

The original settlers were all construction workers, chiefly on the railway which had to be built across a difficult mountain boundary. The English company doing the work eventually sold out, and lost its transhipment rights, when labour troubles were added to the physical difficulties. The railway line to Kiruna was completed in 1902, having taken nine years, but this was ten years behind the Swedish route to Luleå. The Ofotbanen, as the Narvik-Sweden line is called, was officially opened on 14 July

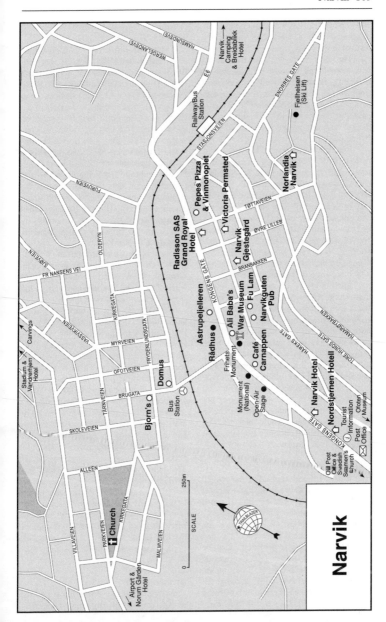

1903 and the railway's construction is still celebrated with a week-long late-winter festival in the town.

The early years were tough and the new town found its very survival full of problems. Political as well as economic troubles led to periods when no ore was being carried through Narvik. The electrification of the railway in 1923, heralded as the key to future prosperity, was necessary but no panacea.

Even the occupation of Norway in the period 1940–45 was in large measure due to the strategic importance of the Swedish ores to the German war machine. The ill-fated Narvik Campaign has been the subject of controversy ever since. The three short months between the German invasion of Norway and the Allies' evacuation from Narvik were far more critical than is often realized. Not least is the fact that the Campaign was instrumental in the change which occurred in Britain's leadership.

The railway is still the town's lifeline. The Arctic Highway is not an irrelevance but is seen as more of a local road than as a national or international road. The dependence on Swedish iron ore is much diminished and new light industries have been introduced. The town is evidently thriving today and there is a sense of purpose in its people. Many of the buildings date from the post-war reconstruction made necessary by the wartime bombing and shelling but many more are even more modern. Even its most loyal citizens would not describe Narvik as especially attractive to look at: it is essentially workaday.

Services

The tourist information office has moved in recent years and is now less conveniently placed along Kongensgt (which is also the Highway) but south towards the direction of the harbour. Walking down the Highway, the office is to the left of the road where the park (right) finishes. It cannot be rated especially highly as tourist offices go but it will be able to offer guidance on the town's attractions. A word of warning: the office doesn't seem to keep to its advertised opening hours (10.00 to 16.30) so an early

visit may be frustrated (☎ 76 94 33 09; 🖹 76 94 74 05; 🖳 post@narvikinfo.no).

The **post office** (☎ 76 92 36 00) is even further down the Highway, between Bribakken and Brattbakken, turnings left off the Highway. Both **railway** (☎ 76 92 31 79) and **bus** (☎ 76 92 31 21) **stations** are in the opposite direction and to the right of the Highway. Going north, look for Tottaveien and then take the next turn right, Stasjons veien. To reach the small airport, **Framneslia Lufthavn** (☎ 76 92 22 00), go to the extreme west of the peninsula, through Frydenlund and into Framnes district. Larger aircraft have to touch down at the airport at Evenes (☎ 76 98 10 00) which Narvik shares with Harstad. It is now called Harstad-Narvik Airport and is reached by turning off the Highway (E6) at Bjerkvik on to the E10 (see Part 6).

Narvik's main **police station** (☎ 76 92 34 00) is at 14–18 Kongensgt and the main **hospital** (☎ 76 96 80 00) is on Sykehus veien close to the **Stadium** and on the north side of Frydenlund district.

The **library** is at the back of the town hall (**Rådhus**) which is located by the bridge across the railway in the centre of town. It offers free internet access but has somewhat eccentric opening hours which seem to change daily. There is a modern public **swimming pool** (*idre henshus*, ☎ 76 92 27 89). It is open from 15.00 to 19.00 in summer and 17.00 to 20.00 in winter. It's located in Frydenlund; keep straight on after crossing the bridge over the railway and turn right into Villaveien.

Narvik is a good place to shop for necessities but less so for anything special. Two blocks north of the Grand Hotel (see p167) is a hideous new shopping centre, the Narvik Storsenter. The alcohol store is here as is a variety of small eating places.

The town isn't particularly large and most places of interest are within walking distance of the square. If a taxi (*drosje*) is needed, there's a central call number (☎ 76 94 65 00).

Around town

The Arctic Highway enters the town from along a narrow cliff-edge route after crossing the Beisfjord to the Fagernes headland. This is a rather difficult path and the new engineering works are designed to improve the situation here.

The dock area is clearly seen to the west of the road. After the Highway crosses a mineral line, a few hundred metres or so further on is the **Swedish Seamen's Church (Svenska Kyrkan)**. Despite the recent decline the great harbour still claims to be the busiest in the world for the handling of iron ore (it is Norway's second port in tonnage). It certainly dominates the south-western quarter of the town and its work-like appearance does little to improve Narvik's attractiveness.

The town is split in two by the railway which runs in from Sweden and down to the harbour. To the west, on the seaward side of the railway and Highway is Frydenlund, the residential district. Here you'll find the town's main church, the town's very large indoor sports centre, the main sports stadium and the hospital. By the very edge of the coast, north of the harbour, is Narvik's airport, one of the network of short-take-off airfields that has been developed over the past three decades. There are also some new industries in Frydenlund for Narvik has diversified its economy into clothing, wood products and soft drinks, among others, to reduce its dependency on iron.

To the east of the Highway is Oscarsborg (Oskarsborg) which includes the central business district and most of the hotels. Oscarsborg district is sandwiched between the Highway and the steep slopes of Fagernesfjellet. This mountain rises to over 1000m in less than 2km from the coast and most of the district roads run along the slopes, contour-fashion, and parallel to the Arctic Highway.

Down to the south of the town, where the Highway enters Narvik, is the **harbour**. Iron-ore production, processing (pelletizing) and shipment are all in the hands of the giant Swedish company LKAB. In spite of improvements made at Luleå (the rival Swedish port), nature sees to it that Narvik retains year-round advantage and its harbour can take vessels up to 350,000 tonnes.

However, the great ore-handling plant at the harbour is less busy than in the past and the number of ships to be seen has fallen.

It would be a pity to pass through Narvik without stopping. In fact that may be impossible because it is a town in which the pedestrian is king. I have never experienced anywhere else in the world where traffic is seemingly so ready to stop for each and every pedestrian who decides to cross its path. The effect on traffic flow is to slow everything to a crawl but no one shows any sign of impatience.

In the centre of the town to the right of the Highway is a small pedestrianized square (Torget) in which you'll find the famous **Frihets (Freedom) Monument** by Eriksen. The nude woman and child are evidently hardy souls as they survive the Arctic winter and the summer fountains. Torget is Narvik's hub.

With some time to look around, there's quite a lot to see. In the square, Torget, is a small but fascinating museum. It is in the right-hand corner of Torget by the steps. Run by the Red Cross, this **War Museum** opened in 1964 and was enlarged in 1980. It isn't a museum on the grand scale but an intimate and moving display tracing the short history of the Narvik Campaign and the subsequent period of occupation in World War II. Each time I have visited the museum I have come away wondering how the citizens of Narvik felt in early June 1940. After just two months of fighting, leading to victory over the Germans, they found themselves suddenly condemned to five years of brutal occupation as the Allied forces withdrew and the Germans reoccupied the town. Entry to the museum is NOK25 and the money goes to the Red Cross. Opening hours are 10.00–22.00 on weekdays from mid-May to late August but it closes during the rest of the year. The museum is also open at weekends (12.00–15.00) in summer.

In contrast is **Narvik Church** in Frydenlund. To reach it, cross the bridge over the railway and continue on Brugata taking the second left turn leading into Kirkegt. The church stands in its own well-kept grounds. It is open to visitors, rather than worshippers, only in summer (June–August) from 10.00 to 15.00 except Sundays and Mondays. This is a church of cathedral size; it seats 750. Narvik Kirke dates from 1925 but the organ is more recent. The architect was Olaf Nordhagen and it is unmistakably Scandinavian in style. There is some fine stained glass in addition to well-crafted sculptures. The most beautiful feature is the painting, behind the altar, of Christ at prayer. This is the work of Elif Pettersen.

Older than the church, and not to be missed, is what is called the **Old Post Office**. The oldest building in Narvik, it is situated on a grassy bank opposite the Swedish Seamen's Church at the southern end of Kongensgt, beyond the modern post office and to the left of the Highway going south. This quaint little building dates from the mid nineteenth century when it was a workshop for the original farm which was Narvik's origin. In 1888 it became the Victoriahavn post office but served this purpose for about a decade only and was then disused. Remarkably, the building survived the war and in 1995 it was restored. Today you are looking at all that remains from the days when Narvik was just a couple of farms on the peninsula.

Something of those long-gone days is also preserved in the **Ofoten Museum**. It is easiest to combine a visit to the Old Post Office with one to the museum. Turning back up Kongensgate from the Old Post Office, you take the first right turn into Vahallabakken, then right again into the unforgettably named Administrasjonsveien. The museum is at the end of the road housed in what, until 1995, was the railway company's headquarters. It is a beautiful 1902 house, another survivor of wartime air raids and misuse by the occupying army. The museum's collection traces the story of the area's early settlement – a scattering of farms and Sami reindeer grazing – to its explosive growth through the last 120 years. The museum is open from 10.30 to 15.30 on weekdays but in July it also accepts visitors at the weekend from 12.00 to 15.00 (☎ 76 96 00 50).

On the western side of the Highway, near the centre of town and going south from the square, is a small park. There are two main attractions here, the **National Monument** and a delightful piece of sculpture. The Norwegian inscription on the triangular monument translates as: *Thanks to our Allies 1940–45 For Peace and Freedom. Thanks to those who Fought in the War.*

At the other end of the gardens is a charming metal cast **sculpture** of six naked children with a dog. It is wonderfully lifelike and carefree: Scandinavian street sculpture at its best. Close by is an **open-air stage** where there are occasional performances.

If staying in Narvik for more than a day, you might find a visit to the **harbour** and the iron-handling plant to be of interest. After all, this is what Narvik is all about. The one-hour guided tours on weekdays start at 13.00 and cost NOK30 (☎ 76 92 38 00). On the other side of town, at Vassvik, are rock carvings (*helleristninger*) including a fine specimen of a reindeer. To reach the carvings, cross the bridge over the railway into Frydenlund, take the fourth right turn into Tårnveien, then look for a left turn into Einerveien. The carvings are located in Brenholtet (*holtet* = wood).

Visiting Narvik in summer, it is easy to forget that it is an important ski centre. The only reminders are the **Fjellheisen** (mountain lift) and the sight of men, women and children on roller-skis weaving in and out of the traffic in the town.

There are some really excellent **ski slopes** above the town. **Rallar'n Sports Hotel and Alpine Centre** is on Fagernesfjellet. There are eight prepared slopes, half of them floodlit, and the ski-pulls and lifts can cope with 3500 persons an hour. Close to Narvik are other ski centres and there is a wide variety of other winter sports including telemark skiing and even helicopterskiing! For information it is best to call the tourist information office at the **Narvik Skisenter** (☎ 76 94 27 99).

In summer, the new **mountain lift** carries visitors up to 656m on Fagernesfjellet. The views from here are outstanding: down to the town below, across to the great Ofotfjord and beyond to the Lofoten Islands. If you wish to take photographs, it may be best to walk back down a little slope from the café to avoid too much of the mountain slope in the frame. It is a wonderful place to see the midnight sun in midsummer.

This great mountain which stretches east to an even higher peak, Rombakstotta (1200m), has been called the 'Sleeping Queen'. From the sea the outline of the mountain's crest is, given a little imagination, supposed to recall the profile of Britain's Queen Victoria on her deathbed.

There's a restaurant and viewing platform at the upper lift station. To find the lower lift station, turn up Tøttaveien, just up from the Grand Royal Hotel. At the top take the left turn at the T-junction and continue on this road bearing round to the right. Operating times are: mid-June to end of July, 12.00–01.00; August, 13.00–21.00. The trip takes seven minutes and the cost is NOK70. In winter, the operating times vary according to the weather conditions and it's best to check with the Skisenter (see above) or call the lift company (☎ 76 96 04 94).

Accommodation

There's an especially broad range of accommodation in Narvik mainly brought about by the demands of the business community.

The oldest and largest hotel is the **Radisson SAS Grand Royal** (☎ 76 97 70 00; ▤ 76 97 70 07; ▣ grand@grandroyalho telnarvik.no). It fronts the Highway (Kongensgt) to the right as the road rises away from the square. It is over a hundred years old but has lost a lot of its charm in the post-war reconstruction. Not before time, there's major rebuilding which will eventually increase its capacity from 107 rooms to over 150. In early 2003 the hotel was taken over by the Radisson SAS chain. There's an impressive restaurant but the service is slow and the bedrooms vary from luxury to frankly pokey. There's a sauna and a locally popular bar. The hotel might be considered to be rather overpriced but under the new management this may be rectified. There is limited parking on the street outside.

The **Nordlandia Narvik Hotel** (☎ 76 94 75 00; ▤ 76 94 28 65) has great views on one side where rooms overlook the town. It is up by the mountain lift (*telecabine*) station and has all the atmosphere of a ski resort hotel with lots of wood, good-sized rooms, a restaurant open from 15.00 to 22.00 and a café. There are 91 rooms but for the best views ask for the new 'tower' block. It is quite expensive, up to NOK1045 for a double room at weekends but significantly cheaper during the week. Prices include breakfast and it is good value for money. In winter many of the rooms are used by students which suggests that Norwegian undergraduates live a pampered life!

On Dronningensgt, which runs parallel to the Highway and behind the Grand Royal, is **Victoria Permsted** (☎ 76 92 54 70; ▤ 76 92 54 72). This hotel has 35 rooms, all en suite. The rooms are rather small and simply furnished, reflecting perhaps an emphasis on business guests and conferences. For some reason best known to the management five rooms don't have TV. The restaurant, open to the public, shuts down early (last orders 17.00) and you have to order in advance if you're going to be arriving later. However the Victoria is not expensive and you get what you pay for.

Back on the Highway (Kongensgt) is the **Narvik Hotel** (☎ 76 94 70 77; ▤ 76 94 67 35; ▣ firmapost@narvikhotel.no), just south of the turning into Mimer Bakken. About the same size as the Victoria (34 rooms) it is rather more attractively furnished but is also rather more expensive. A double room in summer will be around NOK900 with another NOK200 added in winter. There are tea- and coffee-making facilities in the rooms but breakfast is not included in the room price. Remarkably, a 24-hour room service is not charged for. There's a café, bar and restaurant/bistro. Again, this is a comfortable hotel although at a price.

Narvik Gjestegård (☎ 76 94 75 40) is on Dronningensgt, down from the Victoria. It is a large old house with bric-à-brac in the windows and antiques in the cellar. It is also very inexpensive: just over NOK200 per person. There are just 3 rooms and no restaurant.

Another guesthouse, accessible by steep steps up to its hilly site on Tore Hundsgt, is **Breidablikk** (☎ 76 94 14 18; 📠 76 94 57 86; 🖳 breidablikk@narviknett.no). Its lofty position gives good views over the town. The street is one of those parallel to the Highway. It is best reached by turning up Brannbakken, just north of the square, then taking the third right on to Tore Hunds. Prices here are modest and there's a range of accommodation from single rooms to a dormitory. It's all pretty simple. There's no restaurant but you can buy breakfast and lunch packets. A double room will cost about NOK450 and a dormitory bed is NOK150. There are just 22 rooms.

Nordstjernen Hotell (☎ 76 94 41 20; 📠 76 94 75 06; 🖳 nhnarvik@online.no) is just past the post office on Kongensgt (see p164). It's a fairly simply city hotel, no frills. There are 24 rooms of which eight are singles. Doubles cost about NOK700 and singles NOK600. Breakfast is included but there's no restaurant.

For really exclusive accommodation you can't beat **Norum Gården** (☎/📠 76 94 48 57). The house dates from the 1920s and it retains its original character and features. There are just four en-suite rooms, with two having attached kitchens for self-catering. Breakfast is available but no other meals. The whole house is beautifully furnished and there are its antiques and curios for sale in the cellars. All this luxury is surprisingly modestly priced at up to NOK550 including breakfast in the self-catering suites. To find Norum Gården, take the directions to Narvik Church (see above), continue past the church along Kirkegt then join Framnesveien; the guesthouse is at the junction with Melloveien.

The cheapest place to stay is probably the **Vandrerhjem** (Youth Hostel, ☎ 76 94 25 98; 📠 76 94 29 99) on Tiurveien which is about as far as you can get from the centre of town. Take the directions to the hospital but continue past it, turn up towards the stadium, go left into Lillevikveien and left again into Tiurveien. Because the old youth hostel, down by the harbour, is currently a refugee centre, the Vandrerhjem is in a student hostel and offers accommoda-tion from June to late August only. Prices vary from NOK150 to NOK400 and it is open for booking only between 07.00–10.30 and 15.00–21.00.

For campers there is **Narvik Camping** (☎ 76 94 58 10; 📠 76 94 58 20), about 2km north out of Narvik and to the left of the Highway. This is a large site with 30 cabins. Ten can sleep four persons and the rest have two bedrooms sleeping up to six. All cabins are en suite with bunk beds. There's plenty of room for caravans and tents. The facili-ties are excellent. There's a sauna and a shower block as well as a café. The views are wonderful across the fjord and there are boats for hire. The cabins are good value with top prices around NOK600.

Where to eat

Narvik is not short of cafés and restaurants. Apart from those hotels which have restau-rants (see above) there are cafés in the big stores and shopping complexes such as **Domus** (cross the bridge over the railway and go to the right). The new shopping complexes north of the Radisson SAS Grand Royal Hotel have various food out-lets and this is now home to Narvik's **vin-monoplet** (alcohol store). Narvik is proud of its new shopping malls. When there's late-night shopping, the town band turns out!

In the Steen og Strom Narvik Storsenter, north of the Grand Royal, is **Pepes Pizza**. It is open until midnight week-days and to 01.00 on Fridays and Saturdays. The pizzas are good, the apple pie is worth the NOK44 they charge and Pepes is a cut above the average pizza parlour.

Of the independent restaurants, **Fu Lam** (☎ 76 94 40 38) is the place to eat Chinese. Fu Lam's looks out towards the fjord from Dronningens gate. Go up Kinobakken off the Highway in central Narvik and turn right. Kinobakken also runs across the other side of the Highway, where you'll find **Astrupkjelleren** (☎ 76 94 04 02). Some say it has character; others say its just dilapidated. It's as much a bar as a restaurant but it has good pizzas and, unusually, rooms to let. Up Dronningensgt from Fu Lam's is the **Narvikguten Pub** (☎ 76 94 79 20). It closes at 01.00 on most days but an hour later on Fridays and Saturdays. Like many other eating places, it is shut on Sundays. It's a fairly basic restaurant but the prices are attractive.

On the Highway is *Café Carnappen* (☎ 76 94 39 70). Next to a bakery, it's not surprising that baguettes are a speciality. Opening hours are 10.00–16.00 with closure at 14.00 on Saturdays – this is Norway.

Longer hours (closing at 04.00 on Saturdays) are found at *Ali Baba's* (☎ 76 94 20 46) on the north-west side of the town square. Some tables are outside in summer.

Perhaps the most upmarket restaurant in town is *Bjorn's Mat og Vinhus* (☎ 76 94 42 90) just across the bridge to the left, next to the Baptist Church and overlooking the Domus car-park. Don't be put off by the entrance or the ground-floor bar. The restaurant above is very pleasing with a full à la carte menu.

For takeaway meals try the *Express Pizza and Grillbar* (☎ 76 94 42 44) on Fosseveien.

The next 200-plus kilometres of the Arctic Highway run through some of the more populated areas of North Norway and the path is often further from the coast than it has been since it crossed the Saltfjell (see Part 4). The road still follows many an ancient route for this area has been settled and farmed for centuries. This is a short stage because, like most travellers up the Highway, you are likely to want to extend your journey with a side trip from Nordkjosbotn to Tromsø, a further 73km.

The Highway: Narvik to Nygård
MAP 6

The Arctic Highway leaves Narvik through its northern suburbs, rising then following a winding path down to the Rombaksfjord. On the edge of the town (to the left of the Highway) is a small lay-by and in it one of the many monuments to the Narvik Campaign. This is a French war memorial, a must for the increasing number of French tourists to North Norway.

The road as it curves down to Rombaksfjorden can be quite difficult in bad weather and you need to drive it with care. The Highway bypasses Vassvik just two kilometres out of Narvik. Until 1964 the Highway ran down to the pier at Vassvik and a ferry crossing of Rombaksfjorden to Øyjord was necessary. Although the crossing was at a narrow point at the fjord entrance and only took 20 to 25 minutes it was an unwelcome interruption to continuous road transport. Narvik and the economy of the northern side of Ofotfjorden are closely linked and this was long recognized in plans to build a bridge. Furthermore, the road from Sweden and through to the Lofoten Islands, the E10, joins the Highway north of Rombaksfjorden. A bridge was the logical solution.

As part of the improvement scheme a new road was built to a high standard down the southern side of Rombaksfjord, at about 30m above sea-level, to a point where the inner Rombaksbotn arm of the fjord is separated from the open outer section by narrows. Here, two facing promontories create a narrow neck: Rombakstraumen. The choice of this site for Rombaksbru reduced the crossing to a minimum but it still required what was Norway's largest suspension bridge when it was constructed between 1961 and 1964.

The Rombak bridge (18km) has a length of 756m and the central span is 325m. It clears the waters of the fast running Rombakstraumen by over 40m. Impressive towers of 76m and 88m support the bridge on the southern and northern sides respectively. The Highway meets the bridge without a steep approach for it is built into the north-facing slopes of the southern cliffs. Despite the fact that the shoreline is north-facing it is rarely seriously affected by winter snows.

The bridge, on the other hand, is subject to strong winds but it does give you splendid views to west and east along the line of the fjord. The Ofot Railway is now left behind. It has followed the same route out of Narvik as the Highway up to this point, although largely through tunnels, but now continues on the southern side of the Rombak inlet on its path into Sweden.

To offset the cost of the expensive Rombaksbru a toll used to be charged at the northern end of the bridge, though no longer. The Highway continues on a route along the south-facing side of Rombaksfjorden. At **Nygård/Trædal** (21km) sea-level is reached and there is the junction with the E10 formerly known as the Nordkalott road and now known as King Olav's road.

SIDE TRIP FROM NYGÅRD/TRÆDAL TO THE BORDER   Map 6a

This is a trip up to the Swedish border. It would take you about two hours for the journey from the Highway and back again. It's probably best done if you're staying a day or two in Narvik. The round trip from Nygård is about 54km.

This is an entirely modern route and road. The E10 was built in the late 1970s and early 1980s. It opened to traffic in 1984. The Swedish authorities built a 132km section of road on their side of the border to give Narvik its first road link with Kiruna nearly a century after the railroad was built and Narvik's iron trade with Sweden commenced.

In order to minimize gradients, the road takes a path which curves north-wards around the Haugfjell, a dome-like mountain. The principal attraction of this side trip is the wild scenery through which the road passes. There is virtually no settlement along its length and the scene is of unending cascading streams running over bare rock, often into placid lakes which are strewn across the area on either side of the road. The largest of these lakes is Sirkelvatnet (8km) which you can see to the right of the road. At **Skogsvatnet** (13km) there is a mountain hotel (to the left of the road). The E10 winds relentlessly onwards and upwards to an altitude of over 500m as it reaches the border with Sweden. There is a customs post just before the border. Along the final few kilometres before Sweden the road and railway come together. Near the border there is also a railway station and a rather austere looking tourist centre.

Across the **border** (27km) the Swedish section of the E10 (formerly Swedish route 98) continues to Kiruna, and eventually to Luleå. Across the border it runs along the edge of the Abisko National Park.

As an alternative to driving this road, there is the old path from Rombaksbotn up to and beyond the international border. This path is **Rallarvien** (*rallar* = immigrant worker) but is more commonly called the Navvies Road. When

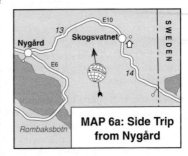

MAP 6a: Side Trip from Nygård

the railway was built, the 5000 or so workers on the line used this path and lived alongside it. Today the 'road' has been restored and is a tourist walk with guides.

There is evidence of the navvies' work and camps. It is usual to take the train up to either Bjørnfjell or Katterat stations and then trek down to the fjord. Details of these guided walks can be had from the tourist office in Narvik or from the Katterat Fjellstue (Mountain Lodge, ☎ 90 85 44 84). In late February or early March, there is the week-long Winter Festival to celebrate the achievement of the railway workers and their legendary cook (actually, more than one) known as Svarta Bjørn (Black Bear).

The Highway: Nygård to Bjerkvik
MAP 6

The Arctic Highway continues along the northern shore of Rombaksfjorden from the hydro-electric station at Trædal. The fjord walls are steep and it has been necessary to build a tunnel section for 550m just before Leirvik (26km). Beyond the tunnel the Highway turns inland to cut across the small peninsula which separates Rombaksfjorden from Herjangsfjorden. The col across the peninsula is largely bog and forest and the road rises to about 30m to find a path. The old ferry point of Øyjord, which previously served Narvik and was on the former Highway, is bypassed at the head of the peninsula.

Running along the eastern shore of the Herjangsfjord, the Highway is fringed by farms as it crosses over a narrow lowland strip which forms the coast of the fjord. The shore is rocky and attractive with good views not only across the Herjangsfjord but also towards Narvik and Ofotfjorden. At the head of this fjord is **Bjerkvik** (36km).

Today Bjerkvik is a major village with a population of over 1500 and with all major services including a hotel. The Nordlandia Bjerkvik Hotel is about 200m along the E10 after the Highway has turned right. There is a hamburger bar closer to the T-junction and most of the other services, such as the **post office** and bank, are clustered around this point where the two major roads meet.

The village was smaller and less important in 1940 but became the scene of some of the fiercest fighting in the course of the Narvik Campaign in World War II. In the second week of May 1940 it was recaptured from the German forces in what was the first amphibious landing of Allied troops under fire in the course of the war. The actual landing was about 800m to the west of Bjerkvik but the village was badly damaged and most of its buildings set on fire in the fighting that followed. A total of 27 villagers were killed. At Bjerkvik the E10 leaves the Arctic Highway which goes northwards while it makes its own way westward to the Lofotens.

Accommodation: Nygård to Bjerkvik
There is just the one hotel in Bjerkvik, the *Nordlandia Bjerkvik Hotel* (☎ 76 95 83 00; 🖹 76 95 83 01). It is situated 200m west of the junction between the E6, the Highway, and the E10, the Lofoten road. It faces on to the E10. There are wonderful and uninterrupted views into the fjord. There are 51 well-equipped

rooms, a lower-ground-floor swimming pool and a sauna. It is not cheap but good value at between NOK500 and NOK750.

SIDE TRIP FROM BJERKVIK TO THE LOFOTENS

This side trip has to be seen as a journey in its own right. The **Lofotens** are magical. I've always regretted that the Arctic Highway could not be routed through the wonderland of Norway's famous archipelago. This string of islands large and small is home to 25,000 whose livelihood is fishing.

Unfortunately, to leave the Highway and travel to Å (what a splendidly magical name that is!) would be to journey 700km there and back to Bjerkvik. Given the time it would take properly to appreciate the Lofoten Islands, such a journey could not be done in much under five days.

The new link road for the E10, due to be completed in 2005, will eliminate the last ferry and speed up the journey but once in the Lofotens it's not difficult to find an excuse to stay.

The scenery of the Lofotens is magnificent. Mountains rise straight out of the sea and wavecut platforms provide sites for countless picturesque fishing villages. The rocks are some of the oldest in the world as well as some of the youngest in Norway (for an explanation, see p41). Over eighty islands make up the chain that is the Lofotens and Vesterålen. Even the modern bridges have become, in typical Norwegian fashion, part of the beauty of the scene.

Fishing has been the lifeblood of the Lofoten islanders for the last 6000 years although agriculture has been practised for over four millennia. Only in relatively recent times has the beauty of the islands become a major attraction to travellers. Now, tourism is a significant part of the economy. There is plenty of accommodation from camping places to small hotels, but for an experience which is essentially true to all that the Lofotens mean, the only option to choose is a *rorbu* (plural *rorbuer*). The rorbuer are fishermen's cottages which can be rented over the summer. Renting can be for one night or for a week or more.

And Å? Well that is the village that is the terminus of the E10 and almost at the very extremity of the archipelago.

For a straightforward but comprehensive account of these islands, there is little better than Leif Ryvarden's *Lofoten and Vesterålen Norway*. The Lofoten Tourist Board can be contacted on ☎ 760 73000 or ▤ 760 73001.

The Highway: Bjerkvik to Elverum
MAPS 6–7

The Highway runs into the centre of Bjerkvik and then turns right to begin a climb up through Gratangseidet, a col linking Herjangsfjorden with the Gratangen inlet. This used to be quite a difficult section of road and a number of re-routings have taken place to give more gentle curves than the earlier hairpin bends which characterized this path through the Prestjord valley. On the climb upwards you can see some of the old road to the left at a lower level than the present Highway. The narrow tracks through thin forest contrast with today's beautifully engineered road.

As the road makes its winding ascent to the top of the plateau, it threads around the mountains and gullies, past waterfalls that decorate the steep slopes with their ribbon-like cascades. Once on the top, you cross the water divide at an altitude of 330m and you leave Nordland to enter Troms fylker. Around this point (41km), looking back towards Narvik, you can have good views of Herjangsfjorden and, beyond, the Ofot mountains.

The plateau top is part of the Gratangseidet, a col with a steady but gentle downward slope. It is an area with a high snowfall and the road can be difficult even in spring. There is a scattering of lakes along the Highway's route and this is a popular place for the inhabitants of Narvik to build their summer cabins, discreetly hidden in the forest. At **Foldvik** (47km), a waterfall passes under the road.

Just after the junction with Route 825 (48km), to the left of the Highway, it is possible to park off the road. There used to be a more substantial parking place here but the authorities deemed it to be a dangerous place for vehicles to pull in and out. All the same, it's worth stopping because a small path off the road leads down to a point where there are excellent views of the inner arm of the Gratangen fjord and the village of Gratangsbotn. Scattered farms are perched on terraces cut in the weak glacial drift by streams which followed the retreat of the ice responsible for carving the fjord. A substantial white building, the school, stands among the trees which give the settlement a park-like appearance.

Route 825 can be seen running the length of the southern shore of the fjord. Eight kilometres from Gratangsbotn a magnificent bridge, Straumsnesbru, almost 400m long, connects Route 825 with Route 848 at narrows that separate the inner arm of the fjord from its wider mouth. A short trip down the 825 might make an interesting diversion if you've got the time. Gratangsbotn was settled by Finnish immigrants in the middle of the nineteenth century and the large *gamme* they built can still be seen. A gamme is a turf hut and was a common form of dwelling in northern Scandinavia in times past. The Sami, however, retained its use and 40 years ago you would occasionally see one in use on the Sami summer pasture grounds.

Beyond the Gratangsbotn junction, the Arctic Highway turns eastward to run through some very pleasant mountain scenery, many of the peaks keeping their snow caps throughout the summer. At 51km is the entrance to the **Gratangs Tourist Hotel**, on the left of the road. Even if not stopping to use the hotel or its **café**, it's worth turning off the Highway because the views into the fjord from the hotel are quite stunning. Also at the hotel is the monument which has been relocated from its previous position back down the Highway. This is another war **memorial**, this time to the Norwegian soldiers who lost their lives hereabouts in 1940.

A little further on, the Highway reaches an altitude of 428m (at 55km). This is Bukkemyra, where the Highway begins its descent to **Lapphaugen** (62km).

To the right of the Highway, at Lapphaugen, is a **memorial** to one of Norway's great war heroes, General Carl Gustav Fleisher. It was here that his forces had a famous victory over the Germans during the Narvik Campaign. Advancing on Bjerkvik he joined forces with the British 24th Guards Brigade and was involved in the recapture of Narvik. Described as 'determined and aggressive' he was keen to continue the war with the Germans after the Allies withdrew from the Norwegian front.

There are cabins and camping at **Lapphaugen Turiststasjon**, just beyond the memorial and on the opposite side of the Highway. At the junction with Route 84 (left), as you leave Lapphaugen, there is a large **café**, Fossbaken Veikro. It is just off the road but it, and its adjacent **cabins**, are not especially attractive.

From Lapphaugen, the Highway competes with a tumbling stream in its rush to reach the bottom of the Salangs valley. As it does so, the Spans River, which runs into Lavangsfjorden to the west, passes under the road by way of a naturally cut tunnel in the limestone rock.

About 3–4km from the R84 junction is a turning, right, towards **Bones**. Three kilometres up this road is the world's most northerly wildlife park, the **Polar Zoo**. It has wolf and wolverine, lynx and brown bear, as well as the more common reindeer and elk. It's an open zoo rather than a wildlife park; all the species are in separate areas. Children like it, others hate it. It is open between June and August and admission is NOK110 for adults with children charged at NOK60. Servicemen also pay the lesser charge! This is in recognition of nearby military bases.

The floor of Salangsdalen is generally sufficiently broad to accommodate farms or allow for forestry. At the beginning of the century it was expected that the valley would become a second Dunderlandsdalen (see p115). This was not to be so, for the iron ore which could be economically extracted was worked out by the end of World War I.

The Highway follows the river through Salangsdalen. Sport fishing is important to the local people and to tourists. The river runs white with foam in its turbulent passage over its rocky bed. To the east, great hanging valleys look down on Salangselva and the river itself breaks through hummocky moraines which disturb the flatness of the valley floor.

The Highway crosses the Salangselv at **Lund** (65km) and in some places the rocky slopes forming the valley sides are pinched together to give the river a gorge-like passage. At nearby **Solbakken** (left) is a small **campsite**.

Salangsdalen is an especially beautiful valley with a unique quietness. So much of the Highway's path is through magnificent scenery that there is a danger of being overawed by its beauty. But no matter how tired the eye, no matter how familiar you are with the grandeur of the topography, you cannot be unresponsive to the loveliness of Salangselva. Stop occasionally along the road and let the scenery speak to you. **Fossengen Camping** (73km) is a possible stop along here.

As the Highway approaches the northern end of the valley there is a slow change in the scene. The mountains dip towards the road and the valley broadens. Now the mountains' sides are no longer bare but clothed in stunted birch. The ground is marshy and subject to flooding in spring when the snows thaw. Its marshiness probably accounts for the fact that there are far fewer farms than might otherwise have been expected.

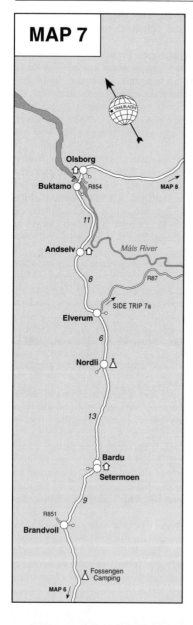

MAP 7

Olsborg

Buktamo   R854   **MAP 8**

11

Andselv   Måls River

8   R87

SIDE TRIP 7a

Elverum

6

Nordli   △

13

Bardu
△
Setermoen

9

R851
Brandvoll

△ Fossengen
Camping

MAP 6

At about 79km and to the right is Bardu Bygdetun, an **open-air museum** of old farm buildings and a small **museum of minerals**.

As you reach **Brandvoll** (80km) the Highway turns north-eastward leaving the Salangselv to follow its seaward path. Almost immediately, Route 851, to the left of the Highway, takes a similar route down the valley. The Arctic Highway soon begins a gentle descent into Setermoen and you can see the high peaks of Istindan for the first time to the north-east. This glaciated mountain mass has summits in excess of 1400m. To the east of the Highway is the deep valley, Kobbryggskaret, which descends from the ice-capped Lifjell, itself only a few metres below 1400m.

Setermoen (89km) is reached by way of a marshy gap. Even in these post-Cold War days, it is still very much a garrison town. The military are in evidence from Setermoen to **Bardu**: soldiers, trucks, camps and firing ranges. Since the 1950s this area, and northwards beyond Andselv, has been an important one for the training of NATO forces as well as Norwegian conscripts. Their presence has brought a high level of prosperity to the region as witnessed by the standard and profusion of services and the high quality of the roads.

Today the town is the headquarters of the 1st Brigade (North Norway) of the Norwegian army and there's a military museum in the town: **Troms Forsvarmuseum** (☎ 77 18 56 50).

(**Opposite**) **Top:** Sagelvvatnet (see p182), an excellent area for wild camping south of Tromsø. **Bottom:** A little off-road driving on the Finnmark *vidde*.

The accent is clearly on defence and there's even a ***Peace Café***. It is open all day in summer but closes at 15.00 in winter. To find the museum, turn off the Highway in the centre of town up the R847. The museum is just 150m up this road.

Setermoen lies at the point where the mountain course of the Barduelv begins its more sedate journey northwards through a broad valley, Bardudalen. The town has some 2750 inhabitants which means that it dominates the district by housing about two-thirds of its total population. The settlement is roughly T-shaped with the stem and the left-hand cross being along the Arctic Highway. The rest of the town spills up the right-hand cross towards the upper reaches of the Barduelva. Originally this was two villages, Setermoen and Bardu, but growth through early nineteenth-century immigration, as well as its post-war

---

 The origins of settlement in the Barduelv and Målselv valleys
Until almost the end of the eighteenth century, Bardudalen was simply a route for the Sami who migrated with their reindeer from the plateau to the coast each summer.

Then, in the 1780s, the districts around Østerdalen in southern Norway suffered from severe flooding and the farmers looked for new lands. In Bardudalen, they found a climate and topography which allowed cultivation and pastoral activities on a scale unparalleled elsewhere in North Norway. In 1791 migration started from Østerdalen, to be followed later by peoples from the great Gudbrandsdalen. Despite a certain loss of population in the mid-nineteenth century, through emigration to North America, Bardudalen and other nearby valleys quickly became established as the largest and most widespread farming community north of the Arctic Circle. The villagers built roads alongside the river courses in the broad valleys. Tributary streams were crossed by wooden bridges and the wider Målselv had a ferry at Fredriksberg. Those sections of road which were eventually to become part of the Arctic Highway kept fairly close to the riverbanks for most of their lengths, but often there were alternative parallel roads on higher and drier ground which could be used in the spring floods. The Bardu and Målselv had no less than 56km of road which were to be incorporated into the Arctic Highway. Moreover, the importance of the valleys had a singular bearing on the final path of the Highway, causing this route to be chosen rather than a coastal road through Lavangen, Salangen and Finnsnes. Much of the evidence of this 'foreign' origin of the people in Bardudalen and Målselva has long since been lost and my Norwegian is not good enough to detect the accents of Hedmark although I'm told they're still to be heard.

Most visible of all relics of the earlier immigration is the church. In 1825, the inhabitants of Bardudalen were given permission to build a church and one Ole Lundberg returned to his birthplace in Østerdalen, a village called Tynset. There he sketched the design of Tynset church on a piece of wood, returned to Bardu and oversaw the building of a replica, though smaller, church. The octagonal wooden building was consecrated in 1829, a belfry was added in 1840 and an organ (since replaced) installed in 1870. The church can be seen to the right of the Highway as the road leaves the town. (Look for the graveyard which is alongside.)

(Opposite) Top: Hamnes headland near Rotsundet (see p204) with a background of the Lyngen Alps. **Bottom:** Oksfjordjøkelbreen (see p210), the only glacier in Norway which calves directly into the sea.

expansion, has merged the two. Although Setermoen is strictly the town's correct name, Bardu is more often used for the enlarged settlement.

The town shelters in an amphitheatre of mountains but it was farming along the Bardudalen that attracted settlers from south-eastern Norway in the 1800s, many coming from Hedmark fylker.

The town's **tourist office** (☎ 77 18 10 97) is to the right of the Highway (look for the Shell petrol station), in a shop, as the E6 turns down Fogd Holmboesgt, after the junction with Route 847. Just before the tourist office is *Patricia's Café* and there's a further **café** and a **pizza bar** a little further down on the left. A large **Domus** store is just off the main road after passing the **post office** that is opposite the tourist office. All the usual services are in the busy town. There's one **hotel** and a **guesthouse** within easy reach of the Highway. The octagonal **Setermoen church** is worth a visit. It is open in mid-summer from 10.00 to 16.30. The church is the venue for occasional concerts.

The Highway makes its exit from Bardu by taking a left turn in the centre of the town and branching north-eastwards up Bardudalen along the left bank of Barduelva. The broad valley floor offers opportunities for farming and many of the small farmhouses stand on mounds of glacial moraine looking like little fortresses. While the valley floor is plastered with glacial debris, its sides rise steeply from the hummocky floor. The lower slopes are thinly covered with pine and birch but as slopes and altitude increase, the bare rock shows through. All around the valley the mountains rise to 1000m or more. To the right of the Highway is Gråhøgda (1002m) and, further north, Istindan (1489m). To the left you can see the two 'ala' peaks, Storala (1238m) and, as the name suggests, the slightly lower Veslala (1106m; *stor*=big; *vesl(e)*=little). The mountains dominate the scene but the valley is wide enough to prevent any feeling of being enclosed.

The Highway has quite significant fast stretches along this part (but beware of speed traps). There's a **camping place** to the left at **Nordli** (102km).

At **Elverum** (108km) there is a junction, to the right, with Route 87. Using Route 87 will bring you back on the Arctic Highway at Øvergård, covering a distance about 10km shorter than the Highway's route. However, if the side trip to Tromsø is to be taken (see p185) there is no saving in distance. Route 87 is described on p179 as a side trip but really it is an alternative to the Highway and it is certainly worth considering as such.

Accommodation: Bjerkvik to Elverum

Just off the Highway and overlooking Gratangsfjord is the *Gratangen Hotel and Turistsenter* (☎ 77 92 02 40; 🖹 77 02 02 70) which can lay claim to one of the best views in the region, down into the fjord from its lofty perch. It has 40 rooms, with the best views from the front, and prices range from NOK450 to NOK600 in summer, NOK100 more expensive in winter. It's a good place for a break in a journey on the Highway.

Lapphaugen Turiststasjon has seven cabins and places for tents or caravans. It is just off the road on a pleasant tree-clad slope. There's a **café** and the prices are good at NOK200 for a two-person cabin and NOK600 for six people. It is open at Easter but then only from mid-June to late August.

Fossbaken Veikro (☎ 77 17 71 20), if you're desperate, is just north of Lapphaugen at the junction with Route 84. There are six unattractive cabins, open all year, and a large **café**.

Before reaching Bardu, there is **camping** at *Fossengen* (☎ 08 98 51 80), to the right of the Highway. This is a pleasant site set among birch trees. There are 12 neat cabins (four en suite of which two sleep six persons). All the cabins are well equipped and include fridges.

Bardu-Setermoen has a choice of accommodation. Most expensive is the *Bardu Best Western Hotel* (☎ 77 18 10 22; 🖹 77 18 14 01) where a double room in summer may be around NOK1050. Even with 39 rooms it is often fully booked. Like many Norwegian hotels, it's best to ignore the drab exterior. Once inside, the entrance lobby is hung with animal skins, there's a big restaurant, a swimming pool and sauna and even a Turkish bath. All rooms have showers but not baths. The hotel is reached by turning up Route 847 at the centre of town and taking the first right turn. Also up the R847 is *Annekset Gjestegård* (☎ 77 18 13 04; 🖹 77 18 24 00). After passing the library, nearly opposite to the turning for the Best Western, Annekset is on the left alongside *Nills Café* and *Jeppe's Pub*. There are just 12 rooms which can be a little noisy on the main road but it does have the convenience of a café and restaurant.

The *Barduturistsenter* (☎ 77 18 15 58; 🖹 77 18 15 98), with cabins arranged in regimental lines, is off the Highway on the right leaving the town. The last time I was there most of the best accommodation had been commandeered for use by refugees from Kosovo. It has a swimming pool and was ideal for family groups.

Nordli Camping offers tent spaces and five cabins with showers. If you've got a choice, drive on; this is a dull and dismal site.

SIDE TRIP FROM ELVERUM ALONG ROUTE 87   Map 7a

The road is Route 87 and it takes about 90 minutes to do the trip back on to the Highway at Øvergård. It is an attractive alternative to the Highway: not only is it marginally shorter but also the route passes through the beautiful Tamokdalen.

Turning off the Highway at Elverum, Route 87 follows the Målselv valley eastwards. The road bridges the Barduelv and cuts north-eastwards at first until it meets the flat and marshy valley bottom of Målselva. Much of this part of the journey is forested with a sprinkling of farms. You can see little of the Måls River from the road. This is a pity because it follows an interesting contorted path in a broad meander belt. Many of the meanders cut back on their courses, leaving the valley filled with alluvium mixed with glacial gravel. After just 9km there is a minor road leading off to the left. This is worth investigating because only 3km along its path is a waterfall: Målselvfoss.

Målselvfoss is not noteworthy for its height, which is only 22m over three steps. By Norwegian standards this is a relatively modest drop, but it is the length which is impressive: 600m. The plunge pool at its base is one of the best salmon fishing spots in this part of Norway. Those salmon that escape the fisherman's hook are helped up the fall by a 450m salmon ladder. It's the longest ladder in Europe and dates from 1910.

Route 87 continues along the southern terraces of the river until it bridges the stream at **Rundhaug** (20km). It is joined by Route 854 on the northern side

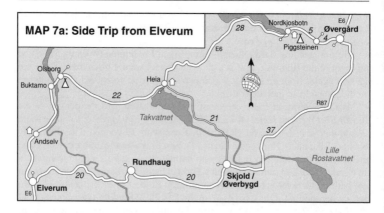

MAP 7a: Side Trip from Elverum

and both continue eastward keeping close to the right bank of Målselva. Mountains rise on both sides of the valley and small cirque glaciers have carved their niches into the rock faces on the north-facing sides.

The road turns northwards to **Skjold/Øverbygd** (40km) where it is joined by a road from **Heia** (21km away) which is on the Arctic Highway (see p182). Route 87 just touches the village before climbing to Lake Rosta. This lake is visible from the road but if you want to see it at close quarters it is necessary to take a minor road (at 50km) across Tamokbru and signposted Eidsvoll. The lake is rich in salmon and is a favourite place for local anglers.

Route 87 turns north at the bridge and begins its path through the captivatingly beautiful Tamokdalen, surely one of the most wonderful valleys in Troms. The narrow corridor, through which flows the Tamokelv, is bordered on both sides by mountains rising to over 1400m. This is Route 87's major attraction.

The road rejoins the Arctic Highway in Balsfjordeidet at **Øvergård** (77km). At this T-junction a turn to the right on to the Highway leads you to the great Lyngenfjord. However, if you are taking the Tromsø side trip, then turn to the left and travel back down the Highway to Nordkjosbotn (9km away) and take the E8 to Tromsø (see p185).

The Highway: Elverum to Nordkjosbotn
MAPS 7–8

From **Elverum**, the Arctic Highway continues with the Barduelv another eight kilometres to **Andselv/Bardufoss** (116km). This little town of rather more than 3000 inhabitants is in some ways not unlike Setermoen. The military are to be seen in the streets and in a large camp bordering the road. Their tracked snow vehicles proclaim this an important training area for Arctic warfare. The southern accents to be heard in Setermoen can be detected here for many of the families had their origins in Østerdal, Oppdal, Gauldal and the Gudbrandsdal before moving north nearly two hundred years ago. In fact Andselv/Bardufoss and Setermoen/Bardu can be thought of as twin settlements at each end of Bardudalen, the valley which attracted the early nineteenth-century immigrants. The whole area, even to the north of Andselv, is quite well settled and there is all that you might need: provisions, fuel and a range of **accommodation** from simple campsites to small hotels.

On arrival at Andselv/Bardufoss, there's a small **café** to the right of the Highway and then the first signs of the military, in the form of a large barracks. Nearby are a **petrol station**, **stores** and a **bistro-pub**. This is the district of Hellgelia. The road then sweeps left to **Rustahogda** where, to the left, is a **monument** to Colonel Ole Reistad (1898–1949), a wartime hero. At the same point is the **Polarbadet** (☎ 77 83 08 30), an ultra-modern swimming pool with a complex of slides, chutes and small pools. It is said to be the biggest swimming centre in North Norway. If staying in Andselv/Bardufoss, it's worth a visit. It costs NOK75 for adults and NOK45 for children but there are family tickets for NOK175. Once in the complex, everything is free including Turkish baths and saunas. It's best to telephone for opening hours because they alter through the year. In winter it is open only in the evenings on weekdays.

Nearby there's accommodation at **Bardufosstun** which describes itself as 'more than a hotel...' and it is (see p184).

The Highway has been rebuilt to bypass Andselv which now lies to the left of the road. Access, clearly marked, is by way of a bridge over the Highway reached by turning off right and looping back. In the sentrum is the **Bardufoss Hotel** and all the usual services. Opposite the Domus store in a group of buildings set back from the road is the **tourist information office** (☎ 77 83 42 25) in a travel agency. A little further up the street are the **library**, **post office** and **police station**. Beyond them is a **café**.

As the Highway leaves the town it passes through **Fagerlidal** (121km), notable as the place where the first farm of the southern immigrants was established in 1789. Onwards is a little settlement, **Haraldvollen**, to the right of the Highway. It is a little service point with a **café**. The road continues along the Målselv, which has been joined by the Barduelv to the east of the town, and falls gently towards **Olsborg** (129km). At this point there is a collection of villages. Olsborg is the best known but it is **Buktamo** which is reached first. Just after bridging the Måls River there is a turning to the right (Route 854) which leads directly into **Moen** where there is a memorial to Jens Holmboe who was instrumental in the development of the area in the late eighteenth century. Olsborg itself lies to the left of the Highway and there's a **guesthouse** here. Also in Olsborg is the **North Norway Riding Centre** and a **bronze sculpture** to *Nybyggerkona* ('The Settler's Wife'). This monument was unveiled by the King, in 1988, on the occasion of the bicentenary of the first settlement of the area by peoples from South Norway. Perhaps King Olav will have recalled other memories. The red house nearby was where he took shelter when, as crown prince, he was fleeing, with his father King Haakon, from the advancing Germans in 1940.

There have been a number of road improvements and re-routings along the next section of the road as far as Balsfjorden. Indeed all the way from Setermoen to Nordkjosbotn the Arctic Highway is a superior road with excellent surfaces and widths. Between Setermoen and Andselv the Highway carries quite a lot of traffic but it is less well used further north and especially beyond Olsborg.

Out of Olsborg the Highway turns to run across an inter-montane col and on to a low plateau at about 200m. High mountain ranges stand back from the road. To the right is the Mauken range exceeding 1200m in places and to the left, on the northern flank, Breitinden is a hundred or more metres higher. The col is occupied not only by the Highway but also by the Takelv, to the right of the road. Farms are scattered along the route but by the time you reach Takelvdal (141km) they are replaced by open forest and peatbog. The military uses this area as a firing range. A **camping place** lies to the right of the road.

The Highway runs close to the shore of a large lake, Takvatnet, on the right of the road before it reaches **Heia** (151km). Here there is a junction (to the right) with Route 857 which leads down to Øverbygd (see side trip p179) some 21km away. This road has been improved (ruining a favourite wild camping site of mine!) and makes an alternative way to Tamokdalen. It is an attractive route with small farms situated above Takvatnet. The lake itself is placid much of the time but a wind along its long axis can whip up the water into sea-like waves. By the side of the Highway at Heia is a granite **monument** to the engineer Paul Holst.

Two kilometres beyond Heia the Arctic Highway has been re-routed. Previously it ran into Storsteinnes but this path is now Route 858 and the modern Highway bypasses the village by taking a rather more southerly route. The re-routing saves little or nothing in distance but it is a superior road and, having been built where no road went before, it is largely through unpopulated countryside of forest and marsh.

If you take the old Highway route (Route 858), you will find it to be a pleasant alternative descending into **Storsteinnes** via Sagelvdalen. Just before entering the village there is a view, to the right, of Markenesdalen (see below). Storsteinnes shelters in a small bay, Sørkjosen, which indents the shore of Balsfjorden. There are many farms here on a talus platform which also supports the road. To rejoin the Highway you should turn right along the shore road after entering Sørkjosen.

The path of the new Highway takes it to the west of a high range of mountains, Holtinden and Kvitinden, whose summits exceed 1000m. The new road meets the old by the shore of Balsfjord where the giant Markenesdalen (to the right of the Highway) hangs above the level of the fjord. This is an exceptionally good example of a glacial hanging valley.

Now, across the great fjord, can be seen the magnificent scenery for which Tromsødistriktet is justly famous: parabolic valleys of glacial origin, sharp peaks shattered by ice weathering, sheltered cirques and the fjord itself. The highest ground, especially if facing north, retains its snow in summer and some of the cirques are occupied by glaciers. In winter, only the bare peaks thrust through a thick mantle of snow.

Balsfjord is noted or, depending on your taste, notorious for its goat's-milk cheese.

Shortly after reaching the fjord, the Highway runs eastward along one of its inner arms, the mis-named Nordkjosen. This section of the road has been reconstructed, widened and given an improved surface but the sight of the fjord with its enclosing mountains is a reason to slow down.

To the right of the road are the overshadowing mountains of Rakeltinden (1403m) and Istindan (1489m). Despite the names, it is the former that is ice-capped. Across the fjord rises the great Piggstind at a few metres above 1500m. At these great heights the peaks may frequently be shrouded in cloud but temperature inversions often give rise to strips of cloud hanging like garlands along the mountain slopes. At other times the peaks sprout banner clouds clear against a blue sky. Across the water you can see the E8 road to Tromsø following a parallel course on the opposite shore.

The Arctic Highway also passes (to the left of the road) an enormous building at **Bergneset** (172km), one of the few industrial or commercial buildings along the Highway which is something of an eyesore (*No Aqua*, please note).

The Highway runs into a scattered village at the end of the fjord: this is **Nordkjosbotn** (179km). To go into the village, bear right when you see the Shell garage to the right and a bridge ahead. Nordkjosbotn is at the western exit of a low lying col. Its site is across flats of deltaic origin. The fjordhead is gradually silting up and as it does so the village migrates

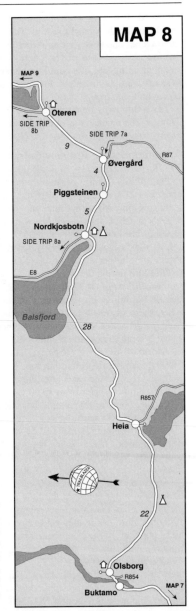

westward. It is an important communication node and is usually a bustle of activity in the short tourist season. The village has all the necessary services for the traveller and it is wise to refuel here, especially if you are not taking the Tromsø side trip (see p185). There is **accommodation** in the village, and a small **camping site**. It would also be possible for you to park a camper or caravan off the road overnight. For hotels the preference might well be Tromsø if taking that side trip.

Two **side trips** are described on p185. The first, using the E8, takes you into Tromsø. The second is an alternative route back to the Arctic Highway without having to retrace the road back to Nordkjosbotn.

Accommodation: Andselv/Bardufoss to Nordkjosbotn

The *Bardufoss Hotel* (☎ 77 83 05 00; 🖹 77 85 05 01; 🖳 b-hotell@online.no) is in the *sentrum* (centre) of Andselv next door to the Domus store and **café**. It's about one kilometre from Polarbadet, the swimming pool. The fifty rooms are quite spacious. All are en suite but only a few have baths rather than showers. There's a pub, cafeteria and bar with a grillroom which is open into the late evening. The hotel is independently owned by the Jensen family and may seem a little old-fashioned, especially the rather dark corridors, but it is well-run. Prices are cheaper at weekends (NOK900 for a double) but quite expensive (NOK1200) during the week.

Bardufosstun (☎ 77 83 46 00; 🖹 77 83 34 68) is alongside the Polarbadet, outside Bardufoss. It is a complex of cabins and rooms, with a total of 33 units where there's been no holding back on equipment. It has been built to suit the needs of the active holidaymaker whether they be into winter sports or angling. There is a range of sports facilities close by.

North of Andselv is *Olsborg Gjestestue* (☎ 77 83 11 84). After crossing the Måselv, take the first main left turn into the village, go past the petrol station (left) and the guesthouse is just 20m or so further on the same side of the street. The restaurant is open from 10.00 to 22.00. Nearby is a **pizza bar**. There are just eight rooms in this simple but adequate guesthouse and with doubles at NOK550 it is very reasonable.

Takelv Camping (☎/🖹 77 83 51 14) is 12km east of Olsborg and to the right of the Highway. It is a simple but acceptable site with 19 cabins and electrical connections for up to 36 caravans. Its limited facilities do include washing machines. Prices are around NOK300.

In Norkjosbotn is *Vollan Gjestestue* (☎ 77 72 23 00; 🖹 77 72 23 30), unmissable in the centre of the little village. It's a popular place for local people to gather in the **café**. Conveniently, the café is open from 07.00 to 22.00. With just 13 rooms it does get fully booked in summer due to Nordkjosbotn's nodal position. It's nothing special but a convenient place for an overnight stay. Rooms are en suite and prices are around NOK800 for a double.

Bjørnebo Camping (☎ 77 72 81 61) is in the centre of the village, immediately after the Shell petrol station, but is open only from early June to mid-August. Its ten cabins are simple but washing machines and tumble dryers are on site. The price is a modest NOK300.

Just outside the village, on the road to Tromsø, is another, more attractive, small **camping site** (see side trip to Tromsø below). Seventy-three kilometres up the E8 is Tromsø with a wealth of accommodation options.

SIDE TRIP FROM NORDKJOSBOTN TO TROMSØ   Map 8a

This side trip to Tromsø is a 'must' unless time is really short. Otherwise who could ignore the 'Capital of the North' and the beautiful Balsfjord? The road is fast with a singular lack of steep gradients. However, it is fairly heavily used. It is fascinating to recall that this road, linking Tromsø to the interior, dates only from 1936.

The distance is some 73km, needing about an hour or so of driving. You'll need at least one full day in Tromsø to see something of the town.

A second side trip, from Fagernes, off the E8, is also described on p194. Using the two trips in combination allows you to go into Tromsø, back track to Fagernes, take the second side trip and re-join the Arctic Highway at Olderdalen. Certainly, if you intend driving the Highway in both directions, this is an option not to be missed.

The E8 and the Arctic Highway (E6) join in Nordkjosbotn just after crossing a straight causeway on the edge of the village. Turning right at the junction will take you along the combined E6/E8 (see Part 7, p197) but to reach Tromsø, turn left. In less than a kilometre is Sjøvollen, a **campsite**, to the left of the road.

To begin with, the E8 is never far from the very edge of the fjord. The first 20km out of Nordkjosbotn have been reconstructed in the last couple of years. This has reduced curvatures on bends and increased widths to make this a quite fast road. Much of the new course lies high above the old path with links between the two. In places the new road is up to 100m above the old. There are some extraordinary feats of engineering but also the loss of some good viewpoints. The narrow littoral strip is farmed but it is the opposite shore which attracts attention. There is an exceptionally good viewing point at **Seljelvnes** (9km). Across the fjord are the mountains that overshadow the Arctic Highway: Istind, Store Russetind and Rakeltind.

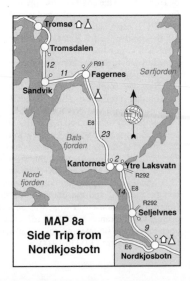

At Seljelvnes there is a minor road (Route 292) leaving the E8 to the right. This runs through Lakselvdalen towards the head of Sørfjorden and into the Lyngen peninsula. It is possible to use this route to rejoin the E8 at Ytre Laksvatn. It will add an extra 37km to the journey but gives very good views of the Lyngen and Lakselv Alps. You can see the

MAP 8a
Side Trip from
Nordkjosbotn

highest peak, Jiekkevarre (1833m), to the north. If making this detour, be certain to take the left turn at Lakselvbukt where the road meets Sørfjorden, otherwise you will be forced to drive the whole length of the fjord without there being another turning.

From Seljelvnes, the E8 runs northwards along the main fjord, Balsfjord. The fjord narrows near **Slettmo** (15km) and on the other side of the water is the village of Balsfjord, recognizable by its church, and behind the settlement towers Føgltind (1034m). The new path of the E8 rejoins the old near Laksvatn (22km). Between the village and **Ytre Laksvatn** (23km), where the minor road, Route 292, referred to on p185, rejoins the E8, it is possible to see a little of the Lyngen Alps. The E8 uses a causeway to avoid going through the village.

At **Kantornes** (25km) the E8 turns abruptly northwards again and forsakes the fjord edge. A minor road leaves the E8 here (to the left) and runs round the shore of Balsfjorden to rejoin the main road at Sørbotn. This minor road (Route 294) continues to give excellent views of the fjord and the mountains of Troms but to follow it will almost double the distance to be travelled to reach Sørbotn (40km rather than 22km).

The E8 loses sight of the fjord from Kantornes as it strikes a path through two forested valleys separated by a broad col. This is Lavangsdalen which is formed by the south-flowing Smalatelv and the north-running Mellemdal River. The col takes the road to just over 80m and within the col is a good example (left) of a cirque glacier. Near here (35km) to the left of the road, is the **Sarastein**. The boulder is a Sami **ritual stone**, a reminder that the whole area has strong Sami connections.

When you reach **Sørbotn** (where the 294 re-joins it) the E8 is back with the water. Indeed, it is difficult to get away from water in the whole of this part of Troms where the coast is so deeply fractured and the coastline is remarkable for its collection of peninsulas and islands. The Norwegian for peninsula, incidentally, is especially graphic: *halvøy* (half island). The water here is an inlet off Balsfjorden, called Ramfjorden. The E8 follows its eastern shore where there is a **campsite**, Ramfjord Camping (42km). At **Fagernes** (48km) it is joined by Route 91, an alternative road back to the Arctic Highway. (See side trip from Fagernes, p194.)

Near the south of Ramfjorden the E8 cuts across a gap in the hilly Ramfjorden promontory above **Sandvik** (59km). The road runs above the level of the fjord and you'll have quite good views to the west to Kvaløya (Whale Island). Islands and peninsulas block the view further west to the sea, and to the east the Lyngen Alps rise to over 1800m. Five kilometres further on, the road drops back to fjord-level and in another seven it is into **Tromsdalen** (71km). To the right, signposted but off the E8 up a winding path, is **Forsvars Museum** (the Tromsø Defence Museum; ☎ 77 62 88 36). This houses the *Tirpitz Sanlingen* (*Tirpitz* Collection). The museum is still being developed and the emphasis on the *Tirpitz* artefacts may diminish. Currently it is housed in what was an artillery position during the German occupation. Entrance is NOK20 for adults with half-price for children. It is open only in the summer months and at weekends only in May and September. Opening hours are 11.00 to 19.00.

Accommodation: Nordkjosbotn to Tromsø

There may be the urge to press on to Tromsø once on the E8 at Nordkjosbotn but, if the intention is to explore Tromsø, there are cheaper alternatives than staying in the town. After all, Tromsø is only an hour's drive from Nordkjosbotn.

Just outside Nordkjosbotn off the E8 is a campsite hidden away among the trees. This is *Sjøvollen Camping* (☎ 77 72 84 70). There are just three cabins but there's space for tents or caravans. There are showers and television in the cabins and the site is open all year. Two cabins take six persons in one or two bedrooms and the third sleeps three people. Prices range from NOK350 to NOK600 and there's a very friendly management.

On Ramfjord, just south of Fagernes and the junction with Route 91, is *Ramfjord Camping* (☎ 77 69 21 30; 📧 77 69 22 60). It is closed in mid-winter (mid-November to February). The cabins are simple, without even water, but there are plenty of shared facilities. The site's a bit cramped but the caravan area is pleasant. The kiosk, sauna and **café** are a plus. Prices range from NOK500 for a six-person cabin to NOK220 for a double cabin.

TROMSØ

Tromsdalen isn't quite Tromsø although it might be seen as a suburb. The city of **Tromsø** is built, like almost all the other major settlements of North Norway, on an island. There are some major exceptions such as Narvik (a modern town), Alta (a collection of villages) and Vadsø (which did actually start life on an island, see p47). But island sites offered some of the best harbours and, more importantly, were nearer the rich fishing grounds of the Norskehavt – the Norwegian Sea.

My own feelings about Tromsø are somewhat ambivalent. It is attractive as a lively, even cosmopolitan city but it has an air of introspection. Although it lays claim to be the capital of North Norway it is difficult to reconcile this with its detachment, physical and psychological, from the rest of Arctic Norway. As it loses its old elegance it becomes more aggressive and self-important. Certainly Tromsø should be visited. It has a lot to offer and there is much to see, but somehow it is not the authentic Arctic of the Highway.

History

Tromsø received its charter as a town in 1794 and became the Hålogaland bishopric in 1803. Today it is an especially proud, even boastful, city. It seems to attract a host of hyperbolical titles: Paris of the North, Gateway to the Arctic, Norway's largest fishing 'village', the world's most northerly university city, Capital of North Norway, and Norway's largest city.

The last is something of a spoof. It is true that it is Norway's largest city-municipality (actually about the size of Luxembourg at 2558 sq km) but this includes the Lyngen Alps and fjord and the island, Kvaløy. This vast area is home to over 60,000 inhabitants but, although most live in Tromsø/Tromsdalen, the built-up area of the city is not significantly bigger than that of unpretentious Harstad. Pre-World War II, its de facto population was scarcely more than 10,000. It was not until 1964 that it absorbed its neighbouring kommunes into a Greater Tromsø. The population continues to grow at a greater than average rate and is further swelled by large student numbers.

The town has had an eventful history. The area has been settled for thousands of years, probably since the Pleistocene ice sheets retreated. It has also long been a meeting place for a variety of peoples. The Sami have traditionally used the area as summer pastures for their reindeer. The Finns found an easy crossing into Norway via Skibotn (see p201) and even the Russians arrived to exchange timber and

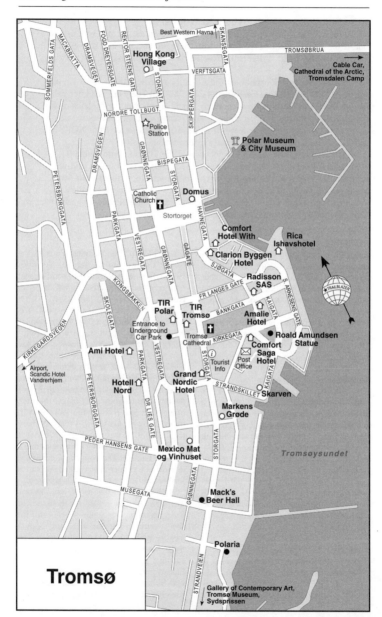

Tromsø

agricultural produce for fish. Even so, the town's population was only 2–3000 at the beginning of the 19th century. It grew more rapidly from the 1850s when shipbuilding was introduced. Another notable date was the opening of Mack's Brewery in 1877.

In more recent times, the town became world famous overnight as the new 'capital' of Norway when the king and crown prince, together with the government, retreated to Tromsø from Oslo in May–June 1940. Soon afterwards, the royal court and government moved to exile in Great Britain for the duration of World War II. Some four years later on 12 November 1944 the giant German battleship *Tirpitz* was finally sunk in Tromsøysund in an air raid by the British Royal Air Force. The ship was already so disabled by earlier attacks by the RAF and the Royal Navy that it was no longer of any use except as a floating fortress. The raid of November 1944 was by no less than 32 Lancaster bombers armed with 12,000lb 'tall boy' bombs. About 1000 of the ship's crew perished.

In May 1969 a great fire swept through the city and a large number of the old wooden buildings that had given the town so much of its character were destroyed. Property, worth in excess of NOK60 million at that time, was lost as fire raged in the City Square and along Storgata.

The most recent date of note is 1972 when the university opened its doors for the first time.

Until 1960 it was necessary to cross Tromsø from Tromsdalen by a short ferry. In March that year a new, elegant bridge of 1016m span was opened to traffic. It is a splendid sight with its steep curves carrying it above the fast-running Tromsøysund. Ocean-going ships can glide under the great arch but have to beware of a current which has been known to smash smaller boats against the slender pillars.

The bridge transformed communications between the island, Tromsøya, and the mainland. Traffic doubled overnight and its rate of growth has continued to be unparalleled in North Norway. It gave a special boost to the development of Tromsdalen on the mainland side of the bridge.

The bridge is no longer the only way to reach the city centre. By the 1980s it was clear that another bridge or a tunnel would be needed and in the mid-1990s a tunnel had been completed. The tunnel is reached by continuing along the shore, past the bridge, for about 2km to the suburb of Tomasjord. In fact there are two separate, lined tunnels for each direction.

On reaching the tunnel exit on the island, which is Tromsøy, the road leads right, briefly through the suburbs of the city which include the university quarter. At the third roundabout the road plunges into an extraordinary labyrinth of tunnels which even include roundabouts and car-parks. It is like a vast underground road network. The main path runs parallel to the city's high street, Storgata, and the tunnel connects with surface roads in the centre of town.

It is all incredibly ambitious for a town of only 60,000, but it's typically Norwegian and, of course, it works.

Services

If using the bridge, the centre of the town is approached by turning left off the bridge and driving down Skippergata. Tromsø is not a town to drive around. The roads are congested in summer, there are many restrictions and, in any case, it is small enough to be explored on foot. There are surface parking places but they quickly fill up and a better plan might be to use the large 800-place underground car-park. To reach the centre of the town, continue along Skippergata to a triangular road-island and branch right. This takes you on to **Storgata** which, as the name suggests, is the High Street. Most attractions lie to the right or left (harbour-side) of this road.

The **tourist office** (☎ 77 61 00 00, 📠 77 61 00 10; 🖳 info@destinasjontromso.no) is on the left of Storgata if driving or walking from the bridge, in the block after its junction with Kirkegata. The office is open all year but its opening times are variable. On weekdays it opens at 08.00 every day but stays open two hours later than normal, until 18.00, in the high season (June through to mid-August). At weekends it is closed from mid-September to mid-May but opens from mid-morning until early afternoon for the rest of the year. The office can be contacted by phone but it would be wise to call in and collect a map and other information before embarking on a sightseeing tour of the town.

The main **post office** is on Strandgata (turn off Kirkegata by the cathedral) and the **police station** (☎ 77 66 77 66) is at the northern end of Grønnegata.

To reach the **underground car-park** (see p189), turn right off Storgata into Fr. Langes Gate then left into Vestregata. The entrance is first left. This car-park does not take caravans.

The regional hospital is in the university quarter near the northern exit from the tunnel under the sound. (For emergency medical care, ring ☎ 77 68 30 00.)

The town's **airport** (☎ 77 64 84 00) can be found by following Route 862 as far as the university. Beyond the airport there is a bridge to Kvaløy Island.

Around town

The E8 runs through the southern fringes of Tromsdalen, which are largely residential. North of the bridge, there is a mixture of industry and commuter homes. Just before the bridge there are two attractions. The first, signposted to the right of the E8, is a **cable car** (☎ 77 63 87 37) to Storsteinen. The name of this hill literally means 'big rock' and, at 420m, no one can argue with that description. The four-minute trip to the top is not to be missed. You'll get spectacular views which include the whole of Tromsø and its island, as well as the neighbouring islands and peninsulas. The cable car runs from 10.00 to 17.00 from April to September inclusive, but on sunny days in June, July and August it is also operating to an hour after midnight. At that later time it is possible to experience the midnight sun from 21 May to 23 July. In winter, Storsteinen is noted for its skiing between 25 November and 21 January, when the sun never rises, and at these times the town can be seen sparkling with electric light. There's a **café**, kiosk and bar at the top where you can post a card or letter with

special franking. If not travelling by car to Storsteinen, it's only a half-hour walk from the centre of town. Alternatively, the No 26 bus runs from the city.

The other attraction before crossing the bridge is more visible from the road. It is the famous **Cathedral of the Arctic**. To reach it you must turn off the E8 to the right instead of bearing left to cross the bridge. There is a small car-park behind the cathedral. Strictly it is not a cathedral at all, but is impressive none the less. From across the sound it looks like a giant white ridge tent sagging in the middle. In fact, it consists of 11 major triangular sections which are joined by windows. Each section represents an apostle (the 12 minus Judas). It has the largest stained-glass window in northern Europe and, at the other end of the building, a fine pipe organ. A charge is made for adults (NOK20).

It is not possible to stop to take photographs when driving across Tromsøbrua. However, there is a pedestrian pathway over the bridge and it may be best to walk some way across it from Tromsdalen, leaving the vehicle at the church, if you want to photograph the church or the town from the bridge's highest point.

The attractions of Tromsø are not only its museums and churches. There are still a few of the **old wooden buildings** that survived the 1969 fire. There are some wonderful examples in Skippergata and in Sjøgata (near the harbour). Many of the old buildings are luxury shops. Down near the harbour by the Comfort Saga Hotel (see p192) is a statue of **Roald Amundsen** who was the first man to reach the South Pole. The statue is a favourite perch for seagulls which have given Amundsen a guano cap. In the same little green triangle is a **memorial** to the Jews who died in World War II and another commemorating Norwegian-Franco comradeship.

Tromsø Cathedral is on Kirkegata (off Storgata). It dates from 1861 and is one of the largest wooden churches in Norway. It is close to the site where, in 1250, King Håkon Håkonsson built a church to convert the Sami. The cathedral is closed on Mondays.

The **Catholic church** is also of interest. It is located off Storgata, on the right up the hill from Stortorget (the harbour square). Despite its diminutive size, it is actually a cathedral – the most northerly Catholic bishopric in the world. It was visited by Pope John Paul II in 1989.

Of Tromsø's many museums, two are easily accessible on foot in the Skansen quarter. To reach them, walk along the harbour-side towards the bridge. One is the **Polar Museum** (☎ 77 68 43 73) housed by the harbour in an old customs warehouse. It has exhibits demonstrating Tromsø's link with the polar regions. It is open from 10.00 to 17.00 from mid-June to mid-August and from a minimum period of 11.00 to 15.00 for the rest of the year. It is open at weekends. Entrance is NOK30. Behind is the **City Museum**, housed in a late-eighteenth-century customs house. The story told here, largely through pictures, is of Tromsø's history.

There's also a general art museum, the **Gallery of Contemporary Art** (☎ 77 65 58 27), off Muségata. This can be reached by continuing along Storgata until it becomes Strandveien. Muségata is on the right (west) and the museum is down a short road on the left of Muségata. It's closed Mondays but open from noon to 17.00 otherwise. Entrance used to be free but is now NOK40.

The best museum, however, is not in the town but at the southern end of the island. This is the **Tromsø Museum** (☎ 77 64 50 00), also called the University Museum. To reach it, continue down Strandveien (by car) towards Lanes. If travelling by bus, use the No 28 from the town centre. The museum is in a splendid building set in a park (Folkeparken). It is part of the university and houses a most interesting cultural, ethnic and scientific collection. Nearby is a typically Scandinavian open-air folk museum of old buildings. In June, July and August it is open from 09.00 to 20.00 every day but it has shorter opening hours for the rest of the year. Entrance is NOK20.

Near the harbour on Hjalmar Johansensgt is the **Polaria** (☎ 77 75 01 00), a celebration of all things Arctic. It is all rather well done and includes an audiovisual display in a circular cinema. There are showings of a panoramic video film. Children like the Polaria particularly because of its interactive displays and its aquaria. The Polaria is open from 10.00 to 19.00 in summer but only for five hours, from noon, in winter. Entrance is NOK70.

On the other side of the town, at Breivika, is the **Northern Lights Planetarium** (Nordlysplanetariet, ☎ 77 67 60 00). Breivika is the university area and is accessible by Route 862 going north out of the city centre. The displays are not all astronomical and there is an excellent multi-image audio-slide show. The Planetarium has somewhat unreliable opening arrangements so it's best to telephone to check.

There is an unusually wide variety of entertainment in Tromsø: cafés, discos, bars and cinema, probably reflecting the demands of a large student population and

---

🦌 Summer in the North

This may be the point to remind visitors to North Norway that the high season, summer, which is most popular for visitors, is very short. It is usually defined as June to mid-August. The 'early' finish to this season often catches visitors from other parts of Europe unawares. You may find that after mid-August some guesthouses and campsites will be shut down; museums and other attractions may be closed or open only for limited periods in the day. It is always worth checking opening times and periods if visiting the region outside of the high season.

More encouraging, visitors to museums and similar attractions usually find that there are concessions for children, students and pensioners outside of high season.

port. The local beer, Mack's, has its own **beer hall** (☎ 77 62 45 00) towards the southern end of Storgata (on the right going south). Native English-speakers should note that 'muck' is simply the Norwegian pronunciation and not a comment on the beer's (excellent) quality. There are tours of the Mack brewery but they have to be booked in advance.

Accommodation

As befits an important administrative, commercial and university city, Tromsø has a wealth of accommodation options. All the same, it is best to book ahead at any time of the year, especially because it is a favoured centre for conferences, beloved of the Norwegian business community.

The **Radisson SAS Hotel** (☎ 77 60 00 00; 🖷 77 65 62 21; 🖳 sales@toszh.rdsas.com) is the most expensive and, arguably, the best in town. It is situated close to the harbour on Sjøgata (turn off Storgata down Fr Langesgt and it is on the right). There are nearly 200 rooms although I've always found them on the small size. There is a good choice of places to eat and the hotel is efficiently run. Rates are between NOK1400 and NOK1700 but summer and weekend prices are about NOK400 lower. There is limited parking.

Just slightly less expensive is the **Rica Ishavshotel** (☎ 77 66 64 00; 🖷 77 66 64 44; 🖳 rica.inhavshotel@rica.no), close by the Radisson SAS but nearer the harbour. In fact it has superior views to the latter because rooms and restaurant overlook the water and the Coastal Steamers dock nearby. There's a pay car-park (NOK85 for 24hr). There are a couple of bars including a piano bar where snacks are available. The bars stay open until the early hours. For luxury, it is probably the best in Tromsø.

There are two 'Choice Hotels', the Comfort Saga Hotel and the Comfort Home Hotel With. **The Saga** (☎ 77 68 11 80; 🖷 77 68 23 80; 🖳 comf.hotellsaga@tromso.online.no) has 66 rooms and rates are NOK1000 to NOK1250, NOK300–400 cheaper in summer. There's no restaurant but the café serves a buffet dinner which,

like breakfast, is included in the price. Parking is limited to twelve spaces. The Saga is just beyond the Rica and Radisson SAS, very close to the Coastal Steamer jetty.

The **Hotel With** (☎ 77 68 70 00; 🖷 77 68 96 16; 🖳 bookings@with.no), named after Richard With, is much better appointed than the Saga but the summer prices are similar. Again, there are limited dining options but, with its maritime theme, it is a very pleasant place to stay. A nice touch is the provision of umbrellas in all the rooms! One has to assume they're for outdoor use.

Next door and under the same management as the With is the brand new **Clarion Byggen Hotel**. It has yet to settle down and establish a reputation.

The **Grand Nordic Hotel** (☎ 77 75 37 77; 🖷 77 75 37 78; 🖳 resepsjon.gnt@nordic.no) on Storgata, the main High Street, is very much a city-centre hotel with a '60s look although the original hotel was Tromsø's first, in 1879. It is a bit overpriced at NOK1200 to NOK1400 (summer prices are NOK300–400 less) but an evening meal is included except on Fridays and Saturdays. There are 100 rooms but parking can be a problem. It has a nightclub 'for adults only – no loud music' so a good night's sleep should be assured!

There are two Tulip Inn Rainbow Hotels, the **TIR Polar** and the **TIR Tromsø** (Polar: ☎ 77 75 17 00; 🖷 77 75 17 10; Tromsø: ☎ 77 75 17 20; 🖷 77 75 17 30; Polar/Tromsø: 🖳 polar@telia.no). These two hotels are opposite each other on Grønne-gaten, the street which runs parallel to Storgata (left turn off Fr Langes gt). With a total of 114 rooms, rates are NOK800 to NOK1000 but these are halved at weekends or with a 'summer hotel pass' from TIR. The Polar and Tromsø share the same facilities. The Polar provides an evening meal for both hotels and there's a shared car-park at the back of the Tromsø. These mid-market hotels are reasonable value so don't be put off by the unattractive exteriors.

Amalie Hotel (☎ 77 66 48 00; 🖷 77 66 48 10; 🖳 booking@amaliehotel.no) on Sjøgata (near Radisson SAS) is quite new, converted from offices. It has 48 rooms (mostly singles). At about NOK650 to NOK850, including breakfast and an evening meal, it is good value even if the rooms are a trifle small.

The *Hotell Nord* (☎ 77 68 31 59; ▤ 77 61 36 05; ▢ stig.hansen@hotellnord.no) on Park-gata (a turning off Fr Langesgt) is a simple and inexpensive option. Rooms start at NOK300 including breakfast. Some rooms have no bathroom.

The *Ami Hotel* (☎ 77 68 22 08; ▤ 77 68 80 44; ▢ email@amihotel.no) is an attractive guesthouse. It used to be called the Kongsbakken Gjestgiveri. It is to be found by continuing up Fr Langesgt and turning left into Skolegt. There are wood-panelled walls and a sort of cosiness that makes you feel you're living in a private home. There's limited parking and light meals have to be ordered in advance. Some redecoration appeared to be needed when I was last there. The hotel is closed at Christmas and Easter.

Away from the centre of Tromsø, there are further options.

One kilometre from the airport is the impressive *Scandic Hotel* (☎ 23 15 50 00; ▤ 23 15 50 01; ▢ tromso@scandic-hotels. com). Built to serve the airport and business conferences, it also caters for those wishing to explore the region, including trips to the Lyngen Alps. There is a swimming pool and sauna, bars and a nightclub, (although the club shuts in summer). There are 146 rooms, parking and a good restaurant (the Måken, on the second floor). If you want to abandon your vehicle, this hotel is attractive because the city can be reached by bus. The Scandic isn't cheap. Singles are from NOK1000 but weekend and summer prices are reduced by about 40%. Breakfast is included. To reach the hotel, take Route 862 out from the centre of town towards the airport. When almost there, the hotel is clearly visible, off Route 862, to the right, near a big shopping centre.

A small hotel is the *Sydsprissen* (☎ 77 62 89.00; ▤ 77 61 89 77) at the very southernmost tip of the island. Continue along Strandvegen (the harbour road and continu-

ation of Storgt) to almost its very end. Prices are from NOK400 but there's no restaurant: it should be seen as a simple hotel for an overnight stay.

The *Best Western Havna Hotel* (☎ 77 67 59 99; ▤ 77 67 50 33; ▢ havna@online. no) is close to the exit from the tunnel under Tromsø Sound (Tromsøysundet). After emerging on the island, turn towards the city at the first roundabout (see p189) and the hotel is just by the next roundabout, on Terminalgt. (The terminal is Brevika harbour.) The Havna is a small 38-room hotel, near the university and the planetarium. It is good value from NOK650 with breakfast in summer but – always to be remembered – summer finishes in mid-August in Tromsø. Buses run from here to the city centre.

Far and away the cheapest accommodation is to be had at the *Tromsø Vandrerhjem Elverøy* (☎ 77 68 53 19), the youth hostel. It is out of town and not easy to find but the tourist office will provide a map. A dormitory bed here costs NOK125 to NOK150 but nothing else is provided. Even the bedding has to be hired. There are limited self-catering facilities on each floor. The hostel shuts during the day (11.00 to 17.00). Accommodation is available between 1 June and mid-August only. For the rest of the year, it is filled by students.

On the other side of the Sound, in the mainland suburb of Tromsdalen, is a guesthouse, the *Nye Tromsdal Gjestgiveri* (☎ 77 63 99 00; ▤ 77 63 98 97). It is signposted off the road between the bridge and the tunnel. After passing the bridge, look for Evjenveg on the right. Follow this road (left) to Tytteaervegen. There are only 27 rooms in this simple guesthouse but the price is just NOK400 and meals can be had here.

Tromsdalen Camp (☎ 77 63 80 37) is next to the guesthouse. There are 48 cabins which vary in size and facilities. At NOK300 there are one-room cabins sleeping two with no water. But at NOK900 the cabins are en suite with two bedrooms. All cabins have cooking facilities and most have a fridge. There's plenty of space for tents, caravans and campers, with electricity for just NOK20 per day. The mountain background to the site is beautiful.

Where to eat

There is a wide choice of cafés, restaurants and bars in central Tromsø. Most are a mix of dining places plus bars and the majority are found on the two main roads, Storgata and Strandgata (near the harbour-side).

For a good meal in pleasant surroundings, try *Markens Grøde* (☎ 77 68 25 50) near the junction of Fiskegata and Storgt. It is described as a *vilt-og fiskerestaurant* and *vin-og Kaffebar*, which says it all: game and fish with a wine and coffee bar. The fish, seafood and venison (reindeer) are well worth the price.

An alternative at something like the same level is *Emma's* on Kirkegata, opposite the cathedral. Here too, there is a café: *Kaffe Lars*. The main restaurant is open from 16.00 to 01.00 but closed on Sundays. The coffee bar serves wine and beers and, remarkably, it is open from 07.00 to 02.00 on weekdays, opening a little later at weekends.

Skarven (☎ 77 60 07 20), by the harbour at the bottom of Strandskillet, is strong on fish and seafood (try the seal and whale meat for a change) but its full name, Biffhuset Skarven, is justified by its beef dishes. When the weather's good, there are plenty of pavement tables at this popular eating place.

It is possible to get Mexican dishes at the *Mexico Mat og Vinhuset* at the southern end of Storgt, as it becomes Strandgt, opposite the Spar supermarket. There are some vegetarian dishes on the menu. A main meal will cost NOK150–200.

Those preferring Chinese food can try the *Hong Kong Village* which is at the other end of Storgata by the junction with Verftsgt.

A pleasant little café-bar with character is *Påttjørne* on Sjøgata by the Radisson SAS. As usual, the **Domus** store, on Torget, also has a café. Across the harbour, at the foot of the cable car (see p190) in Troms-dalen, the *Allegro* is a café and pizza bar.

Around town there are plenty of pizza bars and takeaways. No one need go hungry in Tromsø.

SIDE TRIP FROM FAGERNES TO OLDERDALEN   Map 9a

After a visit to Tromsø, this can be an alternative way for you to return to the Arctic Highway at Olderdalen. The journey will take under two hours (including two ferries: 20 minutes and 35 minutes). The road is Route 91 and the driving distance from Fagernes is 46km.

This side trip gives an alternative not only to retracing the E8 back to the Arctic Highway but also to 117km of the Highway itself. Taking into account the journey back to Nordkjosbotn from Fagernes (48km) which you also save, the net saving in road distance is 119km to Olderdalen. It is difficult to decide on the merits of using this road rather than going back to Nordkjosbotn but if time is short there is no contest. This is the road to take, but refuel before starting out.

To reach Fagernes from Tromsø, some retracing of steps is inevitable. Take the E8 out of Tromsdalen towards Nordkjosbotn and travel 23km back to **Fagernes**. (Distances will hereon be given from Fagernes.) Turning left from the E8 on to Route 91 takes you up into Breivikeidet. The road rises to **Fuglemo** (2km from Fagernes) where it crosses a ridge and then runs along the very broad depression, hugging the steeply rising edge of Gabreilfjellet to avoid the marshy valley bottom. On the other side of the depression, Tromsdalstind (1238m) and Skardlifjellet (966m) dominate the north-western flank of this great glacial trough. Small hanging valleys score the steep sides of Breivikeidet. Despite the marshy ground, this is an area where wild camping is possible. It is a most beautiful setting.

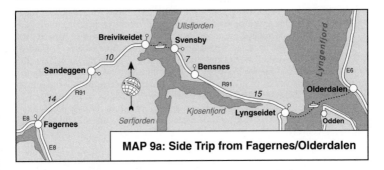

MAP 9a: Side Trip from Fagernes/Olderdalen

At **Sandeggen** (14km) there are two river crossings, first the Breivikelv, then Russevankelva. The col remains wide for a while but the road is now on the western side. Gradually the pass narrows as the road drops gently down through a birch-filled corridor to the **Ullsfjord** and the **Breivikeidet** ferry point (24km). There's a small **kiosk**. Fourteen crossings a day are made by the ferry in each direction in summer. The crossing takes about 20 minutes with first and last departures around 06.30 and 21.00 from Breivikeidet and 07.00 and 21.30 from Svensby.

The Ulls is a particularly wild looking fjord. North from Breivikeidet its shore is uninhabited and few have their homes on the opposite shore. The ferry crossing is rewarding. Views northwards are to the open, broadening Ullsfjord; to the south is the narrow entrance to Kjosen, a slim inlet off the main fjord.

The ferry docks at **Svensby** where there is a **café** (which may not be open), an information point and a few houses. Turning right from the ferry quay leads to the continuation of Route 91. The road runs along the fjord's edge to **Bensnes** (31km excluding ferry) from where it turns south-easterly along the Kjosen inlet. This is a splendid, if short, stretch. On the other side of the water rise the majestic peaks of the Lyngen Alps (see also p201). By the roadside the great Tyttebær screes provide road gravel for many of the minor roads of Troms fylke. The mountains here are etched by cirque glaciers whose blue ice is revealed by the summer sun. In bad weather this valley can present a somewhat forbidding countenance but in bright light it will be a wonderful experience driving through.

As the head of the Kjosen inlet is left behind, the road rises then falls on a steady gradient to the little village of **Lyngseidet** (46km) where the ferry leaves for Olderdalen.

The village has attracted traders for three centuries and its church is worth a visit. The original building dates from 1731 but it was extended fifty years later and, in contrast to so many of North Norway's churches, given a cruciform shape. Much of the village lies off Route 91 and along Route 868 (see p198).

Until the 1970s, Lyngseidet was on the Arctic Highway. There was no continuous road along the eastern shore of Lyngenfjord; the Highway led up the western side and the ferry was a necessity not an option. It provided then, as now, a welcome respite from driving. Today, the ferry is far less used and there must be a danger that it will cease to operate. I hope not because Route 91 is a shorter and interesting alternative route to or from Tromsø.

The ferry crosses Lyngenfjorden at a particularly broad point. Looking south it is impossible to see the fjord-head because of a bend in the valley but, to the north-west and south-west, there are good views of the Lyngen Alps. As the ferry passes the headland separating Lyngenfjorden from its arm, Kåfjorden, the widening mouth of the Lyngenfjord is clearly visible to the north and to the south-east you can see the Arctic Highway threading its way around Kåfjord.

The ferry ties up at a simple quay at **Olderdalen** (see p204) on the north shore of Kåfjorden. The crossing takes about 35 minutes with eleven ferries per day in each direction. There are no crossings before 09.15 from Lyngenseidet, or 08.15 from Olderdalen. Last crossings are at 21.30 and 20.45 respectively.

PART 7: NORDKJOSBOTN
TO ALTA

Nordkjosbotn holds a very special place in the Highway's path through the Arctic. From just beyond Mo i Rana the road has been north of the Polar Circle but it is from Nordkjosbotn that there's something about its path that really does mark it out as one of the world's great highways. It could be because from here the population thins, farms become more scattered and the need to check the fuel gauge becomes more important. Perhaps it is because the Highway now begins to take a more easterly route and you really do feel to be at the top of Europe. Whatever it is, as you set out from Nordkjosbotn, the sense of adventure heightens.

The Highway: Nordkjosbotn to Oteren
MAP 8

From the village the Arctic Highway (E6) shares a path with the E8 which has joined it from Tromsø. Their combined route is through an L-shaped pass between the mountains which conveniently links Balsfjorden with the Lyngenfjord. The defile is only 18km long and cut by two broad valleys. Despite its flatness, interrupted only by eroded glacial drift, the road is narrow in places and certainly not one of the best engineered sections of the Highway.

The Highway has very few farms to keep it company. Scattered along the road they look attractive enough in summer but in winter this is a lonely, harsh environment. To the south of the road, mountain cusps break the skyline like bared teeth but below the peaks the valley sides are smooth and incredibly beautiful. Few of the valleys running away from the Highway lead anywhere but they are none the less inviting. The naked sides of the peaks and of Kilafjellet (1083m) to the north are gullied by torrential streams on the higher slopes, but the lower slopes are clothed in birch. The contrast between the north- and south-facing sides of the valley is clear. The north-facing slopes show the expected valley glaciation and this side keeps its snow all summer.

A short way down the road out of Nordkjosbotn you'll see what must rank as the most bizarre feature of the whole of the Highway. Standing just a few metres to the left of the road (5km) is a glacial erratic boulder about five or six metres high. This is **Piggsteinen** (the Painted Rock). For decades, this has been a travellers' memorial. It used to be partly hidden by vegetation but it is now very visible. From top to bottom, the rock is decorated with the names or initials of those who have passed by, recording where they have come from and where they are going. Only the occasional slogan is included. It makes a change from the customary graffiti which is the tourist's usual contribution to the countryside, but quite where they find the paint and how they scale the rock to reach the top, remains a mystery. Strangely it does not seem incongruous but maybe I have got used to it.

At **Øvergård** (9km), the Highway crosses the watershed, at about 95m, between Nordkjoselva and Balsfjordeidet. It is also the point at which Route 87 from Tamokdalen joins the E6/E8 (see Part 6). The valley broadens northwards and, shortly before **Oteren**, there is a small **hotel**, Lyngskroa (18km), with a store and bank opposite. This is a convenient place to stay if you've not taken the side trip to Tromsø. If you are camping, there are good sites at Skibotn (see p201).

The Arctic Highway meets the inner arm, Storfjorden, of Lyngenfjorden at Oteren. Here the Stordalelv meanders through terraces and is discharging its load of silts and sediments in the fjordhead, gradually extending the land in a delta. There has been some reconstruction of the Highway around Oteren and towards Kvesmenes. Much of the work has been focussed on straightening the path.

At Oteren it is possible for you to use Route 868 and thus follow the Arctic Highway's old route along the western shore of the Lyngenfjord.

Accommodation: Nordkjosbotn to Oteren

Partly hidden and lying back from the Highway at Oteren, is the *Lyngskroa Turisthotel*. It's not especially grand but very acceptable for an overnight stay. There are just 30 simple rooms, all en suite but not well soundproofed. The floors are not wood or carpeted but made from some composition that adds to the noise. Best to choose a room at the far ends of the corridors.

There is a restaurant and bar and the meals are very reasonably priced. Although the hotel is often quite empty, it's best to book ahead because Lyngskroa is popular with coaches. Summer rates should be around NOK400 but if you find that the car-park area is empty it may be worth bargaining. There are reductions for longer stays and good rates for accommodation plus board. It's worth checking the functioning of the TV before unpacking in your allotted room.

SIDE TRIP FROM OTEREN TO LYNGSEIDET Map 8b

Like some of the other side trips that have been described, this is really an alternative to the Arctic Highway. Using Route 868, a turning left off the Highway at Oteren, the journey is some 42km to Lyngseidet (see Part 6, p195) and from there it is possible to rejoin the Arctic Highway by taking the ferry to Olderdalen. This will effect a saving of 57km but with the extra time needed for the ferry there may not be a commensurate saving in total journey time. The 868 takes you along the steep-sided western shore of Lyngenfjorden and was the original route of the Highway up to the mid-1970s. It is a narrow road in places but without gradient.

Leaving behind the Highway at Oteren, you can see the silting of the fjordhead, then the great U-shaped valleys of Signaldalen and Kittdalen framing conical mountains. Looking back from Route 868, to the south, there is a good view of Norway's 'Matterhorn', the twin pyramidal peaks of Otertind (1360m). Driving up the fjord, two features impress, one natural, the other man-made. The natural landscape is dominated by exceptionally steep slopes to the left of the road. The human landscape is characterized by a scattering of tiny fishing-farming communities, hamlets of a dozen or fewer houses. Because of the shortage of level ground for buildings or fields, sites have been chosen where rivers tumble off the mountains and have spilled out forming delta flats in the fjord. These great fans of alluvia have been terraced by the rivers which laid them down and farms stand on these ledges like doll's houses in a shop display.

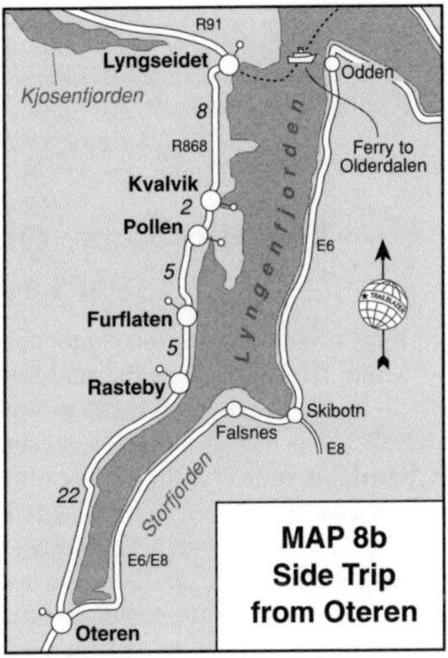

Fish farming is a fairly recent activity but you can still see some old fish-drying racks. In the tiny fields, hay is set out to dry on wire fences during the summer days. In winter, the rivers are reduced to a trickle but in summer their milky meltwater contrasts with the dark depths of the fjord waters.

MAP 8b
Side Trip
from Oteren

At **Rasteby** (22km), the fjord widens and the mountain walls which flank the road get even steeper as they rise towards Rastebyfjellet and Pollfjellet. The steepness of the slopes and the upper convexity of their faces obscures the glacier-capped summits. **Furflaten** village (27km) is much like its neighbours but has unusually high terraces and a somewhat larger jetty.

It is just beyond Furflaten that Route 868 abandons the old Arctic Highway route and takes to a new pair of parallel tunnels (28km) through the mountain face rather than staying in front of it. The tunnels, largely unlit, are over 3100m long. The reason for tunnelling is interesting. It is the solution to an old problem on this part of the road: avalanches. Snow and rock were liable to thunder down on to the road at almost any time in winter or spring. Local people knew the warning signs and rarely was there loss of life. However, during World War II, the occupying German forces built an avalanche shed over the road but this did not prove successful. The story is told of two German soldiers who stopped to take photographs of the falling snow and were killed by their folly. The villagers did not see it as their duty to warn the enemy.

On leaving the northern end of the tunnel, you'll see two settlements occupying what would be an island site were it not for the fact that sediments have filled the gap between the island and the mainland shore. The villages are **Sandvika** and **Ørnes**. They are now linked by minor roads to Route 868. **Pollen** (32km) and **Kvalvik** (34km) stand at opposite ends of this alluvial 'bridge' which carries the road on to a broader terrace.

From Kvalvik, the mountain wall stands back from the road and farming is more extensive. Now it is possible to appreciate the great height of the Lyngen Alps which form a massive spine of peaks along the length of this peninsula, Lyngshalvøya. Looking west and south from the road, you can see its glaciated summits, including North Norway's highest, Jiekevarre, at over 1800m.

Route 868 runs into the village of **Lyngseidet** (42km) past the village school and to the ferry point. For ferry details and a description of Lyngseidet see p195.

For a really fascinating account of this area in World War II, you can read David Howarth's book, *We Die Alone* (Lyons Press, 1999).

The Highway: Oteren to Alta
MAPS 9–12

This is a long stretch without the distractions of major side trips.

The Arctic Highway, since the mid-1970s, has shared the route of the E8 and turned to the right after leaving Oteren. The path is winding as first Signaldalselva and then Kittdalelva are bridged. There are three minor side roads at **Kittdal bridge** (22km) leading off to the right. The first (Road No 321) cuts back to take a route up Signaldalen. To go the whole length of this road entails a 40km round trip but, if you've got the time to spare, this beautiful valley is worth the effort. The gradients are low because the road keeps to the valley bottom but on either side tower mountains, all in excess of 1300m. These include the famous Otertind (see p198). In the valley is a cottage surviving from when this valley was first settled by southerners in the 1700s. At Signalnes the road branches; the right-hand is the better surface. The road ends at Paras, at the foot of a 1400m peak of the same name. There are many footpaths leading up to the mountains from here.

The other two minor roads are actually the ends of a loop road of some 14km running up Kittdalen (Road No 322). This is a similar but less spectacular version of Signaldalen.

The Arctic Highway has had to slip inland to cross the rivers but quickly returns to the fjord side as it makes its way down Lyngenfjorden. This first section of the fjord is called Storfjord or Big Fjord (confusingly, because it is the smaller part of the main fjord).

This part of the fjord is not as deep as the outer valley and is less good for fishing. Few settlements line the path of the Highway here. At **Falsnes** (40km) the promontory affords you the first really good views northwards up the Lyngenfjord. The uninterrupted view attracted the attention of the German occupying forces in World War II. Choosing a site on the slopes of Falsnesfjellet and using Russian prisoners to build a service road up the steep side of the mountain, they constructed a massive artillery emplacement. A more peaceful use of this viewpoint up the fjord is as a place to see the midnight sun between 22 May and 22 June – weather permitting.

Beyond Falsnes the Highway turns inland to the silted estuary of the Skibottselva. After crossing the river, the Highway and the E8 go their separate ways at **Olderbakken** (45km). The E8 chooses a south-easterly route up the gently sloping Skibotndalen before climbing steeply through wild uninhabited country. This part of the E8 is known as the Road of Four Winds. It is the route used by the German army of occupation when they retreated into Finland in 1944.

Today, as for centuries, the Sami use it for the seasonal migration of their reindeer. Just before reaching the frontier it attains 550m at Galgojavrre (34km after leaving the Arctic Highway). The Finnish–Norwegian border is reached 5km further on. The E8 crosses into the Finnish Panhandle. Beyond, the road leads to the head of the Gulf of Bothnia (564km) where the E8 meets the E4. Turning west at this point, along the E4, the road leads along the Swedish coast to Stockholm after 1612km; turning east, again on the E4, the road runs south through Finland to Helsinki (1313km).

But all this is a diversion. The Arctic Highway continues on its own into the village of **Skibotn** (47km). The village is on rising ground and is a historic meeting place for Sami, Finn and Norwegian.

Today the village is scattered over a wide area with pleasant buildings located among the trees. The site of the old market is being developed as a modern market complex, complete with exhibitions illustrating the history of the village and its district. Skibotn has its own **tourist information** (☎ 77 71 54 77). There is a wide range of services including alternatives to the hotel accommodation at Lyngskroa (see p198), **campsites** as well as a tourist **hotel**. Skibotn is known as the caravan capital of North Norway.

North of Skibotn no road existed along Lyngenfjorden until the re-routing of the Highway in the mid-1970s. The next road would not have been encountered for a further 32km round the headland and into Kåfjord. Today it's very different.

The Arctic Highway now hugs the shore of Lyngenfjorden. It is immediately clear why this is a modern road. There is little or no natural shelf for the roadway: it all had to be blasted out of the steep wall of the valley side. Much of the Highway is on a ledge just a few metres above the waters of the fjord. In other places it shelters behind a rock wall. Only in one place, just north of Skibotn, has a tunnel been constructed. This is 600m long and well lit. This stretch of the Highway is uninhabited but there is fish farming in the fjord. You will see that there are some delightfully situated picnic spots constructed at intervals along the Highway's path and these make excellent places to stop to admire the **Lyngen Alps** across the fjord. This great mountain range rising majestically from the deep waters is a truly wonderful sight. Small glaciers spill off the peaks and the higher ground retains its blanket of snow throughout the summer.

The Lyngen Alps make for challenging climbing. Mountaineering here was pioneered by the British and even today many of those tackling the new climbs come from Britain. The most famous of the pioneer climbers was William Cecil Slingsby. Much of his climbing was at the beginning of the century and his book *Norway, the Northern Playground* makes interesting reading. It was Cecil Slingsby who coined the name 'Mont Blanc of the North' for Jaeggevarre. Known as the 'father of Norwegian mountaineering', he first visited Norway in 1872 and returned more than a dozen times to make the first ever ascents of a number of peaks.

From the Highway you can get the best views of the Alps in the morning when the light is right; but in almost any light, and even in any weather, the Alps are one of the highlights along the whole length of the road.

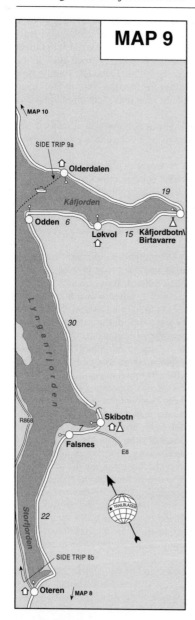

MAP 9

MAP 10

SIDE TRIP 9a

Olderdalen

Kåfjorden

19

Odden 6

Løkvol 15 Kåfjordbotn\
Birtavarre

Lyngenfjorden

30

R868

Skibotn

Falsnes

E8

7

TRAILBLAZER

22

Storfjorden

SIDE TRIP 8b

Oteren /MAP 8

You can see the more northerly summits of the Lyngen Alps from **Odden** (77km) where the Highway swings eastward around Kåfjorden. I always find this a rather frustrating section of the road. I suppose it is because throughout the next 40km you are aware of the Highway on the other side of this narrow fjord and there is a sense of having to retrace one's steps, albeit on the opposite shore.

At **Løkvol** (83km) there are two minor roads leading off to the right. These are in fact both Road No 332, a 5km loop road. It is possible to drive beyond the loop up into a steep but pleasant little valley, Manndalen, but this would add another 20km or more. The settlement lies in a broad re-entrant valley. There is a petrol station and a shop at Løkvol. There's also a **café**, which has **rooms** to let, but it's not especially attractive.

Worth a visit is the Domestic Craft Society Shop. On sale here are the products of an ancient form of weaving. These are *grener*, a sort of mat-cum-blanket which the Sea-Sami of this region have made and used for centuries. Nowadays these are more often displayed as wall hangings. The Sea-Sami's economy contrasted with that of the nomadic Sami. Reindeer formed little or no part of their lives. Rather it was fishing the rich waters of the fjords and sea coast. Up Manndalen the Sami influence is strong and ancient crafts are still practised. The making of goat cheese is famous.

The **Manndalen Sjøbuer** stand right in the middle of the settlement. *Sjøbu* means boathouse. There are eight turf-roofed cabins with little loft bedrooms – all very Lofoten-like.

This side of Kåfjorden is north facing and, with its steep sides, it is almost uninhabited and little farmed after Løkvol. There is a tiny village, **Skardalen** (89km), tucked into the valley of the same name, but the next substantial settlement you'll reach is at the head of the fjord: **Kåfjordbotn/Birtavarre** (98km). Again there is a shop and petrol supplies although there was no diesel the last time I was there. The **post office** is on the turn in the road round the fjordhead and the church is at the junction with Route 333. **Camping** is provided; turn right just after crossing the bridge over the river.

The village grew in the late nineteenth and early twentieth centuries when mining was taking place in the mountains surrounding Kåfjorddalen. Ore was shipped out from the little harbour but by 1920 the workings became uneconomic. Now the valley produces hydro-electric power. There are old boathouses at Birtavarre that have been restored and three or four kilometres up the Kåfjordal is an old Sea-Sami farm: Holmenes. This, too, has been restored. The outbarns have been converted into a small **museum**, Nord-Troms Sjøsamiske Museum, devoted to Sea-Sami cultural exhibits.

There is a long steep and winding road up Kåfjorddalen (Road No 333) from the village but the latter section is not open for public use. If you want to explore this fascinating valley, there are footpaths up to the old mining area from Ankerlia (9km) or there is an old mining road up to Moskojaisa. The higher you go, the more wonderful are the views of this deeply dissected valley region. The end of the valley is the Norwegian–Finnish border.

Turning to take the northern shore of the fjord the Highway is now in quite different country. This is the sunny side of the valley. What is more, the slopes are less steep. As a consequence this is a more settled and farmed route. The road runs a little way from the waterside; farming takes place on the hillsides but the economy is one of fishing plus farming as evidenced by the large number

---

Skibotn and the Laestadians

Skibotn has been a noted marketplace from ancient times. The November and March fairs were well established before the village became an authorized market in 1840. The attractions were not confined to trading. When times were hard, fishing in the fjord brought immigrants from Finland, particularly in the mid-eighteenth century, and their descendants can still be traced through their Finnish surnames common in the Lyngen district. The great glaciated trough of Skibotndalen was the obvious way into the area. The merchants' houses are mostly gone from Skibotn but one link with the past is the Læstadian religious rally held in Skibotn every two years.

This is usually very well attended. The sect, named after Lars Levi Læstadius who was Pastor of Karesuando in the middle of the nineteenth century, combines Lutheranism with some of the old Sami rituals. It appealed to those Sami who were dissatisfied with orthodox Lutheranism but it had unfortunate consequences especially arising from the Likkatus (ecstasy of group communion – see p228). All the same, Læstadianism does something to preserve the old values and social structures of the Sami.

of boathouses and small jetties. On the other side of the fjord, only just left behind, it is possible for you properly to appreciate the steepness of the valley slopes broken only by some superb hanging valleys cut by smaller glaciers as they joined the ice which forged Kåfjord in the past.

Olderdalen (117km) is the ferry point to and from Lyngseidet (see Part 6, p195). Despite the reduction in the importance of the ferry since the Highway's re-routing in the early 1970s, the village has grown and has all the usual services including a **guesthouse** and fuel. The **post office** is to the left just before the ferry. The village **tourist office** is open only in summer (☎ 94 54 85 44).

The Highway turns north from Olderdalen for the next 20km as it runs along the shore of the gradually widening Lyngenfjord. As it reaches the Lyngenfjord from the narrower Kåfjord, you can again get good views of the Lyngen Alps on the far side of the water. By the side of the Highway there are, here and there, the isolated and simple homes of fishermen. This area is still dependent upon the harvest of the sea rather than the land but there are now few of the gigantic drying racks which used to be a feature here. The market for dried fish has almost disappeared.

At **Djupvik** (137km), as the Highway turns eastward, there is a minor road, down a slope to the left, and a **camping** place. This simple four-kilometre detour takes you to the very point of the headland separating Lyngenfjord and the stretch of water known as Rotsundet. The Germans, in World War II, appreciated the significance of this headland's view, positioning a heavily armed gun position here; the bunkers still remain. The most impressive views from here are those across the mountains and northwards to the fjord mouth. To the west is the Lyngen peninsula and to the east a scattering of islands. In the distance, looking straight up the fjord, it is possible to see Fugløya, an island noted for its bird colonies. The island is some 50km away so there have to be very good conditions of visibility in order to see it. A certain amount of luck is also needed to see the midnight sun from here. When visible, it is a marvellous sight as the disc touches the fjord's surface before rising again.

From Djupvik the Highway now turns eastward and, in very general terms, this is its path for the rest of the journey. A glance at even a simple atlas shows Norway's coast from here aligns to a west-east direction in contrast with its previous south-north orientation. An immediate consequence is that the Highway now becomes exposed to cold airflows from the Pole. The warming effects of the North Atlantic Drift are less evident.

A change also occurs in the fjords. Already, as with Lyngenfjorden, the deep and penetrating inlets point their open mouths to the north rather than to the west, as is common further south. But another difference with the fjords may be observed as you continue along the Highway. The narrow, steep-walled, drowned estuaries you've seen further south become increasingly broader and their sides shallower. Indeed the whole landscape becomes softer, more subdued, as plateaux tend to replace high mountain peaks.

Fishing dominates the economy along the shores of Rotsundet. From the Arctic Highway the shelving beach runs down to the quiet waters of the sound and, at a small ferry point, **Rotsund** (143km), there is a link with Uløya, the island across the water. The ferry point is called Rotsund although the village is another three or four kilometres further on. The ferry crosses over the sound to Hamnes which you can easily see from the Highway.

Hamnes is hardly big enough to be called a village yet it has had significance in the past as a trading centre. Perhaps its strangest claim to fame is as the home of a certain Ovida Lyng who, in the first half of the nineteenth century, became the unelected leader of the community. As well as rearing twelve of her own children, she adopted another thirty-two. Not surprisingly she was known as 'Mother' Lyng.

The main settlement of Rotsund stands at the mouth of Rotsundalen, a pretty, tree-filled valley stretching southwards from the coast. There is another one of those frequently found loop roads leading into the valley and I have used this valley for wild camping a number of times.

Just 4km later the Arctic Highway passes its half-way point between Mo i Rana and Kirkenes.

Two kilometres further, the Highway runs into **Langslett** (149km) and to the left is a junction with Route 866. This road leads to Skjervøy, a substantial settlement on an island of the same name. The village is worth a visit but it is 30km from the Highway, giving a round trip of 60km. Allow an hour and a half if you decide on this detour.

The journey out to Skjervøy has been made easier by the quite recent (1991) construction of a 2km tunnel to replace the ferry across Maursundet.

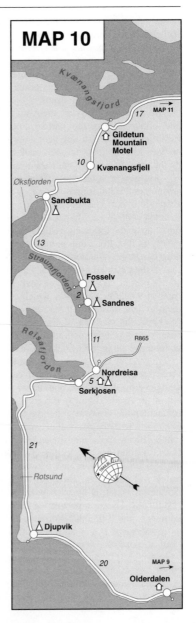

In the village is an early eighteenth-century church and the old trading post, the Kiilgården, has been partly restored. The fish factories and small shipyard leave no doubt about the *raison d'être* of the village. The harbour also provides a stopping place for the Coastal Express – the Hurtigrute. On the journey, to the west of the northern end of the under-sound tunnel, is Maursund. Maursund Gård, an old eighteenth-century trading post, has been reconstructed as a coastal cultural centre for North Troms.

As you leave Langslett, the Arctic Highway moves away from the coastline and climbs across the narrow neck of land separating Rotsundet from Reisafjorden. The journey here contrasts with the flat shore-path as the road ascends to over 200m through thick birch woods. The area is sometimes used by the Sami in summer when their reindeer feed among the trees.

You may well have seen reindeer from the Arctic Highway much further south than this but from now on they are in greater numbers and it is as well to keep a look out. The deer are often seen on the roads that they use with an ill-founded confidence. They are most easily seen if they are moving in the same direction as the following vehicle, their white tail and rump hair showing quite clearly as they trot along in that ungainly, almost comic, bobbing fashion. The most dangerous situation arises when they dart across the road seemingly oblivious to the traffic. If one crosses, there is a good chance that another will follow so it is best to slow down to a crawl. The rule is quite simple: the reindeer have right of way. On a highway which carries so little traffic, you cannot expect them to have developed a road sense.

From the crossing of the peninsula ridge, the Highway descends quite steeply on a winding path to Reisafjorden. There is an important and growing community along the western shore of this fjord. To the right of the road, just before entering Sørkjosen, is a somewhat incongruous Lapp Shopping Centre. From **Sørkjosen** (158km) to **Nordreisa** (163km) the area along the Highway is well developed. The total population of these settlements is about 5000. To the left of the Arctic Highway is Sørkjosen **Airport**. This has a STOL (short take-off and landing) runway and there are link services to Tromsø and Hammerfest to connect with the national network. To the right of the Highway are the kommune offices and a modern community centre. The administration building, Bjørklygården, has a collection of historic pictures and archival material. There are services aplenty in and between both settlements including a couple of **hotels** and **campsites**. There is a signposted **tourist office** at Storslett, part of Nordreisa, which is open all year (☎ 77 76 56 76). It is next to a **Chinese restaurant**. There's a **post office** about 150m up the Route 865. Of the two little towns, you'll find that Nordreisa is the best place to refuel and shop.

Sørkjosen has a small man-made harbour-cum-marina but the head of the fjord at Nordreisa is gradually filling in with sediment brought down by the rivers which spill into it. At low tide vast flats are exposed and at their landward edges vegetation has already colonized.

Should you need to join Route 865, you'll have to take a turning right in the middle of Nordreisa. The 865 runs down Reisadalen for 44km before it becomes a minor road and then a track for 10km. It is not recommended as a side trip because, although pretty enough with its waterfalls and lakes, it is a long way to nowhere. If you do decide to make this diversion, you'll find that the landscape is largely forested and pleasant enough if driven for a few kilometres up-valley. If the whole length of the 865 is followed to Bilto (44km) the objective might be for you to take a boat trip along the river from here to Nedrefoss. Although it takes nearly three hours, there is sight of one of Europe's highest waterfalls: Mollesfoss (273m). At the end of the boat journey a path leads to another fall, the Isnofoss, and the river runs through a one-kilometre gorge some 70m deep. These features are all part of the Reisa National Park.

Leaving Nordreisa and Reisadalen behind, the Arctic Highway runs behind the fjordhead sandflats and on to a little village, **Flatvoll** (166km). The village lies in a small embayment in the main fjord. The Highway's path then turns inland to make yet another crossing of a peninsula neck with a rise of some 30m. This short (3km), wooded section of the route brings you to **Straumfjorden**. The mouth of this fjord has a narrow opening to the broad Reisafjord. The green waters sweep through the gap giving fishermen some real sport with its rich harvest of coalfish, cod and haddock. Small fishing communities along the shore here managed to resist the temptation to abandon their traditional economy and make a new life in south Norway or in towns like Alta or Tromsø. A little forestry and dairy farming supplement their income from fishing. Also along the fjord are two attractive **campsites** at **Sandnes** (174km) and at **Fosselv** (176km).

The Highway runs along the fjord edge only a few metres above the water. This stretch of the Highway used to be something of a switch-back but it has been greatly improved in recent years all the way round into the next inlet. This is **Sandbukta/Øksfjorden** (189km). To the north-west you can see the islands of the Skjervøy group and ahead is the Trolldalstind. The grey-pink 1100m Nuovas peak dominates the view.

Øksfjord is interesting because a moraine ridge has effectively cut the fjord in two leaving a lake, Øksfjordvatnet, on the landward side and giving the Highway a path across the fjord. A new bridge, man-made this time, crosses the river which allows the lake to drain into the open fjord.

Øksfjordvatnet is a lake of unique beauty enclosed by mountains on three sides. As the Highway climbs away from Sandbukta the little settlement by the water's edge looks like a toy village. There is **camping** by the lake.

The Highway from here begins one of its more difficult sections. Until relatively recently, winter closure was common and even today there is still a risk as you'll guess from the road-closure barriers. The problem is one of altitude and exposure to northerly winds rather than steep gradients. In avoiding what would be a long coastal route round the Trolldalstind range, the road has to climb on to the **Kvænangsfjell**, a plateau that forces the Highway up to over 400m above sea-level. At a latitude of nearly 70°N and with little shelter from winds blowing off the Arctic Ocean to the north, this is a fine, even audacious, piece of engineering.

As the Highway threads its way towards the top of the plateau-like col, what little shelter was afforded by the Trolldalstind is lost and, at 300m, thin birch gives way to open peat bog. Over the years all the usual expedients of protective measures have been taken: massive snow fences, road widening and straightening and, especially, the raising of the highway to permit snow to be blown off into the marginal ditches.

This is a particularly exposed stretch of the Highway and snow flurries are not uncommon even in summer. In poor weather the road may well be below the cloud base. Just below the summit the open waters of Kvænangsfjorden come into view and to the right and above the road there is a small hotel, **Gildetun Mountain Motel**, (199km) with **cabins**, a busy **café** and, most recently, a **tourist information office** (☎ 77 76 99 58). The office closes in winter. The hotel building is interesting and a favourite stopping place for travellers along the Highway. This is where to get your cameras out of their cases, for the views out into the Kvænangsfjord are quite stunning. The broad waters of the fjord are broken by islands large and small. To the far north is the Loppa peninsula, half in Troms and half in Finnmark; south are three small ice-caps and attendant glaciers. The largest of the ice-caps, Øksfjordjøkelen, has an outlet glacier which dips down to sea-level. This is the only glacier in Norway actually to calve into the sea.

To get the best views of this beautiful fjord and its islands you should go on the slopes below the Highway on the other side of the road to the hotel.

The Kvænangsfjell is more of a ridge than a plateau and the Highway drops sharply down from the top and winds its way back to the edge of the fjord. The biting cold Arctic air sweeps across the Highway and ensures that birch trees do not appear until below 200m and then only where there is some shelter. You remind yourself that, now the alignment of much of the coast is west-east, there's nothing north of you except the polar ice. Another snow-closure barrier is passed before the Highway reaches the fjord edge but at 100m above water level. A precipitous drop borders the Highway on the seaward side but more gentle birch-covered slopes, on the other side, separate the road from the steep bare faces of Gaggavarre.

Scree spills off the mountains and the Highway carves a passage through the boulders. At times it is difficult to distinguish the natural talus from the detritus of the road engineers' dynamited construction works. It is not only scree which falls from the mountains. Many tumbling streams are crossed by the road and the Highway is forced on to an undulating path carrying it to sea-level at one point and back to 100m at another.

Eventually the Arctic Highway settles for a near sea-level altitude before bridging the narrow Sørstraumen outlet of Kvænangsfjordbotn, the inner arm of the fjord, at **Karvik/Sørstraumen** (213/216km). There is a shop and fuel to the right of the Highway at Sørstraumen and 3km further on is a **camping** place.

For years, the fast waters of Sørstraumen were crossed by a short ferry. But in 1960, the Arctic Highway was re-routed in a 39km detour round the head of the inlet. Eventually an elegant 300m arch bridge was built, in 1975, and 32km was cut from the Highway's route. What has not changed is the excellent fishing in the tidal race of Sørstraumen where saithe are a speciality. A small harbour here is used for the export of local slate.

Of course, you can still take the old road round to the head of Kvænangsfjordbotn and back to its present path. This journey is an easy one for the gradients are shallow. At Navit (9km from Karvik) there is a 20m waterfall within 100m of the road. The lower valley from here to the head is filled with cotton grass in summer and the shallow waters of Kvænangsbotn are gradually filling with silt. A hydro-electric power station is sited near Seljevoll (21km). The head of the inlet is surrounded by the denuded slopes of Corrovarre, Rossavarre and Ordavarre. Clear of regolith and soil, they are scarred by ice action. Rocky islands litter the fjordhead. On the northern side of the inlet this road, the old Highway, rises to just over 100m and, in places, you will lose sight of the fjord. There are some homes of farmer-fishermen along the shore but it is an isolated community that has been forsaken by the Arctic Highway.

Having crossed the Sørstaumen bridge, the Highway now runs through the village of **Sekkemo** (220km) and into **Badderen** (222km). There is a shop at Badderen but the old petrol station is closed. There was a small but important port here when copper was mined in the nearby Badderdalen. Today, the drift-filled inlet, Badderfjord, is used by fishing craft. Farming, too, is quite prosperous on glacial drift from here to **Undereidet** (226km) where the Highway cuts off another headland by choosing to follow a col, Baddereidet.

You will find that the scenery along this pass is varied although much is utter wasteland. First there are rocky slopes, supporting gorse or thin birch, then come treeless bogs as the Highway climbs to 250m and snow fences are needed. Descending at the northern end of Baddereidet the Highway's path is abrupt and partly wooded though bog persists down to 100m. As you approach **Kåsen** (234km), the road's gradient lessens and to the left (west) the slopes of Ridevarre (722m) appear to have been attacked by some Brobdingnagian chopper, its bare rock face crossed by sharp horizontal ridges.

Beyond Kåsen the Highway reaches its next fjord, Burfjorden. This is a particularly well sheltered fjord and the village, **Burfjord** (237km), was a local market centre before the days of good road transport. It is still important enough to have shops, a bank, a petrol station and a small hospital. Accommodation is available in a **guesthouse/café** and in **cabins**. Gone, though, are the connections with the now defunct copper-mining industry. It is from Burfjord that boat trips are organized to view the glacier Jøkelfjordbreen (☎ 77 76 81 31). It is also from about this point on the Highway that the Sami set up their stalls on the roadside. If the weather is bad, no one will be in sight. The Sami are fair-weather salesmen.

Along the fjord edge, the Highway just above the level of the water, there are farms. It is difficult to make a living here simply from farming so the usual tri-part economy of fishing, farming and forestry is the norm. Cattle and sheep are kept by the farms, but grazing is often along the roadside and you will have to keep a sharp look out.

Slipping across a small headland the Highway makes for Alteidet. Just before reaching the village, a turn left down a minor road (245km) takes you to Simonsen Gårdsferie (Simonsen's Holiday Farm). This working farm has **cabins** but its real claim to fame is that it offers a great variety of activity holidays.

As well as being able to enjoy the farm work and fishing, there is skiing, mountain tours, dog sleighs and snowmobile trips. The farm has a little **museum** with some old tools and farm equipment. Among the stock on the farm are llamas, not an everyday sight in Norway. Almost best of all are views to the jagged peaks of the Kvænangstind seen across the fjord. It's a gem of a place. This is somewhere to stay at any time in the year. Run by Nelly and Willy Simonsen, the farm will offer you a holiday to remember.

Alteidet village (248km) is snugly placed at the head of an even more sheltered inlet than Burfjord. This is still a quite important little village but its heyday was in the past when migrating transhumant Sami used the Alteidet valley. There are still some attractive old buildings but it has lost its market function to Burfjord and it is unlikely to resume ascendancy. There is a pleasant **camping** place with **cabins**.

Striking east from Alteidet the Highway follows the valley of the same name. About a kilometre out of the village there is a road leading off the Highway to the left towards Jøkelfjorden. Look for the sign *Jøkelfjordbreen*. A short drive down the road, about six kilometres, there's a turn right towards Saltnes which leads to a farm after some 2000m. It's possible to park near the yellow house and walk along a track along the fjord edge. All the way along this path you will have excellent views of **Øksfjordjøkelbreen**. This glacier is the only one in Norway to dip down to sea-level and calve into the fjord. If you walk the whole length of the path – not especially easy going – you find yourself just the fjord's width from the snout of the glacier. To reach the glacier itself is a 7.5km trek.

Continuing with the Highway you cross a col. There is a little farming here despite the marshy character of the pass and the shallow slopes on either side are tree clad. A little more than half way along the valley the Highway crosses the fylke boundary, leaves Troms and enters Finnmark.

The Arctic Highway's 650km journey through Finnmark begins just short of Langfjorden which it joins at the eastern end of the Alteidet pass. The Highway meets the fjord at its head and takes a sharp turn southwards with the pretty Russelva valley behind it. The Langfjord is remarkable for its length, narrowness and straightness. From vantage points on the road, as it runs round the head, you can see the whole 30km or more of the fjord's length. Sedimentation is taking place rapidly at Langfjordbotn and, at low tide, shallow flats are uncovered.

The Highway turns right at the head of the fjord. Straight ahead is Route 882 leading after 40km to the village of Øksfjord, the ferry point for an incredible number of sea routes to the outlying islands and even to Hammerfest (see p233). All these ferries are a reminder of the isolation of these northern communities.

At the southern corner of the fjord's head is **Bognelv** (257km), the only settlement of consequence along either shore of the fjord. The exceptional shelter that this east-west fjord provides enables a little farming to take place but the steep walls of the fjord, elsewhere than at the head, rule out any activity except on a small scale. You'll find petrol, shops and a **café** in the village and there is also an excellent fjord-side **camping site** with **cabins**.

Apart from the almost inevitable tourist-season Sami 'kiosks' selling skins and largely factory-made Sami clothing, the Highway's next 50km is almost deserted. The Highway along the southern shore of Langfjord has undergone reconstruction in recent years. The undulating path of the early road, rising and falling 15m or so over the fretted shoreline, is now replaced by a flatter surface and somewhat straighter alignment. Some 4km out of Bognelv there's a 2500m tunnel which protects the Highway from heavy winter snowfalls.

Across the fjord you have excellent views which wonderfully illustrate the extraordinary perseverance of the people in this harsh environment. On the opposite shore to the Highway runs Route 882 and along it is a string of tiny farms. True, they enjoy a favourable south-facing aspect, but this hardly compensates for the isolation and the climate. Hay is grown on seemingly impossible slopes and later put out to dry in conditions of unreasonable humidity and precipitation. A little white-painted church with a simple spire symbolizes their faith. Beyond Rivabukt, about three quarters of the way to the fjord's mouth, even faith cannot overcome the challenge of a near vertical cliff-face and the mountains win the battle for the land.

On the Highway's southern side of Langfjord, the slopes of Lassefjellet, of the Langfjell and of Høyfjellsnosa tower above the road. Facing almost due north and deprived of the sun, the slopes above 100m are bare even of scattered birch. Enormous screes rest as monuments to freeze-thaw weathering. At

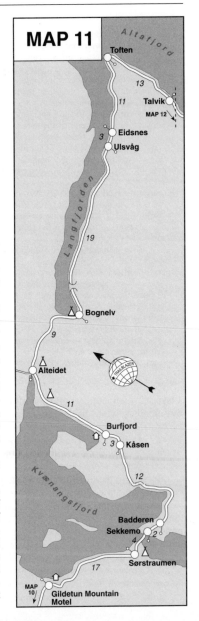

Finnmark

Finnmark (the land of the Finns) is the traditional meeting place of the northern peoples: Sami, Finns (*Kvens*), Russians and Norwegians. Norwegian sovereignty was not finally established until the early nineteenth century. The Norwegians were, in fact, latecomers to the region, their first settlements probably dating from the fourteenth century. The earlier settlers in this most northerly part of Scandinavia were from the Komsa culture (see p218). These people were largely trappers and they exploited the opportunities afforded as the fauna moved northwards on the retreat of the Pleistocene ice sheets.

There are many Stone Age finds in Finnmark and the Sami people were almost certainly here about the time of Christ's birth. Their early econo-culture was a mixture of herding, fishing and hunting and only in the sixteenth century was the nomadic way of life, with reindeer, established.

Finnmark has experienced good times and bad. It has not escaped conflict but despite the mixture of peoples, harmony has generally been the order of the day. Some of the most difficult times in Finnmark's history occurred as recently as World War II. The retreat of the German forces of occupation saw the total destruction of almost all buildings in the policy of 'scorched earth'. It is difficult, today, to appreciate the enormous task that was Finnmark's reconstruction after 1944.

Along with north Troms, Finnmark's population today enjoys enterprise zone status giving a range of concessions. The origin of this special treatment was to prevent or at least slow the de-population of these northern territories. The young, especially, are attracted to what they see as 'the good life' offered by the south of Norway. The incentives are mostly in the form of reduced taxes. For example, most trades are exempt from the payroll tax, there are higher child benefit payments and student loans are on a more favourable basis than the rest of the country.

Neither of the other two fylker through which the Highway runs has developed its adventure tourism so extensively as Finnmark. Although some mention of this will be made, for comprehensive information you should contact the Finnmark Tourist Board (☎ 78 44 00 20; 🖷 78 43 51 84; 🖳 post@visitnorthcape.com).

Ulsvåg (276km) a stream off Høyfjellsnosa has cut a series of deep terraces into the morainic waste blocking its entrance into the fjord and, near **Eidsnes** (279km), a striking gorge from the same mountains gushes water into the fjord by way of a waterfall. The Høyfjellsnos, as its name suggests, is very steep and in winter avalanches are a serious problem. Snow fences prove inadequate and require frequent replacement.

Because of these difficulties, which increase as the Highway becomes more exposed and is forced to climb, a very ambitious tunnelling scheme is being considered. The idea is to drive a 9km hole under the mountains to link Eidsnes with Talvik. This would cut 14km off the Highway's present path, solve the climatic problems but deprive travellers of some superb views. The cost can't be measured in kroner, but it is the cost-benefit in financial terms that will decide the issue.

Without the tunnel-to-be, you continue along the Langfjord. A new section of the Highway bypasses and runs above the village of **Storsandnes** (285km). A road cuts back, left, into the village if you need to refuel or shop. Fish farming along the fjord is the village's interest. Onwards you can see across the fjord into the forbidding Ytre Kaven. This mountain-girt cove breaks the otherwise regular and vertical cliff line. From Storsandnes the road begins to climb towards the headland that separates Langfjord from the great Altafjord.

At **Isnestoften** or, more usually, **Toften**, (290km) the road's altitude is about 65m and the views are most certainly worth a halt. The contrast between the narrow Langfjord and the broad Altafjord is manifest. Ignore the rather untidy Sami stalls which are usually found here in summer and go to the left of the road to look out over the broad Altafjord. The German occupying forces appreciated the view and mounted a major artillery battery here. The dug-outs, trenches and emplacements are still visible just 20m from the Highway.

Evidence of earlier recognition of the strategic importance of the entrance to Altafjord is provided by the 17th-century construction of a fort on Årøy, the small island to the immediate east of Toften. At that time it was the Swedes who were the enemy. Pre-dating even the fort are Stone Age sites on the shoreline below Toften. The shore here, as so often in northern Scandinavia, is rising as a consequence of the retreat of the great ice sheets (isostatic recovery). The exposed marine platforms below the headland have shown evidence of Stone Age man dating back to 3–9000BP. The Sami also settled this area at least 1000 years ago.

It is possible to get a view of Alta from Toften even though it is still almost 50km away. In winter, in the half light which is the Arctic's shadowy illumination, the town's twinkling lights announce that this wasteland is not without a haven.

The Highway descends from Toften along a section of road which is not one of its best constructed paths. There is some need for widening and reductions in curvature which will no doubt be done if the Eidsnes-Talvik tunnel is not built. The road does not drop back to sea-level in one single descent but rises and falls with the topography. Across the waters, to the east, the opposite coastline looks uninviting, even sinister, its blue-black cliffs plunging into the apparently bottomless waters of the fjord.

At **Talvik** (303km) the Highway is back at sea-level. The village is set in a small bay at the mouth of the River Stor. Alta is hidden from view and it seems extraordinary today that, centuries ago, Talvik, rather than Alta, was the centre of the fjord's trade. In the late 1960s Talvik finally gave up the unequal competition and became incorporated into Greater Alta.

The bay is surrounded by hummocky hills of uncertain origin and the village has a number of minor roads leading up-valley. There is a shop and a bank but the petrol station was closed on my last visit. The particularly fine church is worth a visit. The village has an air of self-containment about it.

The Highway climbs a little away from Talvik and you'll get the best views of the village from this more southerly position. Alta reappears as the road rounds a promontory at **Flatstrand** (311km) and this is perhaps the only place on the Highway from where you can see both Alta and Talvik. From Flatstrand the Highway heads towards an arm of the main Altafjord, Kåfjord. Crossing a low col between Storvik (318km) and Flintnes (320km) the Highway passes one of the Kautokeino Sami reindeer summer-grazing areas before slipping to the water's edge of Kåfjord (323km).

From Kåfjord the Arctic Highway runs round the infilling head of the fjord by way of a causeway. To the right is a minor road leading up the pretty Mattisdalen. The river, Mattiselv, has cut into the sediments, leaving terraces of drift and alluvium to mark the successive levels of erosion. The minor road (326km) up the valley takes you seven kilometres along it and past a lake (to the left). The river provides excellent fishing but you need a licence.

The Highway bridges the Mattiselv and takes a path away from the coast swinging northwards behind the eastern slopes of Sakkovarre. The lower slopes are wooded but, higher up, the rock is bare of any vegetation. This part of the road is built across drift and deltaic deposits which block what might be another long arm of the great Altafjord. To the right of the Highway, two lakes, Storvatnet and Kvænvikvatnet, and their marshy surrounds are all that is left of what would have been an even larger inlet than Kåfjord. Now, to the left of the Highway, there is only the relatively diminutive Kvænvik bay.

From **Kvænvik** (330km) a minor road leads left off the Highway to the headland separating the two inlets, Kåfjord and Kvænvik. The Highway now returns to the fjord-side after avoiding the Kvænvik bay by crossing bogland and then rising 60m along the flank of Skaddefjellet. Looking back, you can see the village lying below a huge moraine which shuts off the valley of the river which feeds into the bay.

As the Highway approaches **Alta** (338km) it climbs sufficiently to give splendid views north (to the left) along the length of the Altafjord and across its scattered rock flats and small islands. The road enters the town at Hjemmeluft where there are some interesting rock carvings and a museum. There is car-parking space and an **information office** down the slope towards the sea (see p219).

Accommodation: Oteren to Alta

Apart from near Alta, there is a regular scattering of camping sites, small hotels and guesthouses along this 320km stretch of the Arctic Highway.

There is choice at Skibotn: hotel or cabins. *Skibotn Turisthotell* (☎ 77 71 53 00; 🖹 77 71 55 06) is centrally placed, nothing special in appearance but with 24 rooms and both a cafeteria and restaurant it rivals Lyngkroa at Oteren. Alongside there are two-bedroom cabins with kitchens. Rooms or cabins will cost around NOK700 or less and the hotel is open all year. Down by the fjord there is *Skibotn Camping* (☎ 77 71 52 77). The site is open only five months each year from May. The ten cabins do not have toilets but there is tap water in the kitchens. There's a sauna and showers on this well located site.

By the river down a rough road is *Strandbu Camping*. It is near the junction where the E8 leaves the E6. This is mostly a large caravan park but there are eight cabins. No 8 is very large with a loft bedroom and it has a shower and toilet. Prices range from NOK300 to NOK600. There's a sauna on site but the whole place looks rather untidy. On the outskirts of the village is yet another camping place, *Olderelv Camping* (☎ 77 71 54 44). This is a pleasant site among the pine trees. It's open only from May to September. Again, it's mainly a caravan site (there are no less than 300 permanent caravans). The eight cabins include two with lavatories and another three with water. All have kitchens.

Kåfjord

Kåfjord rose to fame early in the nineteenth century when it became the largest settlement in the whole of Finnmark. The reason was copper. The ore was mined between 1826 and 1909, though mining was already in decline when, in 1878, the founding mining company left the area. This company, called Altens Kobberverk, was formed by two Englishmen, Crowe and Woodfall, in 1826 and later taken over by another of their countrymen, a Mr Robertson, whose descendants still live in the fylke. Englishmen, many from Cornwall, were among the five hundred or so workers who mined the copper and one, a Mr Thomas, had the unique distinction of being elected to the Norwegian parliament, the Storting. There was great jubilation among the Kåfjord community and, it is recorded, much champagne was drunk.

The British connection is still to be seen. In 1837, they built a fine church (to the left of the Highway), the second oldest in Finnmark. It was restored in 1969. In the little graveyard behind the church are memorials bearing the names of a James Trelease and a Samuel Monk among others. Two young brothers of the Trelease family have their graves here. Both died in the 1860s, one aged three and the other aged eight, from a drowning accident. Unlike other regions in North Norway where the British were led by mining interests, they were generally made very welcome here.

Today the population is just a couple of hundred people. The massive Kåfjord Kobberverk and jetty lie derelict, an untidy scar from a short but impressive period in the past. As the copper began to be worked-out, many families emigrated to the USA.

Occasionally, descendants from those families return to Kåfjord to walk the crumbling paths through the old mines and up to the Haldde range. There is a marked trail about 300m north of the church on what is now called the Copper Walk (one of many *Fotefar mot nord* – Footsteps northwards). Details of the walk are in a booklet obtainable from the Alta Museum (see p222).

Just over one and a half kilometres from the end of these paths, perched on the peak of Halddetoppen at 1149m, is the old **Nordlysstation**. The world's first aurora borealis (northern lights) observatory was established and functioned here until its transfer to Tromsø in the early years of the nineteenth century. Remarkably, it is possible to rent the observatory; details are with the Alta Museum.

Kåfjord is also in the history books for the shelter it provided for the German navy in World War II. The fjord was ideally placed to give harbour to ships that could quickly sail north to harass the convoys of war materials, destined for the Russian Front, as they crossed the Barents Sea. The most notorious of these was the *Tirpitz*, in her time the largest and most powerful battleship afloat. The *Tirpitz* first found shelter in Kåfjord in July 1942 but it was in September 1943 that the British made a daring and justly famous attack using X-craft – midget submarine minelayers. The raid was only a limited success and through the later part of 1943 and early 1944 Kåfjord saw a succession of air attacks on the battleship by the British and the Russians. Despite this concerted effort the *Tirpitz* survived to limp to Tromsø before finally being sunk in November 1944 (see p189). Kåfjord was the scene of one of the major tragic farces of World War II. The *Tirpitz* never played a major part in the war at sea yet it defied the Allies' innumerable attempts to destroy it over many years of the war. The tragedy was the loss of life, on both sides, which the raids involved.

There is a memorial to this action to the left of the Highway where the Copper Walk starts. The inscription on the plaque ends with a statement that '*A team of British sub-aqua club divers dived in these waters in 1974 and 1976 to discover a little more about the attack and to pay tribute to the bravery of the crews.*'

Despite the abundance of choice at Skibotn, the accent on caravans may well be a reason why those seeking an unspoilt location will press on to **Birtavarre Camping** (☎/🖹 77 71 77 07) at the head of Kåfjord. Off the Highway to the right, after the bridge in Birtavarre village, there are 17 cabins for 2 or 4 people. There's no water in the cabins and the site's open only from mid-May to mid-August. The setting is pleasant and the prices NOK230–300 reflect the simple nature of the cabins.

The ferry point at Olderdalen has accommodation at the **Olderdalen Gjestgård** (☎ 77 71 82 60; 🖹 77 71 81 66), just a hundred metres or so up the slope on the right from the ferry. There are 19 rooms, nine with shower and toilet and ten without. The busy **café**, which is part of the guesthouse, is open from 10.00 to 21.00 in summer and from 11.00 to 19.00 in winter. Prices for the rooms range from NOK350 to NOK450 and include breakfast. There are also nine cabins sleeping 2–4 persons at NOK200–300. This is an especially convenient place to stay if you arrive in Olderdalen on a late ferry or you miss the last crossing.

Close to the turn for Djupvik and the viewpoint at Spåkenes is **Lyngenfjord Camping**; about a dozen cabins are on site. They don't have water and the kitchen is pretty basic but, with bunk beds for four and only NOK180–300, they are realistically priced. Best of all are the views from this valley side. The majesty of the Lyngen Alps is overwhelming.

The substantial settlement of Nordreisa has two hotels and nearby camping sites. On entering Sørkjosen (the start of this linear town) there is the **Best Western Reisfjord Hotel**, on the left of the Highway by the marina. There are 54 rooms, 17 of which are single-combi rooms (that is, they will sleep two) with all the rest doubles. All rooms are en suite and of generous size. There's a big open restaurant and a fitness centre. Parking space is ample. The prices are quite high, from over NOK400 per person, but breakfast is included.

Also in Sørkjosen is a small guesthouse, **Henriksens Gjestue**. It's on the Highway, a neat and new-looking building. It has just ten double rooms at between NOK450 and NOK650 with breakfast. Simple but well maintained, it has a **café** and bar on the ground floor.

A little further on in Storslett, just off the Highway to the right, is an L-shaped, yellow building. This is **Nordlandia Storslett Hotell** (☎ 77 76 52 00; 🖹 77 76 52 90). It has an interesting history. The hotel building was originally in Lillehammer, in southern Norway, and was constructed for the winter Olympics of 1994. With the Olympics over, the building was redundant, so it was dismantled and rebuilt here. Not as difficult as it sounds as it is a wooden construction. All 93 rooms are en suite; 89 are doubles and four are triples. There are also two suites. Prices are some NOK100–200 less at weekends when a double will be about NOK800. Breakfast is included. The large dining-room is a little dark and the whole hotel looked as if it would benefit from some refurbishment when I was last there. The hotel closes in early September and reopens in mid-May. The small **Reisa Hotel**, to the right of the Highway in Storslett, was occupied by refugees when I was last in the town.

There are three restaurants of note in Storslett. *Xinya*, in the shopping precinct, serves Chinese and Norwegian dishes and prices are very reasonable. A full meal will cost some NOK110 only. *Bios* is in the park square at the junction of the Highway and Route 865. It is very large, inexpensive with an attached café. On the Highway is *Grillstun Mat og Vinhus*. It could be described as a burger-bar/pub.

There are two camping sites, a little over 10km out of Nordreisa. The first to be reached is *Sandnes Camping* (☎ 77 76 49 15) on the left of the Highway. The site, overlooking the fjord, has ten simple cabins. Two-bed cabins cost NOK200; NOK350 is the price of a four-bed cabin. The washing and lavatory facilities are communal. Sandnes is open from mid-June to late August.

Two to three kilometres further on, again to the left of the Highway, is *Fosselva Camping* (☎ 77 76 49 29; 🖹 77 76 76 09). The sloping site has fine views across the fjord. The larger cabins will sleep five and include their own showers and two bedrooms. At NOK650, they are inexpensive for their quality. There is plenty of space to pitch a tent.

What should be a good site at Øksfjord, by the lake, is actually somewhat scruffy. *Øksfjord Camping* (☎ 77 76 67 48; 🖹 77 76 68 59) has caravan places and tent space but the eight cabins are disappointing. They vary in size from 4-bed to 6-bed and the larger ones have toilets and showers. The site is open for two months from mid-June only. The large cabins cost NOK550.

A very popular choice of stopover is *Gildetun Mountain Motell* (☎ 77 76 99 58; 🖹 77 76 99 59) on the top of the Kvænangsfjell. There are 29 rooms in the hotel and a further 26 in cabins. There's a **café**, open from 09.00 to 22.00. All cabins and rooms are en suite and there's a sauna. The weather can be severe up here, at over 400m, and you'll welcome the turf roofs. Prices are around NOK620 for a double room and NOK520 for a two-person cabin. Without breakfast the price drops by NOK60. Gildetun closes from October to April.

Sekkemo Camping (☎ 77 76 84 43), at Sørstraumen, is on a ledge overlooking the fjord. The site is more attractive than the cabins but, if staying there, go for the smaller new cabins. Prices may be as low as NOK200.

In the village of Burfjord, look out for a **café** to the left of the Highway. It is also the *Burfjord Gjestgiveri* (☎ 77 76 84 48). The guesthouse is a separate building with just six simple rooms. If you want a meal you have to use the café but there is a refrigerator and coffee-making facilities in the rooms. There's just one bathroom but the prices are low. A single is NOK260, a double is NOK380.

Just 8km further on, a contrast awaits you. The delights of *Simonsen Gårdsferie* (☎ 77 76 93 86) have already been described (see p209). The accommodation is in three cabins of varying size or in rooms in a house. It is possible to rent the whole house (four bedrooms). All are well equipped. The real problem is that an overnight stay is likely to extend into a week, especially as prices reduce with length of stay. Prices vary according to the accommodation selected but as a guide, a 4–5 person cabin will be about NOK850 including bed-linen for a one- or two-night stay. Activities are charged extra (not the farm experience) but prices are reasonable.

The last accommodation before entering Finnmark is *Alteidet Camping* (☎ 77 76 93 57). The views are good but the 20 cabins are set in regimented rows. There's no water to the cabins but there is a sauna. (The further north one goes the greater the likelihood of finding a sauna.) Costs of NOK250–350 depend on size of cabin. The camp is open only during the summer, defined as June to mid-August.

Finally, now in Finnmark but before reaching Alta, there's a treat in store. This is *Altafjord Camping* (☎ 78 43 28 24; 🖹 77 65 88 48). The location is Bognelv, with the sloping site to the right of the Highway, a backdrop of forest giving way to towering mountain slopes and an outlook across Langfjorden – an arm of the great Altafjord. The campsite is on a farm, one of the oldest in Finnmark, with strong Sami connections. Remarkably there are 110 beds available in 26 cabins, each cabin having its own balcony. The largest cabins sleep six and have three rooms with toilet and shower. All cabins have kitchens but only a few are fully en suite. There's a little kiosk, a sauna, a farm museum and trips arranged to visit the mountain and forest Sami. The wonderful site is complemented by a very friendly and efficient management. The site is open for caravans all year but the cabins are let only at Easter and the three months of summer. Cabin prices range from NOK270 to NOK550.

ALTA

Alta can, with justification, lay claim to be the most interesting town actually on the Highway, although Narvik might object. Yet it's not at all well-known outside Norway despite being one of the fastest growing of all the settlements of the north. Although on the coast, it is essentially a 'land' rather than a 'sea' town. Unlike many of the other old settlements in North Norway, it is not on an island. More to the point, its economy looks inland, not out to sea. It has never been a regular port of call for the Hurtigrute; it is more like an overgrown Sami village, a sort of expanded Kautokeino (see p227) or Karasjok (p262).

History

The earliest settlers arrived soon after the retreat of the ice some 8–9000 years ago. Their dwellings have been traced to the Komsafjell promontory which juts into the fjord in the middle of the town. It was in 1925 that the archaeologist Anders Nummerdal established the former presence of Stone Age people. These were the Komsa people who, with their palaeolithic culture, probably came from the region of the Gulf of Finland. Whether they were the progenitors of the Sami is less certain but

amongst the finds have been what are thought to be primitive skis.

Exactly what attracted these people to the Altafjord may never be known but, as hunters, it was probably the herds of reindeer which migrated north as the Quaternary ice sheets ablated. Later settlers were almost certainly attracted by the area's potential for some forms of agriculture. The summer is longer and warmer here than almost anywhere else in Arctic Norway. With a longer growing season as well as higher accumulated temperatures, Alta must have seemed something of an oasis. Precipitation is lower than in much of North Norway although higher than in interior Finnmark. Snowfalls are less of a problem here and summer rainfall is adequate.

The area around the head of Altafjorden is singularly well suited to cultivation. Three rivers, the great Altaelv and the smaller Tverrelv and Transforelva, have fashioned the land. Sediments have been laid down to mix with glacial drift and the rivers have carved giant terraces in the weak materials that choke their mouths. It is on these terraces that much of the farming takes place, on a scale unparalleled in Finnmark and rarely surpassed in all of Arctic Norway.

The rivers and their valleys give access to the Finnmark vidde to the south and it is by these routes that the early settlers came. Not until the Tanaelv is reached in East Finnmark is there such a clear natural route into the innermost parts of Lapland. It is the vidde which is the natural hinterland of Alta.

Alta's history in the period between Palaeolithic times and the sixteenth century is unclear. By the 1500s there were some fishing/farming settlements around the fjord but not until the late seventeenth and early eighteenth centuries were the nucleated villages at the head of the fjord established. It was these villages which were destined to become today's town. In 1703 the Alta Kommune was set up. This included much of the fjord's shore as far west as Talvik. Around the same time there was an influx of large numbers of Kvæns who had been driven out of Finland by political unrest and high taxation. The people descended on the coastal low ground from the vidde bringing with them their own distinctive language and culture which are still in evidence today. With their own non-littoral origins they strengthened the agricultural economy and introduced the cultivation of grain. Many of their descendants still live in the area and account for the prominence of Finnish names.

For decades the region was Finnish and Sami rather than Norwegian. Even in the census of 1801, of the 1800 people in the Alta parish only 500 were Norwegian. Alta benefited from the cosmopolitan mix of its population. In the 1830s, mining, first by the Dutch and the British, brought prosperity as well as introducing large numbers of workers from the Dovrefjell in Sør-Trøndelag. As mining declined, these workers turned to farming and the Sør-Trøndere have become the farming élite.

The three villages at the head of Altafjord remained physically separate until fairly recent times. Bossekop (Whale Bay), Bukta (Bight) and Elvebakken were spread, west to east, along eight or nine kilometres of a track which was to become part of the Arctic Highway. Their functions were as markets, especially for the Sami, and, combined, they constituted the most important centre in West Finnmark, officially recognized as such from 1791. The main market moved from Elvebakken, in the east, to Bossekop, in the west, in 1844, largely because the latter was already established as the most important Sami trading centre in all Lapland. The great December and March Sami fairs ceased here only after World War II.

Most of the old buildings in Alta were destroyed as the German army burnt everything in sight as it retreated in 1944. The war brought hard times to Finnmark but the most cruel blow of all came when the entire population – less some forty who took to the forests – were forcibly evacuated by sea while their town was set aflame. Now a new Alta has grown on the sites of the three villages that have merged to form a single contiguous settlement. A population of 6000 in 1970 has risen to around 17,000 in the municipality and every time I visit the town I find something new. The rate of change is astounding but much of its old charm remains.

Even in its earliest days, Alta impressed the visitor. That most observant of Lapland travellers, von Buch, wrote in July 1807 of an Alta 'so beautiful and so diversified'. He might not recognize it today but it has retained much of its beauty with buildings set among trees giving it its rural rather than urban character: a big village.

Services

The town's **tourist information office** was in the middle of making a move in early 2003. Previously based in Bossekop, it was being relocated to the museum (see p222) at the western entrance to the town and on the right-hand side of the Highway coming into Alta. This will be far less convenient for visitors because you will have to drive out to it from the centre of town. The contacts have yet to be decided but you can try the museum (see p222) or telephone ☎ 78 45 77 77. Failing this call the Finnmark Tourist Board (☎ 78 44 00 20; 🖷 78 43 51 84; 🖳 post@visitnorthcape.com).

The Arctic Highway runs like a spinal cord through the whole of the town. From the turning at Hjemmeluft it descends gently to **Bossekop**, the first of the old villages. As it does so it passes, on the right, the former hotel which is now an old people's home, set back from the road amongst the trees. Bossekop was for a long time the nearest Alta came to having a sentrum. It was here that Route 93 (see side trip to Kautokeino p225) used to meet the Arctic Highway. It is an important service centre with banks, shops, a post office and petrol stations. Alta seems to have more than its fair share of petrol stations – some open 24 hours.

Most of the shops and services lie in a complex of minor roads to the left of the Alta Highway where there is ample car-parking. To the right of the Highway is the **post office** and the **telephone exchange** which provides facilities for international telephone calls. After passing these two buildings there is a crossroads. The turning right is Thomasbakkveien (the old Route 93) and the left turn takes you into the shopping area. Bossekop, apart from the widening of the roads and the additional street furniture, has not changed too much in recent decades and its busy sense of purpose is its hallmark. I always think of it as the hub of Alta despite all the new building elsewhere.

A short climb away from Bossekop, followed by a gentle descent on the Highway, and the modern **Alta City** is reached. Many of the citizens of Alta objected to the term 'city' when it was first used but it is still heard, along with Sentrum. Alta City is a product of the town's planned growth in the 1970s and 1980s. It lies (signposted) to the right of the Highway and consists of a collection of modern buildings partly grouped around a square. The site, as well as the architecture, is new; no village antecedents here. It looks what it is, functional and efficient. The dominant building is the Rica Hotel and the kiosk in the square is the only one now to stock **foreign newspapers** in the tourist season. There is a **health centre** to the left of the entrance road from the Highway and a cluster of useful services including a bank and car-repair garages as well as further accommodation options and places to eat. The very modern Parksenteret proudly claims to be "the largest shopping centre in

Finnmark". No one's likely to contest the claim. The city/sentrum is still being added to. It hasn't the sense of purpose that characterizes Bossekop and there's always the thought that perhaps it would be better to come back when it is all finished.

The Highway does not enter Alta Sentrum but continues towards **Bukta**, the main harbour area, where industrial buildings separate it from the water's edge. A straight section of road carries it down and through to **Elvebakken** where again there is a range of services and shops. Past the **barracks** (left of the road) of the Alta Battalion with its simple **war memorial**, the Highway reaches the junction (signposted), to the left, with a minor road leading to the airport.

Alta Airport (☎ 78 48 25 00; 📄 78 48 25 80) is built on the deltaic flats of the River Alta. The runway uses the full length of the flats plus a man-made extension. There is a small terminal building for the daily services to Kirkenes and Oslo.

After the junction with the airport road, the Highway swings south-east to bridge Altaelva and runs through the district of **Kronstad** which stretches some distance south from the road. This area is particularly well wooded and comprises largely of the houses of those who work in the town. Finally, after crossing the Tverrelv by the **Tøfossen Bru**, the Highway leaves Alta for its journey eastwards and northwards.

Around town

Alta is an ideal place to take a few days' rest from travelling the Highway. It is not that the town is alive with entertainment; it isn't, but there is a wide choice of accommodation and plenty of interesting side trips. In addition to the side trips described on p225, there are excursions to Alta's famous **slate quarries** (☎ 78 43 33 35), opportunities for **river boat trips** (☎ 78 43 33 78) and for **fishing** in the fjord (☎ 78 43 13 67). Unless one has a small fortune to spend, it's best to forget the **salmon fishing** on the River Alta. It is one of the world's best salmon rivers but the closest most get is to view the anglers when on a visit to the **Alta Canyon** (see p230).

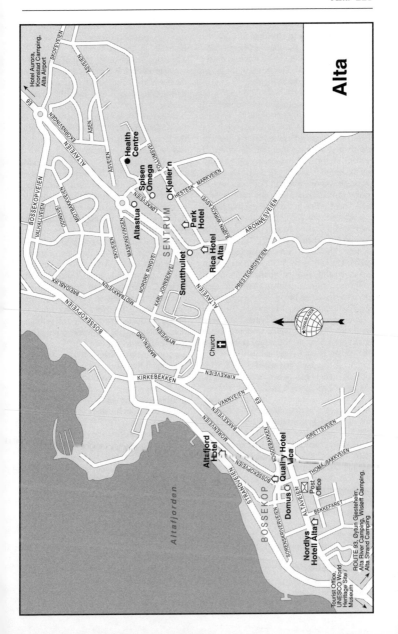

In the town the single biggest attraction is the **UNESCO World Heritage Site** with its attached museum. The site is at Hjemmeluft, on the edge of the Highway where it enters the town (see p214). This is where the information office is to be re-located.

The **museum** (☎ 78 43 63 30; 🖹 78 43 63 50; 🖳 alta.museum@alta.kommune.no) is new (1991). In 1993 the building won the European Museum of the Year award. On two floors are exhibits retelling the story of Alta's past up to the times of World War II and its aftermath. Exhibits also tell the story of the cultural and physical history of the area. The Sami's place in Finnmark is also given prominence. There is a **café**, a shop and a **post office** in the museum building.

Outside you can tour the Stone Age site on raised walkways to view the largest collection of **rock carvings** in northern Europe. They were discovered as recently as 1973. The oldest are thought to date from about 6000BP and the youngest from just 500 years before the birth of Christ. Here are depicted scenes of life in this remote part of the world thousands of years ago. They tell a fascinating story. The carvings have been made into the rocks which were previously under the sea. As the ice melted at the end of the Pleistocene Ice Age, and its weight was removed, the land has slowly risen. This phenomenon is known as isostatic recovery. As more and more wavecut rock became exposed above sea-level, the carvings continued lower down the slope leaving the oldest on the highest ground. All the carvings can be viewed from a five-kilometre wooden walkway which threads though the site. Most of the 3000 or so carvings have been highlighted in red. Purists who object to this are told that this was probably how they were originally coloured.

The entry charge for the museum and site is NOK60 but children under 16 are admitted free. In summer the opening hours are 09.00 to 18.00 at the beginning and end of the season but it stays open progressively later to the time of the midnight sun when it closes at 23.00. It can take a whole day to view all the exhibits and carvings. In winter, the hours are more restricted (09.00 to 15.00 on weekdays and 11.00 to 16.00 at weekends). With the carvings probably obscured by snow or invisible in the darkness of winter, the admission charge drops to NOK35.

The **church** is worth visiting as one of the few old buildings to survive the war-time destruction, though considerable changes were made in 1950. The original church had been inspired by the English management of the Kåfjord copper works (see p215). It is to the left of the Highway between Bossekop and the 'new city'/sentrum.

Alta has become a base for a wide range of **adventure holidays/experiences** in all seasons. These often require small groups to be organized and the various trips on offer change from time to time. Many of the arrangements involve the local Sami population and provide interesting – if not always authentic – insights into the life of these people. Snowmobile trips in winter, canoe trips up the River Alta in summer, treks over the vidde, cross-country skiing; there is a variety which is always being extended. It is best to check some time before leaving for Norway and again on arrival in Alta to obtain up-to-date information. Contacts can be made through the tourist office in Alta (see p219) or through agents in the two Sami villages Masi (also Maze) and Kautokeino (see p227).

Alta is also a good stepping-off point for the kommune of Loppa, the collection of islands off the coast. Again, information can be had from the tourist office.

Accommodation

Alta has an exceptionally wide range of accommodation for travellers along the Highway but it should be borne in mind that there's a reduced choice in winter and that summer may be deemed to be over as early as mid-August.

The grandest hotel is the *Rica Hotel Alta* (☎ 78 48 27 00; 🖹 78 48 27 77; 🖳 rica.hotel.alta@rica.no), situated in the heart of the new sentrum. In fact it was one of the first buildings to be erected there. There are 155 en-suite rooms and it's very well managed. Although it boasts three restaurants, it's likely that only the café (with a limited menu) near reception will be open. The

Rica is favoured by conferences which results in the hotel looking towards that trade rather than the overnight traveller. It also means the hotel may be fully booked in winter. There's a sauna, but beware: the wooden benches have some exposed metal – contrary to all the rules of sauna construction. Rates are high: between NOK700 and NOK1300 in summer.

Across the square and occupying the same block as the shopping centre is the *Park Hotel* (☎ 78 43 62 11; 🖹 78 43 63 80; 🖵 post@parkhotel.no). This 30-room hotel is a welcome new addition. There are doubles that convert to triples and the usual Scandinavian option of singles that are combis, sleeping two. There's a homely atmosphere about the park. Coffee and waffles are available all day and included in the room price. A sauna is available and some rooms have baths rather than showers. On the down side, there is no proper restaurant although breakfast and a snack evening meal are included in the charge of around NOK700 (single) to NOK900 (double). For NOK1400 there's a double suite with its own sauna. For anyone driving the Highway in winter, it's encouraging to know that there's an underground car-park.

Quality Hotel Vica (☎ 78 43 47 11; 🖹 78 43 42 99; 🖵 post@vica.no) is in Bossekop. Turn left into the Bossekop sentrum from the Highway and continue along this road. The hotel is on the right. This is a smaller hotel than it looks; only 24 rooms. Parking is at the front of the hotel. The hotel is spotlessly clean, very well decorated and has a warm feel. There are separate smoking and non-smoking parts to the restaurant which is open all day. A sauna, bar and honeymoon suite complete the facilities. Summer rates are from about NOK700 (single) to NOK970. Winter rates are NOK300–400 more. All prices include breakfast. Ask for one of the 'new' rooms.

If you continue past the Vica down to the fjord you can loop back to *Altafjord Hotel* (☎ 78 43 70 11; 🖹 78 43 70 13). With 68 rooms and a restaurant, and prices around NOK500, this is an inexpensive option. However it is open to the public only in summer. By mid-August it is back

to doubling as student accommodation. Don't expect luxury.

What was the Alta Gjestestue is now the more grandly named *Nordlys Hotell Alta* (☎ 78 43 55 66; 🖹78 43 50 80; 🖵 e-post @nordlyshotell.no). It lies back from the Highway (on the right as you come into Bossekop). It is especially good for families or small groups. Some rooms are linked to provide beds for five people. The corridors are narrow but the rooms, all en suite, are adequately sized. It was built in 1978 but renovated in 2000. There's a café on the front and a restaurant which stays open until 22.00. Rates are reasonable at NOK900 for a double in summer and just NOK50 more in winter.

At the eastern end of Alta is the suburb of Saga. Continue along the Highway, past the airport, cross the bridge over the Altaelv, then the bridge over the Tverrelv and take the next main road on the right, Tverrelvdalsveien. *Hotel Aurora* (☎ 78 43 78 00; 🖹 78 43 78 01), formerly the Sagatun, is on the left, on a rise. The two inter-connecting buildings date from 1991. The 30 rooms are en suite with the bathrooms rather like a cabin within the bedroom. There's a pleasant little à la carte restaurant, a sauna and solarium. The restaurant is decorated with some interesting abstract photographs. Sagatun's location may not be ideal for access for the rest of the town but you may consider its semi-rural position to be an attraction. Rates are NOK680 to NOK840.

The only other hotel in Alta is the Ongajoksetra which caters only for groups.

Just outside Alta is the *Øytun Gjesteheim* (☎ 78 43 55 77; 🖹 78 43 60 40). This simple guesthouse is reached by taking Route 93 towards Kautokeino (see p225). About 4km after leaving the Arctic Highway take a turn right opposite the camping places at Øvre Alta (see p225), along Skoddevarre, for this summer-only guesthouse. In winter it is student accommodation. The 81 simply furnished rooms are not en suite but there's one shared bathroom for every 7 guests. It is good value at around NOK500 with breakfast. Even here, there's a sauna – well, this is Finnmark.

Campers are well served but be prepared for large sites. I prefer to wild camp in the forest some 15km out of Alta. There are three big camping places at what is called Øvre (outer) Alta along the banks of Altaelva. Finding them is simple: take Route 93 off the Highway west of Bossekop and after about 4km you reach the first camp, *Alta River Camping* (☎ 78 43 43 53; 🏠 78 43 69 02). This camp has 15 well-constructed cabins including one adapted for the disabled. Six of the cabins had all facilities when I was last there and I know the owners planned to upgrade more. There are also six rooms available and plenty of space for tents and camper vans. There's a sauna and a shared washing machine and dryer. Open all year, Alta River Camping charges between NOK250 and NOK400 for cabins.

Just 400m further on is *Wisløff Camping* (☎ 78 43 43 03; 🏠 78 44 31 37). The reception here has a kiosk. Of the 14 cabins, all sleep four except for one small two-bed cabin. The cabins nearest the entrance (Nos 8–14) are en suite. All have cooking facilities. It's a popular site for caravans. Rates are roughly the same as at Alta River except for the biggest cabins which are some NOK100 more expensive.

Moving on another 500m brings you to *Alta Strand Camping* (☎ 78 43 40 22; 🏠 78 43 42 40). Of the 34 cabins, 15 are classed as apartments. These come at between NOK580 for 1–2 persons to NOK850 for the largest, sleeping seven. Prices of the other cabins depend upon whether they have a water supply and how many they sleep. A two-person cabin without water will be about NOK250 but a cabin sleeping six and having water will cost nearer NOK700.

These three camping sites along the river are all popular despite their large size and location outside Alta. Within the town, and just off the Highway, is *Kronstad Camping* (☎ 78 43 03 06; 🏠 78 43 11 55) in a nicely wooded site close to the mouth of Tverrelva. To find the site, continue on the

Highway though Alta almost to its eastern exit. The site is visible on the left of the Highway. There's a variety of cabins, 29 in all, with rates starting around NOK300. Some of the cabins at this long established site need upgrading. You will need to check, too, that the refugees housed here have vacated the site.

On the way out of Alta, driving north, to the left of the road is *Solvang Camping*, a neatly laid-out site with little red cabins among the pine trees.

All the camps in Alta are open all year.

Where to eat

As with accommodation, there is lots of choice in Alta. The relatively new Alta City or Sentrum has spawned a host of eating and drinking places. Pride of place has to go to *Smutthullet* which is in the Parksenteret and is really a complex of four separate establishments. The name means 'The Leaphole' but the significance escapes me. It really needs its own guidebook with complicated opening days, times, and age-limits. Smutthullet 20 is on the ground floor. No one under 20 is admitted at night. It's a nightclub at weekends and serves meals (NOK100–180) at lunchtime and in the evening. It is open every day, and until 03.00 on Saturdays. Then there's Smutthullet 18 which serves pizzas and Mexican dishes on the first floor but is closed on Mondays. On the same floor, Smutthullet 23 is largely a bar and is often rented out. This one closes on Wednesdays.

Far more straightforward and under the same management is *Altastua*, a restaurant serving all meals and drinks in the evening. In case that's too simple, it closes Sundays and doesn't open again until Wednesday.

Also in the Sentrum is *Spisen Omega*, a well presented café, and *Kjeller'n* on the edge of the square. The latter, as the name suggests, is mainly a bar. It stays open very late (03.00 on Fridays and Saturdays) but is closed on Mondays. If you want a meal it can cost between NOK50 and NOK150.

(Opposite) Top: Masi (see p226), a small Sami village on the way to Kautokeino. **Bottom left**: A World Heritage Site: the Stone Age rock carvings at Alta (see p222). **Bottom right**: The tundra, land of the cotton grass.

Within the senteret there is a collection of cafés: **Toppen** (meals from NOK50 to NOK200) and **Park Kafé** (NOK20–70), both on the second floor. The Park is especially attractive. On the ground floor, drinks, especially coffee, are the speciality of **Gabiten Kafé** and **Kaffe Larsen**.

In Bossekop, the **Domus** supermarket has a very popular café and, to the right of the Highway before you reach the crossroads, there is **Harry's Bistro**. There is talk of this Bistro closing but that would be a pity. It serves 100gm burgers for NOK60 and potato chips are about NOK30. There's a drive-though option for those in a hurry.

The larger hotels' restaurants will usually serve non-residents.

SIDE TRIPS FROM ALTA

There are three interesting side trips that can be made off the Highway from Alta but two are alternatives to the same destination. Although you probably need to be staying in Alta to take these side trips, if you fail to take a trip to Kautokeino you'll be missing a wonderful experience.

1 Side trip to Kautokeino via Route 93   Map 12a

Kautokeino via Route 93 is a whole day trip. The distance is 130km and the road is generally very easy driving. As said, this side trip should not be missed. There is interesting scenery and, with Kautokeino as the goal, the long journey is well worth the effort. Kautokeino is possibly the most important Sami settlement of all. Unlike Karasjok (see p262) it has not yet capitulated to tourism.

Route 93 leaves Alta at its junction with the Arctic Highway, just before reaching Bossekop. It's best to refuel before setting out as the journey is through largely uninhabited country. Parts of the road were built as recently as 1964. The pre-war road stopped just 18km short of Kautokeino at Mieron. The rest of the journey could be accomplished in winter only on the snow roads that led beyond Kautokeino and into Finland. Now the re-routed road is kept open for most of the year.

Route 93 follows the same path as the Alta River for the first few kilometres of its southerly path. Little of the river is seen but here and there the giant terraces into which the river is incised are evident, some being cut into to extract road gravels. At **Øvre Alta** (4km), the river is visible, broad, turbulent and worthy of its other name: Storelva (Big River). The area to the south of Alta is farmed and forested, characteristic of the whole of the Altafjord head.

At **Skillemo** (7km) a minor road leads towards the river. This takes you to Jøraholmen and 'Vina', the riverside villa where from 1862 the dukes of Roxburghe spent their summers pursuing the salmon of Altaelva; at one time they had the exclusive fishing rights over the whole river. The Alta remains one of the best salmon rivers in the world but American millionaires have replaced the British peerage. The cost of a day's fishing licence is upwards of NOK3000 and seaplanes ferry the anglers and their catch to and from the best stretches.

A kilometre further on at **Tangen** (8km), Route 93 veers to the right and a minor road swings more sharply left (see Side trip 2). Route 93 now follows the path of Eibyelva, a left bank tributary of the Alta. At **Kløftan** (22km) there

---

(Opposite) Top: The midnight sun skims the horizon at the North Cape (see p251). **Bottom**: Sami church at Kautokeino (see p228). Traditional costume is now kept almost exclusively for special days.

is the rocky confluence with Vesterelva, with the road clinging to the edge of a small gorge, Trangdalen. Rapids and falls cascade down to the right of the road as it winds and climbs up the gorge. This is the only moderately difficult section of this route.

At the top of the gorge the road comes out into the open country, the plateau or vidde, and runs alongside the gleaming ribbon that is Lake Trangsdal. The vidde, crossed at altitudes between 300m and 400m, is wild. This is Lapland at its most untamed. Dwarf birch, where there is shelter, reindeer moss, bogland and glacial gravels make up the scene along with countless streams winding their way through a patchwork of lakes. Large herds of reindeer graze this plateau in winter but few will be seen in summer. Sami tents (*kåta*) may be spied occasionally in among the trees or, more likely, near the road where there will be half-hearted attempts to sell you skins and horn.

There is a small **mountain hostel** (fjellstue), with a **café**, which is popular with those trekking the vidder at **Suolovombe** (50km). It is here that the pre-war Kautokeino–Alta road joins the modern Route 93. The old road can be used (see side trip, p230). Just two kilometres further and Route 93 reaches its highest point, 418m.

A small road turns off to the left rather less than 20km later. This leads down to **Masi** (Maze, 68km). This is an important, totally Sami, village. There is a 3km loop road through the village leading back to Route 93 so a detour adds little to the journey time.

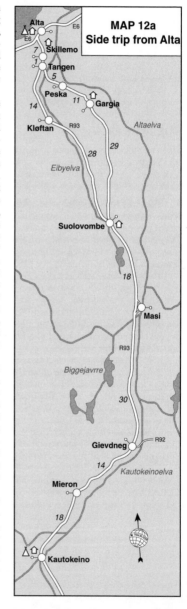

Masi suffered the fate common to almost all Finnmark's settlements in World War II. It was burnt to the ground. However, unlike most other villages this was not as the Germans retreated in 1944 but was the result of a vicious firing of the village one night during the occupation. Some two hundred or so Sami live in the village and there is a general store, petrol station and clinic. I have reason to be thankful for the latter. It was to this clinic that I was taken after a serious accident some years ago. The village was also where I first met Ellen-Anne, the Sami girl who was to become my interpreter in the years to come.

The single most interesting building in the village is the **chapel** which dates from 1965. It stands on rising ground to the right of the loop road through Masi. Services are held here when there is none at Kautokeino and the occasion is an ideal one to see the full and colourful Sami costume.

The village is probably not as old as Kautokeino but it has a longer history as a 'Norwegian' Sami settlement. The original chapel was erected in the early seventeenth century partly to establish Norwegian sovereignty at a time when Kautokeino still lay within Swedish jurisdiction.

It is a pretty little village in the summer. The area around and down to the nearby Kautokeinoelv (as the River Alta has become by this point on the vidde) is farmed. A livelihood based entirely on reindeer herding is hardly viable in the twenty-first century.

Route 93 from Masi southwards continues over the plateau and is never far from the Kautokeinoelv which is to the left of the road. At **Gievdneg** (98km) there is a junction (to the left) with Route 92 which leads to Karasjok where it would be possible to rejoin the Arctic Highway.

Another small Sami settlement is reached at **Mierojohka** (Mieron, 112km) where there is a small shop and **café**. This was the terminus of the pre-war road from Alta. Fortunately Route 93 knows no such limits and the road runs over the plateau before descending into **Kautokeino** (130km), the largest Sami village and the most scattered.

Accommodation: Alta to Kautokeino There is only one place to stop on this route: the **Suolovuopmi Mountain Inn** (☎ 78 48 75 10), 50km out of Alta. There are cabins and rooms in the main building. It's worth stopping for a meal here. The **café** serves local specialities, especially reindeer dishes and fish. Their reindeer tongue sandwiches are famous. Catering for skiers as well as walkers, it is open all year. Small cabins cost around NOK200 and larger ones NOK375.

KAUTOKEINO

Kautokeino, or Guovdageaidnu, lies in a sandy basin, cut by the river in the glacial sands and gravels left after the ice age. So sandy is the landscape that exposed parts resemble a desert. The Sami houses are sprinkled in apparently random fashion around the basin; only the church, standing on a knoll, gives the village any real focus.

The old Sami name for the settlement was Guovdageaino, meaning 'Halfway House', and this gives a clue to its origin. It probably began life as a resting place on the route between the Norwegian coastal Sami settlements and those of interior Lapland, that is, Sweden and Finland. Winter encampments from at least as far back in history as the thirteenth century gradually evolved into a permanent settlement of note by the seventeenth century. Growth was slow. By 1880 it is recorded that there were still only about a dozen houses, yet the school catered for seventy pupils in winter.

Today's village is the centre of the largest reindeer district in Norway and houses about 1700 people, most of whom are Sami. Descendants of the Kvæns, from Finland, still dominate trade in the village.

The church, built in 1958 to replace the one burnt down by the German occupying forces in World War II, is close to the site of the original chapel. In fact, the first permanent building, set on a bluff on the right bank of the river, was a house for a priest and for visiting government officials. The original church was put up alongside on rising ground called Goattedivva (which means 'Tent Knoll') when the village had grown to eight or nine houses.

One series of incidents connected with the church, or at least with religion, disturbed the peace of the village in 1852. These have become known as the Kautokeino Riots.

Preacher and botanist Lars Læstadius, founder of the Læstadian sect (see also p203) had many followers in Kautokeino. The most fanatical decided that the time was right to rid the village of its 'sinners'. The move resulted in a riot in the autumn of 1852 in which first two Norwegians then two of the Læstadians were killed. The authorities clamped down on the sect and two of its leaders eventually suffered the death penalty.

More than a century ago, in Paul du Chaillu's *The Land of the Midnight Sun*, Kautokeino was described as a meeting place for the Sami about Easter time before they moved with their reindeer to the summer pastures near the coast. '*Every house was full of Laplanders, coming to see their friends and relatives*.' The village was still quite small then but the Sami, who lived in scattered settlements over the vidde in winter, saw it as their spiritual home. It has much the same attraction today even though fewer of the Sami live outside the village.

Services

The main shops are along Route 93 through the village, mainly in a cluster on the left opposite the ESSO station. There are two other petrol stations. Taking the turning left off Route 93 before the bridge leads you along a minor road near to the river. There is a **tourist information office** (☎ 78 45 65 00). Also here is a **bank** and, further on, the Kautokeino Museum which serves as a Sami community centre for a variety of activities.

Around the village

Its prominent position will often make the **church** the first place to visit. It is usually left open for visitors to see the simple painted interior. On Sundays there may be a service and an excuse for the Sami to wear traditional costume. Even more impressive will be a wedding ceremony but these, by custom, are usually at Easter before most foreign travellers are passing through the village. Easter is festival time. It is *the* time to be in the village.

Behind the church there is an interesting Sami graveyard with wooden, stone and wrought-iron memorials. The high ground around the church also gives a good view over much of Kautokeino.

Within the village there are a number of other important buildings, none more significant than the Sami boarding **school** (to the left of Route 93 on entering the village). This excellent school has done much to raise the general standards of education among the Sami. Its reputation extends not only throughout Lapland but as far south as Tromsø. It has its own swimming pool, library, cinema and ski jump, facilities which are shared with the local community.

Close to the school is a sports centre with a large bronze of a running reindeer.

There is an important reindeer-meat factory on the eastern side of the village and a radio station near the school.

Particularly worth a visit is the **Sámi Instituhtta** (Nordic Sami Research Institution, ☎ 78 48 80 00; 🖷 78 48 80 30; 🖳 info@nsi.no). Take the first left after passing the ESSO station and continue about 300m on this road. The Institute is on the left. Its prime purpose is research but the staff are usually willing to spend time with visitors who are interested in the culture of the Sami people. The modern buildings, including a theatre, are the focus of a number of village activities.

There is more than one **silversmith** in Kautokeino, for the plateau yields a number of precious and semi-precious ores. But quite the most extraordinary is the silversmith and artist **Frank Juhls**, a German whose workshops and galleries are situated on the hill above the village to the right of Route 93 (signposted at the junction with a minor road just after entering Kautokeino and before crossing the river).

Juhls, not without considerable local opposition, set up his workshop just after World War II making largely silver jewellery in the style and patterns of traditional Sami pieces. Walking down the steep path to the galleries you are confronted by what must be one of the most unusual buildings in all Lapland. The outward appearance is of a series of interconnecting, large, strangely shaped, wooden and glass tents. Every time I visit there seems to be an addition to the building. The entrance is through the silversmiths' workshop where skilled and student craftsmen fashion intricate pieces for sale in the galleries here or in the smart shops of Scandinavia and Germany.

There is a collection of Sami artefacts and paraphernalia (not for sale) but the main galleries are full of expensive jewellery, paintings and ceramics. In recent years, there have been added imported items from the Near East, especially Afghanistan. The latter items are housed in a gallery below ground level. The whole building is richly furnished and quite beautifully laid out. The music of J S Bach may be playing quietly in the background and there is an air of elegance and sophistication. To visit Kautokeino and not see the Juhls' galleries is to miss seeing a curious community of craftsmen at once alien to, yet part of, Lapland.

Route 93 continues southwards from Kautokeino to the Finnish border, a further 44km, and on to Karesuando.

Accommodation

There is one hotel in the village, the **Nordlandia Kautokeino Hotel** (☎ 78 48 62 05; ▤ 78 48 67 01). Opened in 1968, it stands on high ground to the right as Route 93 enters the village. It is a simple but com-

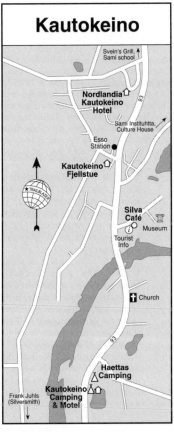

fortable hotel which also acts as an activity centre. All 50 rooms are en suite and there's a sauna. The restaurant is unexciting but adequate and its views are good. Prices include breakfast with costs for a double ranging from NOK1200 on a winter weekday down to NOK780 at a weekend in summer.

Taking the first turning right after the hotel turn-off will bring you to **Kautokeino Fjellstue** (formerly Alfreds, ☎ 78 48 61 18; ▤ 78 48 58 55). There are eight cabins with cooking facilities but no water. They cost NOK300. The main building has eight rooms, half of which are en suite. Rooms start at a modest NOK200. This is a very inexpensive alternative to the hotel but prices accurately reflect quality. There's also a **café** which is open all day.

There is a large camping area south of the river bridge and to the left of Route 93. This large operation is *Kautokeino Camping and Motel* (☎ 78 48 54 00; 📠 78 48 53 01). Twenty-five cabins are scattered over the place, with eight having shower and toilet. These cost NOK480. Those without water come at NOK280. All cabins have cooking facilities and the site is open all year. The adjacent **café** closes in winter.

This is a well-run camping place. Next door is *Hættas Camping* (☎ 78 48 62 60). This is a smaller and simpler site, with no water in the 11 small cabins. Cooking facilities are provided. A cabin costs NOK250, or NOK400 for two nights.

Where to eat

There is not much choice for food although the hotel serves non-residents. On entering the village there is a little café, *Svein's Grill* (formerly Ellen's Grill). The plus point here is that it stays open until midnight. In the little complex of shops is *Silva Café*.

2   Side trip to Kautokeino over the plateau (a 4x4 route)   Map 12a

Kautokeino can also be reached by driving across the vidde. There is little difference in the distance covered, just three kilometres each way, compared with using Route 93 all the way. However, if you have four-wheel drive and the weather is good, then this is the more interesting route. It will take perhaps an extra hour on the minor plateau road but more if you take in Northern Europe's deepest canyon.

To take this route, follow Route 93 as far as Tangen (8km) – see Side trip 1, p225. At the junction turn left off Route 93 and follow the minor road which crosses a narrow bridge over Eibyelva. This road is well surfaced, winding in parts, but adequately wide. It follows the path of the Altaelv and there are occasional glimpses of the river, particularly fine where the road rides high along the gravel terrace. At **Peska** (13km) there are the famous Skifebrudd **slate quarries** visible high on the mountainside to the right of the road.

Much of the journey here is through thin forest with small farms set at wide intervals beside the road. Farming is less prosperous as you move away from Alta. There is excellent wild camping along parts of this section of the road but the temptation to fish in the Alta must be resisted; remember it costs thousands of kroner a day! The scenery is pretty rather than spectacular, with streams spilling off the high ground to the east and into the Alta River.

One of the streams entering the Alta is the Gargiaelv and at **Gargia** (24km) there is a mountain inn or **fjellstue**.

Immediately after the fjellstue the minor road stops and the path up to the top of the vidde is a very simple track. This is not really suitable for the average car but might just be possible without four-wheel drive in good, dry weather. With four-wheel drive there should be no problem.

The track climbs fairly steeply through ever-thinning forest to come out on top of the plateau where the most prominent features are the snow-road cairns. This is true treeless tundra: boggy, rocky and wild. Although strictly without trees (even dwarf varieties cannot survive), there is often a network of creeping horizontal birch which, when bent upwards, may reach two metres. Here and there you may see the wooden tent poles and stone markings of a Sami camping place where the herders and their reindeer will have rested on their migrations between summer- and winter-feeding grounds. The silence and primitive beauty of the windswept plateau is awesome.

At about 30km from Alta, there is a small marked plot to the left of the track where vehicles can be parked. From here you can walk the six or so kilometres (path marked to the left of the road/track) to the **Sautso gorge**. The canyon is cut in the Bæskades mountain plateau by the Alta/Kautokeino River. Three hundred metres or more deep and six kilometres long, it is worth the trek.

The plateau track continues away from the parking place on an undulating surface, which may be flooded after rain. Take care with any bridge encountered: they are not well maintained. Finally, the track begins its descent into Suolovombe (53km) where it joins Route 93 (see Alternative Route on p226) for the final 80km to Kautokeino.

Accommodation Famous and popular among all who revel in the Finnmark vidde is the *Gargia Fjellstue* (☎ 78 43 33 51; 🖳 post@gargia-fjellstue.no). Twenty-four kilometres out of Alta, there has been a mountain lodge here for almost 150 years. The present building dates from just after World War II. There are 4 cabins and 11 rooms, giving a choice of self-catering or use of the **restaurant**. The meals are excellent, using fresh local ingredients. In addition to the restaurant (closed on Mondays) there is a **cafeteria** which is open all day. This is the place from which to explore the plateau and canyon or to take part in a variety of activities organized by the fjellstue. There is even horse riding. The management has its own stables of sturdy Icelandic ponies. Gargia is open all year except Christmas to February. Room prices are from NOK275 and the en-suite cabins range from NOK350 to NOK600.

3   A trip along the Altafjord

A trip to the Altafjord can be made in about half a day although a full day would be better. The round-trip distance involved is 130km. This trip is best made in fine weather when the beauties of the fjord can be seen to advantage. It has the disadvantage, for those travelling the Arctic Highway, of repeating some 29km of the E6.

To take this trip, follow the Arctic Highway east out of Alta to **Leirbotnvatn** (29km). This part of the journey is described on p233. At Leirbotnvatn there is a very sharp turn to the left on to Route 883 which climbs steeply away from the Highway along a lake-strewn path, past innumerable rivers and rapids. The journey here is through forested country but the road quickly slips down to the fjord, reached at **Leirbotn** (36km), a little village sheltering in a bay off the main Altafjord.

MAP 12b: Side Trip from Alta

From here the road follows a coastal path clinging to the side of the fjord and giving excellent views to the west (left). This is a very beautiful stretch of coast with good sea-fishing (no licence required) and off-track to most travellers. The island of Årøya lies just off the mainland and there are small fishing hamlets and isolated farms along the roadside.

The road winds into a small inlet off the main fjord, Skillefjorden, then returns before swinging into another inlet, Korsfjorden. It reaches a village, **Nyvoll** (65km), and stops short of the head of the inlet. There are shops and petrol in the village. From Nyvoll there is an infrequent ferry linking to the remaining 24km of Route 883 on the other side of Korsfjorden. It is probably wise to turn back at Nyvoll but if you take the ferry then in a couple of kilometres you'll come to the tiny village of **Komagfjord**. Here there are three rorbuer, fishermen's cottages typical of the Lofoten Islands. Each rorbu can sleep six and is for rental. They are very well equipped.

PART 8: ALTA TO KARASJOK

For much of the journey to Karasjok, the Arctic Highway turns to inland routes over the vidder which separate the fjords before finally heading southwards into the interior of Finnmark. Most of this path is, not surprisingly, uninhabited – except by the Sami in their summer camps. It will be prudent, therefore, to fill fuel tanks when the opportunity occurs even if they are already half full. Accommodation, too, is not easy to come by and choice is limited even in those settlements such as Skaidi, Lakselv and Karasjok which are on the Highway's route.

The Highway: Alta to Skaidi
MAPS 12–13

The Arctic Highway leaves Alta through the district of Kronstad, crosses the Tøfossen bridge over Tverrelva and rejoins the coast just after passing the mouth of the narrow Transfordalen. Back with the shore means a return of views out to the fjord and, sharply westward, to the town of Alta. The Highway is now running along the shore of Rafsbotn, an easterly arm of Altafjorden which, with Kåfjorden, gives the whole fjord the shape of an inverted T.

Rafsbotn (18km; NB distances from Alta assume the Bossekop junction as the centre of Alta) is a small fishing village, with a store (right), but the Highway skirts by to begin its climb through a gorge away from the fjord. From here to Skaidi, 80km away, the country is wild and desolate.

Slopes on either side of the Highway are steep but birch trees often manage to find a root-hold in the scree. The road's gradient lessens at about 200m and the forest thickens. By the time you reach the top of the rise, there are only scattered trees and bog. Thus begins 'the land of the cotton grass', the tundra, true Lapland. Cotton grass is typical tundra vegetation, seeking out the damp ground and growing round, and even in, shallow ponds and lakes, which rest on the peaty surface or in the ill-drained active zone above the permafrost.

Along the roadside, and especially at a place called **Nibijavrre** (24km), you begin to see the summer huts of the Sami whose reindeer find food and shelter in the thin forest of this wasteland. The huts, mostly to the right of the Highway, are the houses for the short summer of Sami from the Kautokeino district. Often the whole family will be in residence, sometimes just the young adults. The huts here are poorer than those on Sennalandet further along the Highway. Typically the area around the huts will be an untidy collection of snow scooters, the occasional sledge and the detritus of family living. You may find a tent erected near to the road as a tourist-lure, with skins and antlers for sale.

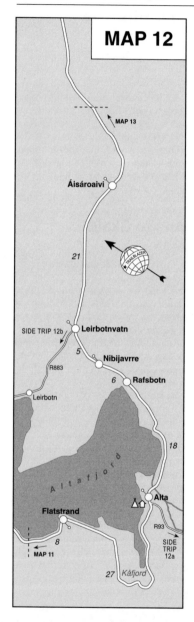

MAP 12

MAP 13

Áisároaivi

21

Leirbotnvatn

SIDE TRIP 12b

5 Nibijavrre

R883

6 Rafsbotn

Leirbotn

18

Altafjord

Alta

Flatstrand

R93

SIDE
TRIP
12a

8

MAP 11

27 Káfjord

From this higher ground the Highway descends 50m to Leirbotnvatn (29km) in the company of a stream (to the right of the road) which matches the Highway's gradient with its shallow falls over a rocky bed. Leirbotnvatn, a large lake at the head of Lakselvdalen, is at the junction with Route 883 (see Side trip 3 from Alta, Part 7, p231).

The Highway's route continues up Stokkedalen. This requires a steady climb on a consistent gradient. The road has been built above valley level such that there are steep slopes up to the left of the Highway while, to the right, the land falls away down to the largely unseen river. The valley is tree-filled and a favourite place for the Sami's reindeer to forage. Despite the erection of some fences and crude reindeer-scares, the deer quite frequently dash wildly across the road and an unexpected encounter with a car will leave the animal dead and the vehicle damaged. It is best to watch carefully and always give the reindeer right of way.

Below the Highway, to the south-west, the river runs in a gorge which narrows towards the head. As the road climbs towards the plateau above the gorge the forest begins to thin and at about 375m the path levels and the Highway is ready to cross the Senna vidde. Now you'll see no trees, no habitation, simply bare rock, patchy grass and bog. This tundra scenery is reminiscent of the Saltfjell where the Arctic Highway crosses the Polar Circle (see Part 4, p131).

The route taken by the Highway to cross the vidde is mostly close to the plateau's watershed. This is no mountain ridge; the rivers scarcely cut into the landscape. It is all remarkably flat and this adds to the desolation. When I first travelled the Highway many years ago it was little more than a waterbound gravel track which, after spring thaw or rain, was difficult to negotiate as it became rutted by the few vehicles that used it. Its only redeeming feature was that it was straight.

Today's Highway is even straighter but it is raised, widened and well surfaced. It used to be impossible to keep the Sennalandet section open through the winter. Now there will be temporary closures in the worst of the winter snowfalls but it is essentially an all-weather road.

No one lives on the vidde but in summer between late May and early September, the Sami from Kautokeino and Masi (see Part 7, p226) move here to watch over their reindeer after the spring migration. There is a scattering of huts at first and then, towards **Áisároaivi** (also called Aisaroiui; 50km), there is what comes close to being a Sami village. This concentration of huts is explained not only by the people's wish to live in a more socially coherent community but also by the presence of a small chapel, a slaughterhouse and springs for water supply.

When I made the first study of Áisároaivi in the 1970s (*Nomads of the Arctic*) many of the Sami families had just begun to move their huts to this area where the Highway crosses the head-waters of Repparfjordelva. Now this loose agglomeration is established but the huts and the primitive living conditions are much the same. The loneliness of the tundra is ameliorated by living in this community but, when the sleet is blown across the vidde from leaden skies, there is little to envy in the life of the Sami at Áisároaivi.

The little **chapel** lies to the left of the Highway and you can see it clearly. It is usually kept locked except when, on the occasional Sunday in summer, a service is held. Then the Sami walk down the tracks that link their widely separated huts with the Highway and assemble in the tiny wooden building for a service in Norwegian and Sami. Afterwards they move back to the huts to share endless cups of coffee with their neighbours. Theirs is a very private life and if you wander off the Highway into their settlement, you are not generally welcome. Not so those who buy whatever they have for sale in tents and crudely erected wooden lean-tos that are set up against the road.

Beyond Áisároaivi the Sami encampments are fewer but, as you descend to 250m and below, the birch woods reappear in the shelter of the valley and, tucked in among the trees, are the summer cabins belonging not to the Sami but to Norwegians who fish the river. The river is the Repparfjordelv and the Highway shares its valley, running high above the stream and its salmon-rich waters.

As the Highway approaches Skaidi the valley of the Repparfjordelv, here called Breidalen, narrows. The river is entrenched in a gorge within a gorge. At first the road follows the river but at about 200m it levels out and drops less steeply, eventually running on a shelf some 60m above the river. Much resurfacing and straightening of the Highway has taken place here in recent years and many of the more difficult sections have been rebuilt by the simple expedient of explosive charges placed in the rock walls. The gorge, however, still acts

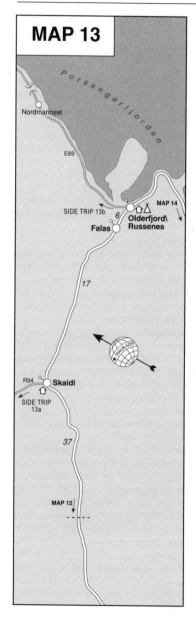

MAP 13

Porsangerfjorden

Nordmannset

E69

MAP 14

SIDE TRIP 13b

Olderfjord\
Russenes

Falas

17

TRAILBLAZER

R94   Skaidi

SIDE TRIP
13a

37

MAP 12

like a funnel, strengthening the winds blowing through it. As a consequence, the trees are stunted, almost stump-like, and above the gorge there is only rock and bog.

The gorge broadens into a valley as you reach **Skaidi** (87km). Skaidi is a textbook example of a service settlement resulting from a major road junction. The name means 'River Meeting'. The Highway turns right into the village but to the left is Route 94 leading to Hammerfest. The village is well served by a **hotel** and a **motel**. There is a store and the village is an ideal place for you to stop and re-provision. There is a **tourist kiosk** (☎ 78 41 62 80), to the right of the road, open in summer.

Accommodation: Alta to Skaidi

There's not a lot of choice other than to stop at Skaidi. Even wild camping isn't very practical. At Skaidi the *Skaidi Arctic Hotel* (☎ 78 41 61 20; 📄 78 41 61 27) is open all year but, in winter, accommodation has to be pre-booked. The hotel has 44 rooms of which nine are singles. As so often in Norwegian hotels, the singles convert to doubles and the doubles to triples.

The hotel is close to the centre of the village to the left of the Highway. There are smoking and non-smoking lounges, a restaurant which is open most of the day, a swimming pool, sauna and solarium. Four rooms have their own sauna. With rates at NOK400–500 (including breakfast), this is an excellent stopover option.

There is also the *Skaidi Kro og Motell* (☎ 78 41 61 23; 📄 78 41 61 59) just after the hotel. This is really a **café-cum-guesthouse**. It has just eight rooms and the prices are only a little below those of the hotel.

SIDE TRIP FROM SKAIDI TO HAMMERFEST   Map 13a

Using Route 94 this is the way to Hammerfest which lays claim to be the world's most northerly city. The distance is 58km or 116km for the round trip. You could do the journey in one day from Alta but this adds a further 194km and you would have to make a very early start for this to be worthwhile. This is a well-trodden path because of the attraction of Hammerfest and, with a range of hotels in the town, it may be a place to stay before returning to the Highway.

Route 94 branches left (west) off the Highway at Skaidi to follow the Repparfjordelv through its wooded valley. There are usually plenty of reindeer along and on the road, sometimes making driving difficult and slow when they refuse to give way to traffic. The road runs to the mouth of the river where a bridge (7km) takes it along the barren shore of the fjord. There is a little farming and fishing done from the scattered homesteads by the shore but it is a rather bleak and forbidding outlook across the waters.

The road continues in a north-westerly direction towards Kvalsund. At **Leirbukt** (20km) you can look out for a collection of three **rock carvings**. They are not in situ although the largest, dating from about 500BC, was found in the area. It depicts three small deer and what is evidently a boat.

Kvalsund (= Whale Sound/Strait, 26km) is noted as a centre for fishing and there is a processing plant. There's a petrol station (right) here as well as a **post office** and store. There are two camping sites with cabins, ***Repparfjord Ungdomssenter*** (☎ 78 41 61 65) and ***Gargo Camping*** (☎ 78 41 52 28). Both are quite small, but inexpensive and all right in an emergency.

One afternoon, returning to Alta from Hammerfest, a companion and I stopped to fish from a rickety pier just south of Kvalsund bridge. With only one rod we were taking a catch as fast as the other could unhook and return the fish to the water. It should be said that neither of us is more than a piscatory novice. If you've got a rod with you, it makes a nice break in the journey.

Kvalsund bridge (27km) replaced the old ferry in 1977. The ferry used to be great fun, taking only five minutes but always battling against the waters racing through the narrow strait separating Kvaløya from the mainland. Today's bridge is a tamer but more elegant crossing. It is one of Norway's longest suspension bridges with a main span of over 500m and a total length of almost 750m. It reaches a height of 25m above sea-level giving it a rather windy exposure.

Kvaløya (Whale Island) is the home of Hammerfest. It's also a summer feeding area for the Sami's reindeer which, incredibly, cross the turbulent waters in their annual migration to the island.

Route 94 turns left at the northern end of the bridge. A minor road turns to the right for 4km before stopping at Storbukt. From there on there is no road round the whole of Kvaløya's eastern side.

MAP 13a: Side Trip from Skaidi

The road to Hammerfest keeps close to the western shoreline, sometimes high above the water and sometimes just a metre or so from sea-level. At **Akkanjargstabba** (35km) there is a Sami **sacrificial stone** or *stallo*, a relic from the days before the Sami were converted to Christianity. There are text-book examples of permafrost by the road. Cotton grass, hummocky ground, horizontally growing 'trees' and the occasional stunted birch all keep company with the road.

At first the island will seem deserted but as Hammerfest gets nearer you can see the homes of fishermen who brave the waters of the Barents Sea. Eventually, Route 94 winds its way over the top of a col away from the shore and the first sights of the town can be glimpsed ahead. There is the superb natural harbour which is Hammerfest's *raison d'être*.

Hammerfest (58km), at 70° 39' 48", claims to be the northernmost town in the world although Honningsvåg (see p247) fails to claim that title only by virtue of its late official classification as a town.

HAMMERFEST

Kvaløya, is the 'Whale Island' and it was as a whaling station that Hammerfest was founded (to rival Archangel).

History

Its first church was built in 1620 and the settlement achieved the status of town in 1789. In 1807 a traveller to the harbour reported that 'whales were everywhere'. At the same time there were only nine houses and less than forty inhabitants. The dwellings of four merchants, a shoemaker's workshop, a customs house and a school-house: that was Hammerfest in the early nineteenth century. By 1875 there was still only one street of straggling houses, yet four years earlier, another traveller remarked on the hospitality afforded to strangers and found 'comforts and luxuries one would little expect'.

Hammerfest at the start of the twenty-first century is home to about 9000 people whose basic economy remains dependent upon fishing. It is true that tourism, often in the form of cruise-liner passengers, supplements their income but fish is king. It is a proud town and justly so. It has excellent shopping facilities including well-stocked bookshops, modern churches and hotels. Everything is 'the most northerly in the world', from the Catholic Church to the Skogstua forest. It was the first town in Europe to have its streets lit by electricity and a meridian stone commemorates the

early nineteenth-century measurement of a meridian arc to the Black Sea.

The greatest pride of Hammerfest derives from its immense sense of community. This characterizes the people. The town survived a naval bombardment from the British Royal Navy in 1809, a devastating fire in 1890 and, more recently, the complete destruction of the town by the Germans in World War II.

When the German army retreated from Finnmark in 1944, they forcibly evacuated the entire population before systematically burning down every building. When the people returned, and few failed to come back, only the church had miraculously escaped destruction. The rebuilding of Hammerfest is a testimony to its inhabitants' courage and faith.

Hammerfest's future is uncertain but probably lies with oil and gas. Already it supplies the exploratory fields in the Barents Sea and the so-called Snow White development off the port's coast. Oil and gas are likely to take over fishing's pre-eminent place in the future but that industry is fighting back with the rapid development of sea farming with salmon.

The centre of the town in summer is a bustle of activity as local people, fishermen, sailors and tourists mingle along the main road, Kirkegata, and in the small square and market-place. The town is strung out around the bay because building is restricted by the steep cliff-like wall of Salen, an 80m mountain that overshadows the settlement. The streets have to be protected from avalanches by snow fences built across the cliff-face.

Services

The **tourist office** (☎ 78 41 21 85; ▯ 78 41 19 00; ▯ info@hammerfest-turist.no) is open all year and is situated on Kirkegata (Route 94), on the left, just as you enter the main part of the town. Look for the turning to Corn Moes Gata.

The quality and nature of the **shops** down Kirkegata reflect the influence of tourism. There are very good bookshops and souvenir outlets. There is usually an excellent selection of Norwegian pewter although the best pieces may be gone by August. The **post office** is in Parkgata which leads left off Route 94 as you enter the main part of the town. Past the post office is the **police station**. In the opposite

direction, up from the post office by the corner of Parkgata and Kirkegata is an **internet café**, *Polar Webcafé* (☎ 78 42 99 00).

Around the town

There's enough to see to justify an overnight stay.

The most prominent buildings are the modern **church**, completed in 1961, and the large fish-processing plant. The church is to the left of Route 94 on its final approach down into the centre of the town. It is usually open for viewing during the day and is worth visiting if only for its dramatic stained-glass window that forms the southern end of the church. The **chapel**, which survived the German fires, is in the cemetery on the other side of Route 94.

The **Catholic church**, the world's most northerly, is dedicated to Saint Michael who features, with a dragon, in a mosaic on the front of the building. This church is also usually open during the day.

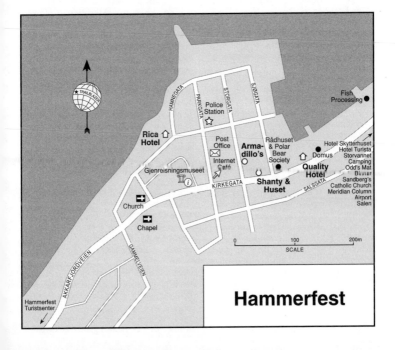

Hammerfest

The Royal and Ancient Polar Bear Society
The Royal and Ancient Polar Bear Society (☎ 78 41 21 85) was founded by two Hammerfest businessmen in 1963, so not quite as ancient as its name implies. Their aim was to make the town and its history better known generally but in particular to the many summer visitors. To join the society you have to visit the headquarters inside the museum. Membership confers no special privileges unless you just happen to be in Hammerfest on the third Sunday in January when you can attend and vote at the General Assembly. However, the NOK150 joining fee does include a tiny silver polar bear pin and a diploma. It's all good fun and the money raised helps to maintain the museum.

The **museum** (☎/🖹 78 41 31 00) has an enormous stuffed polar bear in the entrance. It leaves one in no doubt as to the size of these wonderful animals. There is also a variety of other stuffed animals and birds, pieces of Arctic exploration equipment and an interesting collection of photographs. Entry to the museum is NOK20. The building is open from 11.30 to 13.30 from September to mid-May and from 10.00 to 15.00 in the summer. At weekends the opening times are 11.00 to 14.00. From late June to mid-August the hours of opening are from 06.00 to 17.30.

To reach the church, continue along Kirkegata, through the town. As Kirkegata becomes Standgata, turn right up a steep hill and you can see the church.

In the little square, reached by steps down from the shopping street, is an attractive **fountain**. It was donated by Charles U Bay, who was the USA's ambassador to Norway after World War II. His mother had emigrated to the USA from Hammerfest.

Across the road from the Square is the **Music Pavilion**, erected in 1989, the 200th anniversary of the town's foundation. It is interesting architecturally as an example of a style seen in Hammerfest in the early twentieth century. In the square is a sculpture of an Arctic ship in pack ice, a symbol of the town's commercial heritage.

Rådhuset (City Hall) is in Rådhusplass (turn left out of Kirkegata, the main shopping street/Route 94, towards the harbour). The City Hall is home to the Polar Bear Society and museum. Another fascinating museum is **Gjen-reisningsmuseet** (☎ 78 42 26 30; 🖹 78 42 26 42), on the main street, Kirkegata, with the information office. The museum has exhibits tracing the World War II period of Hammerfest's history, together with others charting the post-war recon-

struction. It is all very well done and really should not be missed. There's also a tower which gives good views over the town.

To view the **Meridian Column** (*Meridianstøtta*) entails driving through the town and around the bay along Fuglenesvn. Go past the **hospital** and then turn left into Fuglenesbukta from where the column is signposted. It was erected in 1854 to commemorate the first international measurement of the earth's circumference in 1852. Norway was joined by Sweden and Russia in this scientific first. The column is close to the end of the Fuglenes peninsula so it's worth continuing to the point from where there are good views back into the town. Also at the end of the peninsula are old fortifications (now restored) dating from the Napoleonic War of 1810.

Hammerfest's STOL **airport** is reached by continuing along Fuglenesvn. When I first visited the town there was no airport and to fly in or out you used a float-plane. Beyond the airport is the suburb of Prærien. A further 10km or so beyond the suburb is the village of Forsøl. This is the place to get the best views of the midnight sun in high summer and there are also some ruins of Stone Age and Iron Age dwellings.

(Opposite): Hammerfest's church (see p239) has an impressive stained glass window.

Some of the best views of the town can be had by driving to the top of **Salen**, Hammerfest's own mountain. It is possible to trek up to the summit but it's a steep climb. At the top is a lake, Storvannet with a camping site alongside. But the highest point, Turista, at 86m above the town, provides splendid bird's-eye views of the town, its harbour and the Arctic Ocean. If your visit coincides with the arrival or departure of a visiting liner it's all quite breathtaking. There is also a hotel here.

It is possible to visit some of the islands off the north-west of Kvaløya by taking one of the regular high-speed ferries which serve them. You can get details from the tourist office.

Accommodation

There is plenty of choice unless you arrive in the middle of the tourist season when booking ahead would have been wise.

Of the four hotels, the most upmarket is the *Quality Hotel* (☎ 78 42 96 00; 🖷 78 42 96 60; 🖳 hammerfest@quality.choice.no). Located by the town square it is one of the few hotels in North Norway which looks as good from the outside as it does inside. There are 50 rooms including suites, mini-suites and what are called cabins (doubles with bunk beds). The suites are clearly better than the rooms and it is best to ask for a room with an outlook to the square or waterfront. Facilities include a **café** which is open most of the day but only in the evening on Sundays. A bar, two pubs, a sauna and solarium complete the attractions but all this comes at a cost. The suites come at a hefty NOK1500 to NOK2500 while the rooms are upwards from NOK1045. Breakfast is included. Parking is very limited.

Rivalling the Quality is the popular *Rica Hotel* (☎ 78 41 13 33; 🖷 78 41 13 11; 🖳 rica.hotel.hammerfest@rica.no) on the corner of Sørøygata and Batteriet (turn left into Sørøygata from Parkagata, by the post office). It has 84 rooms, half of which are non-smoking. There are two restaurants

and the one with the piano bar is small but has good views. The hotel has a fitness room. Rates are from NOK1090 for a single (combi) room to NOK1295 for a junior suite. Breakfast is included. There's a pub, the Pinocchio Pub, and parking is available. Overall, the Rica is good value.

On the top of Salen, the town's mountain, is *Hotel Skytterhuset* (☎ 78 41 15 11; 🖷 78 41 19 26). This 66-room hotel is somewhat unusual. During the winter it caters almost entirely for local clients, including visitors to the town's hospital. Some parts of the building are even let as apartments. In the summer, rooms come at NOK550 for singles and NOK750 for doubles with these rates including breakfast. Skytterhuset is well furnished and has a large bright lounge.

Also on Salen is the small *Hotel Turista* (☎ 78 41 46 11; 🖷 78 41 45 55) at the viewpoint (see above). Built in 1991, it has a certain charm with lots of excellent woodcarving, a galleried restaurant and a café which stays open until 23.00. There are three stuffed polar bears and an elk head to remind you where you are. The six double rooms cost NOK1080 including breakfast while the breathtaking views are free. All rooms are en suite and the bathrooms have bath-tubs. Turista opens at the end of May and closes at the beginning of September.

I once spent the night in a Land Rover by the beach outside Hammerfest. There was a northerly wind blowing and I was convinced I would freeze to death before morning. Those who wish to camp are advised to have good sleeping bags.

There are two campsites and both have cabins. *Hammerfest Turistsenter* (☎/🖷 78 41 11 26) is to the left of Route 94 by the Shell petrol station as you approach the town. The site is a little disappointing with no good views but there is choice. There are 27 cabins at NOK350 and rooms at NOK650. The Turistsenter is well kept and quite new (1998). The season is limited:

(Opposite) Traditional Sami life
Top left: Rarely used today, a *gamme* (turf hut). **Top right**: *Aitte* (food store), raised to protect from wolves and wolverines. **Bottom**: *Kåta*, a forked-pole tent.

May to October. The other campsite with cabins is up on the mountain, Salen, by the lake. This is *Storvannet Camping* (☎ 78 41 10 10). It is better for campers but there are only seven cabins. Prices are similar to those at the Turistsenter.

Where to eat

Odd's Mat og Vinhus (☎ 78 41 37 66) has character and some really interesting dishes. This restaurant is on the left of Kirkegata as you go though the town, just before the turn up to the Catholic church. Its entrance isn't imposing; it's above a tattoo parlour. Look for the cauldron above the door. The variety of dishes is impressive. On the menu is caviar, salmon, seal and snails and they'll even flambé a reindeer. Fish dishes are around NOK150 and meat dishes NOK200. Odd's overlooks the harbour at the rear. To eat Chinese, the best restaurant is *Dinner* (☎ 78 41 38 78), just before Odd's and on the same side of the road. The menu isn't all Chinese and a main meal will cost about NOK110. Try the banana-splits at NOK47. The site is similar to Odd's, on the first floor and with a harbour view at the back. The entrance is between two shops and easily missed. It is open from 14.00 to 23.30. On the opposite side of the street to Dinner is a baker's shop (*bakeri-konditori*), *Sandberg's*, which doubles as a **café**, but there's limited seating.

Between Sjøgata and Storgata but on the main street is a pub, *Shanty*, and restaurant, *Huset Restaurant*. Fortunately, its rather scruffy outward appearance belies its interior. Here it is the beer and pizza that attracts. Mexican dishes are served at *Armadillo's*, on Storgata, and there's the usual café at the **Domus** store, on Kirkegata beyond the Quality Hotel.

The Highway: Skaidi to Olderfjord
MAP 13

Passing the Skaidi Hotel, set among the trees to the left of the road, the Arctic Highway leaves the village to begin what you may feel is one of its less interesting sections, to Olderfjord. After crossing the Guraelv, the road leaves the forest to climb on to a low, bare and uninhabited plateau. The Highway was realigned across the vidde in the 1960s and the old path can still be seen if you look carefully; sometimes to the right and sometimes to the left of the modern route. The bleak appearance of the landscape is attributable to its exposure to northerly winds that affect the area both in summer and in winter.

When the snow clears in spring, mats of sub-Arctic vegetation appear filling the gaps between the rocks, and the narrow river valleys reveal their stunted birch trees. The dwarf birch is a response largely to the desiccating effects of the cold winds. The vidde in summer becomes a patchwork of grey, green and brown.

The watershed of the plateau is at only just over 200m above sea-level. Here the Haiter ridges separate the drainage of Repparfjorden from that of the Porsangerfjord. Again the gradient takes the Highway down to Lake Smøfjord and the road then runs on an almost gradient-less course across the rocky fjell. Finally there is a steep winding descent through a tree-filled valley to reach the great Porsangerfjord.

Porsangerfjorden is North Norway's greatest fjord and, by area, the largest in Norway. Unlike the fjords of West Norway this enormous inlet has no steep sides; it is an altogether softer, though no less beautiful, landscape greets the eye.

At **Olderfjord** (110km) the Arctic Highway turns sharply right to run down the inner arm. To the left is a side trip along European Route 69 to the North Cape. Olderfjord, on the Highway, merges with the village of **Russenes**, which is the beginning of Route 69. Russenes has a post office, **information kiosk** (open only in summer), store, petrol station and **café**. There is **accommodation** in the village.

Accommodation: Skaidi to Olderfjord

Apart from a small food store which has places for caravans to park at Falas, just 6km or so before Olderfjord, there is nowhere to stay on this section of the Highway until Russenes is reached. At Russenes, the ***Olderfjord Hotel*** (☎ 78 46 37 11; 🖹 78 46 37 91; 🖳 old erfj@online.no) lies to the left of Route 69 just after turning off the Highway. Here a single costs from NOK250 to NOK450. ***Russenes Camping***, under the same ownership, has cabins and a campsite. The best cabins are to the right of the road by the fjord. Remarkably, both the hotel and the camp are open all year. In high summer, both are often fully booked by the afternoon as travellers to and from North Cape break their journeys here.

SIDE TRIP FROM OLDERFJORD TO NORTH CAPE   Map 13b

The temptation to leave the Highway for this trip is more than most can resist because the goal is **North Cape** (*Nordkapp*), Europe's most northerly point. All the same it must be borne in mind that this is a two- or even three-day detour. In order to see the midnight sun or, at least, to look for it, an overnight stay on Magerøya, the island on which the North Cape sits, is almost essential.

Route 69 has been greatly improved in recent years. Much of it dates only from the 1960s. The undersea tunnel, which carries the road on to the island, opened as recently as 1999. The route can be quite heavily used in the tourist season (especially towards the end of July). Traffic often moves unnecessarily and dangerously fast, drivers having left too little time to get to North Cape and finish their holidays in time for a return to work. For many, getting to the Cape is the *raison d'être* of a visit to Arctic Scandinavia. This is especially true of a high proportion of those entering Norway from the Finnish Approach Routes (VIII and IX, see p97 and p110) via Karasjok.

If taking this side trip, refuel at Olderfjord/Russenes.

If you are contemplating travelling in winter, you need to take into account that the E69 from Honningsvåg to the North Cape is not an all-weather road. It is closed for most of the winter and even in May it might be necessary to drive in convoy and studs or snow tyres may be needed. (See Part 1, p18 and p23.) Information about the state of the road can be obtained by telephoning ☎ 78 47 28 94. Information is also displayed on some approach roads, especially north of Karasjok.

The E69 starts its 131km journey to the North Cape in Olderfjord/Russenes and much of the route is along the edge of **Porsangerfjord**. At first, the road runs behind a small peninsula to the north of Olderfjord and, to the left, there is a junction with Route 889 (4km). This is quite an interesting road to follow for anyone with time to spare because it runs across the major Porsanger Halvøya (Half Island, ie peninsula) to **Kokelv** (19km) and thence to **Halvøysund** (86km). These settlements, and others through which the 889 passes, wonderfully demonstrate the North Norwegians' acceptance of isolation. The **chapel** at

MAP 13b
Side Trip
from Olderfjord

Kokelv is particularly interesting because it was built by German youths after World War II as an act of expiation for the war crimes committed in Finnmark.

If you stay with Route E69 you'll see none of this but instead will continue along the western shore of Porsanger. The scenery in summer is incredibly beautiful although the harshness of winter may keep the road closed until late May. Although the landscape is less dramatic, the relief less bold, these northern fjords have a loveliness of their own. Throughout the length of the E69's path along the shore it is possible, weather permitting, for you to see the opposite side of the fjord some 20km or so away. Along the road's path the land is mostly treeless except where the shelter of a small valley allows birch to escape the all-destroying winds. The vegetation is fragile here. If destroyed it will take a long time to recover and driving off the road must be discouraged. You just have to exercise a little discipline and not drive off the road unless there is already a clearly worn path.

The preservation of the flora is not the only reason to stay on the road. Off the road, even on rising ground, the summer melt of the active zone (above the permafrost) can be extremely boggy. Even when fit to walk over, the weight of a vehicle will spell trouble (see p27).

One of the most fascinating features of this road is the geology. Exposed in cliff-faces and along the rocky shore are endless mica-schists and slates tilted at every angle. At times the countryside looks like an abandoned quarry but it's all the work of nature, not of man.

There is little to distinguish one section of the road from another but this does not detract from either its interest or its succession of fine views. For much of the route the E69 keeps close to the shore and, at first, there are small hamlets and the individual homes of the fishermen and their families. A cut-out of a reindeer advertises the presence of a **silversmith** (8km) with the occasional bargain to be had if you're there towards the end of the season. At **Nordmannset** (14km) there is a village shop but there is otherwise little to detain you.

As the road swings back to the coast a long tunnel, Skarvbergtunnelen, drives through the cliff and the fjord is lost to view (17km). This 3km tunnel has some deceptive bends as well as some long straight sections. It is lit all the way. In summer, it is quite often used by reindeer for the warmth and shelter it offers. The deer usually keep close to the ends of the tunnel but are reluctant to move and can be a real hazard unless you keep a good lookout. Reindeer may appear unexpectedly at any place along the E69.

Beyond the tunnel two quite delightful bays, Indre Sortvik, also Svartvik, (24km) and Ytre Sortvik (27km) have been linked by a relatively new short section of road close to the shore. There is also a short (496m) tunnel, Sortviktunnelen. No doubt there were good reasons for this but the old road round the back of the headland separating the bays was an especially beautiful stretch. It was also a place I used for wild camping for many years but I like to think that it is not just nostalgia that leads me to regret the relentless re-routing and straightening of Norway's roads.

Steep cliffs form a backdrop to the road north of the bays and, as the E69 comes close to the mid-fjord island of Store Tamsøya, it bridges the Molvik River (41km). The island is one of the lesser-known bird colonies of North Norway. It is also famous for its cloudberries (*multerberries*). The only way you can reach the island is by boat so the birds are undisturbed although the berries are collected by local people at the end of the summer.

A bay, Vedbotn, breaks the shoreline and before the E69 takes its detour around it there is a junction (48km) with a 2km minor road down to **Repvåg**. This interesting little village of some 100 to 150 people was once the ferry port for Honningsvåg and the North Cape. It took the place of Russenes in this respect when the road connection from Olderfjord was built. Later, as the road pushed on to Kåfjord, it lost this function, save in winter when the Kåfjord section of E69 becomes blocked by snow and a ferry is the only way to travel.

There is a small fishing industry in the village and a brief visit will give you a good impression of the life and circumstances of these northerly communities. There is **camping** here and a **motel-cum-guesthouse** with a **café** (see p246). The little church with its graveyard is worth visiting.

From the junction with the minor road to Repvåg, the E69 continues across bleak and open tundra. The ground, affected by permafrost, has a typical hummocky appearance with patches of tussock and cotton-grass. In summer what appears to be dry is often little short of true bog. In winter all is whiteness.

Taking a broad curving path, there are fleeting glimpses of Honningsvåg at around 70km. Three kilometres further on, the E69 turns down towards **Kåfjord** (73km), a small north-facing fjord. This was where the road stopped before the undersea tunnel was built. Now the little harbour, previously so busy with summer tourists, lies off the E69 and watches the cars and trucks sweep by.

The modern road runs round the western side of Kåfjorden to approach the entrance to **Nordkapptunnelen**, the undersea link to the island, Magerøy. There is a toll station (79km) where the charge is NOK125 for a vehicle and driver plus NOK40 for each additional passenger. Motor cycles are charged NOK60 and large vehicles cost NOK400, but there is no extra charge for caravans because so many Norwegians tow trailers. The charges are made in each direction. From the toll station, for nearly seven kilometres, the E69 runs through the North Cape tunnel until it emerges on Magerøya, the Arctic-island home of Honningsvåg and the North Cape.

Emerging from the tunnel (86km), the E69 passes the Veidnes toll station, crosses Veidnes bridge and runs through the short (190m) Sarnes tunnel. The road hugs the shoreline and you'll see some really attractive scenery around Sarnes village and across the water to a strange conical island. The

---

The Fatima Project

The connection of the mainland of Norway to Magerøya was one of the most ambitious projects ever undertaken in North Norway. Called the **Fatima Project**, it was conceived in the 1980s and only completed in 1999. The idea was driven by a belief that there will be an ever-increasing interest in the North Cape by those tourists who wish to visit the 'end of Europe'. In the past, the journey included a ferry crossing, first from Russenes, then from Repvåg and lastly from Kåfjord. The destination was always Honningsvåg but the journey time shortened as the road along the western side of Porsangerfjorden was built in stages as finance allowed and demand dictated. However long the ferry crossing, there was always the problem that impatient tourists wanted a road connection and road safety was compromised as the ferries disgorged their load of vehicles which then formed an ill-disciplined convoy on to the narrow E69. The largest ferry had a capacity of 650 passengers and 140 vehicles. That number of vehicles all hitting the road at the same time was a recipe for chaos or even disaster.

In 1980, a tunnel was proposed but it took another thirteen years before it was agreed to realize the scheme. Like most projects of this magnitude, costs nearly doubled from the original estimate of just under NOK700 million. It is hoped to recoup about NOK200 million from the toll charges.

The main tunnel is 6870m long, with 277m actually under the sea, while the gradient is over sixty per thousand. At its deepest the tunnel drops nearly 230m from the entrance height. This is a splendid piece of engineering in an area that has considerable geological constraints. The tunnel is lit but unlined and is almost straight along the undersea section.

On the island, the Fatima Project included an entirely new road with two other tunnels and a new bridge. The length of this new section of the E69 is all of 28.6km. It's an impressive piece of engineering by any standards; at 71° N it is astounding.

Was it all worth the time and effort? Probably, but, as so often, some drivers miss the welcome respite afforded by the ferry crossing.

Honningsvåg tunnel (92km) is the next section of the Fatima Project. It is 4440m in length, almost straight and is partly lined. It rises at first and then falls as the end of the tunnel is reached. In about 3km the E69 curves to the left up towards the North Cape. The road is open to vehicles from about the end of April until November. There are no exact dates; it depends on the snow cover.

The right curve at this point leads off into **Honningsvåg** (see p247). Make sure you've plenty of fuel as there's none between Honningsvåg and the Cape.

Accommodation: Olderfjord to Honningsvåg

Not on the island but still quite handy for visits to North Cape is the ***Repvåg Fjordhotell og Rorbusenter*** (☎ 78 4734 40; 🖹 78 47 27 51; 🖳 nord.no@ online.no) at the little village on the mainland, Porsangerfjorden, that lies just off the E69 (see p245). It is open from April to October, inclusive. This hotel is really top-rate. Built on the village's wharf, it looks like a set of fishermen's cabins and boathouses. There are no less than 77 rooms and cabins, the latter sleeping up to seven. There's a restaurant, a bar and even a fitness room and sauna. You won't forget you're on the fjord. Some of the rooms even have lifebelts on the wall. It is worth every krone at NOK500–800.

HONNINGSVÅG

If it were not for the fact that Honningsvåg had the official status of a village it would rank as the most northerly town in the world! It is fully twenty minutes of latitude north of Hammerfest. That was the position until quite recently. With a population around 3000, it is now classed as a town. Yet its people have yet to challenge Hammerfest's boast. If they did, what would become of Hammerfest's great tourist attraction? Anyway, Honningsvåg has the North Cape.

Honningsvåg is on the sheltered, southern side of the island and is built within the further protection of a bay. It is not a particularly attractive town and has all the hallmarks of having been hastily and unimaginatively rebuilt following its destruction in World War II.

The E69 to the North Cape does not enter the town but climbs quickly away from it. Coming from the mainland, to enter the town turn right at the signpost where the road divides between its North Cape and Honningsvåg paths. This will bring you into Storgata. The main shopping area of Honningsvåg is around the bay where there is rather more flat land. Like Hammerfest, Honningsvåg stands in the shadow of steeply rising cliffs on which fences protect the settlement from snow and rock avalanches. So close in places is the cliff to the bay that only three parallel streets squeeze between its foot and the shoreline. The inner one of these, Øvregata, sits high above the other two giving it excellent views of the bay.

Services

Typical of these Arctic towns, the range of services is far superior to what might be expected by the size of the settlement. This is the place to have a check on that minor fault with the vehicle, to stock up on fuel and provisions and to purchase another sweater.

The helpful **tourist office** (☎ 78 47 25 99; ▤78 47 35 43; ▣ info@northcape.no) is down by the harbour, near the **bus station**. It's easiest to find by turning off Storgata (the main street) as you come in at the northern end of the town. The office is open from 08.00 to 16.00 Mondays to Fridays but in summer (which here means mid-June to mid-August) it stays open an extra two hours and also opens at the weekends at noon for four hours.

Along Storgata, on the left as the road swings around the harbour, is a **bank** and there's another near the quay where the Coastal Steamer (Hurtigrute) docks. To find it, turn towards the harbour from the roundabout on Storgata. You need to remember that banks close at 15.00. The **post office** is on the northern side of Storgata, by the roundabout. The **police station** is by the bank near the harbour.

Around the town

The town's not really a place to linger but there are a couple of places of special interest. The **church** was the only pre-war building in the town to survive the German's scorched earth policy. It was first consecrated in 1884 and, as the population returned in 1945, many of the townsfolk lived in the church as they began to reconstruct their homes. Opposite the church is a stone **war memorial** with some sixty names. Just off Storgata, in a small garden area, is an interesting bronze of a man holding a fish. Yet another reminder of how important is fishing in this part of the world.

Down by the tourist office (see above) is the **museum** (☎ 78 47 28 33; ▤ 78 47 20 32; ▣ nordkapp@online.no), the Nordkappmuseet. Not too surprisingly, there is a heavy emphasis on fish and fishing. The history of this industry over the last 10,000 years – since the end of the last ice age – is told, as well as the general natural history of coastal Finnmark. World War II and the rise of tourism feature prominently. For art lovers, there's an exhibition of paintings by Bjarne Holst. Entry is NOK20 and, officially, it's open all year but in winter it's best to telephone to ensure someone is there. Opening hours are 09.00 to 20.00 in summer, from 13.00 on Sundays.

The shopping area is along Storgata. The town's **shops** don't compare with the quality and sophistication offered by those in Hammerfest and there are few shops offering much in the way of souvenirs. The few that do stay open until 22.00 in summer while the little kiosks selling tobacco, sweets and newspapers don't shut until midnight. In contrast, like many other parts of Norway, it is common to find most shops closing at 16.00. For souvenirs, try Arctandria down by the harbour or Arctic Suvenir in the same area and sharing the building of the tourist information office.

The town's **library**, a good place to gather general information, is opposite the bank on Storgata and next to the telephone exchange. And, if you're tired from the night up at the Cape, there's a small garden down by the harbour with just three seats but a delightful view of the activity on the water.

Accommodation

The demand for accommodation can out-strip availability in high summer even though some tourists' visits are so short that they don't bother to overnight on the island, except for their visit to the North Cape Hall. As the season tails off, by mid-August, much of the accommodation clos-es down. It is always best to book ahead if you want to avoid the risk of having to retrace your route back to the Arctic Highway without a night's sleep. There are choices of accommodation either in Honningsvåg or along the road to the Cape. My own preference is to stop in town. At least you get to see something of a truly Arctic settlement.

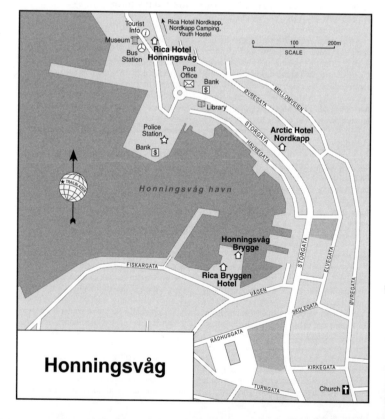

Honningsvåg

The Rica chain has three hotels on the island. In town there's Rica Hotel Honningsvåg and the Rica Bryggen Hotel. The *Rica Hotel Honningsvåg* (☎ 78 47 23 33; 🖷 78 47 33 79; ⌨ rica.hotel.honningsva ag@rica.no) is the town's largest (174 rooms) and is the first you reach as you drive into the town, on the right of Storgata. It is popular with cruise groups having a night on dry land but there's nothing particularly to recommend it. The restaurant is slow, the meals very ordinary. Rooms are rather small and it is showing its age. Doubles cost around NOK1000 so it's not cheap.

Preferable is the *Rica Bryggen* (*brygge* = dock or harbour; ☎ 78 47 28 88; 🖷 78 47 27 24; ⌨ rica.bryggen.hotel@ rica.no). It is tucked away on the far side of the harbour: turn right off Storgata to go down Vågen, then turn right again on to Fiskargata and the hotel is on the right. This is a modern hotel with pleasant rooms (ask for a harbour view) and good en-suite bathrooms. There's a relaxing reception area and an attractive restaurant, open from 17.00 to 23.00 for dinner. Prices are the same in all three Rica hotels (for the third, Nordkapp, see p251). Only the Bryggen stays open all year. The other two Rica hotels close in winter and the Rica Hotel Nordkapp may well be closed by mid-August.

Honningsvåg Brygge (☎ 78 47 64 64; 🖷 78 47 64 65; ⌨ post@hug.brygge.no) is close to the Rica Bryggen and used to be a Best Western hotel. It is now independent and very much a family concern. The hotel, open all year, is built on the jetty with the appearance of a group of fishermen's cabins. It really is the most attractive place to stay on the whole of the island. Prices are similar to those of the Rica hotels and the en-suite rooms are simply furnished but the ambience and the service are superior. The family that runs the hotel owns the Sjøhuset Restaurant next door so this is where you eat (see opposite).

On Storgata is the *Arctic Hotel Nordkapp* (☎ 78 47 29 66; 🖷 78 47 30 10), an unpretentious building with an entrance straight off the street. It has 50 rooms with a cafeteria on the ground floor. It is open all year but, if business is slack, it shuts for Christmas and Easter. The rooms are small and simply furnished. Even though it has recently been given a fresh coat of paint, inside and out, its prices may be seen as bordering on over-charging at NOK960 for a double room.

Where to eat

All the hotels will accept non-residents in their restaurants. A favourite is *Sjøhuset* alongside the Honningsvåg Brygge Hotel (see below). Not only is the à la carte menu one of the best in Honningsvåg but the atmosphere is most attractive. Looking out from the restaurant, the view is into the harbour, but beware: the sight of the craft bobbing up and down on the water may have the same effect as being on board ship. It is open between 14.00 and 23.00 and a main course will be between NOK150 to NOK200.

There are only slightly more modest prices at the *Grillbaren* and the **cybernet café** on Storgata close to the Arctic Hotel. Here a 150gm burger and chips will cost you about NOK110. It's a modern, clean and smart fast-food café that stays open until 01.00 in the morning and until 04.00 on Fridays and Saturdays. Well, you might as well make use of the midnight sun.

In the harbour area is *Nordkapp Konditori* which sells sandwiches, cakes and coffee. It shuts at 17.00 and at 14.00 on Saturdays. Up Storgata, beyond the post office and Hagen's store, is *Sentralen Bar and Disco*, another fast-food outlet which also sells ice cream. Behind the tourist information office is *Corner*, a café, doubling as a pub, specializing in fish dishes but with other choices. It's open until 02.00 on Fridays and Saturdays and until midnight on other weekdays.

Opposite the Rica Honningsvåg is *Bryggerie* (= brewery; it claims to be the world's most northerly). It keeps the same hours as Corner and has a **café** as well as a bar. It's quite smart and much like a modern pub in an English town.

Honningsvåg to North Cape

The journey up to North Cape is largely through wilderness although with an increasing demand for accommodation in the summer season, there has been new building near to Honningsvåg in recent times. To the untutored eye, the island may seem especially barren but, if you're a geomorphologist, this is a delight of classic periglacial landscapes.

The E69 climbs away from Honningsvåg passing a junction (100km) with a minor road, right, leading to the village's busy STOL airport at **Nordmannset**. From here the scenery becomes steadily more wild and truly tundra. The island is treeless and there is clear evidence of permafrost. The environment is technically periglacial, that is, there is melting in summer near the surface, the so-called active zone, but below all is frozen. Weathered rock wastes down the slopes under the action of ice and meltwater while some snow patches last throughout the summer. This Arctic island is not only at high latitude but is also mountainous.

The E69 rises to over 300m above sea-level but falls through valleys which dissect the plateau. Ten kilometres or so from the Honningsvåg turn there is a junction with a minor road down to **Kamøyvær**, a small fishing settlement just 3km away on the east coast.

Beyond the junction to the village, look for the scattered summer huts of Sami whose reindeer migrate to the island each spring. The traditional crossing is by the Magerøya Sound, a 1500m swim, on the island's south-west side.

At 109km there's a minor road to the left, the island's only other long-distance route. For 21km this road travels west across Magerøya to the coast. This is not a road that can be recommended for general exploration but at its terminus, **Gjesvær**, there is a small guesthouse. From the guesthouse, you can take a boat trip to the bird islands off the north-west of Magerøya. There are impressive colonies of petrels, cormorants and even puffins, among other birds. There's a good chance of seeing sea eagles. To arrange a trip, call ☎ 78 47 57 33.

As the E69 turns almost due north there are views out to sea across Tufjorden to the west while a very minor road leads down (left) to the fjord-head (118km), where a rather better road takes a turn right. This is the Skarsvåg summer road to the world's most northerly fishing community, a short 3km

---

Kamøyvær Village

If there's time, it's worth taking a trip down to the village. It's even possible to get bed and breakfast accommodation – look for the sign *rom*. The village isn't old. In fact it is only about a hundred years since anyone settled here. All the same it has an interesting background and you can get a real feel for what living in the Arctic is like.

The attraction for the early settlers was the shelter which the island provides from the worst of the winds of the Arctic Ocean.

It's a mixed population: Norwegian, Russian and the so-called Sea Sami. The common interest and unifying feature was fishing. This little side trip repays the effort if you take a meal in a restaurant in the village square and try one of the fish dishes.

There are only some 150 or so people living in the village but they are especially friendly and will arrange boat trips out to some of the smaller islands for those eager to see more of the 'top of Europe'.

The North Cape

The Cape is undeniably an extraordinary feature: 307 metres of sheer mica-schist cliff with a plateau top. It was first called North Cape by the English voyager Richard Chancellor in 1553 on his quest to redis-cover the sea route to Russia which had been used in Viking days. Its previous name was *Knyskanes*. Another English association was the adoption by Admiral Fraser of the title Lord Fraser of North Cape after the sinking of the German battleship *Scharnhorst*, on 26 December 1943, by his flagship the *Duke of York*. Indeed, it was Fraser who was asked to carry out the opening of the road to the Cape in 1956.

Up to that date the Cape could be visited only by sea, the island being com-pletely road-less. The difficult journey by sea and the even more difficult climb to the plateau had been made by many a famous traveller and a clutch of royal per-sonages. Thomas Cook organized the first tourist visits in the 1870s.

The attraction is the Cape itself and the potential it gives for an uninterrupted view of the sun through the whole 24 hours of each of the 77 days of summer. No guarantee can be given of a sighting; it is at the whim of the weather.

drive. There's accommodation here in the form of two little **hotels** and **camp-ing** grounds.

From these junctions, the E69 turns north-westward and then sharply north-east to approach the **North Cape/Nordkapp** (131km).

Accommodation: Honningsvåg to North Cape

Outside Honningsvåg, the largest hotel is the third of the Rica properties, *Rica Hotel Nordkapp* (☎ 78 47 33 88; 🖹 78 47 32 33; 🖳 rica.hotelnordkapp @rica.no). This hotel is open between May and August only. The exact dates for opening and closing depend on demand, so even if you've booked a room here you may find yourself transferred to the Rica Honningsvåg. The location is Skipsfjord, off the E69 and 30km short of North Cape. It is not especially attractive in appearance but comfortable enough inside. Its function is simply to cater for the overnight needs of those going to or returning from the Cape. With 290 rooms, it's the largest hotel on the island. Unless you're in such a hurry that you can't spare the time to stay in the town, it has little to recom-mend it. Prices are the same as the other Rica hotels.

For campers there's a wonderful choice at *Nordkapp Camping*, close to the Rica Nordkapp Hotel at Skipsfjorden. As well as ample tent space, there are cabins, bungalows, family-rooms, caravan spaces and the island's *Youth Hostel* (☎ 78 47 33 77; 🖹 78 47 11 77; 🖳 heidial@online.no). It is a really big site around a lake and is one of the many NAF (Norges Automobil-Forbund – the Norwegian motoring organization) camps around the country. It is open from mid-May to mid-September. The standards here are high and the site is well run. There's a shop and a sauna, a laundry and plenty of lavatories and showers. Prices are reasonable, considering the quality. A bungalow, with two double bedrooms and all facilities is NOK800. A cabin sleeping four with a kitchen and water supply costs NOK440, while one with a bathroom but no kitchen is NOK500. In the Youth Hostel, dormitory beds cost NOK120. A tent space costs NOK80 but there's an extra charge of NOK20 per person.

In the village of Skarsvåg, there is the *Mini Price Motellet* (☎ 78 47 52 48; 🖹 78 47 27 51; 💻 j-k-karl@frisurf.no), with just ten rooms and no restaurant, and the *Nordkapp Turisthotel* (☎ 78 47 52 67; 🖹 78 47 52 10; 💻 bj.pett ersen@c2i.net). The Turisthotel has thirty rooms and a restaurant. Both charge less than NOK450 and, although the accommodation is simple, a stay here does give you the opportunity to see the village. Note that the motel is open only in the summer.

Camping is also possible at Skarsvåg with a choice of two sites: *Kirkeporten Camping* (☎ 78 47 52 33; 🖹 78 4752 47) and *Midnattsol Camping* (☎/🖹 78 47 52 13). Both have cabins as well as tent spaces and Kirkeporten also has five rooms. The best cabins (and most expensive – up to NOK900) are at Kirkeporten. Midnattsol Camping has the same number of cabins, fifteen, but they're cheaper with a top price of under NOK500. Both camps are open from late May until the end of August.

Havstua (☎ 78 47 51 50; 🖹 47 78 51 91) is a guesthouse in another interesting village, Kamøyvær (see p250). This is a somewhat superior property with a range of accommodation and full services. Open only from May to September, its prices are from NOK450 to about NOK750.

In the same village is *Arran Nordkapp* (☎ 78 47 51 29; 🖹 78 47 51 56), a slightly larger guesthouse (28 rooms) providing simple accommodation at about NOK450 for a double. Again, it's open only in summer.

If you're determined to see the bird islands off the west coast, then Gjesvær (see p250) has cabins at the *Gjesvær Turistsenter* (☎ 78 47 57 73; 🖹 78 47 57 07) open from June to mid-September.

NORTH CAPE

A visit to **North Cape** can be the experience of a lifetime or a great disappointment. Most visitors hope to see the midnight sun (13 May to 29 July) and most are unlucky. Some may have the good fortune to see the disc close to the horizon but it is an exceptional year when large numbers of visitors can watch the whole disc dip towards the sea only to rise again after midnight.

But it is not only the absence of a visible sun that may lead to a feeling of disappointment. It could be the overt commercialization and, it must be said, the tawdry and scruffy appearance of what ought to be a place of natural beauty, a place where nature should be supreme.

At 70° 10' 21" North, the Cape is not quite Europe's most northerly point and, being on an island, is certainly not the most northerly place on 'mainland' Europe. Sorry North Cape. Even on the island the little peninsula of Knivskjellodden is 47 minutes of a degree further north. You know you've arrived at the Cape when you find yourself entering a vast vehicle park crowded with cars, camper vans and trucks from all over Europe. There'll also be buses which have brought passengers who arrived at Honningsvåg on cruise ships.

In a fragile environment in which nothing grows very quickly, this barren landscape is unattractive and off-putting. Press on through the pay-kiosk (NOK175 to enter) and go to the cliffs' edge and you begin to appreciate why so many make this journey. If the price of entry seems high, remember that the season is short (few visit in winter when you need skis or a skidoo) and some of the profits go to a variety of good causes.

The tourist opportunity that the 1956 road gave to the island was quickly seized and a simple building was erected near the edge of the cliff. Various additions and enlargements were made over the years but

Midnight sun

The phenomenon of the midnight sun (*midnattsol*) isn't peculiar to North Cape. The whole length of the Arctic Highway, north of the Polar Circle, experiences at least one day when the sun never sets; the period increasing to two and a half months at North Cape. Practically speaking, and taking twilight into account, the periods during which it will effectively be daylight for all twenty-four hours are very much greater at North Cape.

North Cape is at longitude 25° 47' 40" east, roughly the same longitude as eastern Crete. Some allowance therefore has to be made in calculating midnight rather than being misled by using standard Norwegian time. Midnight comes early at North Cape!

Very few visitors to the Cape will ever experience the complementary phenomenon of total darkness in the winter months, the polar night. Between 18 November and 24 January, the sun fails to rise above the horizon. Although, again, there is some twilight at the start and finish of this period, the consequences of living in perpetual darkness for long periods in the year shouldn't be underestimated. Depression is common, here called the *mørkesyke* (the 'dark sickness'). No one doubts the reality of seasonal affective disorder in the Arctic.

in 1988 an entirely new North Cape Hall was opened under commercial management. This includes a section hewn out of the cliff to give an indoor viewing gallery with an outer terrace. There is a café and a restaurant, souvenir shops and even a chapel. The post office will frank cards sent home and there are showings of video film and slides in a small theatre with a wrap-round screen.

You may, for a fee, join the Royal North Cape Club (there are two registers, one for VIPs and another for the masses) and celebrate your arrival at the Cape in the traditional fashion: with champagne and caviar.

A few simple points are worth noting. There is no accommodation at the Cape nor is it permitted to camp or stay in campers/caravans. The only exception is for any couple who might be married in the chapel; they can spend their wedding night at a special suite at the top of the Hall. *Chacun à son gout.*

It can be quite exceptionally cold when the wind blows from the north; after all, there is just sea and ice between the Cape and the North Pole, 2000km away. The best

views of the Cape's face are from the corner of the vehicle park away from the Hall or even from outside the fenced area, to the left of the approach road. Certainly don't expect to have the Cape to yourself: it is very popular in high summer. The total number of visitors each year gets close to a staggering quarter of a million and most of those come in summer.

All the commercialism may make the Cape seem to be just another tourist magnet, not worth the effort of visiting. What makes it all worthwhile are the views across the Arctic Ocean, the knowledge that there's no land between you and the North Pole, and, if you're lucky, a chance to experience the phenomenon of the midnight sun. There's no night here in mid-summer. You are at the top of Europe.

To get back to the Arctic Highway from North Cape, you have no choice but to retrace your route. This takes you back to **Honningsvåg** where most visitors to the Cape take the opportunity to find accommodation for at least one night. In fact, quite a few will spend the morning catching up on the sleep they missed seeking the midnight sun.

The Highway: Olderfjord to Lakselv
MAP 14

Back at Olderfjord the Arctic Highway continues its path along the western shore of the inner arm of Porsangerfjorden. The fjord is in two distinct parts. The outer arm, which you'll have seen on the journey to North Cape, is exceptionally broad and almost unbroken by islands. This southern arm, followed by the Highway, is narrower and littered with uninhabited islands.

The Highway keeps close to the shore of the fjord; there is little space for an alternative. It is bordered by mountains to the west and it is only when it crosses the necks of small promontories, five in all, that it leaves the shore and loses sight of the water. This used to be a poor section of road to the head of the fjord but a programme of straightening and widening has improved the road to a generally high standard.

Rivers punctuate the path of the Highway giving rise to numerous bridges. These streams arrive at the fjord's edge heavily laden with silt and gravel. In springtime, when melting snows add to their volumes and velocities, these rivers carry such a large load that the bridge abutments act as traps and the detritus is prematurely deposited. You can see some large gravel terraces have been formed near the shore and these are excavated for building materials. At other places the rivers' load is spilt out into the fjord itself.

Few people live along this western shore of Porsangerfjorden. Fishing is the main occupation of those who do, but their economy is usually supported also by farming, particularly dairy cattle. The Highway is their lifeline, easing their isolation.

Kistrand (118km) is just around the turn in the Highway as it leaves the Olderfjord to run south towards Lakselv. It used to be on the Coastal Steamer route; no less dependent on the sea, it now has to rely on its small fishing industry for its livelihood. There is a pleasant little church in the village by the edge of the fjord and with a small graveyard. The church dates from 1856; it was one of the few buildings in Finnmark not to be destroyed by the Germans in their retreat at the end of World War II. You can still see some signs of the war including concrete gun emplacements.

A minor road leads left off the Highway (125km) south of Kistrand. This crosses on to a small peninsula where there is a small fishing community.

Two bays, Ytre Billefjord and Indre Billefjord, break the line of the coast to the south. The second of these, Indre Billefjord (139km) is interesting. It claims to be the innermost part of the Porsangerfjord that has a guaranteed ice-free harbour. Certainly it is true that towards the head of the large fjord, its shallowness makes ice a real possibility in winter. The village, **Indre Billefjord**, is situated in a picturesque cove sheltered to the north and south by peninsulas. The southern headland is broad and a number of fishermen-farmers have settled here, particularly on the southern side which combines gentle slopes with a more favourable aspect. Four roads lead off to the left of the Highway and on to the headland. Only the second and fourth are worth exploring. This is the last chance you have to refuel before Lakselv. You'll see the filling station and a store to the right, but don't be surprised if it is shut, especially if it happens to be a Sunday. There's a **café** just beyond the filling station and another store about a kilometre further on.

Towards the southern end of the headland where the Highway begins to return to the fjordside (144km), a short road to the right runs around a lake, Gåradakvatn, and back on to the Highway. It is an interesting detour off the Highway, even if it does add about 7km to the journey.

The Highway bridges an important river, the Stabburselv, just north of **Øvrenes** (158km). The valley, Stabbursdalen, is very attractive but, unfortunately, there is only a short, 3km road up the valley (turn right on to a minor road at 156km before reaching the bridge).

However, if the valley is to be explored there is a very good camping site with excellent cabins to the right of the Highway some 800m or so after crossing the bridge. This is *Stabbursdalen Camp and Villmarksenter* (Wilderness Centre, ☎ 78 46 47 60). A small **shop/café** is on site. Stabbursdalen, which stretches away from the road to the right, has been declared a national park.

Near to the camping place but on the other side of the road is the **Stabbursnes Nature Museum**. It has been developed since 1990 and now

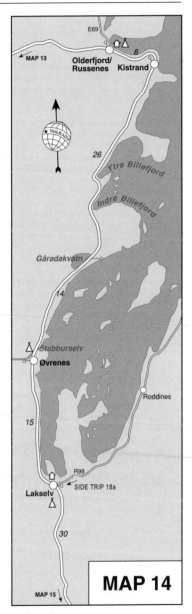

MAP 14

Stabbursdalen and Stabbursnes

 The valley (*dalen*) is a national park and the headland (*nes*) is a nature reserve. The park, at nearly 100 sq km, is one of the smaller of Norway's nineteen designated national parks and only one of two which abut or are crossed by the Arctic Highway. The other is the massive Saltfjellet-Svartisen park at the Polar Circle. The number of national parks is set to be greatly increased.

Stabbursdalen takes in the greater part of Stabburselva and its tributaries. The park's main claim to fame is that it contains the world's most northerly coniferous (pine) forest. In fact, the pine forest is only one tenth of the area and is mixed with birch which otherwise has the area to itself. The pine forest is ancient and some of the trees have been dated as over 500 years old. The Stabbur River is unusual in that its course is a mix of rapids and falls together with other stretches which scarcely seem to be flowing at all. These pools are known as *pombola*. The largest of the falls is Njakkafoss, tumbling through a narrow gorge. The landscape was formed by glacial forces and by the outpourings of morainic materials. The meltwater did as much work as the ice and produced the splendid Ravttosavzi canyon.

As well as forest and woodland, there are wetlands and high areas where lichens are all that can survive. It's a great place to view the birdlife of Finnmark with osprey and black grouse being just two of the species.

For the sportsman, there is excellent salmon fishing and elk hunting, but you do need a licence. Salmon fishing has improved since two salmon ladders were constructed on the river allowing the fish to get as far upstream as Njakkafossen.

If the idea of real wilderness attracts you then call in at the museum (see p255) and ask for guidance. There are marked paths and places to camp but there are also lots of rules to be obeyed. It's too large an area to just wander around without knowing where you're going.

The nature reserve was declared a protected area in 1983, thirteen years after the park was established. It comprises an area of wetland and part of the delta area of the Stabbur River as it spills into Porsangerfjord. It will not be very evident as you drive along the Highway although you may see some notices proclaiming Stabburnes Naturreservat. The reserve is at the mouth of the river but stretches nearly 9km along the coast and almost 2km into the fjord. Most of the reserve and all of the wetland is south of the estuary.

Entry to the wetland is forbidden in the period 1 May to 30 June to protect the large numbers of migratory birds that rest and feed here. Some of the species are quite rare like the lesser white-fronted goose. Other birds found here include the dunlin, the bar-tailed godwit and the knot. In winter, it is the eider that is prominent.

The reserve protects one of the largest salt and brackish marshes in the whole of North Norway.

has attractive exhibits illustrating the natural history of this part of the Porsangerfjord area. There are four sections called: riverscape, viddascape (the plateau), fjordscape and coastscape. There are also traditional Sami handicrafts (*duodji*). The museum is open between 09.00 and 20.00 (afternoons only in winter) and the volunteers who man it are especially helpful. If you intend going into the national park, it really is unwise unless you've called in here first and talked with the curators.

There's coffee available and a lavatory. The museum also acts as a **tourist information office**. Entrance is NOK30 with children charged NOK10 (☎ 78 46 47 65; 📄 78 46 47 32; 🖳 stabburs@online.no).

The Highway keeps close to the shore as it continues towards Lakselv but only here and there is Porsangerfjorden visible. Stands of birch or the curvature of the road otherwise screen the head of this great fjord.

Where it can be seen, it's worth leaving your vehicle to look at the boulder-strewn alluvial flats of Vesterbotn, the arm of the fjord along which the Highway is built. In good light this is a wonderfully picturesque scene of contrasting but subdued colours.

To the right of the Highway, there is greater contrast. Here the land rises steeply to over 300m with steep and impressive rock faces scarred by weathered clefts and erosion gullies. These form the edge of the massive Finnmark vidde which is cut by broad valleys of typical glacial concavity.

At 170km, just short of Lakselv the steep cliffs to the right of the Highway were used until recently for the storage of military arms and ammunition. The area was designated a controlled military zone and was a first reminder that the Highway was getting closer to the Soviet border. These post-Cold War times have seen a relaxation of the regulations and an abandonment of the cave stores although you might still be able to pick out their entrances.

The small town of **Lakselv** (173km) is tucked in between the mouth of the river and the infilling fjord-head. As you drive into the town you'll see the main church on your right.

Accommodation and food: Olderfjord to Lakselv

The choice is between self-catering at Stabbursdalen or waiting to get to Lakselv.

Stabbursdalen Camping (see p255; ☎ 78 46 47 60; 📄 78 46 47 62; 🖳 info @stabbursdalen.no) is excellent. Although the site may seem a little bare (vegetation doesn't grow quickly in these parts) the 26 cabins are very good. The largest are especially well equipped and all except the six smallest are en suite. All have kitchens with water. There is ample space for camper vans and electricity is available. The camping site should be open all year but the smaller cabins aren't available in winter. In a severe winter the camp may close during January and February. There is a **café** (closed in winter) and a **shop**. In summer, the largest cabins are NOK610 and the smallest NOK310. Prices fall in winter and if the camp isn't full you might try bargaining.

LAKSELV

The name, Lakselv, translates as 'Salmon River' and the Arctic Highway forms the little town's main street. Almost anything you might need is available along here even though the population is only about 3000.

Services

There are a number of petrol stations along the Highway and it's wise to fill up in the town. There is a very modern shopping complex on the left of the Highway and there are **banks** as well as **shops** here. The **post office** is next to the *vinmonopolet* in the shopping centre. The **tourist office** is off the Highway in Husflidsbygget, opposite the police station (☎ 78 46 21 45). It is open to visitors in summer only (09.00-17.00), summer being defined as early June to mid-August. Yes, they have long winters in this part of Norway. The tourist authority can be reached all year (☎ 78 46 07 00; 🖹 78 46 07 01; 🖳 info@porsanger-arrangement.no).

There is an **airport** (☎ 78 46 45 00) close by at **Banak**; this is a suburb of Lakselv reached by turning left off the Highway at a signposted junction towards the eastern end of the town. Confusingly, it has taken on the name North Cape Airport in recent times. It is quite important airfield. During World War II, German aircraft used it as a base from which to harass the Allied convoys to Murmansk. Today it is the most northerly stop on the main domestic route through North Norway.

Around the town

Unless you're a **golf** fanatic, there's little to detain you in the town. No one would describe Lakselv as anything but strictly functional. However, if you would like a round on what must surely be the world's most northerly golf course, then you'll find it to the east of the town, 3km from the airport. It isn't yet completed. The last time I was there, just six holes were playable.

Aside from golf, the only places of interest in the town are Gårdstunet and the world's most northerly winery. At **Gårdstunet** (The Farmyard; ☎ 78 46 20 49) there is a Sami tent (*lavvu*), a sauna, complete with bath outside and a lounge serving coffee.

These are intended to represent the three cultures of Finnmark, the Sami, the Finnish and the Norwegian. To be fair, there are other Sami artefacts. It's all rather quaint as is the little herb garden in which it is set. Officially, it is open all year but it's best to telephone if you want arrange a visit. To find it, drive 200m beyond the turn to Karasjok and turn left, signposted Ildskog. Go about 2km up this road, turn left again and you'll find Gårdstunet at the end of the 500m road.

The **winery** (☎ 78 46 27 52) also needs notice if you want a tour and tasting. It is on Meieriveien which the last turn to the right off the Highway before the major turn to Karasjok. The winery mainly produces an aperitif called Nordkapp (now there's a surprise). It is made from crowberries which grow in abundance in the thinly forested areas of west Finnmark. There are tours at noon and 16.00 between late June and early August. They cost NOK95 but you do get a tasting. Under-18s can go in free but there are no drinks for them.

Accommodation

In Lakselv there are three hotels. The best is a little way out of town, about 2km along the Arctic Highway after you've turned south towards Karasjok: the *Best Western Lakselv Hotel* (☎ 78 46 54 00; 🖹 78 46 54 01; 🖳 hotell@lakselvhotellene.no) is to the right of the road and clearly signposted. There has been a general upgrading of the hotel in recent years as well as extensions to the building. Its history is interesting because it was the first new building put up after World War II and, at that time, it was used for a range of community purposes, including local council meetings and baths for the people who had returned to rebuild the settlement. The baths are now strictly for guests. There are 44 en-suite rooms, of which six are single and the rest doubles or combi. There's a sauna and a restaurant but, be warned, if the number of guests falls below an undisclosed level, you have to find your evening meal in the town. In midsummer this is a popular stopping place for travellers coming up from Finland to the North Cape and you'll have to book ahead.

At other times, the hotel can be almost empty and it's worth negotiating terms. Prices are around NOK800 with breakfast and the hotel is open all year although, in the absence of any advance bookings it closes from Christmas to the end of January.

Lakselv Gjestestue (☎ 78 46 15 04; 🖹 78 46 23 91) is off the Highway opposite the filling station, Statoil, to the right if you're going towards Karasjok. The street name is Idrettsveien and it's the last turn but one before the junction to Karasjok. The last time I was there I could get no service and then saw a notice: 'You'll find me in the pub'. It has just eight rooms and a bar, but no restaurant although there's a pizza bar alongside. It's definitely overpriced at NOK500–700.

In the sentrum by the Statoil filling station is the *Porsanger Vertshus* (☎ 78 46 54 15; 🖹 78 46 54 01; 🖳 hotell@lakselvhotell ene.no) which is managed by the Lakselv Hotel. It's a rather strange, unwelcoming place and, even in summer, most of its clients are business people. It's open all year 'if needs be'. It has 40 rooms at NOK600 –900. This is again rather pricey for what you get. The *Åstedet Bistro* is part of the hotel and serves decent à la carte three-course meals at about NOK250. It seems to be where Lakselv's youngsters 'hang out' and it describes itself as an internet café.

Just outside the town is the *Lakselv Vanderehjem* (Youth Hostel) and *Karaslaks Camp* (☎ 78 46 14 76; 🖹 78 46 11 31). Take the Karasjok road out of Lakselv, driving about 5km from the major turning at the eastern end of the town. This is, of course, the Arctic Highway. The hostel and camp are signposted up a dirt road to the left of the Highway. It's a 2km drive up this road. The accommodation is typical of a hostel but the price starts at NOK500. For casual visitors, the hostel is open only from 1 June until the end of August, but groups can book all year. It's a well-maintained hostel, complete with sauna and a Sami tent. The campsite is intended largely for camper vans. The whole complex is an *utfartssenter* which, in case you were wondering, means an outdoor or activity centre. There are opportunities for hunting, canoe-ing, boating and fishing, among other activities; it's a good place from which to explore the countryside.

Until 2002, campers and those looking for cabins relied heavily on Banak Camping. Now that is closed, *Solstad Camping* (☎ 78 46 14 04; 🖹 78 46 12 14) is the only option, close to the town and on a very pleasant site along Route 98. To reach it, simply stay with the Highway through Lakselv but, instead of turning right to Karasjok, join the 98 and the camp is just one kilometre down the road.

There are five apartments and seven cabins as well as camping space. The apartments are open all year but the cabins have yet to be insulated against the cold winters so they're available only from May to September. Standards are high and the prices are reasonable for the quality you get. All apartments are en suite and fully equipped. The largest, sleeping up to six, are NOK800 and the three-person cabins are NOK500. The cabins have cooking facilities but are not en suite. The one-bed cabin is NOK300 and a four-bed cabin is NOK450. Bedding is for hire at NOK70. Solstad offers some activities including riding. It's convenience for Lakselv and its attractive site make it very popular.

Where to eat

The hotels all serve food either in their own restaurant (Lakselv Hotel) or in attached restaurants (the pizza bar at Lakselv Gjestestue or the bistro at Porsanger Vertshus) as described above.

The most popular and reliable eatery is the independent *Lorry's Veikro* (roadhouse) *og Drive In*. This is on the right of the Highway just before the traffic island in a new single-storey building. There's a large car-park but there's no drive-through counter. Surprisingly, it closes at 16.00 on Fridays and Saturdays but otherwise remains open until 23.00. It's a bit like an American diner, simply furnished but clean and with a fast-food menu. Prices are as good as anywhere else in town. The *Mecca Superstore* close to Lorry's has a café open in shop hours and there are also small cafés in the sentrum shopping malls.

The Highway: Lakselv to Karasjok
MAPS 15–16

It is at Lakselv that the traveller along the Highway has a major decision to make. If you had been driving to Kirkenes in the mid-1980s you would have had no choice. The Arctic Highway (E6) led round the eastern side of Porsangerfjorden, crossed a couple of high vidder and entered the Tana valley from the north. Then all changed. The gaps in the route between Karasjok and Tana Bru were closed and the Arctic Highway was re-routed south through Karasjok. This allowed it to avoid the high fjells and greatly improved its chances of being an all-weather road.

What then is the difficulty over the choice you can make today? Simply, that the old path (now Route 98) is possibly more interesting than the new and is 42km shorter. However, despite the greater distance, the new Highway route is probably faster because of its few steep gradients. And then there is Karasjok. If the old route is followed, Karasjok will not be visited. I suggest that, if you are making a round trip to Kirkenes in summer, take the Highway in one direction and Route 98 in the other. (A description of Route 98, from Tana Bru to Lakselv is given in Part 9, p274.)

Staying with the Arctic Highway, your route is south out of Lakselv, passing the Lakselv Hotel on the right (176km). The road is heavily used in high summer because it is the short route from much of Western Europe to the North Cape. There is scope for some improvement in the road's surface and alignment but it is safe and relatively fast.

Striking south from Lakselv you pass the marked entrance to Lakselv Vanderehjem at 179km on the left. On this part of the Highway you are driving through scattered hamlets which are part of the well-settled head of Porsangen. As the Highway crosses the 70°N latitude it climbs gently through birch forest to Nedrevatnet (right), a lake in the course of the Laks River. It is this river whose valley you'll be following for much of the way to Karasjok. Near the lake is **Porsangermoen** military camp. You'll see the warning signs in Norwegian, English, Russian, Finnish and German. There's a map showing the area and the injunction: 'Camping and photograph and stop (sic) is restricted'. This is an important garrison for the Norwegian army and also known to NATO troops on Arctic training exercises. Most of the barracks are to the left of the road but there are married quarters and stores to the right. Although there is a shop and a post office, this is not an especially popular posting. The military zone lasts for about 12km along the Highway and the exit is again marked by signs.

The scenery in the military zone and further south is pretty, especially the views to the west (right of the road). There are numerous lakes, many of which have small, interesting-looking islands breaking through their calm waters. Further west you can see the high fjell which rises by a seemingly vertical wall to some 1000 metres. To the east, scarcely half that height is reached.

About a kilometre after leaving the restricted area is **Skoganvarren** (202km). There is a Sami village to the west of the Highway and, nearby, on the same side of the road is the marked **Porsanger Museum** (☎ 78 46 00 00). It is yet another war museum with an extraordinary collection of photographs and artefacts put together by Johan Kåven. Kåven is described as 'the medicine man' from Billefjord. The origin of this sobriquet isn't clear. This museum is interesting for the insight it gives into the horrors of the German occupation of this remote part of Europe in World War II.

There's also a mini-shop and **post office** at the museum. Opening hours are from 13.00 to 18.00 during the season 25 June to 11 August. The museum is closed on Mondays. Visits are possible outside these times and period but you need to telephone first.

Another kilometre further on and you'll see a vehicle park and information board at the right of the Highway. This is the start of the **Lasarettmoen** (**203km**) trail, one of the *fotefar mot nord* (footprints in the north) which is the name given to both natural and man-made attractions in North Norway. There's a small collection of log **cabins** here and a **café**. The trail leads though thin forest to another extraordinary war relic.

When you get to the end of the 600m path you find yourself in the remains of what was the largest German military field-hospital in North Norway. It served the needs of the German forces in Finnmark, in north Finland and on the Russian front. On their retreat in 1944, the

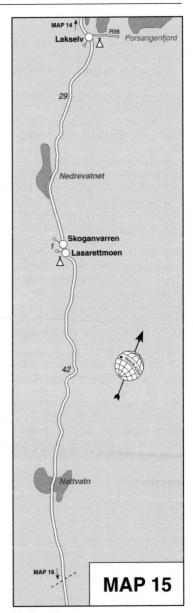

German army blew up and set fire to the hospital but the layout is still identifiable and the area's cold temperatures have ensured that not everything has rotted away. The wounded and sick were often brought here using Banak airfield (see p258) which was north Europe's biggest airport in World War II.

From Lasarettmoen, the Highway ascends by increasing gradients through the narrowing valley. As altitude increases, the woodland, which has bordered the Highway so far on this stretch, begins to thin and the immediate scenery becomes bleak marshland.

Near to the district border between Lakselv and Karasjok kommunes (210km) at an altitude of just over 300m you'll have especially good views to the west and moderately good views to the east. To the north-west the mountains rise to over 1000m and are totally unvegetated. The road is now on the Rivnesidde plateau and it has to make a descent to **Nattvatn**, a lake which spreads either side of the road. This section of the Highway has some good straight stretches but speeding isn't recommended. In summer you should see reindeer near the road and maybe elk too. Sami often set up roadside stalls a little way out of Karasjok.

After rising again to over 350m (238km) you begin to descend into Karasjok. There are steep and flat sections to this path but the road is largely through forest with the occasional marsh and innumerable streams to cross. There is a fall of over 200m in 8km into Karasjok which lies in the broad basin of the Karasjok River. In fact the scenery is so very different from that of the vidde that it comes as a bit of a shock to be confronted by green fields and landscape reminiscent of Kautokeino, the twin Sami village to the west (see Part 7, p227). At 245km you enter **Karasjok**.

Accommodation: Lakselv and Karasjok

There's just one possibility, the ***Skoganvarre Turist og Camping*** (☎ 78 46 48 46; 🖹 78 46 48 97) which is by the side of the Highway at Skoganvarren, by the entrance to Lasarettmoen and the marked trail to the old German military hospital. It's inexpensive with 30 log cabins under NOK500 served by a central shower and lavatory block. There's a café, a games hut with billiards, a camping site and a shop. Although it claims to be open all year a lack of visitors may see it shut. It's difficult to see any particular attraction unless it is to savour the wilderness which is the camp's setting.

KARASJOK

Karasjok, or Kárasjohka, lies on the Karasjokka, a major head-stream of the mighty Tana River which it joins only a short distance from the little town. Karasjok is a major Sami settlement comparable with Kautokeino (see p227) and Utskoji (in Finland). It seems more of a town than Kautokeino and it claims to be 'the capital of Lapland'. If you've visited Kautokeino, it will be interesting to compare and contrast the two settlements. Even if most visitors declare Kautokeino to be the more authentically Sami, Karasjok is worth an overnight stop.

The climate of Karasjok is interesting. It is exceptionally dry, its annual total precipitation is around 300mm, the sort of figure you would find at Alice Springs in the Australian Desert. Unlike Alice Springs, however, it can be exceptionally cold in winter. Karasjok's mean minimum temperature is -14.5°C but temperatures down to -30°C or less are not uncommon. In summer temperatures rise to respectable figures, often reaching the twenties Celsius during the day. The dryness and cold winters are largely a result of the more continental location of Karasjok on the Finnmark vidde compared with places nearer the coast.

History

The earliest settlement dates from the early sixteenth century although Sami had been hunters in the area for centuries before this. Attracted by the broad and sheltered river plain, the early hunters used the location for their winter quarters. With the semi-domestication of reindeer, hunters became transhumants, and the Sami began to supplement their reindeer herding with farming. By the end of the sixteenth century a traditional *siida* (a Sami village based on co-operative living) had been established by the river.

When the traveller-explorer, Paul du Chaillu, visited the village over one hundred years ago he estimated the population at 125. There were then twenty farms. By

the 1880s there was a church and a school. By the start of World War II, in 1940, the population was estimated at 350 and the river remained unbridged, relying on a ferry.

Today, the population is around 2200 with another 800 in the district.

The village has become a town although it has remained predominantly Sami. Unlike Kautokeino but in common with Masi (see p226), it was always a Norwegian Sami village not one of the Kvæns.

With the bridging of the river and the improvement to the roads, Karasjok is an important node on the E6, the Arctic Highway and on Route 92 which goes west to Kautokeino and south to Finland where it links with the Finnish Route 92 (see Approach Routes VIII and IX – Part 3, p97 and p110). The building of the E75 link (see p270) with the Arctic Highway to the east does not seem to have diminished Karasjok's importance.

The days when Karasjok was full of Sami in their traditional dress are gone. If you want to see the colourful costumes, even if somewhat less decorated than those of Kautokeino, you will need to be in the town

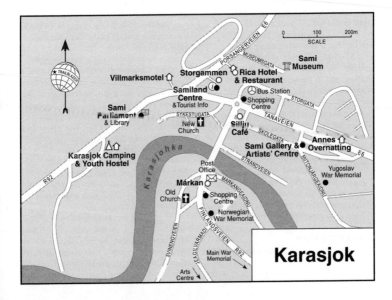

Karasjok

at the time of a wedding or other special event. All the same, Karasjok is the place to get to know something of the culture and history of these tradition-conscious people.

Entering the town

Coming into Karasjok, the Arctic Highway descends into the town and you turn left at the first major junction to go towards the centre. (To carry straight on is to go towards Kautokeino on Route 92.) At the next roundabout, at the start of the sentrum, there's another choice. If you go straight on you remain with the Arctic Highway and arrive at the hub of Karasjok. If you turn right, you'll cross the river and be on your way to Finland.

Services

The **tourist office** (☎ 78 46 88 10; 🖹 78 46 88 11; 🖳 koas@koas.no) is in the Samiland Centre (see above) to the right of the Highway as you enter Karasjok from Lakselv. It is open all year but closes at weekends between September and early May. Opening times are from 09.00 to 16.00 but it stays open until 19.00 from mid-June until late August.

There's never a shortage of **petrol stations** in this part of Norway and Karasjok is no exception. Significant price differences are rare but it is worth looking round.

Most of the usual services are in the sentrum. Here you will find **banks**, the **bus station** and a range of shops. A second **shopping centre** is down the Route 92, just the other side of the° river where there is another supermarket, some craft shops, a silversmith and the main **post office**. In this part of Norway, where gold and silver are found locally, you can find some beautifully crafted pieces of jewellery.

For free **internet** access, go to the Samisk library (*SámiSierrabibliotehka*) which is near the school. Turn right along Niitjárgeaidnu from the Arctic Highway as it leaves the centre of town on its way east.

Around the town

Karasjok is really quite small so almost all its attractions can be reached easily on a walk round the town. A good start is the

Samiland Centre (first opened in June 2000) that houses the tourist office. All of Sámpi (Lapland or Sami Land) is here. There will be some who don't like it and consider that it debases an ancient culture, turning it into a theme park. All the same you do get a flavour of that culture. The best place to start is the information centre, across to the right from the entrance and car-park. Here you can get a descriptive leaflet and picture-map of the centre.

The Sámpi shop has a variety of souvenirs which are of a better than usual standard. Nearby are washrooms and a café. For something out of the ordinary you can have coffee, sitting on reindeer skins, in one of the tents (*lávvu*) which are part of the centre's displays. There are different sorts of tent as well as Sami turf huts (*gammen*) and modern Sami huts. Children particularly like the tame reindeer and trying their hand at lassoing. In the corner of the site is what is called the Magical Theatre or the spirit rock (*stálobákti*). This very well-designed building has widescreen shows of Sámpi in all its moods. As with similar shows at the Arctic Circle and at North Cape, the standard of the presentations is high and really shouldn't be missed.

The theatre building, dating from 1989, was used for sittings of the Sami parliament until the new purpose-built building (see p265) was opened a couple of years ago.

The Karasjok Guesthouse (see p266) stands at the edge of the site and the Rica Hotel is close by. You may find part of the car-park occupied by an old car or two with the boot open. This will be a Russian car-boot sale; after all, the Cold War's over and the border's not far away.

The Samiland Centre is open all year from 09.00 but closes at weekends from September to June. Closing time is 19.00 in mid-summer but 16.00 for the rest of the year. Entry is NOK90 with reductions for children and families.

If you find the Samiland Centre a little too much of a theme park, the **Sami Museum** (*Sámiid Vuorká-Dávvirat*) is rather more 'serious', with plenty of glass cases. Turn back up the Highway from the Samiland Centre and then go past the Rica

Hotel and turn right; the open-air museum is on the left with the museum building alongside. The only signpost uses the Sami name.

The displays tell much of the history of the Sami and their culture from the traditional to the contemporary. Entrance is NOK25. Opening times are variable according to the time of year and the day of the week. If you're here between 12.00 and 15.00 you can be sure that it is open but the hours are much longer in mid-summer.

The new **Sami Parliament** (*Sametinget*) building is on the road towards Kautokeino (Route 92) on the left about 200m from the roundabout. It is a really beautiful structure, executed in a variety of woods, and housing not only the parliamentary chamber but also a magnificent **Sami Library** containing almost 40,000 books. It is possible to view the interior by taking one of the tours which are available on the half-hour from 08.30 to 14.30. Each tour lasts about 30 minutes but, if you're in Karasjok in winter, there's only one tour daily, at 13.30.

The town's two churches should be visited. Karasjok's **Old Church** is on a turning off the road towards Finland (Route 92). Follow this road from the roundabout at the town centre, cross the river and the little white church can be seen on the right. Built in 1807, it's the oldest church in Finnmark. Remarkably, it survived the German scorched earth policy at the end of World War II; nothing else did. The **new church** is also off the same Route 92 but on the town side of the river bridge, to the right of the road coming out of town. The best time to visit these churches is when there's a service and the Sami are present in their traditional dress. Easter is best of all: the marriage season. If you attend a service, beware. They last a very long time.

There are three **war memorials** in the town. The main one is along the road towards the Finnish border but the most moving are those to Yugoslav prisoners of war and to those Norwegians who died on their return to the town after being forcibly evacuated at the end of WWII. They died in attempting to clear the mines that had been left behind by the retreating German army. The Yugoslav memorial (*Serbegrav*) is a small garden by the town's sports centre on Niittonjárgeaidnu, a turning off the Arctic Highway as it goes east out of the town. The Norwegian memorial is south of the river to the left of Route 92 on its way to Finland.

There are two arts centres in Karasjok. The **Sami Gallery and Artists' Centre** (Sámi Dáiddagouvddás, ☎ 78 46 90 02) is near the turn off from the Highway towards the Yugoslav memorial (see above). There is a variety of exhibitions through the year and entrance is free. The centre is open from 10.00 to 15.00, closed on Saturdays but open on Sundays from 12.00 to 17.00. The other arts centre is a little way out of town. Take Route 92 towards Finland, cross the river and turn down the third road to the right. The centre is at the end of this road. The centre is open for special exhibitions so you need to ask at the tourist information centre to check for the current situation.

If you want to see the making of the Sami's traditional knives, you need to go even further out of town. Go past the old church (see above), turn off right down Svinengveien and the **Knivsmed Strømeng** is signposted right after about one kilometre. The standard of craftsmanship is very high. Check with the information centre before a visit but it is usually open from 08.30 to 16.00 on weekdays.

Karasjok is the place to be for all sorts of activity holidays. There's every thing from panning for gold to snowmobile safaris in winter. For details of these opportunities it's best to email 🖳 info@finnmark.org.

Accommodation

The *Rica Hotel* (☎ 78 46 74 00; 📱 78 46 68 02; 🖳 rica.hotel.karasjok@rica.no) is signposted to the left of the Arctic Highway as you enter the town from Lakselv. It stands just alongside the Samiland Centre. It's the best in town, comfortable rather than luxurious. There are 56 rooms but it is very popular in summer and booking ahead is necessary. The two restaurants serve some Sami dishes and there's a large Sami turf-roofed hut (*gammen*) in the Samiland Centre in which the hotel holds the occasional party. There's a fitness room, a sauna and usually plenty of parking space. Rates are a little high for what you get: from NOK750 to over NOK1000.

Next door is the 28-roomed **Karasjok Guesthouse** (for contact details see Rica Hotel, p265) which is also run by Rica and used for groups or as an overflow for the hotel. Rates are lower than the hotel by about NOK200 but you lose the en-suite facilities.

If you drive into Karasjok from Lakselv and continue past the roundabout to go on to Route 92 towards Kautokeino, you'll see the **Villmarksmotel** (☎ 78 46 74 46; 🖹 78 46 64 08) on the right up a fairly steep slope. There are both cabins and rooms with accommodation for 34 people. It's nothing very special but very satisfactory for the price. A double room is about the same as a four-person cabin at about NOK700.

All three hotels or guesthouses are open all year.

Karasjok Camping and the **Youth Hostel** (☎ 78 46 61 35; 🖹 78 46 66 97; 🖳 hal onen@online.no) are also along the road to Kautokeino (Route 92), to the left of the road as it leaves town. The Youth Hostel has only six beds at NOK115. If it's full then guests are transferred to the cabins on the camping site. In total there are 21 cabins sleeping between two and eight persons. The largest cabins include shower, lavatory and even a sauna and a TV. There is space for tents and the outlook is over the river, towards the town. Prices for cabins range from NOK230 to NOK850 according to size. A place for a tent or camper van is NOK70.

In the centre of town, just left off the Highway on its way to the east, is **Annes**

Overnatting (☎/🖹 78 46 64 32). Just a couple of cottages and four rooms sleep eleven. There are no meals served here but it is so near to the centre of town that it hardly matters. Prices are around the NOK500 mark with the en-suite rooms the most expensive.

Where to eat
Rica Hotel has two restaurants and there are a number of cafés including those in the supermarkets in the town centre and just across the river bridge. The best of these is probably **Márkan Café** near the post office (see p264). It is on the first floor of the Rimi Building opposite the Esso filling station. There's a Sami longboat for decoration and picnic-table seating. it's basic, neat and tidy and good value.

On a traffic island opposite the Statoil station on the Arctic Highway is the **Sillju Café**. This serves grills and burgers, the latter at NOK38. Look for a single-storey, red, wooden building with a small second-floor tower.

Within the Samiland Centre, but separate from it, is **Storgammen** (☎ 78 46 74 00). This restaurant is a complex of four Sami turf huts (*gammen*) where diners sit on reindeer skins around an open fire. From the outside it seems hardly possible that over a hundred can be seated for a meal. The menu chiefly comprises Sami dishes with very fresh ingredients. The choice is from reindeer meat and fish, game birds and locally gathered berries. Look out for the *multerberries*. This must be *the* place to eat in the so-called capital of Samiland, Sámpi.

PART 9: KARASJOK TO KIRKENES

This is the last lap of the journey. It is also through some of the most remote and wild parts that the Arctic Highway travels on its way to the Russian border. There will be no mistaking that this is the Arctic, the tundra.

The Highway: Karasjok to Tana Bru
MAPS 16–18

Just as the previous stage of the Arctic Highway ended on a re-routed section of road, so too the final stage begins on a similarly redirected Highway. However, unlike the Lakselv to Karasjok road, which has a long history, the Karasjok to Tana Bru section includes some completely new stretches. A quarter of a century ago, you wouldn't have had this option of getting to Tana Bru by road.

Until the mid-1970s a gap of some 33km between Valjok and Levajok broke the continuity of what was then Route 92. Only a track linked the two small settlements. When the gap was closed there was another two years before it was finally upgraded and designated as the Arctic Highway (E6). A significant portion of the Highway from Karasjok to Tana Bru has the high speed limit of 90km/h. This reflects the low traffic volumes as well as the state of the road. You still need to keep a good look out for reindeer and remember that the road is quite narrow.

Beyond the Tana the Arctic Highway enters East Finnmark, the most remote region in Norway with a distinct and magical character.

The petrol stations are few and far between along the whole of this stage and you should refuel before leaving Karasjok.

The Arctic Highway leaves Karasjok by following the Karasjokka along its left or northern bank. Two large buildings stand away from the Highway, To the left is the hospital and to the right the school. Passing small houses, the homes of the Sami where snow scooters and sledges sit in the garden waiting for the return of the winter's snow, the road soon puts the village behind it. Along the first 20–25km the road is quite narrow and its path undulating. Although the river is never far away you'll get only an occasional glimpse of it, to the right. Where you can see it, its broad waters are fringed by massive beds of sand and gravel. These river beaches, broadening on the insides of meander bends, are visible throughout the summer, but in spring when the river discharges the meltwater of the winter's snow the swollen Karasjokka is almost twice its average width.

On the other side of the river is Route 92 running into Finland and at about 11km out from Karasjok, down a small path to the right and parallel with the

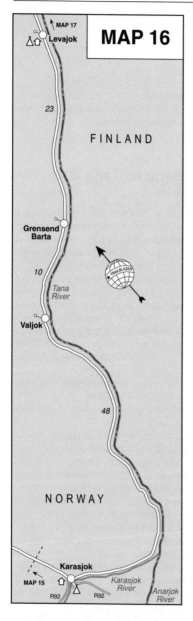

Highway, is one of the many reminders that this is Lapland or Samiland. By a small stream running into the Karasjokka are the remains of a bridge that was built by the Sami decades ago and is still called the 'White bridge' although little now remains.

The Highway swings left and northwards as you reach the confluence of the Karasjokka and Anarjokka (13km). These two great rivers, the latter forming the boundary between the Finnish and Norwegian Samilands, become the Tana from this point and this continues to function as the international boundary. Strictly speaking, the Tana and the Anarjokka are the same river of which the Karasjokka is a mere tributary.

From here, when you look out to the right, the view across the river is into Finland. The next section of the Highway follows the Tana and you can get good views of the river. Fishing is excellent and both sport and commercial fishing are practised. You'll see the long boats of the fishermen beached on both sides of the river and the silence will be broken by the splutter of an outboard motor as a boat negotiates the shallow water running over huge beds of gravel.

Much of this part of the valley, and beyond, was filled with a lake as the ice retreated from the area 10,000 years ago. Great sandbanks are evidence of the old lake, and the Highway runs along the former lake terrace, often as much as 30m above the river level. Access to the river is restricted and, here and there, the sands and gravels are quarried for the building and construction industries. The Finnish side of the river is more heavily settled than is the Norwegian and the old terraces are less obvious. Gradually the Highway descends back to river level and you can appreciate the Tana's immense width. As with the Karasjokka, the summer width is only some fifty percent of what it becomes in spring when the sandbanks and point bars are covered by torrential meltwaters.

Alongside the river forests of birch mask the sandy terraces but occasionally rocky outcrops break the monotony of sand, river and trees. Only rarely can you see the parallel Finnish road on the right bank.

At **Valjok/Válljohka** (48km), to the right of the road, is a little Sami chapel half hidden behind the trees. The small red building can be reached by driving or walking off the Highway up a path leading through the trees. There is a bell-tower by the chapel but both are usually kept locked. The chapel is on a terrace above the river and down by the water's edge there is a farm. This part of the Highway is sparsely inhabited so it may be worth noting that there's a telephone for public use to the left of the road in Valjok.

Leaving Valjok, the Highway bridges one of the Tana's many tributaries. Just before the bridge to the right is a small Sami open-air museum. It probably isn't worth stopping unless the offer of waffles or a *rom* is irresistible. A *loppe-marked*, or flea market, is also advertised here. Quite who uses this facility in these remote parts is unclear.

The Highway's standard improves from this village, a reminder that this is part of the mid-1970s new road. There are two long straight sections of the road but little settlement either here or on the Finnish side of the river. The Finnish road is also modern on this stretch and the former isolation of this district, without a motor road for so long, has left it wild and undisturbed.

The road is not only straight, but quite flat with the undulations subdued and hardly noticeable. At **Grensend Barta** (58km) there is another public telephone (to the right of the Highway in a house). After crossing another river, the Highway begins to wind but cuts through a rocky spur as it runs 20–30m above the Tana. The river valley is now clearly narrower and hills rise on either side. Trees clothe the Norwegian slopes but the more gentle gradients across the river in Finland are farmed. If you're driving the Highway here in mid-August, the leaves of the birch trees will already be turning golden yellow, a reminder of how short is the summer in these parts.

Crossing the boundary between the Karasjok and Tana kommunes/districts (62km) the valley narrows still further with the Tana incised in a deep cleft. You can now see the Finnish road clearly and, looking up at the hillsides, it is remarkable to find that the tree-line reaches almost to the top of the vidde.

The modern, 1970s, road, which has given you easy driving with plenty of straight sections, comes to an end as you reach **Levajok** (81km). Here there is another, quite substantial fjellstue (mountain lodge). This is Levajok Villmarkstue and Levajok Fjellstue with a range of accommodation and lots of activities.

As the Highway continues beyond Levajok, the valley opens a little and the terraces are less marked. In spring, the Tana is in flood and carries a heavy load. But, in summer, when the water is low, much of the boulder-strewn bed becomes visible. On the other side of the valley, the Finnish road runs on a

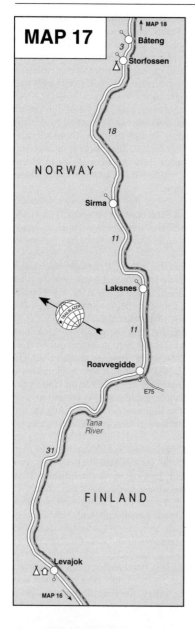

parallel course to the Highway. After 4km (85km) the Highway crosses a major tributary of the Tana which has a number of falls along its course. Here, on the Tana, are the Ailestrykene, a five-kilometre stretch of rapids and a favourite spot for salmon fishermen.

With good views across the valley, the Highway threads its way close to the Tana following every twist and turn of the river. In places the river bifurcates as its course negotiates rocky outcrops in its path. At **Roavvegidde** (112km) a short road leads off the Highway to the right and down to the river. Here there used to be a ferry across the river and into Finland. The ferry ceased to operate and once the Arctic Highway was re-routed along the Tana it became clear that a bridge should be built to give the only crossing of the Tana between Karasjok and Tana Bru, a distance of over 200km. Finland upgraded its approach road to a European Route, E75, but the construction of the bridge met with difficulties and a scheduled opening planned for 1993 had to be delayed by a year.

Now there is an elegant suspension bridge called *Samilandsbrua* (the Samiland bridge) with a notice proclaiming that the *riksgrense* (border) with Finland is just 300m away. This crossing is increasing in importance and, for some purposes, rivals the Finnish–Norwegian link through Karasjok. (See also Part 3, Approach Routes VIII and IX.)

On the Finnish side there is a customs post and the village of Utsjoki. Ivalo is 165km away to the south.

The other Arctic Highway

Finland, attacked by the Soviet Union in November 1939 in the famous Winter War, became allied with Germany during the rest of World War II. The Finns paid a heavy price for being on 'the wrong side'. There was much destruction of property, especially in the north, and it was 1945 before this tragic period in the county's history was over.

The peace terms, confirmed by the Treaty of Paris in 1947, saw the Soviet Union annex important south-eastern territories in the Karelian region. Finland also lost the so-called Petsamo corridor, an important strip of territory that stretched north to the Barents Sea forming a buffer zone between Norway and the USSR. This corridor gave Finland access to an ice-free port and was served by a road which, pre-war, was called the Arctic Highway.

From a Norwegian point of view, the fact that they now had a road which would become known as Norway's Arctic Highway was something of a mixed blessing. There were times, in the Cold War, when they might have preferred the Finns to have remained a bulwark between themselves and the Soviets.

This new crossing of the Tana River by the Samilandsbrua may be something of a compensation for Finland's loss of Petsamo, but there are many Finns who are still resentful of the USSR's annexation of their important outlet to the northern tip of Europe.

Beyond the river crossing the Arctic Highway becomes the E6/E75 as far as the head of Varangerfjorden where the E75 and the Highway part company again. At **Laksnes** (123km), there used to be a café but it was closed the last time I was there, as was the rather scruffy camping site. However, there's still something for you to see. On the left-hand side of the Highway there are interesting kettle holes. These are rounded hollows in the sand and gravel that were deposited by the meltwaters of the retreating ice. In places, as here, bodies of ice, which had yet to melt, blocked the deposition but, when melting did occur, the hollows were left behind to fill with water. You have to drive off the Highway, through the very open birch forest, to see the kettle holes. If you're not in a four-wheel drive, it may be better to walk the 2–300m.

Sirma (134km) is a small Sami village set at a point where the valley has broadened and the birchwood forest is dominant. There are numerous farms here on the broad terrace. The village has a chapel (built in 1959) and a school. A petrol station, shop, **post office** and small **café** are more than you might have expected.

The aspect has now changed. The valley is broad, the terraces are settled and farmed. The Arctic Highway's path no longer seems quite so remote; if you look down to the river you'll see the river-bed has sand banks instead of boulders. There is a riverside **camping** site at **Storfossen** (152km) where caravans are accepted and there are cabins high above the river. There's also a small shop.

It is another favourite place for salmon fishing partly because the long rapid stretch of river of some 6km allows for fishing from the shore without the need of a boat. The Tana, Alta and Laks rivers rival each other as the world's best salmon river, but I think the Alta must be given the title.

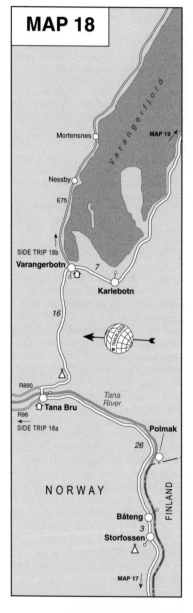

When you reach **Båteng** (155km) you are at another small Sami settlement. It lies to the right of the Highway close to the river but clearly visible from the Highway. A minor road loops off the Highway, through the village, and back again. You'll see a small shop to the left of the Highway with most of the village to the right.

Six kilometres or so further on and the other side of the river becomes Norwegian territory, not Finnish. You can see the Sami village of **Polmak** on the other side of the Tana as it turns to flow in a northerly direction. Polmak can be reached from a point further along the Arctic Highway (see p281).

Now running almost due north the Highway bypasses **Syd-** and **Nord-Holmsund** (167km) which lie, like Båteng, on a minor road just off the Highway and by the riverbank.

From about 179km you can get views of **Tana** (or **Tana Bru**) just 3km further away. As the Highway reaches Tana, you have completed the 1970s section of the Highway's path to East Finnmark.

Tana Bru is the 'capital' of the Tana River community. It has a number of new buildings but to enter the village you need to continue downriver, beyond the bridge and along Route 98 for a few hundred metres instead of crossing the river along the Arctic Highway (E6). If you decide to visit the village, the 'town' hall is worth seeing with an arts exhibition hall and theatre. Tana is a place to stay overnight (there's a **hotel**), to refuel or to make use of the village's array of services. Because this is the last convenient place to restock before you get to Kirkenes, it's worth checking your provisions. There's a good store, bank, **grill bar** and kiosks. The **post office** is just behind the **tourist office** (☎ 78 92 53 98; 📄 78 92 53 09; 🖳 postmottak @tana.kommune.no) which is clearly signposted to the left of the road going north, just beyond the hotel. The information office seems to keep unusual and unpredictable opening times.

Accommodation: Karasjok to Tana

There isn't a lot of choice in this remote part of Finnmark.

Eighty-one kilometres out of Karasjok there's one of those surprises you keep finding in Finnmark: an activity centre and a riding school. At a clearly marked point on the Highway you turn right down a path to find Levajok Villmarkstue to your right and Levajok Fjellstue Rideskole, down a further path to your left. The *Villmarkstue* (Wilderness Hostel, ☎ 78 92 87 46; 📄 78 92 87 79; for the riding school: ☎ 78 92 87 14) is actually an excellent small hotel on the bank of the Tana. The older part is nearest the river and includes a nice sitting-room and dining-room with good views. Non-residents can usually get a meal and there's a café open most of the day. The new building has the better rooms (doubles at NOK700 with breakfast) all en suite. Only four of the rooms in the older buildings are en suite (with the shower actually in the bedroom) but prices are lower (NOK450). There's a total of 10 rooms in the new section and 11 in the old; but it's very popular and you would be wise to book ahead. This part of Norway is very popular with Finnish visitors.

There's plenty to do: fishing, boat trips, wilderness walks or horse riding next door. The Tana is one of the great salmon rivers of the world. The riding is from the fjellstue which has 9 cabins and a camping site. The cabins are simple with kitchens but no other facilities and prices range from NOK250 for a two-bed cabin to NOK390 for a five-bed one. There are horses to suit children, as well as satisfying the needs of experienced and novice riders. The riding school runs one-week courses. There are also kayaks.

Everything closes down at Levajok between November and May.

Storfossen Camping (☎ 78 92 88 11; 📄 78 92 88 99) is to the right of the Highway. There are just 12 cabins, strung out along the river, with space for caravans and tents. There's a small shop. Four of the cabins are en suite and prices range from NOK250 to NOK800. One cabin sleeps five, another has two beds and the rest sleep four. It's a popular place for people fishing the river but is nothing like as attractive as Levajok. The fishing is on a 600m stretch in the season June to mid-August. It's worth noting that licences are required for river fishing in Norway and there are many regulations governing the sport. Sea fishing is free from restrictions.

Tana is big enough to boast a hotel. The *Comfort Hotel Tana* (☎ 78 92 81 98; 📄 78 92 80 05; 🖳 info@tana-turisthotell.no) is near the centre of the village. It lives up to its name and provides comfortable accommodation in 30 en-suite rooms. The restaurant is good and the hotel is open all year. There is also a **café** and a sauna. The hotel can be quite busy because of its location so it's best to book ahead. Double rooms cost almost NOK1000 (NOK1200 with evening buffet meal) which is a bit on the expensive side, even for Finnmark. Unusually, the hotel also has 16 cabins and a camping site. The cabins are a little tired looking and cost NOK250 (or NOK350 with a freezer). Water and toilets are communal.

There's further camping at **Tana Famillecamping** (☎ 78 92 86 30; ☎/🖹 78 92 86 31) in Skipagurra. This village is actually outside Tana, some six kilometres along the Highway towards Kirkenes. As the name suggests, the camp is family friendly; there's even a 'quiet time' between 23.00 and 07.00. There are 19 cabins and plenty of space for tents. Although there is a good range of shared facilities, even including a TV room and sauna, the cabins are only simply equipped with electric cookers but no shower or toilet. Prices range from NOK250 to NOK350 according to cabin size. A tent site costs NOK50 and there's a kiosk at the entrance to the camp.

SIDE TRIP FROM TANA BRU TO LAKSELV   Map 18a

This isn't strictly a side trip but **an alternative route** between Tana and Lakselv (see p258). In fact, it is the former route of the Arctic Highway before the Karasjok to Tana road had been completed. If you have come to Tana, via the modern Highway, and are returning south after a visit to Kirkenes, this route is well worth considering for your onward journey rather than repeating what you've already done. In any case most travellers will probably find this alternative the more interesting, the 'scenic route', and it's the shorter at 211km.

The route is not well served by petrol stations so you should watch the fuel gauge and fill up when the opportunity occurs.

The whole of this journey is by Route 98. Instead of staying with the Arctic Highway and crossing the bridge over the Tana, go straight on through Tana as Route 98 continues where the Highway left off. You are now travelling northwards along the west side of the river skirting the village.

The road swings away from the river, which is lost to sight. A series of terraces form the Tana's left bank. The lower ones are farmed but the upper terraces are devoted to pasture or, more often, are forested. Route 98 stays with the lowest terrace as it returns to near the riverside at **Vestre Seida** (=West Seida, 4km).

This was where, in World War II, the Germans erected a pontoon bridge. Beyond Seida, the road, still on the lowest terrace, follows the river downstream. Tanaelva and its valley are quite exceptionally broad and the mountains stand back a respectful distance from the river. For kilometres the road travels over a gently undulating path with little or no gradient. Even the bridges over tributaries to the Tana, like the Maskejokka which has incised spectacular meanders into the giant terraces, fail to cause the road to deviate from an almost perfectly straight path. The farms are less evident on this stretch as they are separated one from another by tracts of forest.

You reach **Rustefjelbma** (23km) just as the road turns away from the Tana to begin a largely westerly path. A minor road continues northwards to the head of the Tanafjord. If there is time, it is an attractive detour of about 16km (32km round trip). The road passes through Bonakas (3km), home of the world's most northerly agricultural college, and Langes (9km), the location of the old Tana church. The road ends at **Nordre** (16km) where there is an unobstructed view into the whole of the outer Tanafjord and the Arctic Ocean. It's the view that makes this detour worth considering.

Rustefjelbma is a Sami name meaning 'The Cove of the Rusty Coloured Water'. There is no compact settlement here; instead houses are scattered along the terraces. However, close to the road (to the left) is the Tana church. Built to the design of Esben Poulsson, the church was officially opened on 21 June 1964. It is a rather plain wooden building with a steeply canted roof, but it has a most attractive, tall (26m) belltower. This pyramid of wood stands away from the church but is connected to it by a corridor. The whole structure is very modern in appearance and in singular contrast to the old Tana church at Langes.

There's a **guesthouse** in Rustefjelbma.

The road climbs out of Rustfjelbma across a high neck of land which separates the Tana River valley from Smalfjord, a narrow arm of the great Tanafjord. A minor road leads off (right, at 31km) to **Smalfjord** village where there is a sizeable jetty, but Route 98 runs around the head of the inlet and turns northwards to reach its most northerly point, just 3km from latitude 70° 30' North.

Turning west to **Torhop** (41km), Route 98 then follows a south-westerly path to another of the Vestertana inlets. The hilly divides between these inlets are bleak and treeless but the lower slopes carrying the road gently down to the fjord-arms are clothed in birch which is remarkably thick for this latitude.

You'll find that each of the inlets has some settlement and along the fjord-arms' edges are isolated homesteads finding a living from river and sea fishing and from the limited amount of farming that can be practised this far north. The fishing vessels used are incredibly small, many scarcely 10m long. With their little box-like cabins they appear almost comic and certainly unseaworthy. That they set out in almost any weather, and invariably return with a catch, is a tribute to the skill of both fisherman and boat builder.

Vestertana, part of the larger Tanafjord, is shallow and sand-filled. The views across the fjord towards the mountain peaks to the west are quite wonderful. Two peaks, Flattind and Perletind rise to well over 600m.

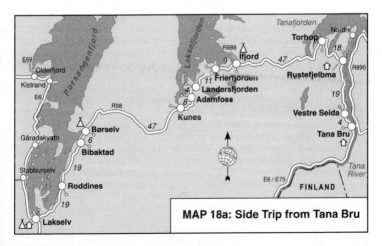

MAP 18a: Side Trip from Tana Bru

From **Vestertana**, Route 98 begins its climb up on to Ifjordfjellet. A road barrier reminds you why the new Arctic Highway/E6 route was developed.
Closure is inevitable at times in winter because of heavy snow cover. In many
ways this used to be a most difficult section of road but, over many years,
improvements have been made to widths and the radii of curvature of the
bends has been increased. The road starts its ascent alongside the fjord but
pulls away from the water through a series of near-hairpin bends. At the top of
this section of the road the view back towards Vestertana is a reward for the
climb. You will get only a fleeting glimpse of the glistening waters of the fjord
because the road then pulls away across a barren rock-strewn path alongside
but out of sight of the Storelv gorge. Finally, close to the top of the plateau, the
road joins Storelva and uses its valley to reach more level ground.

Ifjordfjellet is forbidding. The path of the road across the vidde is never
more than 8km south of latitude 70° 30' North. The winters here are severe and
Route 98 is closed during that season, reopening, in a good year, in mid-May.
The treeless landscape is roughly hewn; monotonous and bare yet somehow
always interesting. On the flatter surfaces lie large shallow lakes and snow
patches survive the summer sun. For the most part, rivers run in broad valleys
of little depth but, where small vigorous streams flow on steep slopes or masses of glacial drift lie on the surface, then the rivers are incised into narrow V-
shaped cuts. There is no shortage of water in summer when the streams feed
off melting snow, but in winter there are no streams, no lakes, no rock; just a
thick white coat to give a sameness and a silence to the plateau.

The road crosses the divide at 370m, a little more than halfway across the
plateau. There is no permanent settlement on Ifjordfjellet but the Sami use the
area as summer pasture for their reindeer. These Sami migrate here each year,
after Easter, from Karasjok. Close to the Gamik-Lebesby kommune boundary
(63km) is one of the Sami's camping areas. It is comparable with Áisároaivi on
Sennalandet (see p234). It scarcely merits the description of a village but there
is a jumble of huts, a little white **chapel** and a large **corral**. Keep an eye out for
the chapel, to the left of the road, because it may be possible to see large numbers of reindeer in the corrals here when the Sami round them up for marking.
Each owner has his own identification mark which is cut into the deer's ear.

The best time to see the marking is at the end of summer, from mid-
August to early September. No one seems to mind if you go right up to the corral, or if you take photographs. You may see quite young boys learning to catch
reindeer and holding them while the marking is done. The corral stands back a
little from the road and to the right, There's plenty of ground to park a vehicle.

The chapel, resembling a tent and set on rising ground, is enchanting. It is
situated among a thin stand of stunted birch trees. There is a separate belfry
and reindeer skins decorate the wall behind the altar.

While no one ventures on to this Arctic wilderness in winter, lakes and
streams are fished when the snows have largely gone. It is not uncommon, as
elsewhere in Norway, to see a car parked just off the road, the driver – the
angler – having walked off to his favourite stretch of stream or lake.

To leave the plateau, Route 98 bridges a stream which links the Iskløver
Lakes, passes over a col at 250m and then falls steeply down the valley of the
River Ifjord. Eventually the almost treeless vidde is left behind and the scenery
is forested piedmont.

Ifjord (88km), a fishing village, lies at the head of a narrow arm of Ifjorden which itself is an arm of the great Laksefjord. It is a larger village than most on Laksefjorden. There is a **guesthouse** as well as a caravan park with **cabins**. **Petrol** and a **café** make this a convenient place to stop if you are driving all the way between Tana and Lakselv. There's a triangular church for you to look at if you do stop here.

Leading north (turning to the right) off Route 98 is a new and interesting road, Route 888. Not all of Route 888 is new but an important link was built in the late 1980s to allow traffic to cover the 76km to the northern extremity of the Nordkyn peninsula. A further 20km on a minor road takes you on to Gamik which has wonderful views to the Barents Sea and is a place to view the midnight sun. Unfortunately, there is no road to Kinnarodden, to the northwest of the peninsula. It is this point which is the most northerly on the European mainland at 71° 08' North. Remember, the North Cape (see p251) is actually on an island.

Route 98 ignores the peninsula and continues westward, running near the shore of Laksefjord. Climbing to a small windswept plateau, the road passes great humpbacked *roches moutonnées* which separate the shallow lakes. These are rock masses, shaped as ice passed over the surface. Glacial erratics lie abandoned on spurs and hilltops like the cast-off playthings of a mountain giant. An eerie gorge leads down from the plateau to **Frierfjorden** (97km) where there is a fishing hamlet two kilometres off the main road.

As you cross yet another plateau, you are deprived of views into the fjord until you reach a delightful cove at **Landersfjorden** (108km), yet another arm of Laksefjorden. The little village here is again one of those small fishing communities which pay the penalty of isolation for the rich harvest of the fjord.

The road now keeps rather closer to the main fjord. The landscape is stark rather than harsh, untamed but not menacing. Its primeval quality is its fascination. There is a unique beauty about bare rock when, after being washed by the rain, it is caught glinting in the sun. Its grey face is transformed into a surface of freshly polished pewter.

At **Adamfoss** (112km), twin bridges cross two branches of the same waterfall. Unfortunately, these falls, called Adamfossén and Evafossen, have been almost completely deprived of their waters. You may have seen a clue as to why this is so if you noticed a minor road which leads left off Route 98 a kilometre before the falls are reached. This minor road goes up to the Adamselv power station and it is that which has taken the waters which by right and by nature would cascade over a 40m drop from the Adamsdal into the fjord. Adamsdalen hangs in respect of the fjord (see glossary p42: *hanging valley*) so this is a natural knickpoint in the river's profile. What was a very impressive feature is no longer there.

All the same the views from the bridges into the fjord are pleasant enough. The fjord has a special quietness and serenity here. The low Arctic sun gives a wonderful light quality and this is the place to take your photographs. Down on the low ground by the fjord there are rapidly weathering turf huts (*gamme*) built in the traditional manner of the Sami but dating only from World War II when their homes had been burnt down.

From Adamfossen, the road descends through a landscape of weather-sculptured rocks and thin forest by way of a valley to fjord level. You are now at **Kunes/Storfjordbotn** (120km). Ringed by black frost-shattered mountains in an aged and weathered landscape, the settlement seems even more isolated than similar fjord hamlets. The whole place always seems to me to have a sad, even dingy appearance. There is a **post office** in the village as well as a chapel and some bunkers and trenches from World War II.

Leaving Kunes, Route 98 goes south-west and you are on your way towards Børselvfjellet. The first part of this section is along the broad valley of the Storelv. The river is broad in its lower reaches and its channel is braided in summer's low water. The width of the valley is such that it has the appearance of a broad plain. There are some quite exceptionally straight stretches and, on the much improved road, gradients are low. This fast road rises over a series of shallow steps with hardly a bend in sight. Resist the temptation to speed!

The landscape is one of lakes and streams, birch and bare rock. As the altitude increases, vegetation suffers. The birch becomes noticeably more stunted and seeks shelter in hollows. At nearly 200m and where the border between the kommunes of Lebesby and Porsanger (144km) is crossed, the Sami graze their reindeer in summer. This is the highest point on the Børselvfjell but there are dwarf birch trees growing and, to the left of the road on gently sloping ground, is a **Sami chapel** almost hidden in the vegetation. A belfry just shows above the trees but the white-painted, black-roofed wooden building can easily be passed by unnoticed unless you keep a good lookout.

The Sami here, as on Ifjordfjellet, come from Karasjok. The whole of Børselvfjellet is used for grazing. Only a coil of smoke may identify the position of the Sami's summer camping places but the occasional stockade or reindeer-scare will more clearly mark this as Sami territory. The reindeer-scares are simple pieces of cloth or plastic attached to fencing near the road. The intention is to separate various herds and also to keep the deer off the road. On a long journey through northern Scandinavia it's a common experience to see the body of a reindeer killed by traffic. Foreigners, especially, take too little care when driving in reindeer country. It is sad, too, that a dead reindeer complete with its magnificent antlers is very rare. More often, the antlers will have been crudely removed while the deer's body is left to rot.

Route 98 continues on a more-or-less westerly path partly along the valley of the Børs River which is incised into glacial drift. Following the course of the river, the road turns to a more southerly direction and there are some deep waterfalls: Silfarfossen and the Meksafoss. Only 20m separate the road from the river according to a brief glance at a map but the fact is very different, for the river is flowing over 100m below Route 98 in a truly magnificent dolomite limestone gorge. Thin birch shields the view but there are gaps here and there and it is most certainly worth stopping, crossing to the left of the road, and looking down into the gorge. You'll see the river's crystal-clear waters tumbling over small falls and into silent pools. The river is rich in salmon and trout but, if it is late summer, the tiny speck you can see at the bottom of the gorge is probably an angler seeking the red char for which Børselva is famous.

Soon the road starts its steep, winding descent from the vidde. At about 150m the birch begins to thicken and the road's path becomes less steep as it enters the village of Børselv through farmed and forested country. The Porsangerfjord has been reached.

Route 98 almost bypasses **Børselv** (167km) as it crosses to the left bank of the river, leaving the village to its north and west. Fuel is available in the village and you might stop to visit the interesting **church**. It lies just off the minor road (Route 183) which has a junction with Route 98 and you'll see it quite clearly. The white painted wooden building is in the general shape of an octagon with two lateral extensions giving it bi-axial symmetry. A central spire crowns the church.

The village is home to a community which farms the alluvial soils at the river's mouth. Many of the villagers are of Finnish stock, still using the Finnish language. Just outside the village, to the right of Route 98, is a quite large boarding school which serves both Norwegian and Sami children.

A small road leads off Route 98 to the right (170km). This runs down to a little peninsula which stretches into the great Porsangerfjord. On it stands a small fishing hamlet, **Vækker** (also Surrukopp). At **Bibaktad** (173km) is another small fishing-farming village which lies in the partial shelter of Hestnes point and thus avoids the biting cold winds which sweep down the fjord from the Arctic when the wind is from the north.

After Bibaktad there is scarcely any settlement to line the path of Route 98 on its journey down the fjord to Lakselv. The road, now of very good quality, is never very far from the edge of the fjord. This is actually the narrow inner arm of Porsanger.

With the water to the right of the road, the contrast to the left is marked. A short distance from Route 98, in the east, rise the great mountains of Børselvfjellet, Munkkovarre and Tverrfjellet. Reaching altitudes of 500m so close to the coast, the slopes are rugged and steep. The bare faces are exposed like a section on a geological map. The torrential rivers which drain these mountains are arrested as they meet the still waters of the fjord. Moraines which block the river mouths are being eroded by the streams making gorge-like incisions into the gravels and carrying boulders on to the beach. Avalanches are quite common on this section of the road.

The views into Porsangerfjorden are quite spectacular. In bright sunshine the waters become inky blue and small uninhabited islands litter the fjord. The blue of the water is matched by that of the dolomite rock which streaks through the brown sandstone which is the basic geology of the islands. At **Roddines** (192km) there is a small and fairly new nature reserve. It is here that you will be able to see a result of the Pleistocene Ice Age on the coast, namely raised beaches. The enormous mass of ice caused the land to be depressed and, effectively, sea-level rose.

Now that the ice has gone, the land is steadily rising again (known as isostatic recovery) and the old beaches are gradually being exposed. Ten thousand years ago, sea-level stood just short of 70m higher than today and at Roddines you can see the beach ridges very clearly. There's a helpful information board which explains the features you see. Of course, this phenomenon is not peculiar to the Porsangerfjord but it is especially conspicuous here.

As you get close to **Lakselv**, the road leaves the fjord edge and farms return to the scene. Finally, Route 98 rejoins the Arctic Highway just east of the centre of the town (211km).

For a description of Lakselv, see Part 8, p258.

Accommodation: Tana Bru to Lakselv

There is little choice. You may well decide to make this journey without an overnight stop; after all it is a journey of only just over 200km.

Only a short way out of Tana is *Johnsens Gjestgiveri* (☎ 78 92 70 67; ▤ 78 92 80 10) at Rustefjelbma. There are just 13 double rooms in this simple guesthouse with prices around NOK450. There's a restaurant-cum-café but it is only open from June to September. It's difficult to see why a stop in Tana would not be preferable.

Just under half-way along the route, at Ifjord, is *Nilsen's Gjestgiveri and Camping* (☎ 78 49 9817). There are half a dozen rooms and cabins and the café is run by the same family. The cabins are closed over the long winter. If you need accommodation on Route 98, Nilsen's is acceptable. Prices start at NOK350.

Finally, at Børselv, you'll find *Bungalåven Vertshus* (☎ 78 46 43 95; ▤ 78 46 46 48; ▱ bungalaven@c2i.net). Here there are five simple cabins and a site for tents, open all year. *Vertshus* means inn and there's a fully serviced restaurant, bar and café. Daily rates are around NOK450.

The Highway: Tana Bru to Varangerbotn
MAP 18

When you leave Tana on the Arctic Highway (still the E6/E75) by way of the Tana Bru you are crossing into East Finnmark, Norway's most remote province. From the bridge you can see something of the great width of the river, flowing between the cliff-like terraces it has carved. Massive sand-banks lie exposed when the river is low and salmon of enormous proportions swim upstream towards the Stor falls and the Aile rapids, well known to anglers.

Turning right as soon as you've crossed the bridge, the Highway travels back upriver on a path parallel to that which it has just followed on the opposite bank. If you turn left after crossing the river, the road is Route 890, called the Arctic Ocean Road. On a much improved route, this road leads out to two large fishing villages on Norway's Arctic coast. These are Berlevåg and Båtsfjord. After 75km, much of it along the Tana valley, the road divides, the 890 continuing to Berlevåg a further 60km away. The road to Båtsfjord becomes the 891 and the village is reached in another 31km. These journeys have not been included as side trips because it is unlikely that you will consider a round trip of over 200km worthwhile when it is really only the last coastal stretches which are especially attractive. If you do decide to follow routes 890/89, both roads are easy to use and reasonably fast. There is a small hotel in Berlevåg, *Ishavhotellet* (☎ 78 98 14 15) and camping at *Berlevåg Camping* (☎ 78 98 16 10).

In the opposite direction to Routes 890/891, the Highway reaches **Skipagurra** (185km) after just a few kilometres. There's **camping** here (see p274). If you've not stopped at Tana Bru then there are all the necessary services here. Skipagurra is the landing point for commercial salmon fishing. It is also the junction between the Highway and Route 895 leading to the Finnish frontier via the east bank of the Tana River.

Salmon and Sami

Route 895 is a short stretch of 18km to the frontier and at 14km is a Sami village, Polmak. The river often freezes down to Polmak in winter but in summer it is rich in salmon. In fact, one of Polmak's claims to fame is the 36kg salmon landed by its postmaster, Henriksen, in 1928. The Tana salmon are shorter but fatter than most other species and it's said that local fishermen can tell which of the 35 tributaries of the Tana a particular salmon has come from.

Polmak is also noted for its church, built over a century ago; it has an altar panel dating from 1625. There's a guesthouse in Polmak, dating from 1790; it houses a small museum. It comes as no surprise that the joint theme of the museum is the Sami and salmon. In fact, the village community is mixed Sami and Norwegian.

This area has been important to the Sami for centuries. To the east of the Polmak road there are ancient reindeer traps in the Gollevarre plateau. These traps were used to catch wild reindeer and consist of pits dug in the ground over which were placed slender birch branches. The pits were just deep enough for the reindeer to be trapped but not so deep that injury would be caused. It has been calculated that there were over 500 pits here.

This is also an area where international frontiers mean very little. Norwegians, Sami and Finns mix readily, as do their cultures. You are as likely to hear one language as another. Saunas are common and bi- or tri-lingual notices can be seen. Entries in the telephone directory are often duplicated, in Norwegian and in Sami. The border with Finland is reached a further 4km beyond Polmak and across the border the Finnish Route 970 runs 42km to Utsjoki (see p270).

The Arctic Highway's path from Skipagurra is eastwards across the Seidafjell. It is this vidde which is crossed by the Sami with their reindeer on the migration treks to the summer grazing lands nearer the coast on the vast Varanger peninsula. These traditional routeways have been used by the Polmak Sami for centuries and today some 6–7000 deer cross Seidafjellet in May and again in October.

The Highway crosses these reindeer tracks at right angles as it rises on a winding path away from the Tana valley. This is a rather bleak fjell and for some reason I have never understood it always seems to be raining when I cross it. The road reaches 125m as it runs through a lake-splattered landscape of forest and bog.

Riding high on the plateau there is little to obstruct your view from the Highway. To the north and to the south is open and uninhabited tundra but to the east is Norway's 'last' fjord: Varanger, over 100km long and the only major fjord in the country to have its head in the west and its mouth in the east. A low peninsula extends into the fjord to divide its head into two arms: Meskfjorden and Karlebotn. Driving the Highway you will be making towards the former as the road makes a moderately steep descent from the Seida plateau, reaching the fjord at **Varangerbotn** (198km).

In the village is a new **museum**, the **Várjjat Sámi Musea**. The building, to the right of the Highway, is close to the roundabout in the village centre. It's all very modern, with excellent displays which illustrate the culture of the coastal Sami, that is, the Sami who turned to fishing as an alternative to reindeer herding.

It is said to have one of the best collections of modern *duodji* (Sami arts and crafts) in the whole of Samiland. The standard of museums in the North of Norway is universally high. There's a **café** in the museum.

Varangerbotn's **tourist office** (☎ 78 95 99 20; ▤ 78 95 99 30; ▣ info@ varanger-samiske.museum.no) is at the museum. It is open from 10.00 to 18.00 from mid-June to late August but only on weekdays from 10.00 to 15.00 for the rest of the year.

There are no services along the road between Skipagurra and Varangerbotn but the latter has shops, petrol, a **post office** and a pub, **Jegerstua Verthus**, with rooms (☎ 78 95 80 99). It is also the point from which a side trip can be made along the northern shore of the great Varangerfjord.

SIDE TRIP FROM VARANGERBOTN TO VADSØ & VARDØ Map 18b

This side trip is worth thinking about long and hard. To get to Vadsø is to travel about 49km and Vardø is another 75km. The route has no 'way out' except to return the way you came. There are, of course, compensations and if you get to Vardø you'll be able to boast that you reached the most easterly point in Norway. All the same, it could be one side trip too many.

The road is the E75 which parts company from the E6 Arctic Highway at Varangerbotn. It's an excellent road which takes you through Vadsø, arguably the most important town in East Finnmark, and on to the very eastern extremity of Norway, Vardøya.

The E75 leads eastward directly from the Arctic Highway, travelling at first along the northern shore of Meskfjorden, an inner arm of the Varangerfjord. Just a kilometre down the road is an interesting small **museum**: Amtmannsgammen. The original turf hut was built here centuries ago. Until 1900 it acted as a courtroom and a church as well as a refuge for officials travelling in the area. It is known that the so-called Lapps' Apostle, Thomas von Westen (see p114), used the hut. Today's building is a reconstruction. There is a variety of Sami exhibits demonstrating their material culture. There is a taxidermic exhibition and the

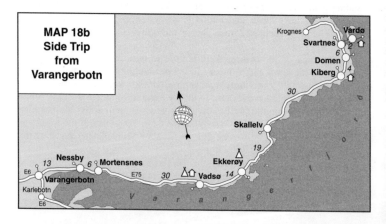

MAP 18b
Side Trip
from
Varangerbotn

private collections of Abraham Mikkelsen, knife-maker to the Finnmark Sami. If you've come all this way, don't neglect to stop here.

A short minor road leads off to the left at **Nyborg** (2km). It runs only a couple of kilometres away from the fjord and it is interesting that there is not a single road which crosses the central or eastern regions of the vast Varanger peninsula. This is Finnmark at its most untouched.

Shortly before reaching **Nessby** (13km) the views to the south begin to improve as you can see the whole of the fjord. A long narrow island, Skåholmen, partly obscures the southern coast but the great size of this fjord is clear enough. Nessby stretches both sides of Route E75 but it is on a minor road, to the right, on a small headland, that you will find the **church**. Built in 1858 and restored in 1983, it is the only wooden church in East Finnmark not to have been burned down in the German retreat in World War II. It is easily seen from the road.

The road keeps close to the fjord edge and the ground rises fairly steeply on the landward side. The partly wooded and boggy slopes reach 300m and look uninviting until they catch the sunlight which sweeps low across the fjord. The higher slopes are treeless and barren. The southern side of Varangerfjorden, with its north-facing slopes, is in shadow for much of the day, even in mid-summer. The Arctic Highway, which uses the southern shore, remains invisible.

At **Mortensnes** (19km) there are the homes of fishermen who set out from the fjord to brave the less tranquil waters of the Barents Sea. Minke whale occasionally seek shelter in Varangerfjorden but sometimes, sadly, become stranded on the beaches. Mortensnes has an Iron Age monolith, the Graksestein, which is surrounded by a stone circle. Grakse is a cod liver oil derivative, but the precise use and meaning of the stone is unclear. The Sami later used it as a ritual stone and there's a marked pathway leading to this **heritage site**.

From Mortensnes, the road moves back a little from the shore but returns to the water's edge at **Vastre Jakobselv** (31km). This is an interesting little fishing village with a fish-product industry. Famous or infamous, depending on your taste, for fish sausages and minced salmon rolls, the village is home to a population of largely Finnish origin. A kilometre further on is a **camping** place, Vestre Jakobselv (see Vadsø)

More, but smaller, fishing hamlets line the path of Route 98 on its next twenty kilometres or so towards **Vadsø** (49km).

VADSØ

The town of Vadsø is an important one. It is the administrative centre for the area and has a long history.

History

The earliest settlers occupied an island, Store Vadøya (formerly Kirkøya), just offshore from the present town. This was common practice throughout North Norway. An island site offered security as well as immediate access to the sea that provided a livelihood. A church was originally built on the island in 1575 but, as the population moved on to the mainland, a new church was erected a little distance from the shoreline in 1710. By 1833, Vadsø had been declared a town by royal charter and it grew in size and importance as a fishing community. Many of the people were, and are, of Finnish origin. Nineteenth-century growth was fuelled by Finns as the population of north Finland outgrew its farming potential during decades of poor harvests. The Varangerfjord, in contrast, was in need of labour as fishing and trade with Russia was growing.

As a consequence of World War II, the town was almost completely burnt down. The task of reconstruction, in 1945–6, was a daunting one but gave the opportunity to re-plan and saw the construction of a host of fine buildings. Most notable is the church.

The modern town is clean and tidy. The public garden used to be tended by school-children but I'm not sure if that's still the case. Flowers grow under glass and there is a sense of pride in Vadsø. The harbour, built around a natural promontory and sheltered by Vadsøya, is a reminder that apart from its administrative function, the town is still dependent for its economy on the sea.

Services

Vadsø is a compact little town so nothing is far away from the centre. The **tourist office** (☎ 78 95 44 90; 🗏 78 94 28 99; 🖳 museum @vadso.kommune.no) is on the main road (E75) a little east from the centre. It is open only from mid-June to mid-August but you can make enquiries at the museum out of season (see below). Opening hours are 10.00 to 18.00 during the week but it closes at 16.00 at weekends. The **post office** is in W Andersens gt, off the main road near the centre of town. There is a choice of **banks**, while **petrol** stations are on Route 75.

Around the town

Vadsø church is a striking example of the work of Magnus Paulsson. It stands on ris-ing ground just 100m from the E75 as it runs through the centre of the town. A tow-ering façade, with a central 'window' fram-ing a small spire, is crowned by a simple triangular pediment. Not to everyone's taste – it has a 1930s' look about it, or children's building blocks (supposed to represent blocks of ice) – it is none the less interest-ing. The interior is more richly decorated than most of North Norway's churches. The painted altar-piece is especially fine, as are the glass paintings in the choir. The church is usually left open during the day and wel-comes visitors.

Down the slope in front of the church is a rather special monument. This is the Kongestein (**King Stone**) which commem-orates the visit on 1 June 1977 of King Olav of Norway, King Karl-Gustav of Sweden and President Kekkonen of Finland. The stone carries their signatures. The visit marked the international character of this part of Norway.

The Finnish connection is also evident in the town's **library** (*bibliotek*, ☎ 78 96 25 00) which has a fine collection of ancient manuscripts not only from northern Norway but also from north Finland.

The Sami connection with Vadsø's past is on the island just off-shore where there are old dwelling sites dating back to AD1000, as well as an old burial ground

The **museum**, on Oscargate (parallel to the E75, just beyond the town centre; turn left up Skolegate and take first right) is a mixture of Finnish and Norwegian cultur-al exhibits. The mixed origins of the popu-lation are further commemorated by the **Immigration** (*Innvander*) **monument** just west of the church. It was the unveiling of this monument which brought the national leaders to Vadsø in June 1977 (see above).

The **Rådhus** (town hall) at the centre of town, to the right of the E75, was built as a reconstruction monument, marking the huge undertaking in rebuilding Finnmark after World War II. Over 10,000 houses and a score of hospitals and churches had been destroyed together with over 100 schools.

A turning to the right in the centre of the town leads you down to a bridge linking the mainland with the island. Not only is this a good way to see the harbour but there is also the *Luftskipsmasten* – the airship mooring mast used by the polar explorer Roald Amundsen in 1926.

Vadsø has a STOL **airport** (☎ 78 95 22 88) just over 2km east of the town and signposted off the E75.

Accommodation

The *Rica Hotel* (☎ 78 95 16 81; fax : 78 95 10 02; 🖳 rica.vadsoe.hotel@rica.no) is the best in town. It stands back from the E75, on the left as you drive eastward with the entrance on Oscargt. It is often fully booked, reflecting the town's importance as a business and administrative centre. It is unpretentious but has 68 comfortable rooms with facilities. Some of the standard rooms are rather small but at least one suite has its own sauna. There is also a sauna in the basement, making it the only sauna in the world that's located in what doubles as a nuclear fall-out shelter. The bar, with a disco, is well patronized by local people and has an old British red telephone kiosk among its furnishings. The restaurant (Oscar Mat og Vinhus) is fairly simple but adequate. There is ample parking outside the hotel. Prices start at NOK850 for a double room and breakfast is included.

On the island, and cheaper, is the *Vadsø Hotell og Konferanse* (formerly Lallas Hotel, ☎ 78 95 33 35; 🖹 78 95 34 35). It has 30 double rooms, simply furnished and not all en suite. The rates here are from NOK550.

Vadsø Apartments (☎ 78 95 44 00) are on Tibergveinen by the harbour. This is a self-catering and inexpensive option with prices around NOK450.

If you're camping you need to stop before you reach the town at *Vestre Jakobselv Camping* (☎ 78 95 60 64; 🖹 78 95 65 32). The site is to the left of the E75 up a slope. There are 18 cabins and ample space for tents. Unfortunately, the rather bare site is somewhat exposed so be prepared if the weather is stormy. Rates are inexpensive. A cabin with 6 beds will cost only NOK350.

Where to eat

Apart from the two hotels, there's not a lot of choice. There's a pizza-bar and the inevitable Chinese restaurant, both down by the harbour, but little else. If you want something better, drive on to Ekkerøy (see below) 15km to the east.

From Vadsø to Vardø

Beyond Vadsø you get a general change to the views from the E75. The fjord begins to widen significantly and the southern shore of Varangerfjorden gradually slips further and further away. Eventually, near to Vardø, the other side of the fjord is no longer Norway but Russia.

On the landward side of the road, the cliffs stand back away from the shoreline and the E75 has a broader lowland from which to choose its path. In fact it runs across the wavecut platform which is characteristic of this coastline. You are seeing another example of an emergent coast, complete with former sea stacks now rising high and dry as outliers of the cliffs. This is the isostatic recovery of the land (see p42). Elsewhere, strong winds which drive into the fjord have blown sand on to the shore creating dunes which choke the sparse vegetation.

There is even less settlement east of Vadsø and for long stretches the road's only company is that of sheep which manage to find a foothold on the near-vertical cliffs to the left of the road. When you come across a small fishing hamlet it often has some feature of special interest. Such is the case with **Ekkerøy** (63km). The hamlet stretches from the mainland via a causeway to Store Ekkerøya. There are **cabins** and a decent **restaurant**. A minor road to the right of the E75 runs just over one kilometre on to the island. The cliffs here form the nesting place of a variety of birds including black-billed gulls and guillemots. The area is easily approached by footpaths and makes an interesting diversion. There are Viking graves on Ekkerøya.

Through **Skallelv** (82km), a largely Finnish speaking hamlet, the road crosses an important river, Komagelva, at **Komagvær** (93km). This little settlement was an important German post in World War II and a joint Norwegian–Russian group raided the valley, Komagdal, in 1941.

On the E75 you occasionally leave the shoreline but at **Kiberg** (112km), where there are **rooms** for hire, a change occurs. Having reached the eastern extremity of Norway, the road turns northwards and slightly inland. Kiberg was another of the German defence posts here in World War II. Heavy artillery was placed to guard the entrance to the fjord and some of the gun emplacements and their bunkers are still just visible (turn right off the E75 and travel through the hamlet).

The road rises away from the coast to reach over 100m near **Domen** (116km) where, unsurprisingly, given the splendid views eastwards into the open mouth of the fjord, yet another German artillery post was built. A minor road down to the right off the E75 leads towards the remains of the fortifications. To the left of the E75 rises Mount Domen, said to be the meeting place of witches in the seventeenth century. According to the ancient story, the witches were said to meet the Devil in a cave at the foot of the mountain at Christmas and on Midsummer's Eve.

After passing the small Vardø **airfield** (☎ 78 98 81 80) at **Svartnes** (122km) there is a choice of routes. You can either continue to Vardø on E75, or take the minor road (341) towards Hammingberg (see p288).

To reach Vardø, the E75 turns right and passes through the tunnel, Ishavstunnelen, under the sea to emerge on the island of Vardøya. **Vardø** (124km) is the most easterly settlement in Norway. It was known as the *Ultima Thule*, the extreme of extremes or end of the world, in the Middle Ages. It is on almost the same longitude as Cairo (31° East).

The tunnel, Norway's first under the sea, was opened in 1982. The road descends almost 90m below sea-level to make the 1.7km link. It was built not to help the islanders reach the mainland, but to keep them on the island! It was considered worth spending about NOK60,000 per island inhabitant on this project in order to persuade them that they were not so isolated as they thought.

Accommodation and where to eat: Vadsø to Vardø

At Ekkerøy there are four cabins. One is the *Ekkerøy Feriehus* (☎ 90 89 15 58) which sleeps six, with rates around NOK600. It is available from March to September inclusive. *Havesten* (☎ 90 50 60 80) has three cabins and a restaurant serving excellent meals: try the fresh fish dishes. The cabins and restaurant are open only from late June to mid-August.

The company which runs Vardø's information office, *Hexeria* (☎ 78 98 84 04; 🖷 78 98 84 05), has rooms to let at Kiberg. None is serviced so there's no choice other than self-catering. The modest and variable prices are all under NOK500.

VARDØ

The town is interesting but not attractive. I once described it as the most unattractive and depressing settlement that I had visited anywhere. Perhaps that was a little unfair but even in the sixteenth century an English account of the settlement called it 'a miserable place' and a sailor mistook its tiny church for a reindeer!

History

Vardø has a place in the history of sorcery. During the seventeenth century, 80 women were tried in the town, found guilty of witchcraft and burned to death. Vardø became known throughout Norway as 'Witches Town' (see also Domen, above). In 1992 a musical was written about witchcraft in Norway. Although successful in Norway, it failed to impress the critics elsewhere.

The most famous landmark on the island is its fort. A church had been built on the island in 1307 and it was followed by a fort as a protection from Russians and Swedes who showed more than a passing interest in fishing the seas around Varangerfjorden. Vardø obtained the status of town in 1789 and shortly afterwards became Norway's largest fishing settlement.

When Paul du Chaillu visited in the late 1870s he reported that there was a population of 1200. Today it is only just double that. He recorded that the town 'had an unfinished appearance; some of the houses painted, others not, and, owing to the ground, there was no symmetry in the arrangements of the streets.' At that time, according to Chaillu, the fort was manned by fishermen and that 'on account of the small pay, six of the garrison fish for the commandant, three for the lieutenant and two for the doctor.' Today, the pay is in kroner and the garrison is from the Royal Norwegian Navy.

During the Cold War, Vardø had a special significance for NATO.

This is as isolated a community as any in all Scandinavia. When the sun reappears after the long period of total darkness (27 November to 20 January) a gun is fired and the school children have a day's holiday.

Two small islands, Reinøya and Hornøya, to the north, just beat Vardøya's claim to be Norway's most easterly territory.

Services

Vardø's **tourist office** (☎/🖷 78 98 84 04; 🖳 contact@hexeria.no) is opposite the Nordpol Kro tavern on Kaigata. Remarkably it is open all year with the hours of 09.00 to 17.00 on weekdays in winter. In summer, the office is open from 09.00 to 19.00 Monday to Saturday, with Sunday opening from 12.00 to 19.00. It's difficult to believe that the office is kept very busy but at least it is customer friendly, perhaps because it is commercially run. The office will sell you a diploma to confirm that by using the tunnel you have travelled under the Arctic Ocean and the Barents Sea!

There are two **banks** on Strandgata, K-Bank and SpareBank 1 Nord-Norge. The **post office** is on Kirkegata and there are a number of **petrol** stations.

Around the town

The **fort**, Vardøhus Festnig, is located off Pers Larssens gate which is on the west side of the island. A direct approach is along Festingsgate from the centre of the town. The octagonal fortress of today replaces the old fort but still dates back to the period 1734–8. (It was dismantled in the late eighteenth century, but re-equipped in 1800.) There's not an awful lot to see but it is open daily from 08.00 to 21.00 in summer and until 18.00 in winter. Entrance is NOK20.

There is a small and well-appointed **museum** (☎/🖷 78 98 80 75; 🖳 vardomuse @c2i.net) 300m from the fort entrance which has exhibits telling the story of the area's natural and cultural history. From mid-June to mid-August it is open from 09.00 to 18.30 every day. For the rest of the year it's open on weekdays from 09.00 to 15.00. The entrance fee is NOK20 with concessions.

Vardøya's only tree is outside the naval commander's quarters. A rowan, it is protected by covers against the harsh winters. In the town square is a **statue** to Fridtjof Nansen.

There are, in fact, two islands making up Vardøya and they are connected by a bridge. On the eastern island is the **church**, rebuilt in 1958 as the fourth on the same site. Kirkegata leads directly to the church across the narrow strait separating the two islands.

Accommodation

There's a hotel, a guesthouse and a camping site.

Vardø Hotel (☎/🖷 78 98 80 75; 🖳 vard omuse@c2i.net) is at the centre of the town. There are 40 comfortable if simple rooms which cater more for business people than tourists. There's a restaurant and café.

Gjestegården (☎ 78 98 75 29) is on Strandgata. There are just five rooms and no services, not even a café. It's cheap but not too cheerful.

The camping site is best ignored.

On from Vardø

The alternative to the tunnel route into Vardø is Route 341, which leads off the E75 towards Hammingberg. This was an important little fishing village before World War II but is now deserted in winter and only comes to life with holidaymakers in summer. The journey to **Hammingberg** is all of 35km. After an inland journey of ten kilometres, the shore of an inlet, called Persfjorden, is reached and the landscape is quite extraordinary. It has been compared by some to the features on the moon, particularly the rock formations; if you've got the time, see what you think.

The Highway: Varangerbotn to Brannsletta
MAP 19

The Arctic Highway turns right out of Varangerbotn running southward behind the peninsula which separates Meskfjorden and Karlebotn at the head of the Varangerfjord. The 126-kilometre section of the Highway between Varangerbotn and Kirkenes is the least heavily trafficked and for more than half of its route it turns its back on the coast and runs inland through wild uninhabited country. You should refuel in Varangerbotn because there is a shortage of petrol stations on this route.

At the head of **Karlebotn** (205km) is a village of the same name which is of considerable historic interest. Almost continuous settlement can be traced here from the Stone Age Komsa culture. The Gropengbakken site has yielded a number of finds, especially in the middle beach terrace where nearly ninety subsites have been located. The Sami used to hunt seal and trap whales in the shallow waters of the inlet; their descendants have settled on the shore and are content with fishing.

Up to the end of the nineteenth century, Karlebotn was the main trading port for East Finnmark. It had its own courthouse and prison and an annual fair was held. Now Vadsø (see side trip to Vadsø p282) has become the fjord's leading settlement. However, Karlebotn has an important boarding school drawing pupils from a wide area. On the hill above the school are examples of *palsas*, huge peat mounds with ice cores. These are typical periglacial features in an area of permafrost.

The Highway has been built to go round rather than through Karlebotn and you quickly turn eastward after the village to travel along the southern shore of Varangerfjorden. This southern side of the fjord is bleak and without the farming or other settlements that fringe the north coast. Aspect is the main explanation as to why there are no inhabitants but the very broken surface of the land is also a deterrent. Inland from the Highway the landscape is almost unearthly. Scarred rock surfaces, weathered and without vegetation, gentle streams flowing from black mountains: it all seems just a little unwelcoming.

Yet if you look northwards from those points where the fjord comes into view, then the contrast is manifest. Illuminated by the weak Arctic sun, the other side of the fjord is altogether different. Here the greens and browns of vegetation form a background to the glistening pink-white and grey-white rock scars. Behind, mountains rise to snow-flecked peaks and the northern fjord coast is lined by a scattering of brightly painted farms. Of course, in winter all will be smothered by snow and obscured by enveloping darkness.

In the fjord, small islands of rock are crowned with white-painted warning beacons and in the bays on this southern shore lie fishing hamlets with a mere handful of farms. These hamlets enjoy sites of unforgettable beauty. Sheltered within the bays, small boats bob up and down on the blue-green waters. Red and yellow, white and blue, wooden houses stand on the shore. Hay is out to dry on the beaches and in the Lilliputian fields.

This is the place to have your camera at the ready, especially if the sun is shining. Because the angle of the sun is never very high at these latitudes, photography can produce excellent results even towards noon.

The two most delightful hamlets you'll pass by on the Highway are **Grasbaken** (219km) in Veinesbukta and **Gandvik** (237km) in Gandvika. Grasbaken has a substantial jetty and its farming includes a flock of sheep. There is evidence here of a Stone Age settlement and there is thought to have been continuous habitation round the bay for nearly 3000 years. Gandvik, 18km further on – and after some of the best views across and

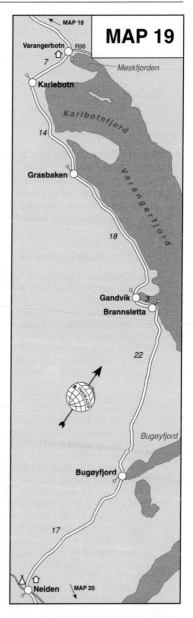

back down the fjord – is delightfully situated. The hamlet is set around an exceptionally well-sheltered cove protected by mountain walls. On the headland to the west there is a Sami **ritual site** of ancient origin. Rather more modern and more visible, there are the near-vertical pipes which channel water off the mountains to feed a small hydro-electricity plant. There used to be camping here but no longer.

You will see many reminders of the Finnish influence in this part of Norway. Overnight accommodation at farms around Varangerfjorden is often advertised in Finnish and much of the population of East Finnmark is not Norwegian but Finnish or Sami.

Accommodation: Varangerbotn to Brannsletta

Apart from the occasional bed-and-breakfast accommodation at farms along the road, there is nothing on this section of the Highway. Even when *overnatting* is advertised along the road you cannot be sure that the farmer will actually be offering anything at the time you're passing. The only options here are to go down to Bugøynes (see below) or to continue on the Highway to Neiden or Kirkenes.

SIDE TRIP FROM BRANNSLETTA TO BUGØYNES

If you've got the time to spare for a 42km round trip, then don't miss this visit to **Bugøynes**. The village is charming, the views wonderful and there's an interesting story.

The turning for Bugøynes is just three kilometres from Gandvik, at **Brannsletta** (240km). A minor road leads off to the left from where (on the left) you can see the raised beaches of the former shorelines which have been exposed as the ice has gone. The road runs along the edge of the fjord for 21km giving you excellent views to the northern shore. Quite suddenly the village comes into view to the left and lower than the road. The road actually stops at this headland and was built with the sole purpose of serving the village which hitherto had been obliged to rely on sea communications. **Bugøynes** is a gem.

Its setting is at the end of the headland formed by the high Bugøynesfjell (rising to 461m) and in a cove itself sheltered by a small island. Not only is the setting quite beautiful but it has the added charm of a collection of old wooden buildings which survived the retreat-and-destroy policy of the German army at the end of World War II. Some buildings, such as the *Lassi* House, date from the mid-nineteenth century. Here then is a small fishing village which still has some of the appearance of a pre-war settlement. The cluster of small houses, competing for space, reminds me of a small Cornish village.

Bugøynes is more Finnish than Norwegian; witness the names on the tombstones in the graveyard, the style of some of the buildings and the language spoken in the street. Today, the village of around 250 people has a fish-processing plant for salmon and, later in the season, king crab. King crab, from Russia, is now being farmed by the villagers. It's claimed that a good specimen can weigh 12kg.

There's a small hotel, ***Bugøynes Opplevelser*** (Experience or Adventure Hotel; ☎ 78 99 03 75; 🖷 78 99 22 27; 🖳 bo-a@online.no). It is on Nesseveien

---

A village is spared

When the German army retreated from North Norway at the end of World War II, its policy was to destroy all buildings, bridges and industrial plants, while the population was either forcibly evacuated to the south or simply left to its own devices. It wasn't difficult to destroy buildings; they were wooden and could easily be burnt down. As a rule, only the occasional stone-built church survived.

There is something of a mystery surrounding Bugøynes. Why was it spared? Was it because of its Finnish connections? This seems unlikely because of the way the German army treated northern Finland. If you question some of the older inhabitants of the village the reason is simply explained.

Just off the shore by the village is a small island which housed a German garrison; the bunkers and ammunition store can still be seen. During the war, the German commander, a Lieutenant Flack, and his troops developed unusually good relations with the village. When the time to retreat came, the commander ignored the order to destroy the village and Bugøynes was too out of the way for the High Command to notice this act of clemency. Bugøynes survived. In return, the villagers ferried the Germans to safety across the fjord.

After the war the villagers were embarrassed by their good fortune and all sorts of stories were invented to explain their situation. Unfortunately, most of the stories tended to show the village in a poor light and the accusation of collaboration was levelled. Today, Bugøynes is rather proud of its old buildings and thankful for its good luck in benefiting from a rare spark of humanity.

---

and also has a clutch of cabins. Rates are generally under NOK500 and it's open all year. If you just want a meal, you can eat locally produced food, including crab, in the hotel's *Lassigården* restaurant situated in an old merchant's house. However, the restaurant is open for non-residents from late May to late September only.

The Highway: Brannsletta to Kirkenes
MAPS 19–20

From Brannsletta, the junction for Bugøynes, the Arctic Highway turns away from Varangerfjord to take an inland and near southerly path. In fact, it never returns to the open fjord, except where it runs tangent to some of the fjord's inlets. You start this part of the route with a climb on a steep gradient to a hilly pass across the neck of the Bugøynes peninsula. It reaches an altitude of over 150m and, momentarily out of the pass, you can get a fleeting view of Varangerfjorden with its shallow bay-head beaches. Then all again is desolate: lakes, frost-shattered rocks, valleys choked with rock debris.

After crossing into the Highway's final kommune, Sør-Varanger (South Varanger), the road runs alongside (to the right) Lake Hauksjøen, sinuous and beautiful. The lake rests on the top of the plateau and drains south-eastward towards Bugøyfjord. The Highway follows the Hauksjøen valley which widens and fills with birch. After crossing the river, the road passes through **Sopnesmyra** (259km) where there is a turning on a minor road to the left towards a little fishing settlement at Karisari. Just over a kilometre further on a similar small road leads to another fishing hamlet at Valen. Both of these short roads are less than two kilometres in length.

The Highway descends into a larger village: **Bugøyfjord** (262km). This is at the head of the fjord of the same name, an inlet from the great Varangerfjord. (Bugøynes is at its mouth.) This is another of those international villages like Skibotn (see p201) and Bossekop (p219), which attracted Finns, Norwegians and Sami to its market; here, too, came Russians. A special importance is attached to Bugøyfjord because it was here that the old winter snow road from Inari (see p107) in Finland reached the sea. You cannot see the main Varangerfjord from the Bugøyfjord; in fact the inlet has such a narrow exit that, from the village, it appears to be enclosed like a mountain lake. There is a public telephone, shop and petrol station in the village.

The southern perimeter of Bugøyfjord is well farmed as far as Vagge on its eastern side but, as the Highway turns away from the inlet, it climbs up the wide valley of Klokkerelva which forms the road's path over the plateau separating Bugøyfjorden from the Neiden fjord. The plateau is ill-drained. Two great marshes, Fødesmyrene (also Fædesmyra) and Sakrismyrene, cover the surface as the road climbs to over 150m.

This area is typically periglacial in character, affected by permafrost. The superficial cover is peaty and, again, there are ice-cored mounds (palsas). Where root-holds exist, there is dwarf birch. This area has always caused problems to the road builders and in the days of the water-bound gravel Highway it used to be very poor and badly affected by frost action. It is much better now but there are still some programmes of improvement to be completed.

As the Highway swings round the mountainous Norskelvfjell, it drops from the plateau to the valley of Neidenelva. This river rises in Finland but in this its lower, Norwegian course, it provides a wide and fertile valley. This is carefully cultivated and has a long history of settlement. The village is effectively divided into two by the river and a waterfall on its course, Skoltefossen.

The Arctic Highway crosses the river above the falls at **Neiden** (279km). A road immediately after the bridge, to the right, runs for 11km to the Finnish border (see Approach Routes VII and IX, Part 3, p91 and p110). This is Route 893. A border crossing is possible to join the Finnish Route 971.

Neiden is a village which has grown rapidly in recent times. Much of the growth is due to tourism and the fact that the Neidenelv is another of Finnmark's famous salmon rivers. It has a range of services: a food store, petrol station, **post office**, a good **hotel**, **camping** and a **cafeteria**. Strictly only that part of the village above the falls is Neiden, the rest of the settlement is Skoltebyen (literally: 'The Town of the Skolts', or of the 'Skolt Sami').

It is this Sami connection which gives the village its major attraction, a tiny log chapel only a few metres square with space for perhaps six or eight people.

It's in a field to the left of the Highway, just before the bridge. This was the Eastern Sami community's **Orthodox chapel**, dedicated to St George and originally built here in the sixteenth century. Over time, disputes over territory and culture led to the retreat of the Eastern Sami into Russia. However, services are still held in the field outside the building and, if you're around on the last Sunday in August, you are in for a treat. This is the occasion of a special mass celebrated in front of a large congregation. If you miss that date, you can usually get the key to the chapel from the farm by the campsite.

There is also a **stave church** in the village, to the left and back from the Highway, which was built at the beginning of the last century. You can also visit a restored **Finnish farmhouse**, the Labahå Farm. Seine fishing takes place at Skoltefossen between the end of June and mid-August. Net-fishing is an old Sami tradition (*lievjeled*) adopted by the Norwegians (*kåppålå*).

The lower part of the River Neiden is deeply incised between sand and gravel terraces as it meanders towards the fjord. On the Highway, however, you move away from the river mouth as the road leaves the village and passes over a low marshy depression to the head of Munkfjorden, an arm of Neidenfjorden. A brand new bridge crosses the Munkelv (287km) then follows and the road turns north-eastward to the steep edge of the inlet to trace an undulating path along its eastern shore. Two or three houses are built on each of the flats that protrude into the fjord and the views from the road are pleasing if not spectacular. If the wind is blowing from the north this can be an especially cold area even in midsummer.

The eastern shoreline of Munkfjorden (the outer part is Neidenfjorden), which you drive along here, is broken by a narrow strait linking this fjord to the Korsfjord. The whole of this part of the Sør-Varanger coast is fragmented by inter-connecting fjords separated by rocky peninsulas and islands. You can see something of the coast from the Highway but the open Varangerfjord is never in view. From **Tusenvik** (307km) the road cuts across the marshy neck of Tømmernes, rising to 100m.

Now that the Cold War seems like ancient history, most of the prohibitions which used to mark these final few kilometres to the Russian border have been relaxed although it is still a military zone for 8km. There are the usual notices, in five languages (now including Russian) warning against camping, photography and stopping. In the past, it seemed just a little ironic that there is a war memorial to the Russians who died in the liberation of Finnmark set beside the Highway.

At **Høybuktmoen** (310km) a road leads off to the left to Kirkenes **Airport** (☎ 78 97 04 00) which has regular services with Oslo and Helsinki. The original airport was built by the Germans during the occupation to serve aircraft which harassed the Allied convoys to Russia. From the airport you descend towards Langfjorden. The river, which links the fjord-head with the lake, Langfjordvatnet – a narrow body of water about 30km long – is crossed by the post-war Straumen bridge.

With a short climb over a rocky ridge, the Highway enters **Hesseng** (317km), a suburb of Kirkenes where the road to Pasvik (see side trip, p299) leads off left and southwards. There are **cabins** here. You enter **Kirkenes** (324km) through a residential district and alongside the old ore railway.

The Arctic Highway has reached its destination. Your journey has been over 1520km or 944 miles from Mo i Rana on one of the world's great roads, all but a small fraction of which is inside the Polar Circle. Unfortunately no one has (yet) thought of providing a certificate to prove your achievement!

Accommodation: Brannsletta to Kirkenes

Only Neiden has accommodation on this leg of the Highway.

Neidenelven Turisthotell (☎ 78 9961 69; ▤ 78 99 61 68) stands to the left of the Highway with a big polar bear pointing the way. The hotel is the best around and although it has something of the appearance of a roadhouse, it is remarkably comfortable with a good restaurant and public rooms. The bedrooms are en suite and simply furnished but there is one suite complete with its own sauna and whirlpool. For those who like their saunas, the hotel has two more, one of which is heated by a wood stove in the traditional fashion. The hotel, popular with Russian guests, is open all year with rates around NOK800.

Also to the left of the Highway, as you come into the village, is *Neidenelven Camping and Motel* (☎ 78 99 62 03; ▤ 78 99 31 44; ⌨ camping @neidenelven.no), partly hidden in trees. This has a big **café** with a bar and no less than six saunas, four of which are wood burning. The site is not especially attractive but it is open all year. There are 13 cabins; three are fully fitted with their own toilets, showers, TV, kitchen and, you've guessed, electric sauna. They cost around NOK900. The other ten cabins have TV and kitchen but no water. These cost NOK350 and have the use of the six extra saunas. There's plenty of camping space.

Away from Neiden but only 5km up Route 893, towards the Finnish border, is *Neiden Fjellstue* (☎ 78 99 61 41; ▤ 78 99 61 88) and **café**, open all year. This comprises 14 simple cabins and a campsite with rates around NOK350. A bonus is that you can eat in a Sami *lavvu* (tent). You are pretty certain to be offered salmon or reindeer.

KIRKENES

Kirkenes lies at latitude 69° 44' North so it is not at the most northerly point on the Highway but it is still as far north as central Greenland. It is, of course, at the most easterly point of the road and, at 30° 10' East it is as far east as Istanbul or Alexandria. Near the entrance to the town is a signpost proclaiming, proudly, that Kirkenes is 5102km from Rome, 2626km from Bergen, 2502km from Oslo and 1154km from Helsinki. It is not without significance and consequence that, in fact, Kirkenes is about as far from Oslo as Oslo is from Rome.

History

It seems almost incredible today that this part of Sør-Varanger did not have clearly defined international boundaries until the mid-1920s. The mix of Norwegians, Finns, Sami and now Russians continues. Kirkenes is a cultural melting pot.

Kirkenes owes its present importance to iron ore. In 1900 there were only four or five houses on the headland which extends into Bøkfjorden. Today the population exceeds five thousand in the area. The discovery, in 1902, of sedimentary iron deposits just eleven kilometres to the south at Bjørnevatn (Bear Lake) quickly led to an influx of people from south and central Norway as well as from Sweden and Finland.

Mining began in 1906 and the first low phosphorus high-grade iron concentrate was produced in 1910. The two world wars brought crises to the mines but they survived, helped in 1948–52 by state loans and Marshall Aid. The railway, carrying ore from the mines to the ore-crushing and upgrading plants in the town and to the port, was possibly the most northerly in the world.

Sadly, the recession in the world's economy in the early 1990s together with increasing costs of production led to the demise, in 1996, of the Sydvaranger mines. Kirkenes' *raison d'être* has gone only to be hurriedly replaced by new state-supported industries. In particular, a new engineering company, Kværnes Kimek, received some NOK200 million and its establishment generated large numbers of new jobs. Ship repairing is now a major employer, too, the ships being largely Russian. The hope is to develop ship building.

No doubt Kirkenes will survive. It has lived through hardship before. During World War II it was subjected to more continuous air raids, 320, than any other place except Malta. At the end of the war, what was left of the town was burnt to the ground by the German army as it retreated along the Highway. As the town lay in ruins from bombing in the summer of 1944 its population was forced to live in the mines. Over 3500 people found shelter there and no less than ten children had the Sydvaranger mines recorded as their birthplace.

The Russian army drove out the Germans but there was a politically tense period of almost a year before they themselves withdrew and reconstruction could begin. Today's town is laid out on a grid-iron plan and has most of the hallmarks of hurried reconstruction. Clearly, its people have a strong sense of purpose and it is unlike most Arctic settlements in appearance.

Despite its isolation, Kirkenes is well served by communications. Notably there is the Arctic Highway and the airport but its port is also the terminus for the Hurtigrute.

In very recent times Kirkenes has grown in importance by virtue of its proximity to the Russian border. Trade of a sort has begun even if it is only the export of second-hand car tyres and other cast-offs. There is also a growing number of Russians who come into Kirkenes to sell all manner of goods from street stalls. It has been estimated that on a good day they can earn the equivalent of six months' wages in Russia. These street markets are now regulated. Around 400 Russian women live in the town, married to Norwegians. The sex ratio favours men in Kirkenes' Norwegian population.

Services

The **tourist office** (☎ 78 99 25 44; 🖹 78 99 25 25; 🖂 postmottak@sor-varanger.kom mune.no) is on Kjelland Torkildsens gate, the same road as the Rica Arctic Hotel (see p297), in the centre of town. It is open all year but only on weekdays out of season (mid-August to June) and between 08.30 and 16.30. In summer the hours are 08.30 to 18.00 except on Saturdays and Sundays when it opens at 11.00. In fact, opening and closing times seem to be pretty flexible.

There are two **banks** on Wiulls gate, the next road down towards the harbour from the information office. The **post office** is on Kirkegt, just west of the town's main church. As befits this 'capital' of Sør-Varanger, there is a good range of **shops**, a **hospital** and plenty of car servicing and petrol stations. This is the place to restock

and to get any necessary repair work done on your vehicle before you turn round for the long drive home.

Around the town

Frankly, there's not a lot to see in the town and, if you're here on a Sunday, you may begin to wonder whether anyone lives here, or why. On weekdays the streets fill but it never sheds its workaday demeanour.

Perhaps it's not too surprising that World War II is the theme of much of what there is to see. In the centre of town, in the square, is the **Mothers' of the War**

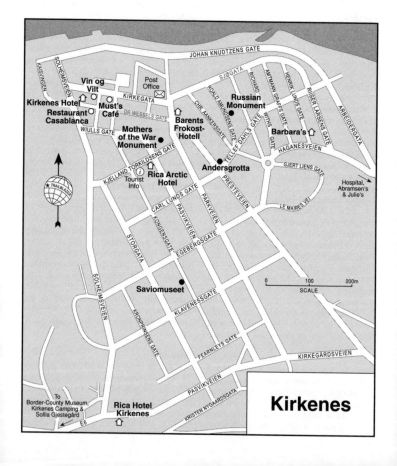

Monument. The women of Kirkenes played a very significant role in supporting the civilian population during the German occupation.

To appreciate the horrors of the war, make a visit to **Andersgrotta** (☎ 78 99 25 44). This is the vast air-raid shelter which protected the inhabitants of the town during the many hundreds of air attacks. The cave was blasted out of the rock early in the war and it is open to the public during the summer with a short film being shown two or three times a day. It's best to check with the tourist office for timings. In winter (mid-August to mid-June) the shelter will be opened on request. Entrance is NOK100.

If you turn into Roald Amundsens Gate (left) from the Andersgrotta you'll find the **Russian Monument**. This is in honour of the Russian liberators in 1944.

Another museum worth looking for is the **Border-Country Museum** (☎ 78 99 48 80). It is located just on the edge of town, off the Highway. As you come into town look (right) for Kristens Nygaards Gt. Turn up here and immediately look for signs. Again the accent is on the war but there's much else of interest concerning the frontier position of the town and its surroundings. There's a **café** at the museum. Entrance is NOK30 and the museum is open all year but closes at 15.00 in winter.

A different sort of museum is **Saviomuseet** (the Savio Museum, ☎ 78 99 92 12). This is really an art gallery exhibiting the work of John Savio (1902–1938). Savio is seen as the first 'educated' Sami artist and something of a role model for the Sami as a whole. The museum has some 300 of his works with some 100 on display at any one time. There are also exhibitions on the art of today's Sami. Open in the summer from 10.00 to 16.00, it shuts two hours earlier at the weekend. To find the building, turn up Kongensgate from the tourist office and it is about 400m up this street on the right. Entrance is NOK30.

Accommodation

There are two Rica hotels in the town. The better, and more modern, is the *Rica Arctic Hotel* (☎ 78 99 29 29; 🖷 78 99 53 25; 🖳 rica.arctic.hotel@rica.no). This is in the centre of town, on the corner of Pasvikvn and Kjelland Torkildsens gate, less than 100m from the tourist office. It's very clearly a businessman's hotel but comfortable and gives good service. There's a sizeable restaurant on the ground floor and the sauna, solarium and swimming pool are a bonus. Even with two suites, 20 double rooms and 68 singles, you would be well advised to book if it's midweek. Strangely, it closes for Christmas week but the other Rica may be open then. Rates are the same for both Rica hotels. Expect to pay around NOK1000.

The *Rica Hotel Kirkenes* (☎ 78 99 14 91; 🖷 78 99 13 56; 🖳 rica.kirkenes.hotel@rica.no) held pride of place before its sister hotel was built. Now it's looking a little tired after almost fifty years but still has a certain charm. Built on the hill behind the town, some of the rooms have good views. Ask for one of these, not those that overlook the car-park. It's easy enough to find. As you come into the town on the Arctic Highway, you should see it to your right before the road dips down to the town centre. There's a good restaurant and the usual sauna and solarium but no pool. It is altogether quieter and more homely than the Rica Arctic. There are 65 en-suite rooms and better parking than for the Rica Arctic where on-street is the only option.

There is a small, slightly scruffy hotel in the town centre on Prestevn, *Barents Frokosthotell* (☎ 78 99 32 99; 🖷 78 99 30 96). It seems to have been taken over by Russians and, as the name suggests, is a bed and breakfast establishment. A few rooms have bathrooms attached. There are just 14 rooms and prices hover around NOK500.

The *Kirkenes Hotel* (☎/🖷 78 99 21 68; 🖳 katinen@on-line.no) has been renovated recently after acting as a refuge for asylum seekers for a year or two. It is on Dr Wessels Gate at the centre of town. It is the nearest that Kirkenes gets to offering youth hostel accommodation. There are 29 rooms and, depending on whether you bring your own bedding, prices are between NOK350 and around NOK450.

There are three small bed-and-breakfast boarding houses in the town. Evening meals may be possible if ordered in advance or you may be allowed to use the kitchen and cook for yourself. *Barbara's* (☎ 78 99 32 07), *Abrahamsen's* (☎ 78 99 12 48) and *Julie's* (book through the tourist office) all have two rooms, a single and a double, and all charge NOK250 for the single and NOK400 for the double. It may make a nice change to stay somewhere that is as small and friendly as these B&Bs. All have parking available.

Outside town near Hesseng, just off the Highway and to the left, about one kilometre from the river bridge and seven kilometres from Kirkenes town centre (see p294), is *Kirkenes Camping* (☎ 78 99 80 28; ▤ 78 99 07 61). There are 16 cabins each with 4 beds but no water in the cabins. It's not especially attractive but one of only two places if you're camping or self-catering. Cabin prices range from around NOK200 to NOK350 according to size and facilities. There is a little **café** at reception which is open from 10.00 to 22.00. The site closes in October and reopens in June.

The road out to the Russian border (see p298) has a gem, tucked away to the left of the road in forest at Sollia. This is *Sollia Gjestegård* (☎ 78 99 08 20; ▤ 78 99 07 61), more of a **restaurant** than a place to stay. However, there are six cabins at around NOK600 and the dining-room in the fine old house is very attractive, looking out over a lake. It's not easy to find so ask rather than driving around.

Where to eat

On Kirkegt is *Must's Café* which serves cakes and bread rolls during normal shop hours. It is quite small, seating only fourteen. Opposite is *Vin og Vilt*, a real gourmet restaurant. Smoked tongue of reindeer is a starter at NOK85 and deserts may cost NOK115. The main course (reindeer, hare, duck, grouse, fish) will cost around NOK270 to NOK360. Certainly it isn't cheap but in this log-cabin-like restaurant you're assured of an excellent meal.

More basic dishes, in sweet chilli sauce, come at around NOK150 at *Restaurant Casablanca*. This is found behind the Shell garage on the corner of Dr Wessels gate. The menu is varied: Mexican, Indian, Thai, Chinese and Spanish. The authenticity may be questioned.

SIDE TRIPS FROM KIRKENES

Having reached the 'end' of the Arctic Highway, it would be a pity simply to turn back without some investigation of Sør-Varanger, the eastern most part of Norway. There are three options: the Russian border nearest the town, the border out at Grense-Jakobselv, on the coast, and the Pasvik valley. If you're staying a couple of days, do all three. If only one day is available, choose between Grense-Jakobselv and Pasvikdalen.

1   Side trip to the Russian Border   Map 20a

This journey begins by returning along the Arctic Highway for about six kilometres to its junction (to the left) with Route 886. At **Elvenes** (11km) there is another junction. The road, to the left, goes down to the coast but the very minor track to the right leads to the Russian border just one kilometre away. This is not the part of the border shown to tourists. At the end of the track is a simple wire fence (not electrified!). There would seem to be no reason why anyone could not climb the fence and enter Russia unnoticed, but it is not advised!

The border point which most tourists visit comes a further 5km down Route 886 at **Storskog** (16km). This crossing is open but prior permission is necessary. Tourists buy souvenirs from a small hut that has been set up close by. The old notice by the gate which used to bar traffic from entering the Soviet Union is gone. No longer is one warned 'not to shout abuse' across the border. The Norwegian Frontier Commissioner has a house here, to the left of Route 886.

With the Cold War consigned to history, a visit to the border takes on the feel of a pilgrimage. Those who can recall just how impenetrable was this frontier zone, marvel at the heavy trucks which now rumble across the border crossing. On the Russian side of the crossing the road leads south to **Nikel**, an important mining town.

2 To Pasvikdalen Map 20a

This is a round trip of over 200km and, again, it's best to refuel before leaving Kirkenes.

It is probably only the most ardent naturalist who will wish to follow the whole length of Route 885 through a valley which lays claim to be unique. You are more likely to be content with a shorter excursion as far as Steinbakk (see p300) and give yourself a round journey of some 100km.

MAPS
20a & 20b
Side Trips
from Kirkenes

Kirkenes
Hesseng Elvenes
E6
27
Ryeng
Skillebekk
Steinbakk
46
R885 Pasvikelv
RUSSIA
Vaggetem
Nyrud

This trip starts on the Arctic Highway in Kirkenes, travelling back down the Highway and turning right to **Hesseng** (7km) rather than left as for Side trip 1 (p298). At Hesseng, the road to follow is Route 885. The road is adequate-to-good throughout its length. Before World War II, the road was being developed as a link with Finland's Arctic road.

The early part of the route is interesting, not for its wildlife, but for the views it gives of the massive mining area around **Bjørnevatn** (a drained lake). The mining activities collapsed in the face of the early 1990s world economic recession and rising costs of production, but the evidence of a once great industry is still clear to see.

After 3km on Route 885 there is a turning off to the left which will give you good viewpoints of the mining area. If this minor road is followed, take the next right turn and it will rejoin Route 885 after a detour of just 3km.

Once the mines are left behind, Route 885 is through very pretty and well-vegetated countryside. Totally unlike much of East Finnmark, this is an area of tall trees and almost lush vegetation, broken only by river courses and lakes. The coniferous forest of the Pasvik valley is similar to the open taiga (sub-tundra) forest of the Siberian tundra. There is a wealth of wildlife although the chances of meeting a bear are now unfortunately (or fortunately?) rare. More birds will be seen here than in almost any other inland part of North Norway.

At **Ryeng** (34km) a minor turning right takes you to **Strand** where there is the **Sør-Varanger Museum**. This quite substantial building houses an exhibition depicting the natural and cultural history of the Pasvik district. It is probably best to check its somewhat unreliable opening times at the tourist office in Kirkenes or to telephone them direct on ☎ 78 99 51 13.

Route 885 presses on to **Skillebekk** (40km) where a side road leads off to the left to **Svanvik**. In just two kilometres the river is reached and, across the lake section, which is the Pasvikelv's course here, is Russia. A short distance from the border is the Russian mining town of Nikel. You can see it from Svanvik although there are better views into Russia later.

Nikel's intrusive appearance in the natural landscape is a reminder that the whole of the western side of the Kola peninsula is an environmental disaster area. The mineral wealth of this annexed land has been exploited with total disregard for the environment. Rivers are polluted and vast areas laid waste. Small hydro-electric plants have replaced waterfalls and contrast with the natural beauty of the Norwegian side of the border could not be greater.

At Svanvik there is a high school and a **chapel**, but most interesting is a preserved **Døla farm** (Bjørklund gård) which dates from the early settlement of the valley.

Beyond the Skillebekk turning, Route 885 moves back from the river and in just over 5km reaches what is known as 'the 96 mound' or Seksognittihoyden, '96' being the height in metres of a hill which is the site of a small Skolt Sami **monument** in a cemetery. This is to the left of the road but none too easy to find in the forest. It is fenced round and you can recognize it by the Orthodox cross at the head of the log-built monument. It is a reminder that the valley is a traditional homeland of the Skolt (Russian) Sami. The hill is a good viewpoint into Russia.

Steinbakk (49km) might be the point to turn back to Kirkenes and the Arctic Highway. It is possible to take a left turning at Steinbakk and follow a minor road towards the river. In 11km this road rejoins Route 885 and a turning right will take you back to Kirkenes.

If you are especially interested in the unique fauna and flora of Pasvikdalen, continue beyond Steinbakk along Route 885 or explore some of the minor forest roads leading off to the right. Route 885 broadly follows the Pasvik River. At **Vaggetem** (also Tjærebukt, 95km) a forest road leads off to the right towards **Ovre Pasvik National Park**. This road does not go into the park but there are marked walking tracks. The park, just 63 sq km in area, contains Norway's largest area of primeval forest. Almost half the park is forest, the rest being bogland and lake.

Route 885 continues to **Nyrud** (104km), a hamlet near to the river. From Nyrud there are only forest roads towards the Russian border.

3   Side trip to Grense-Jakobselv

Map 20c

For this journey, a 120km round trip, it's best to refuel in Kirkenes.

To reach Grense-Jakobselv is to continue on Route 886, eastward from the border crossing (see p298). The scenery becomes increasingly more wild with the ground surfaces hummocky and clearly affected by permafrost. After sweeping round the head of Jorfjorden the road reaches **Vintervollen** (31km). The name means 'the winter field' and it is from here that, in winter, a snowmobile route replaces Route 886. Before World War II the road stopped three kilometres short of Vintervollen, at **Tånet**, and from

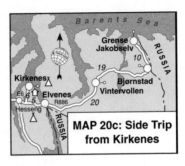

MAP 20c: Side Trip from Kirkenes

there a link road ran south-east and into the Finnish Petsamo corridor. Now that road is a dead-end at the Russian border.

Beyond Vintervollen the feeling of isolation, even desolation, gets stronger. No habitation, little sign of any life, there is just a patchwork of lakes and stunted vegetation. A rise in the road is followed by a descent into the valley of Jakobselva.

At **Bjørnstad** (50km) the road turns northwards and is narrow and poor in quality. (Strictly, this is an unnumbered minor road and not Route 886.) The river is the frontier and Russia lies just metres away from the road, separated only by a broken fence in the trees along the riverbank. There is a small Norwegian guard post at Bjørnstad but on the other side of the river and to the south is a large Russian barracks. On the high cliffs on the Russian side of the river, tall watch-towers still look down on the Norwegian road as it makes its way to the coast and Grense-Jakobselv (60km).

On the left of the road a few hundred metres before the coast is a gaunt stone church. This is King Oscar's Chapel, built in 1869 and later named after King Oscar II (1872–1905). Its construction was symbolic, stressing Norwegian sovereignty over the area and a warning to its Russian neighbours. The little, steepled church has a small cemetery but the building is kept locked. The keys can usually be obtained by enquiring at the small camping site by the shore.

At **Grense-Jakobselv**, apart from the camping site, there is almost nothing but a view to the Barents Sea. With its northern aspect, this is a cold and seemingly a rather unwelcoming place. Maybe, on a rare warm summer's day, the beaches look more attractive and the sea more inviting. On the days that there's a north wind you wonder at the hardiness of the villagers whose home this is.

APPENDIX: LANGUAGES

The words in these short glossaries occur in the text or on maps which the reader is likely to use. Most often they will be found as the suffix to a place name.

NORWEGIAN

The letters æ, ø and å come at the end of the alphabet. The definite article is given to a word by a suffix (-a, -en or -et). Plural forms are generally the suffix -er or -ene.

Norwegian	English	Norwegian	English
bakke	hill	*kjos*	small inlet
bane	railway	*kollen*	knoll
berg	rock	*kommune*	district (part of a fylke)
botn	fjord-head or cirque	*laks*	salmon
bre	glacier	*lille*	little
bru	bridge	*myr*	marsh
bukt	bay	*nedre*	lower
by	town	*nord*	north
dal	valley	*skjær*	skerry
eid	isthmus, col	*skog*	wood
elv	river	*sogn*	parish
fisk	fish	*sted*	place
fjell	mountain divide	*stein*	stone
flat	plain	*stor*	big
flyplass	airfield	*sør*	south
foss	waterfall	*tind*	mountain peak
fylke	county	*tjern*	small lake
gate	street	*topp*	mountain summit
gjestgiveri	guesthouse	*vann*	lake
gård	house, farm	*vatn*	lake
haug	hill	*vei*	road
havn	harbour	*vest*	west
holme	small island	*vidde*	plateau
indre	inner	*vik*	creek, inlet
is	ice or glacier	*vinter*	winter
jokka	river	*voll*	meadow
jord	ground, farmland	*ytre*	outer
kai	quay	*øst*	east
kil	creek	*øy*	island
kirke	church	*ås*	hill

SWEDISH

Swedish is very similar to Norwegian. Even words which are spelt differently but have the same meaning sound almost identical when pronounced. The letters ä and ö come at the end of the alphabet. The definite article is given to a word by a suffix (-n, -en, -t or -et, or -na in some plurals). The plural forms are also generally suffixes (-or, -er, -ar, -n).

Swedish	English	Swedish	English
backe	hill	*liten*	little
bana	railway	*län*	county
berg	rock	*myr*	marsh
bergpass	col	*nedre*	lower
bro	bridge	*nord/norr*	north
bukt	bay	*näs*	isthmus
by	village	*sjö*	lake
dal	valley	*skog*	wood
fisk	fish	*skår*	skerry
fjäll	mountain divide	*slätt*	plain
flod	river	*sten*	stone
flygplats	airfield	*stor*	big
fors	waterfall	*ställe*	place
församling	parish	*söder/syd*	south
gata	street	*tjärn*	small lake
glaciär	glacier	*topp*	mountain peak
gästhem	guesthouse	*vik*	small inlet
hamn	harbour	*vinter*	winter
holme	small island	*väg*	road
höjd	hill	*väster*	west
inre	inner	*yttre*	outer
is	ice	*ö*	island
kaj	quay	*öster*	east
kommun	district	*älv*	river
kyrka	church		

FINNISH

The Finnish language is relatively easy to pronounce (it is largely phonetic with no silent letters) but especially difficult to understand and to use. There are no less than fifteen different case endings for the nouns, no articles and no simple rules for plurals. Swedish is the first language for around 5% of the population and street and place names, particularly in the south and south-west, may be found in both languages.

Finnish	English	Finnish	English
harju	ridge	*ranta kallio*	cliff
joki	river	*rautatie*	railway
järvi	lake	*saari*	island
katu	street	*salmi*	sound
kaupunki	town	*selkä*	ridge
kirkko	church	*silta*	bridge
koski	rapids	*suo*	moorland
kylä	village	*suvanto*	placid waters
laakso	valley	*talo*	house, building
lahti	bay	*tie*	road, route
lautta	ferry boat	*tori*	square
metsä	forest	*torni*	tower
mäki	low hill	*vaara*	hill
palo	fire	*vesi*	water, lake
ranta	shore		

Map Key

	$ Bank		✝ Church / Cathedral
⌂ Place to stay	☆ Police		☿ Bus Station
○ Place to eat	🏛 Museum		⛴ Ferry
✉ Post Office	▤ Library		Λ Campsite
⤴ Internet	(i) Tourist Information		● Other

(Opposite) Top: Karasjok's Old Church (see p265), dating from 1807, is the oldest church in Finnmark. **Bottom**: It's well worth making a side trip from Brannsletta to visit Bugøynes (see p291, *A village is spared*), a relic of pre-WWII days.

(Overleaf) Male reindeer with a magnificent pair of antlers.

INDEX

Notes: **1.** In Scandinavian languages the letters å, æ, ø, ä, and ö are placed at the end of the alphabet. However, for ease of use by readers accustomed to the order of the English alphabet we have indexed words with these letters where they would usually look for them.
2. Suffixes of words often include geographical features. For a list of these see p302
3. Page numbers in **bold** type indicate map references.
4. Abbreviations used: (F) Finland; (R) Russia; (S) Sweden.

Sahara Overland – a route & planning guide *Chris Scott*
1st edition, 544 pages, 24 colour & 150 B&W photos
ISBN 1 873756 26 7 £19.99, Can$44.95 US$29.95
Covers all aspects Saharan, from acquiring documentation to vehicle choice and preparation; from descriptions of the prehistoric art sites of the Libyan Fezzan to the ancient caravan cities of southern Mauritania. How to 'read' sand surfaces, using GPS – it's all here along with 35 detailed off-road itineraries covering over 16,000kms in nine countries. *"THE essential desert companion for anyone planning a Saharan trip on either two wheels or four.'* **Trailbike Magazine**

Tibet Overland – a route & planning guide *Kym McConnell*
1st edition, 224pp, 16pp colour maps
ISBN 1 873756 41 0, £12.99, Can$29.95, US$19.95
Featuring 16pp of full colour mapping based on satellite photographs, this is a guide for mountain bikers and other road users in Tibet. Includes detailed information on over 9000km of overland routes across the world's highest and largest plateau. Includes Lhasa-Kathmandu route and the route to Everest North Base Camp. '..*a wealth of advice...*' **HH The Dalai Lama**

The Silk Roads *Paul Wilson & Dominic Streatfeild-James*
1st edition, 336pp, 50 maps, 30 colour photos
ISBN 1 873756 53 4, £12.99, Can$29.95, US$18.95
The Silk Road was never a single thread but an intricate web of trade routes linking Asia and Europe. This new guide follows all the routes with sections on Turkey, Syria, Iran, Turkmenistan, Uzbekistan, Kyrgyzstan, Pakistan and China.

Trans-Siberian Handbook *Bryn Thomas*
6th edition, 432pp, 52 maps, 40 colour photos
ISBN 1 873756 70 4, £12.99, Can$26.95 US$15.95
First edition short-listed for the **Thomas Cook Guidebook Awards**. New sixth edition of the most popular guide to the world's longest rail journey. How to arrange a trip, plus a km-by-km guide to the routes. Updated and expanded to include extra information on travelling independently in Russia. New mapping.
'*Definitive guide*' **Condé Nast Traveler**

Trans-Canada Rail Guide *Melissa Graham*
3rd edition, 256pp, 32 maps, 30 colour photos
ISDN 1 873756 69 0, £10.99, Can$24.95 , US$16.95
Expanded 3rd edition now includes Calgary city guide. Comprehensive guide to Canada's trans-continental railroad. Covers the entire route from coast to coast. What to see and where to stay in the cities along the line, with information for all budgets.

The Blues Highway New Orleans to Chicago
A travel and music guide *Richard Knight*
2nd edition, 304pp, 50 maps, 30 colour photos
ISBN 1 873756 66 6, £12.99, Can$29.95, US$19.95
New edition of the first travel guide to explore the roots of jazz and blues in the USA. ❑ Detailed city guides with 40 maps ❑ Where to stay, where to eat ❑ The best music clubs and bars ❑ Who's who of jazz and blues ❑ Historic landmarks ❑ Music festivals and events ❑ Exclusive interviews with music legends Wilson Pickett, Ike Turner, Little Milton, Honeyboy Edwards and many more.
'*Fascinating*' – **Time Out**

Europe
Trekking in Corsica
Trekking in the Dolomites
Trekking in the Pyrenees
(and the British Walking Series)

South America
Inca Trail, Cusco & Machu Picchu

Australasia
New Zealand – Great Walks

Africa
Kilimanjaro
Trekking in the Moroccan Atlas

Asia
Trekking in the Annapurna Region
Trekking in the Everest Region
Trekking in Ladakh
Trekking in Langtang
Nepal Mountaineering Guide

Trekking in the Pyrenees *Douglas Streatfeild-James*
2nd edition, £11.99, Can$27.95 US$18.95
ISBN 1 873756 50 X, 320pp, 95 maps, 55 colour photos
All the main trails along the France-Spain border including the GR10 (France) coast to coast hike and the GR11 (Spain) from Roncesvalles to Andorra, plus many shorter routes. 90 route maps include walking times and places to stay. Expanded to include greater coverage of routes in Spain.
'Readily accessible, well-written and most readable...' **John Cleare**

Trekking in Corsica *David Abram*
1st edition, 320pp, 74 maps, 48 colour photos
ISBN 1 873756 63 1, £11.99, Can$26.95, US$18.95
A mountain range rising straight from the sea, Corsica holds the most arrestingly beautiful and diverse landscapes in the Mediterranean. Among the many trails that penetrate its remotest corners, the GR20, which wriggles across the island's watershed, has gained an international reputation. This guide also covers the best of the other routes.
'Excellent guide'. **The Sunday Times**

Trekking in the Dolomites *Henry Stedman*
1st edn, 224pp, 52 trail maps, 13 town plans, 30 colour photos
ISBN 1 873756 34 8, £11.99, Can$27.95, US$17.95
The Dolomites region of northern Italy encompasses some of the most beautiful mountain scenery in Europe. This new guide features selected routes including Alta Via II, a West-East traverse and other trails, plus detailed guides to Cortina, Bolzano, Bressanone and 10 other towns. Also includes full colour flora section and bird identification guide.

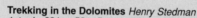

Trekking in Ladakh *Charlie Loram*   Available May 2004
3rd edition, 288 pages, 75 maps, 24 colour photos
ISBN 1 873756 75 5, £11.99, Can$27.95, US$18.95
Since Kashmir became off-limits, foreign visitors to India have been coming to this spectacular Himalayan region in ever-increasing numbers. Fully revised and extended 3rd edition of Charlie Loram's practical guide. Includes 70 detailed walking maps, a Leh city guide plus information on getting to Ladakh. 'Extensive...and well researched'. **Climber Magazine**

The Inca Trail, Cusco & Machu Picchu *Richard Danbury*
2nd edition, 288pp, 45 maps, 35 colour photos
ISBN 1 873756 64 X, £10.99, Can$24.95, US$17.95
The Inca Trail from Cusco to Machu Picchu is South America's most popular hike. This practical guide includes the **Vilcabamba Trail** to the ruins of the last Inca capital, plus guides to Cusco and Machu Picchu.
'Danbury's research is thorough...you need this one'. **The Sunday Times**

West Highland Way *Charlie Loram* **Available now**
1st edition, 192pp, 48 maps, 10 town plans, 40 colour photos
ISBN 1 873756 54 2, £9.99, Can$22.95, US$16.95
Scotland's best-known long distance footpath passes through some of
the most spectacular scenery in all of Britain. From the outskirts of
Glasgow it winds for 95 miles along the wooded banks of Loch Lomond,
across the wilderness of Rannoch Moor to a dramatic finish at the foot
of Britain's highest peak – Ben Nevis. Includes Glasgow city guide.

Cornwall Coast Path *Edith Schofield* **Available now**
1st edition, 192pp, 81 maps & town plans, 40 colour photos
ISBN 1 873756 55 0, £9.99, Can$22.95, US$16.95
A 163-mile National Trail around the western tip of Britain with some
of the best coastal walking in Europe. The footpath takes in secluded
coves, tiny fishing villages, rocky headlands, bustling resorts, wooded estuaries and golden surf-washed beaches.

Pembrokeshire Coast Path *Jim Manthorpe* **Available Nov 2003**
1st edition, 208pp, 80 maps & town plans, 40 colour photos
ISBN 1 873756 56 9, £9.99, Can$22.95, US$16.95
A magnificent 189-mile (304km) footpath around the stunning coast-
line of the Pembrokeshire Coast National Park in south-west Wales.
Renowned for its unspoilt sandy beaches, secluded coves, tiny fish-
ing villages and off-shore islands rich in bird and marine life, this
National Trail provides some of the best coastal walking in Britain.

Offa's Dyke Path *Keith Carter* **Available Dec 2003**
1st edition, 208pp, 86 maps & town plans, 40 colour photos
ISBN 1 873756 59 3, £9.99, Can$22.95, US$16.95
A superb 168-mile National Trail from the Severn Estuary to the north
Wales coast following the line of Offa's Dyke, an impressive 8th-cen-
tury earthwork along the English/Welsh border. The ever-changing
landscape – the Wye Valley, the Black Mountains, the Shropshire Hills
and the Clwydian Hills – is steeped in history and legend.

Pennine Way *Ed de la Billière & K Carter* **Available early 2004**
1st edition, 288pp, 130 maps & town plans, 40 colour photos
ISBN 1 873756 57 7, £10.99, Can$22.95, US$16.95
Britain's best-known National Trail winds for 256 miles over wild moorland and through quiet dales following the backbone of Northern
England. This superb footpath showcases Britain's finest upland
scenery, while touching the literary landscape of the Brontë family and
historical legends along Hadrian's Wall.

Coast to Coast *Henry Stedman* **Available early 2004**
1st edition, 256pp, 95 maps & town plans, 40 colour photos
ISBN 1 873756 58 5, £10.99, Can$22.95, US$16.95
A classic 191-mile (307km) walk across northern England from the
Irish Sea to the North Sea. Crossing three National Parks – the Lake
District, the Yorkshire Dales and the North York Moors – it samples
the very best of the English countryside – rugged mountains and
lakes, gentle dales, wild moorland; sea cliffs and fishing villages.

South Downs Way *Jim Manthorpe* **Available early 2004**
1st edition, 192pp, 50 maps & town plans, 40 colour photos
ISBN 1 873756 71 2, £9.99, Can$22.95, US$16.95
This 100-mile (160km) footpath runs from Winchester to Eastbourne.

❑ TRAILBLAZER GUIDES

Adventure Cycling Handbook	1st edn late 2004
Adventure Motorcycling Handbook	4th edn out now
Australia by Rail	4th edn out now
Azerbaijan	2nd edn out now
The Blues Highway – New Orleans to Chicago	2nd edn out now
China by Rail	2nd edn early 2004
Coast to Coast (British Walking Guide)	1st edn early 2004
Cornwall Coast Path (British Walking Guide)	1st edn out now
Good Honeymoon Guide	2nd edn out now
Inca Trail, Cusco & Machu Picchu	2nd edn out now
Japan by Rail	1st edn out now
Kilimanjaro – a trekking guide to Africa's highest mountain	1st edn out now
Land's End to John O'Groats	1st edn late 2004
The Med Guide	1st edn mid 2004
Nepal Mountaineering Guide	1st edn early 2004
New Zealand – Great Walks	1st edn early 2004
Norway's Arctic Highway	1st edn out now
Offa's Dyke Path (British Walking Guide)	1st edn Dec 2003
Pembrokeshire Coast Path (British Walking Guide)	1st edn Nov 2003
Pennine Way (British Walking Guide)	1st edn early 2004
Siberian BAM Guide – rail, rivers & road	2nd edn out now
The Silk Roads – a route and planning guide	1st end out now
Sahara Overland – a route and planning guide	1st edn out now
Sahara Abenteuerhandbuch (German edition)	1st edn out now
Ski Canada – where to ski and snowboard	1st edn out now
South Downs Way (British Walking Guide)	1st edn early 2004
South-East Asia – The Graphic Guide	1st edn out now
Tibet Overland – mountain biking & jeep touring	1st edn out now
Trans-Canada Rail Guide	3rd edn out now
Trans-Siberian Handbook	6th edn Oct 2003
Trekking in the Annapurna Region	4th edn Nov 2003
Trekking in the Everest Region	4th edn out now
Trekking in Corsica	1st edn out now
Trekking in the Dolomites	1st edn out now
Trekking in Ladakh	3rd edn mid 2004
Trekking in Langtang, Gosainkund & Helambu	1st edn out now
Trekking in the Moroccan Atlas	1st edn out now
Trekking in the Pyrenees	2nd edn out now
Tuva and Southern Siberia	1st edn late 2004
Vietnam by Rail	1st edn out now
West Highland Way (British Walking Guide)	1st edn out now

For more information about Trailblazer and our expanding range of guides,
for where to find your nearest stockist, for guidebook updates
or for credit card mail order sales (post-free worldwide) visit our web site:

www.trailblazer-guides.com

ROUTE GUIDES FOR THE ADVENTUROUS TRAVELLER

Norway's Arctic Highway

MO I RANA - KIRKENES